797,885 Books
are available to read at

www.ForgottenBooks.com

Forgotten Books' App
Available for mobile, tablet & eReader

ISBN 978-1-330-35423-0
PIBN 10038296

This book is a reproduction of an important historical work. Forgotten Books uses state-of-the-art technology to digitally reconstruct the work, preserving the original format whilst repairing imperfections present in the aged copy. In rare cases, an imperfection in the original, such as a blemish or missing page, may be replicated in our edition. We do, however, repair the vast majority of imperfections successfully; any imperfections that remain are intentionally left to preserve the state of such historical works.

Forgotten Books is a registered trademark of FB &c Ltd.
Copyright © 2015 FB &c Ltd.
FB &c Ltd, Dalton House, 60 Windsor Avenue, London, SW19 2RR.
Company number 08720141. Registered in England and Wales.

For support please visit www.forgottenbooks.com

1 MONTH OF FREE READING

at

www.ForgottenBooks.com

By purchasing this book you are eligible for one month membership to ForgottenBooks.com, giving you unlimited access to our entire collection of over 700,000 titles via our web site and mobile apps.

To claim your free month visit:

www.forgottenbooks.com/free38296

* Offer is valid for 45 days from date of purchase. Terms and conditions apply.

English
Français
Deutsche
Italiano
Español
Português

www.forgottenbooks.com

Mythology Photography **Fiction**
Fishing Christianity **Art** Cooking
Essays Buddhism Freemasonry
Medicine **Biology** Music **Ancient Egypt** Evolution Carpentry Physics
Dance Geology **Mathematics** Fitness
Shakespeare **Folklore** Yoga Marketing
Confidence Immortality Biographies
Poetry **Psychology** Witchcraft
Electronics Chemistry History **Law**
Accounting **Philosophy** Anthropology
Alchemy Drama Quantum Mechanics
Atheism Sexual Health **Ancient History**
Entrepreneurship Languages Sport
Paleontology Needlework Islam
Metaphysics Investment Archaeology
Parenting Statistics Criminology
Motivational

TO THE

KING.

SIR,

THE ſtudy and knowledge of the Globe, for very natural and obvious reaſons, ſeem, in all ages, to have been the principal and favourite purſuit of great Princes; perhaps they were,

DEDICATION.

at certain periods, the very sources of that greatness.

But as Pride, Ambition, and an immoderate thirst of Conquest, were the motives of these researches, no real advantage could possibly accrue to mankind in general, from inquiries proceeding upon such deformed and noxious principles.

In later times, which have been accounted more enlightened, still a worse motive succeeded to that of ambition; Avarice led the way in all expeditions, cruelty and oppression followed: to discover and to destroy seemed to mean the same thing; and, what was still more extraordinary, the innocent sufferer was stiled the Barbarian; while the bloody, lawless invader, flattered himself with the name of Christian.

With Your Majesty's reign, which, on many accounts, will for ever be a glorious æra in the annals of Britain, began the emancipation of discovery from the imputation of cruelty and crimes.

It

DEDICATION.

It was a golden age, which united humanity and science, exempted men of liberal minds and education, employed in the nobleſt of all occupations, that of exploring the diſtant parts of the Globe, from being any longer degraded, and rated as little better than the Buccaneer, or pirate, becauſe they had, till then, in manners been nearly ſimilar.

It is well known, that an uncertainty had ſtill remained concerning the form, quantity, and conſiſtence of the earth; and this, in ſpite of all their abilities and improvement, met philoſophers in many material inveſtigations and delicate calculations. Univerſal benevolence, a diſtinguiſhing quality of Your Majesty, led You to take upon Yourſelf the direction of the mode, and furniſhing the means of removing theſe doubts and difficulties for the common benefit of mankind, who were all alike intereſted in them.

By Your Majesty's command, for theſe great purpoſes, Your fleets penetrated into unknown ſeas,

fraught

DEDICATION.

fraught with subjects, equal, if not superior, in courage, science, and preparation, to any that ever before had navigated the ocean.

But they possessed other advantages, in which, beyond all comparison, they excelled former discoverers. In place of hearts confused with fantastic notions of honour and emulation, which constantly led to bloodshed, theirs were filled with the most beneficent principles, with that noble persuasion, the foundation of all charity, not that all men are equal, but that they are all brethren; and that being superior to the savage in every acquirement, it was for that very reason their duty to set the example of mildness, compassion, and long-suffering to a fellow-creature, because the weakest, and, by no fault of his own, the least instructed, and always perfectly in their power.

Thus, without the usual, and most unwarrantable excesses, the overturning ancient, hereditary kingdoms, without bloodshed, or trampling under foot the laws of society and hospitality, Your Majesty's
subjects,

DEDICATION.

subjects, braver, more powerful and instructed than those destroyers of old, but far more just, generous, and humane, erected in the hearts of an unknown people, while making these discoveries, an empire founded on peace and love of the subject, perfectly consistent with those principles by which Your Majesty has always professed to govern; more firm and durable than those established by bolts and chains, and all those black devices of tyrants not even known by name, in Your happy and united, powerful and flourishing kingdoms.

While these great objects were steadily conducting to the end which the capacity of those employed, the justness of the measures on which they were planned, and the constant care and support of the Public promised, there still remained an expedition to be undertaken which had been long called for, by philosophers of all nations, in vain.

Fleets and armies were useless; even the power of Britain, with the utmost exertion, could afford no protection

DEDICATION.

protection there, the place was so unhappily cut off from the rest of mankind, that even Your MAJESTY's name and virtues had never yet been known or heard of there.

THE situation of the country was barely known, no more: placed under the most inclement skies, in part surrounded by impenetrable forests, where, from the beginning, the beasts had established a sovereignty uninterrupted by man, in part by vast deserts of moving sands, where nothing was to be found that had the breath of life, these terrible barriers inclosed men more bloody and ferocious than the beasts themselves, and more fatal to travellers than the sands that encompassed them; and thus shut up, they had been long growing every day more barbarous, and defied, by rendering it dangerous, the curiosity of travellers of every nation.

ALTHOUGH the least considerable of your MAJESTY's subjects, yet not the least desirous of proving my duty by promoting your MAJESTY's declared plan

DEDICATION.

plan of discovery as much as the weak endeavours of a single person could, unprotected, forlorn, and alone, or at times associated to beggars and banditti, as they offered, I undertook this desperate journey, and did not turn an ell out of my proposed way till I had completed it: It was the first discovery attempted in Your MAJESTY's reign. From Egypt I penetrated into this country, through Arabia on one side, passing through melancholy and dreary deserts, ventilated with poisonous winds, and glowing with eternal sun-beams, whose names are as unknown in geography as are those of the antediluvian world. In the six years employed in this survey I described a circumference whose greater axis comprehended twenty-two degrees of the meridian, in which dreadful circle was contained all that is terrible to the feelings, prejudicial to the health, or fatal to the life of man.

IN laying the account of these Travels at Your MAJESTY's feet, I humbly hope I have shewn to the world of what value the efforts of every individual of Your MAJESTY's subjects may be; that numbers

DEDICATION.

bers are not always neceffary to the performance of great and brilliant actions, and that no difficulties or dangers are unfurmountable to a heart warm with affection and duty to his Sovereign, jealous of the honour of his mafter, and devoted to the glory of his country, now, under Your MAJESTY's wife, merciful, and juft reign, defervedly looked up to as Queen of Nations. I am,

SIR,

YOUR MAJESTY's

Moft faithful Subject,

And moft dutiful Servant,

JAMES BRUCE.

INTRODUCTION.

However little the reader may be converfant with ancient hiftories, in all probability he will know, or have heard this much in general, that the attempt to reach the Source of the Nile, the principal fubject of this publication, from very early ages interefted all fcientific nations: Nor was this great object *feebly* profecuted, as men, the firft for wifdom, for learning, and fpirit (a moft neceffary qualification in this undertaking) very earneftly interefted themfelves about the difcovery of the fources of this famous river, till difappointment followed difappointment fo faft, and confequences produced other confequences fo fatal, that the defign was entirely given over, as having, upon the faireft trials, appeared impracticable. Even conquerors at the head of immenfe armies, who had firft difcovered and then fubdued great part of the world, were forced to lower their tone here, and dared fcarcely to extend their advances toward this difcovery, beyond the limits of bare wifhes. At length, if it was not forgot, it was however totally abandoned from the caufes above mentioned, and with it all further topographical inquiries in that quarter.

Upon the revival of learning and of the arts, the curiofity of mankind had returned with unabated vigour towards this

INTRODUCTION.

this object, but all attempts had met with the same difficulties as before, till, in the beginning of his Majesty's reign, the unconquerable spirit raised in this nation by a long and glorious war, did very naturally resolve itself into a spirit of adventure and inquiry at the return of peace, one of the first-fruits of which was the discovery of these coy fountains *, till now concealed from the world in general.

THE great danger and difficulties of this journey were well known, but it was likewise known that it had been completely performed without disappointment or misfortune, that it had been attended with an apparatus of books and instruments, which seldom accompanies the travels of an individual; yet sixteen years had elapsed without any account appearing, which seemed to mark an unusual self-denial, or an absolute indifference towards the wishes of the public.

MEN, according to their different genius and dispositions, attempted by different ways to penetrate the cause of this silence. The candid, the learned, that species of men, in fine,

---

* This epithet given to the springs from which the Nile rises, was borrowed from a very elegant English poem that appeared in Dr Maty's Review for May 1786. It was sent to me by my friend Mr Barrington, to whom it was attributed, although from modesty he disclaims it. From whatever hand it comes, the poet is desired to accept of my humble thanks. It was received with universal applause wherever it was circulated, and a considerable number of copies was printed at the desire of the public. Accident seemed to have placed it in Dr Maty's book with peculiar propriety, by having joined it to a fragment of Ariosto, then first published, in the same Review. It has since been attributed to Mr Mason.

INTRODUCTION.

fine, for whom only it is worth while to travel or to write, suppofing (perhaps with some degree of truth) that an undeferved and unexpected neglect and want of patronage had been at least part of the cause, adopted a manner, which, being the most liberal, they thought likely to succeed: They endeavoured to entice me by holding out a prospect of a more generous disposition in the minds of future ministers, when I should shew the claim I had upon them by having promoted the glory of the nation. Others, whom I mention only for the sake of comparison, below all notice on any other ground, attempted to succeed in this by anonymous letters and paragraphs in the newspapers; and thereby absurdly endeavoured to oblige me to publish an account of those travels, which they affected at the same time to believe I had never performed.

But it is with very great pleasure and readiness I do now declare, that no fantastical or deformed motive, no peevish disregard, much less contempt of the judgment of the world, had any part in the delay which has happened to this publication. I look upon their impatience to see this work as an earnest of their approbation of it, and a very great honour done to me; and if I had still any motive to defer submitting these observations to their judgment, it could only be that I might employ that interval in polishing and making them more worthy of their perusal. The candid and instructed public, the impartial and unprejudiced foreigner, are tribunals merit should naturally appeal to; it is there it always has found sure protection against the influence of cabals, and the virulent strokes of malice, envy, and ignorance.

INTRODUCTION.

It is with a view to give every poſſible information to my reader, that in this introduction I lay before him the motives upon which theſe travels were undertaken, the order and manner in which they were executed, and ſome account of the work itſelf, as well of the matter as the diſtribution of it.

Every one will remember that period, ſo glorious to Britain, the latter end of the miniſtry of the late Earl of Chatham. I was then returned from a tour through the greateſt part of Europe, particularly through the whole of Spain and Portugal, between whom there then was an appearance of approaching war. I was about to retire to a ſmall patrimony I had received from my anceſtors, in order to embrace a life of ſtudy and reflection, nothing more active appearing then within my power, when chance threw me unexpectedly into a very ſhort and very defultory converſation with Lord Chatham.

It was a few days after this that Mr Wood, then underſecretary of ſtate, my very zealous and ſincere friend, informed me that Lord Chatham intended to employ me upon a particular ſervice; that, however, I might go down for a few weeks to my own country to ſettle my affairs, but by all means to be ready upon a call. Nothing could be more flattering to me than ſuch an offer; when ſo young, to be thought worthy by Lord Chatham of any employment, was doubly a preferment. No time was loſt on my ſide; but, juſt after my receiving orders to return to London, his Lordſhip had gone to Bath, and reſigned his office.

This

INTRODUCTION.

This disappointment, which was the more sensible to me, that it was the first I had met in public life, was promised to be made up to me by Lord Egremont and Mr George Grenville. The former had been long my friend, but unhappily he was then far gone in a lethargic indisposition, which threatened, and did very soon put a period to his existence. With Lord Egremont's death my expectations vanished. Further particulars are unnecessary, but I hope that at least, in part, they remain in that breast where they naturally ought to be, and where I shall ever think, not to be forgotten, is to be rewarded.

Seven or eight months were past in an expensive and fruitless attendance in London, when Lord Halifax was pleased, not only to propose, but to plan for me a journey of considerable importance, and which was to take up several years. His Lordship said, that nothing could be more ignoble, than that, at such a time of life, at the height of my reading, health, and activity, I should, as it were, turn peasant, and voluntarily bury myself in obscurity and idleness; that though war was now drawing fast to an end, full as honourable a competition remained among men of spirit, which should acquit themselves best in the dangerous line of useful adventure and discovery. " He observed, that the coast of Barbary, which might be said to be just at our door, was as yet but partially explored by Dr Shaw, who had only illustrated (very judiciously indeed) the geographical labours of Sanson*; that neither Dr Shaw nor San-

---

* He was long a slave to the Bey of Constantina, and appears to have been a man of capacity.

son had been, or had pretended to be, capable of giving the public any detail of the large and magnificent remains of ruined architecture which they both vouch to have seen in great quantities, and of exquisite elegance and perfection, all over the country. Such had not been their study, yet such was really the taste that was required in the present times. He wished therefore that I should be the first, in the reign just now beginning, to set an example of making large additions to the royal collection, and he pledged himself to be my supporter and patron, and to make good to me, upon this additional merit, the promises which had been held forth to me by former ministers for other services.

The discovery of the Source of the Nile was also a subject of these conversations, but it was always mentioned to me with a kind of diffidence, as if to be expected from a more experienced traveller. Whether this was but another way of exciting me to the attempt I shall not say; but my heart in that instant did me justice to suggest, that this, too, was either to be atchieved by me, or to remain, as it had done for these last two thousand years, a defiance to all travellers, and an opprobrium to geography.

Fortune seemed to enter into this scheme. At the very instant, Mr Aspinwall, very cruelly and ignominiously treated by the Dey of Algiers, had resigned his consulship, and Mr Ford, a merchant, formerly the Dey's acquaintance, was named in his place. Mr Ford was appointed, and dying a few days after, the consulship became vacant. Lord Halifax pressed me to accept of this, as containing all sort of conveniencies for making the proposed expedition.

INTRODUCTION.

This favourable event finally determined me. I had all my life applied unweariedly, perhaps with more love than talent, to drawing, the practice of mathematics, and especially that part necessary to astronomy. The transit of Venus was at hand. It was certainly known that it would be visible once at Algiers, and there was great reason to expect it might be twice. I had furnished myself with a large apparatus of instruments, the completest of their kind for the observation. In the choice of these I had been assisted by my friend Admiral Campbell, and Mr Russel secretary to the Turkey Company; every other necessary had been provided in proportion. It was a pleasure now to know that it was not from a rock or a wood, but from my own house at Algiers, I could deliberately take measures to place myself in the list of men of science of all nations, who were then preparing for the same scientific purpose.

Thus prepared, I set out for Italy, through France; and though it was in time of war, and some strong objections had been made to particular passports solicited by our government from the French secretary of state, Monsieur de Choiseul most obligingly waved all such exceptions with regard to me, and most politely assured me, in a letter accompanying my passport, that those difficulties did not in any shape regard me, but that I was perfectly at liberty to pass through, or remain in France, with those that accompanied me, without limiting their number, as short or as long a time as should be agreeable to me.

On my arrival at Rome I received orders to proceed to Naples, there to await his Majesty's further commands. Sir Charles Saunders, then with a fleet before Cadiz, had orders

INTRODUCTION.

to visit Malta before he returned to England. It was said, that the grand-master of that Order had behaved so improperly to Mr Hervey (afterwards Lord Bristol) in the beginning of the war, and so partially and unjustly between the two nations during the course of it, that an explanation on our part was become necessary. The grand-master no sooner heard of my arrival at Naples, than guessing the errand, he sent off Cavalier Mazzini to London, where he at once made his peace and his compliments to his Majesty upon his accession to the throne.

Nothing remained now but to take possession of my consulship. I returned without loss of time to Rome, and thence to Leghorn, where, having embarked on board the Montreal man of war, I proceeded to Algiers.

While at Naples, I received from slaves, redeemed from the province of Constantina, accounts of magnificent ruins they had seen while traversing that country in the camp with their master the Bey. I saw the absolute necessity there was for assistance, without which it was impossible for any one man, however diligent and qualified, to do any thing but bewilder himself. All my endeavours, however, had hitherto been unsuccessful to persuade any Italian to put himself wilfully into the hands of a people constantly looked upon by them in no better light than pirates.

While I was providing myself with instruments at London, I thought of one, which, though in a very small form and imperfect state, had been of great entertainment and use to me in former travels; this is called a Camera Obscura, the idea of which I had first taken from the Spectacle

INTRODUCTION.

de la Nature of the Abbé Vertot. But the prefent one was conftructed upon my own principles; I intrufted the execution of the glaffes to Meffrs Nairne and Blunt, Mathematical inftrument-makers oppofite to the Exchange, whom I had ufually employed upon fuch occafions, and with whofe capacity and fidelity I had, after frequent trials, the greateft reafon to be fatisfied.

This, when finifhed, became a large and expenfive inftrument; but being feparated into two pieces, the top and bottom, and folding compactly with hinges, was neither heavy, cumberfome, nor inconvenient, and the charge incurred by the additions and alterations was confiderably more than compenfated by the advantages which accrued from them. Its body was an hexagon of fix-feet diameter, with a conical top; in this, as in a fummer-houfe, the draughtfman fat unfeen, and performed his drawing. There is now, I fee, one carried as a fhow about the ftreets, of nearly the fame dimenfions, called a Delineator, made on the fame principles, and feems to be an exact imitation of mine.

By means of this inftrument, a perfon of but a moderate fkill in drawing, but habituated to the effect of it, could do more work, and in a better tafte, whilft executing views of ruined architecture, in one hour, than the readieft draughtfman, fo unaffifted, could do in feven; for, with proper care, patience, and attention, not only the elevation, and every part of it, is taken with the utmoft truth and jufteft proportion, but the light and fhade, the actual breaches as they ftand, vignettes, or little ornamental fhrubs, which generally hang from and adorn the projections and edges of the feveral members, are finely expreffed, and beautiful leffons given,

INTRODUCTION.

how to tranfport them with effect to any part where they appear to be wanting.

Another greater and ineftimable advantage is, that all landfcapes, and views of the country, which conftitute the background of the picture, are real, and in the reality fhew, very ftrikingly indeed, in fuch a country as Africa, abounding in picturefque fcenes, how much nature is fuperior to the creation of the warmeft genius or imagination. Momentary maffes of clouds, efpecially the heavier ones, of ftormy fkies, will be fixed by two or three unftudied ftrokes of a pencil; and figures and drefs, in the moft agreeable attitudes and folds, leave traces that a very ordinary hand might fpeedily make his own, or, what is ftill better, enable him with thefe elements to ufe the affiftance of the beft artift he can find in every line of painting, and, by the help of thefe, give to each the utmoft poffible perfection; a practice which I have conftantly preferred and followed with fuccefs.

It is true, this inftrument has a fundamental defect in the laws of optics; but this is obvious, and known unavoidably to exift; and he muft be a very ordinary genius indeed, and very lame, both in theory and practice, that cannot apply the neceffary correction, with little trouble, and in a very fhort time.

I was fo well pleafed with the firft trial of this inftrument at Julia Cæfarea, now Sherfhell, about 60 miles from Algiers, that I commiffioned a fmaller one from Italy, which, though negligently and ignorantly made, did me this good fervice, that it enabled me to fave my larger and more

perfect

INTRODUCTION.

perfect one, in my unfortunate shipwreck at Bengazi*, the ancient Berenice, on the shore of Cyrenaicum; and this was of infinite service to me in my journey to Palmyra.

Thus far a great part of my wants were well supplied, at least such as could be foreseen, but I still laboured under many. Besides that single province of ruined architecture, there remained several others of equal importance to the public. The natural history of the country, the manners and languages of the inhabitants, the history of the heavens, by a constant observation of, and attention to which, a useful and intelligible map of the country could be obtained, were objects of the utmost consequence.

Packing and repacking, mounting and rectifying these instruments alone, besides the attention and time necessary in using them, required what would have occupied one man, if they had been continual, which they luckily were not, and he sufficiently instructed. I therefore endeavoured to procure such a number of assistants, that should each bear his share in these several departments; not one only, but three or four if possible. I was now engaged, and part of my pride was to shew, how easy a thing it was to disappoint the idle prophecies of the ignorant, that this expedition would be spent in pleasure, without any profit to the public. I wrote to several correspondents, Mr Lumisden, Mr Strange, Mr Byers, and others in different parts of Italy, acquainting them of my situation, and begging their assistance. These gentlemen kindly used their utmost endeavours, but in vain.

---

* This will be explained afterwards.

INTRODUCTION.

It is true, Mr Chalgrin, a young French ftudent in architecture, accepted the propofal, and fent a neat fpecimen of rectilineal architecture. Even this gentleman might have been of fome ufe, but his heart failed him; he would have wifhed the credit of the undertaking, without the fatigues of the journey. At laft Mr Lumifden, by accident, heard of a young man who was then ftudying architecture at Rome, a native of Bologna, whofe name was Luigi Balugani. I can appeal to Mr Lumifden, now in England, as to the extent of this perfon's practice and knowledge, and that he knew very little when firft fent to me. In the twenty months which he ftaid with me at Algiers, by affiduous application to proper fubjects under my inftruction, he became a very confiderable help to me, and was the only one that ever I made ufe of, or that attended me for a moment, or ever touched one reprefentation of architecture in any part of my journey. He contracted an incurable diftemper in Paleftine, and died after a long ficknefs, foon after I entered Ethiopia, after having fuffered conftant ill-health from the time he left Sidon.

While travelling in Spain, it was a thought which frequently fuggefted itfelf to me, how little informed the world yet was in the hiftory of that kingdom and monarchy. The Moorifh part in particular, when it was moft celebrated for riches and for fcience, was fcarcely known but from fome romances or novels. It feemed an undertaking worthy of a man of letters to refcue this period from the oblivion or neglect under which it laboured. Materials were not wanting for this, as a confiderable number of books remained in a neglected and almoft unknown language, the Arabic. I endeavoured to find accefs to fome

of

INTRODUCTION.

of thofe Arabian manufcripts, an immenfe collection of which were every day perifhing in the duft of the efcurial, and was indulged with feveral converfations of Mr Wall, then minifter, every one of which convinced me, that the objections to what I wifhed were founded fo ftrongly in prejudice, that it was not even in his power to remove them.

All my fuccefs in Europe terminated in the acquifition of thofe few printed Arabic books that I had found in Holland, and thefe were rather biographers than general hiftorians, and contained little in point of general information. The ftudy of thefe, however, and of Maracci's Koran, had made me a very tolerable Arab; a great field was opening before me in Africa to complete a collection of manufcripts, an opportunity which I did not neglect.

After a year fpent at Algiers, conftant converfation with the natives whilft abroad, and with my manufcripts within doors, had qualified me to appear in any part of the continent without the help of an interpreter. Ludolf[*] had affured his readers, that the knowledge of any oriental language would foon enable them to acquire the Ethiopic, and I needed only the fame number of books to have made my knowledge of that language go hand in hand with my attainments in the Arabic. My immediate profpect of fetting out on my journey to the inland parts of Africa, had made me double my diligence; night and day there was no relaxation from thefe ftudies, although the acquiring any

fingle

---

[*] Ludolf, lib. i. cap. 15.

INTRODUCTION.

single language had never been with me either an object of time or difficulty.

At this instant, instead of obtaining the liberty I had solicited to depart, orders arrived from the king to expect his further commands at Algiers, and not to think of stirring from thence, till a dispute-about passports was settled, in which I certainly had no concern, further than as it regarded me as his Majesty's actual servant, for it had originated entirely from the neglect of the former consul's letters directed to the secretary of state at home, before my coming to Algiers.

The island of Minorca had been taken by the French; and when the fort of St Philip surrendered by an article common to all capitulations, it was stipulated, that all papers found in the fort were to be delivered to the captors. It happened that among these was a number of blank Mediterranean passes, which fell therefore into the hands of the French, and the blanks were filled up by the French governor and secretary, who very naturally wished to embroil us with the Barbary states, it being then the time of war with France. They were sold to Spaniards, Neapolitans, and other enemies of the Barbary regencies. The check* (the only proof that these pirates have of the vessels being a friend) agreed perfectly with the passport filled up by the French governor, but the captor seeing that the crew of these vessels were dark-coloured, wore mustachoes, and spoke no English, carried the vessel to Algiers, where the British consul detected

---

* This is a running figure cut through the middle like the check of a bank note.

INTRODUCTION.

ed the fraud, and was under the difagreeable neceffity of furrendering fo many Chriftians into flavery in the hands of their enemies.

One or two fuccefsful difcoveries of this kind made the hungry pirates believe that the paffport of every veffel they met with, even thofe of Gibraltar, were falfe in themfelves, and iffued to protect their enemies. Violent commotions were excited amongft the foldiery, abetted under hand by feveral of the neutral confuls there. By every occafion I had wrote home, but in vain, and the Dey could never be perfuaded of this, as no anfwer arrived. Government was occupied with winding up matters at the end of a war, and this neglect of my letters often brought me into great danger. At laft a temporary remedy was found, whether it originated from home, or whether it was invented by the governor of Mahon and Gibraltar, was never communicated to me, but a furer and more effectual way of having all the nation at Algiers maffacred could certainly not have been hit upon.

Square pieces of common paper, about the fize of a quarter-fheet, were fealed with the arms of the governor of Mahon, fometimes with red, fometimes with black wax, as the family circumftances of that officer required. Thefe were figned by his fignature, counterfigned by that of his feeretary, and contained nothing more than a bare and fimple declaration, that the veffel, the bearer of it, was Britifh property. Thefe papers were called *Paffavants*. The cruifer, uninftructed in this when he boarded a veffel, afked for his Mediterranean pafs. The mafter anfwered, He had none, he had only a paffavant, and fhewed the paper, which having no check,

check, the cruiser brought him and his vessel as a good prize into Algiers. Upon my claiming them, as was my duty, I was immediately called before the Dey and divan, and had it not been from personal regard the Turks always shewed me, I should not have escaped the insults of the soldiery in my way to the palace. The Dey asked me, upon my word as a Christian and an Englishman, whether these written passes were according to treaty, or whether the word *passavant* was to be found in any of our treaties with the Moorish regencies? All equivocation was useless. I answered, That these passes were not according to treaty; that the word *passavant* was not in any treaty I knew of with any of the Barbary states; that it was a measure necessity had created, by Minorca's falling into the hands of the French, which had never before been the case, but that the remedy would be found as soon as the greater business of settling the general peace gave the British ministry time to breathe. Upon this the Dey, holding several *passavants* in his hand, answered, with great emotion, in these memorable terms, " The British government know that we can neither read nor write, no not even our own language; we are ignorant soldiers and sailors, robbers if you will, though we do not wish to rob you; but war is our trade, and we live by that only. Tell me how my cruisers are to know that all these different writings and seals are Governor Mostyn's, or Governor Johnston's, and not the Duke of Medina Sidonia's, or Barcelot's, captain of the king of Spain's cruisers?" It was impossible to answer a question so simple and so direct. I touched then the instant of being cut to pieces by the soldiery, or of having the whole British Mediterranean trade carried into the Barbary ports. The candid and open manner in which I had spoken, the regard and esteem the Dey always

always had shewed me, and some other common methods with the members of the regency, staved off the dangerous moment, and were the means of procuring time. Admiralty passes at last came out, and the matter was happily adjusted; but it was an affair the least pleasing and the least profitable, and one of the most dangerous in which I was ever engaged.

ALL this disagreeable interval I had given to study, and making myself familiar with every thing that could be necessary to me in my intended journey. The king's surgeon at Algiers, Mr Ball, a man of considerable merit in his profession, and who lived in my family, had obtained leave to return home. Before I was deprived of this assistance, I had made a point of drawing from it all the advantages possible for my future travels. Mr Ball did not grudge his time or pains in the instruction he gave me. I had made myself master of the art of bleeding, which I found consisted only in a little attention, and in overcoming that diffidence which the ignorance how the parts lie occasions. Mr Ball had shewn me the manner of applying several sorts of bandages, and gave me an idea of dressing some kinds of sores and wounds. Frequent and very useful lessons, which I also received from my friend Doctor Russel at Aleppo, contributed greatly to improve me afterwards in the knowledge of physic and surgery. I had a small chest of the most efficacious medicines, a dispensary to teach me to compound others that were needful, and some short treatises upon the acute diseases of several countries within the tropics. Thus instructed, I flatter myself, no offence I hope, I did not occasion a greater mortality among the Mahometans and Pagans, abroad, than may be attributed to

INTRODUCTION.

some of my brother physicians among their fellow-Christians at home.

The rev. Mr Tonyn, the king's chaplain at Algiers, was absent upon leave before I arrived in that regency. The Protestant shipmasters who came into the port, and had need of spiritual assistance, found here a blank that was not easily filled up; I should therefore have been obliged to take upon myself the disagreeable office of burying the dead, and the more chearful, though more troublesome one, of marrying and baptizing the living; matters that were entirely out of my way, but to which the Roman Catholic clergy would contribute no assistance.

There was a Greek priest, a native of Cyprus, a very venerable man, past seventy years of age, who had attached himself to me from my first arrival in Algiers. This man was of a very social and chearful temper, and had, besides, a more than ordinary knowledge of his own language. I had taken him to my house as my chaplain, read Greek with him daily, and spoke it at times when I could receive his correction and instruction. It was not that I, at this time of day, needed to learn Greek, I had long understood that language perfectly; what I wanted was the pronunciation, and reading by accent, of which the generality of English scholars are perfectly ignorant, and to which it is owing that they apprehend the Greek spoken and written in the Archipelago is materially different from that language which we read in books, and which a few weeks conversation in the islands will teach them it is not. I had in this, at that time, no other view than mere convenience during my passage through the Archipelago, which

which I intended to visit, without any design of continuing or studying there: But the reader will afterwards see of what very material service this acquaintance was to me, so very essential, indeed, that it contributed more to the success of my views in Abyssinia than any other help that I obtained throughout the whole of it. This man's name was Padre Christophoro, or Father Christopher. At my leaving Algiers, finding himself less conveniently situated, he went to Egypt, to Cairo, where he was promoted to be second in rank under Mark, patriarch of Alexandria, where I afterwards found him.

Business of a private nature had at this time obliged me to present myself at Mahon, a gentleman having promised to meet me there; I therefore sailed from Algiers, having taken leave of the Dey, who furnished me with every letter that I asked, with strong and peremptory orders to all the officers of his own dominions, pressing recommendatory ones to the Bey of Tunis and Tripoli, states independent, indeed, of the Dey of Algiers, but over which the circumstances of the times had given him a considerable influence.

The violent disputes about the passports had rather raised than lowered me in his esteem. The letters were given with the best grace possible, and the orders contained in them were executed most exactly in all points during my whole stay in Barbary. Being disappointed in the meeting I looked for at Mahon, I remained three days in Quarantine Island, though General Townsend, then deputy-governor, by every civility and attention in his power, strove to induce me

INTRODUCTION.

me to come on shore, that he might have an opportunity of shewing me still more attention and politeness.

My mind being now full of more agreeable ideas than what had for some time past occupied it, I sailed in a small vessel from Port Mahon, and, having a fair wind, in a short time made the coast of Africa, at a cape, or headland, called Ras el Hamra *, and landed at Bona, a considerable town, the ancient Aphrodisium †, built from the ruins of Hippo Regius ‡, from which it is only two miles distant. It stands on a large plain, part of which seems to have been once overflowed by the sea. Its trade consists now in the exportation of wheat, when, in plentiful years, that trade is permitted by the government of Algiers. I had a delightful voyage close down the coast, and passed the small island Tabarca §, lately a fortification of the Genoese, now in the hands of the regency of Tunis, who took it by surprise, and made all the inhabitants slaves. The island is famous for a coral fishery, and along the coast are immense forests of large beautiful oaks, more than sufficient to supply the necessities of all the maritime powers in the Levant, if the quality of the wood be but equal to the size and beauty of the tree

From Tabarca I sailed and anchored at Biferta, the Hippozaritus ‖ of antiquity, and thence went to pay a visit to Utica, out of respect to the memory of Cato, without having sanguine expectations of meeting any thing remarkable there,

---

* Hippo. Reg. from Ptol. Geog. lib. iv. p. 109.   † Hippo. Reg. id. ib.
‡ Aphrodisium. id. ib.   §. Thabarca, id. ib.   ‖ Plin. Ep. xxxiii. l, 9.

there, and accordingly I found nothing memorable but the name. It may be faid nothing remains of Utica but a heap of rubbifh and of fmall ftones; without the city the trenches and approaches of the ancient befiegers are ftill very perfect.

After doubling Cape Carthage I anchored before the fortrefs of the Goletta, a place now of no ftrength, notwithftanding the figure it made at the time of the expedition of Charles V. Rowing along the bay, between the Cape and this anchorage, I faw feveral buildings and columns ftill ftanding under water, by which it appeared that old Carthage had owed part of its deftruction to the fea, and hence likewife may be inferred the abfurdity of any attempt to reprefent the fite of ancient Carthage upon paper. It has been, befides, at leaft ten times deftroyed, fo that the ftations, where its firft citizens fell fighting for their liberty, are covered deep in rubbifh, far from being trodden upon by thofe unworthy flaves who now are its mafters.

Tunis * is twelve miles diftant from this: It is a large and flourifhing city. The people are more civilized than in Algiers, and the government milder, but the climate is very far from being fo good. Tunis is low, hot, and damp, and deftitute of good water, with which Algiers is fupplied from a thoufand fprings.

I delivered my letters from the Bey, and obtained permiffion to vifit the country in whatever direction I fhould pleafe.

---

* Liv. Epit. xxx. l. 9.

please. I took with me a French renegado, of the name of Ofman, recommended to me by Monſieur Bartheleny de Saizieux, conſul of France to that ſtate; a gentleman whoſe converſation and friendſhip furniſh me ſtill with ſome of the moſt agreeable reflections that reſult from my travels. With Ofman I took ten ſpahi, or horſe-ſoldiers, well armed with firelocks and piſtols, excellent horſemen, and, as far as I could ever diſcern upon the few occaſions that preſented, as eminent for cowardice, at leaſt, as they were for horſemanſhip. This was not the caſe with Ofman, who was very brave, but he needed a ſharp look-out, that he did not often embroil us where there was acceſs to women or to wine.

One of the moſt agreeable favours I received was from a lady of the Bey, who furniſhed me with a two-wheeled covered cart, exactly like thoſe of the bakers in England. In this I ſecured my quadrant and teleſcope from the weather, and at times put likewiſe ſome of the feebleſt of my attendants. Beſides theſe I had ten ſervants, two of whom were Iriſh, who having deſerted from the Spaniſh regiments in Oran, and being Britiſh born, though ſlaves, as being Spaniſh ſoldiers, were given to me at parting by the Dey of Algiers.

The coaſt along which I had ſailed was part of Numidia and Africa Proper, and there I met with no ruins. I reſolved now to diſtribute my inland journey through the kingdom of Algiers and Tunis. In order to comprehend the whole, I firſt ſet out along the river Majerda, through a country perfectly cultivated and inhabited by people under the

INTRODUCTION.

the controul of government, this river was the ancient Bagrada*.

AFTER passing a triumphal arch of bad taste at Basil-bab, I came the next day to Thugga†, perhaps more properly called Tucca, and by the inhabitants Dugga. The reader in this part should have Doctor Shaw's Work before him, my map of the journey not being yet published; and, indeed, after Shaw's, it is scarcely necessary to those who need only an itinerary, as, besides his own observations, he had for basis those of Sanson.

I FOUND at Dugga a large scene of ruins, among which one building was easily distinguishable. It was a large temple of the Corinthian order, all of Parian marble, the columns fluted, the cornice highly ornamented in the very best style of sculpture. In the tympanum is an eagle flying to heaven, with a human figure upon his back, which, by the many inscriptions that are still remaining, seems to be intended for that of Trajan, and the apotheosis of that emperor to be the subject, the temple having been erected by Adrian to that prince, his benefactor and predecessor. I spent fifteen days upon the architecture of this temple without feeling the smallest disgust, or forming a wish to finish it; it is, with all its parts, still unpublished in my collection. These beautiful and magnificent remains of ancient taste and greatness, so easily reached in perfect safety, by a ride along the Bagrada, full as pleasant and as safe as along the Thames

between

---

* Strabo lib xvii. p. 1189.   It signifies the river of Cows, or Kine.   P. Mela lib. i.
cap. 7. Sil. It. lib. vi. l. 140.   † Ptol. Geog. lib. iv. Procop. lib. vi. cap. 5. de Ædif.

INTRODUCTION.

between London and Oxford, were at Tunis totally unknown. Doctor Shaw has given the situation of the place, without saying one word about any thing curious it contains.

From Dugga I continued the upper road to Keff *, formerly called Sicca Venerea, or Venerea ad Siccam, through the pleasant plains inhabited by the Welled Yagoube. I then proceeded to Hydra, the Thunodrunum † of the ancients. This is a frontier place between the two kingdoms of Algiers and Tunis, as Keff is also. It is inhabited by a tribe of Arabs, whose chief is a marabout, or saint; they are called Welled Sidi Boogannim, the " sons of the father of flocks."

These Arabs are immensely rich, paying no tribute either to Tunis or Algiers. The pretence for this exemption is a very singular one. By the institution of their founder, they are obliged to live upon lions flesh for their daily food, as far as they can procure it; with this they strictly comply, and, in consideration of the utility of this their vow, they are not taxed, like the other Arabs, with payments to the state. The consequence of this life is, that they are excellent and well-armed horsemen, exceedingly bold and undaunted hunters. It is generally imagined, indeed, that these considerations, and that of their situation on the frontier, have as much influence in procuring them exemption from taxes, as the utility of their vow.

---

* Val. Max. lib. ii. cap. 6. § 15.   † Ptol. Geog. lib. iv.

INTRODUCTION.

There is at Thunodrunum a triumphal arch, which Dr Shaw thinks is more remarkable for its fize than for its tafte or execution; but the fize is not extraordinary; on the other hand, both tafte and execution are admirable. It is, with all its parts, in the King's collection, and, taking the whole together, is one of the moft beautiful landfcapes in black and white now exifting. The diftance, as well as the fore-ground, are both from nature, and exceedingly well calculated for fuch reprefentation.

Before Dr Shaw's travels firft acquired the celebrity they have maintained ever fince, there was a circumftance that very nearly ruined their credit. He had ventured to fay in converfation, that thefe Welled Sidi Boogannim were eaters of lions, and this was confidered at Oxford, the univerfity where he had ftudied, as a traveller's licenfe on the part of the Doctor. They took it as a fubverfion of the natural order of things, that a man fhould eat a lion, when it had long paffed as almoft the peculiar province of the lion to eat man. The Doctor flinched under the fagacity and feverity of this criticifm; he could not deny that the Welled Sidi Boogannim did eat lions, as he had repeatedly faid; but he had not yet publifhed his travels, and therefore left it out of his narrative, and only hinted at it after in his appendix.

With all fubmiffion to that learned univerfity, I will not difpute the lion's title to eating men; but, fince it is not founded upon patent, no confideration will make me ftifle the merit of Welled Sidi Boogannim, who have turned the chace upon the enemy. It is an hiftorical fact; and I will not fuffer the public to be mifled by a mifreprefentation of it; on the contrary, I do aver, in the face of thefe fantaftic prejudices, that I have ate the flefh of lions, that is, part of three lions, in the tents of Welled Sidi Boogannim. The firft was a he-lion, lean, tough, fmelling violently of mufk, and had the tafte which, I imagine, old horfe-flefh would have. The fecond was a lionefs, which they faid had that year been barren. She had a confiderable quantity of fat within her; and, had it not been for the mufky fmell that the flefh had, though in a leffer degree than the former, and for our foolifh prejudices againft it, the meat, when broiled, would not have been very bad. The third was a lion's whelp, fix or feven months old; it tafted, upon the whole, the worft of the three. I confefs I have no defire of being again ferved with fuch a morfel; but the Arabs, a brutifh and ignorant folk, will, I fear, notwithftanding the difbelief of the univerfity of Oxford, continue to eat lions as long as they exift.

From Hydra I paffed to the ancient Tipafa*, another Roman colony, going by the fame name to this day. Here is a moft extenfive fcene of ruins. There is a large temple, and a four-faced triumphal arch of the Corinthian order, in the very beft tafte; both of which are now in the collection of the King.

I here croffed the river Myfkianah, which falls into the Bagrada, and continuing through one of the moft beautiful and beft-cultivated countries in the world, I entered the eaftern province of Algiers, now called Conftantina, anciently

---

* Ptol. Geog. lib. iv. p. 106.

INTRODUCTION. xxvii

ly the Mauritania Cæfarienfis, whofe capital, Conftantina, is the ancient metropolis of Syphax. It was called Cirta*, and, after Julius Cæfar's conqueft, Cirta Sittianorum, from Caius Sittius who firft took it. It is fituated upon a high, gloomy, tremendous precipice. Part only of its aquedudt remains: the water, which once was carried into the town, now fpills itfelf from the top of the cliff into a chafm, or narrow valley, above four hundred feet below. The view of it is in the King's colledtion; a band of robbers, the figures which adorn it, is a compofition from imagination; all the reft is perfectly real.

The Bey was at this time in his camp, as he was making war with the Hanneifhah, the moft powerful tribe of Arabs in that province. After having refrefhed myfelf in the Bey's palace I fet out to Seteef, the Sitifi† of antiquity, the capital of Mauritania Sitifenfis, at fome diftance from which I joined the Bey's army, confifting of about 12,000 men, with four pieces of cannon. After ftaying a few days with the Bey, and obtaining his letters of recommendation, I proceeded to Taggou-zainah, anciently Diana Veteranorum‡, as we learn by an infcription on a triumphal arch of the Corinthian order which I found there.

From Taggou-zainah I continued my journey nearly ftraight S. E. and arrived at Medrafhem, a fuperb pile of building, the fepulchre of Syphax, and the other kings of Numidia, and where, as the Arabs believe, were alfo depofited

---

* Ptol. Geog. lib. iv. p. 111.   † Ptol. Geog. lib. iv. p. 108.
‡ Vide Itin. Anton.

fited the treafures of thofe kings. A drawing of this monument is ftill unpublifhed in my collection. Advancing ftill to the S. E. through broken ground and fome very barren valleys, which produced nothing but game, I came to Jibbel Aurez, the Aurafius Mons of the middle age. This is not one mountain, but an affemblage of many of the moft craggy fteeps in Africa.

HERE I met, to my great aftonifhment, a tribe, who, if I cannot fay they were fair like Englifh, were of a fhade lighter than that of the inhabitants of any country to the fouthward of Britain. Their hair alfo was red, and their eyes blue. They are a favage and independent people; it required addrefs to approach them with fafety, which, however, I accomplifhed, (the particulars would take too much room for this place), was well received, and at perfect liberty to do whatever I pleafed. This tribe is called Neardie. Each of the tribe, in the middle between their eyes, has a Greek crofs marked with antimony. They are Kabyles. Though living in tribes, they have among the mountains. huts, built with mud and ftraw, which they call Dafhkras, whereas the Arabs live in tents on the plains. I imagine thefe to be a remnant of Vandals. Procopius* mentions a defeat of an army of this nation here, after a defperate refiftance, a remnant of which may be fuppofed to have maintained themfelves in thefe mountains. They with great pleafure confeffed their anceftors had been Chriftians, and feemed to rejoice much more in that relation than in any connection with the Moors, with whom they live in perpetual

---

* Procop. Bell. Vand. lib. ii. cap. 13.

INTRODUCTION.

tual war: they pay no taxes to the Bey, but live in conftant defiance of him.

As this is the Mons Audus of Ptolemy, here too muft be fixed his Lambefa*, or Lambefentium Colonia, which, by a hundred Latin infcriptions remaining on the fpot, it is attefted to have been. It is now called Tezzoute: the ruins of the city are very extenfive. There are feven of the gates ftill ftanding, and great pieces of the walls folidly built with fquare mafonry without lime. The buildings remaining are of very different ages, from Adrian to Aurelian, nay even to Maximin. One building only, fupported by columns of the Corinthian order, was in good tafte; what its ufe was I know not. The drawing of this is in the King's collection. It was certainly defigned for fome military purpofe, by the fize of the gates; I fhould fufpect a ftable for elephants, or a repofitory for catapulta, or other large military machines, though there are no traces left upon the walls indicating either. Upon the key-ftone of the arch of the principal gate there is a baffo-relievo of the ftandard of a legion, and upon it an infcription, Legio tertia Augufta, which legion, we know from hiftory, was quartered here. Dr Shaw† fays, that there is here a neat, round, Corinthian temple, called Cubb el Arroufah, the Cupola or Dome of the Bride or Spoufe. Such a building does exift, but it is by no means of a good tafte, nor of the Corinthian order; but of a long difproportioned Doric, of the time of Aurelian, and does not merit the attention of any architect. Dr Shaw never

---

* Ptol. Geog. lib. iv. p. 111.   † Shaw's Travels, chap. viii. p 57.

never was so far south as Jibbel Aurez, so could only say this from report.

From Jibbel Aurez nothing occurred in the style of architecture that was material. Hydra remained on the left hand. I came to Caſſareen, the ancient Colonia Scillitana*, where I ſuffered ſomething both from hunger and from fear. The country was more rugged and broken than any we had yet ſeen, and withal leſs fruitful and inhabited. The Moors of theſe parts are a rebellious tribe, called Nememſhah, who had fled from their ordinary obligation of attending the Bey, and had declared themſelves on the part of the rebel-moors, the Henneiſhah.

My intentions now were to reach Feriana, the Thala † of the ancients, where I expected confiderable ſubjects for ſtudy; but in this I was diſappointed, and being on the frontier, and in dangerous times, when ſeveral armies were in the field, I thought it better to ſteer my courſe eaſtward, and avoid the theatre of war.

Journeying eaſt, I came to Spaitla ‡, and again got into the kingdom of Tunis. Spaitla is a corruption of Suffetula ‖, which was probably its ancient name before it became a Roman colony; ſo called from Suffetes, a magiſtrature in all the countries dependent upon Carthage. Spaitla has many inſcriptions, and very extenſive and elegant remains. There are three temples, two of them Corinthian, and one of

the

---

* Shaw's Travels, cap. v. p. 119.
† Sal. Bel. Jug. § 94. L. Flor. lib. iii. cap. 1. ‡ Shaw's Travels, chap. v. p. 118.
‖ Itin. Anton. p. 3.

INTRODUCTION. xxxi

the Compofite order; a great part of them is entire. A beautiful and perfect capital of the Compofite order, the only perfect one that now exifts, is defigned, in all its parts, in a very large fize; and, with the detail of the reft of the ruin, is a precious monument of what that order was, now in the collection of the King.

DOCTOR SHAW, ftruck with the magnificence of Spaitla, has attempted fomething like the three temples, in a ftile much like what one would expect from an ordinary carpenter, or mafon. I hope I have done them more juftice, and I recommend the ftudy of the Compofite capital, as of the Corinthian capital at Dugga, to thofe who really wifh to know the tafte with which thefe two orders were executed in the time of the Antonines.

THE Welled Omran, a lawlefs, plundering tribe, inquieted me much in the eight days I ftaid at Spaitla. It was a fair match between coward and coward. With my company, I was inclofed in a fquare in which the three temples ftood, where there yet remained a precinct of high walls. Thefe plunderers would have come in to me; but were afraid of my fire-arms; and I would have run away from them, had I not been afraid of meeting their horfe in the plain. I was almoft ftarved to death, when I was relieved by the arrival of Welled Haffan, and a friendly tribe of Dreeda, that came to my affiftance, and brought me, at once, both fafety and provifion.

FROM Spaitla I went to Gilma, or Oppidum Chilmanenfe. There is here a large extent of rubbifh and ftones, but no diftinct trace of any building whatever.

From Gilma I paſſed to Muchtar, corruptly now ſo called. Its ancient name is Tucca Terebinthina*. Dr Shaw † ſays its modern name is Sbeeba, but no ſuch name is known here. I might have paſſed more directly from Spaitla ſouthward, but a large chain of mountains, to whoſe inhabitants I had no recommendation, made me prefer the ſafer and plainer road by Gilma. At Tucca Terebinthina are two triumphal arches, the largeſt of which I ſuppoſe equal in taſte, execution, and maſs, to any thing now exiſting in the world. The leſſer is more ſimple, but very elegant. They are both, with all the particulars of their parts, not yet engraved, but ſtill in my collection.

From Muchtar, or Tucca Terebinthina, we came to Kiſſer‡, which Dr Shaw conjectures to have been the Colonia Aſſuras of the ancients, by this it ſhould ſeem he had not been there; for there is an inſcription upon a triumphal arch of very good taſte, now ſtanding, and many others to be met with up and down, which confirms beyond doubt his conjecture to be a juſt one. There is, beſides this, a ſmall ſquare temple, upon which are carved ſeveral inſtruments of ſacrifice, which are very curious, but the execution of theſe is much inferior to the deſign. It ſtands on the declivity of a hill, above a large fertile plain, ſtill called the Plain of Surſe, which is probably a corruption of its ancient name Aſſuras.

From Kiſſer I came to Mufti, where there is a triumphal arch of very good taſte, but perfectly in ruins; the

merit

---

* Iun. Anton. p. 3.   † Shaw's Travels, cap. v. p. 115.
‡ Cel. Geog. Antique, lib. iv. cap. 4. and cap. 5. p. 118.

merit of its feveral parts only could be collected from the fragments which lie ftrewed upon the ground.

From Mufti * I proceeded north-eaftward to Tuberfoke, thence again to Dugga, and down the Bagrada to Tunis.

My third, or, which may be called my middle journey through Tunis, was by Zowan, a high mountain, where is a large aqueduct which formerly carried its water to Carthage. Thence I came to Jelloula, a village lying below high mountains on the weft; thefe are the Montes Vaffaleti of Ptolemy ‡, as the town itfelf is the Oppidum Ufalitanum of Pliny. I fell here again into the ancient road at Gilma; and, not fatisfied with what I had feen of the beauties of Spaitla, I paffed there five days more, correcting and revifing what I had already committed to paper. Independent of the treafure I found in the elegance of its buildings, the town itfelf is fituated in the moft beautiful fpot in Barbary, furrounded thick with juniper-trees, and watered by a pleafant ftream that finks there under the earth, and appears no more.

Here I left my former road at Caffareen, and proceeding directly S. E. came to Feriana, the road that I had abandoned before from prudential motives. Feriana, as has been before obferved, is the ancient Thala, taken and deftroyed by Metellus in his purfuit of Jugurtha. I had formed, I know not from what reafon, fanguine expectations of elegant

---

* Itin. Anton. p. 2.   ‡ Ptol. Geog. lib. iv. p. 110.

gant remains here, but in this I was difappointed; I found nothing remarkable but the baths of very warm water * without the town; in thefe there was a number of fifh, above four inches in length, not unlike gudgeons. Upon trying the heat by the thermometer, I remember to have been much furprifed that they could have exifted, or even not been boiled, by continuing long in the heat of this medium. As I marked the degrees with a pencil while I was myfelf naked in the water, the leaf was wetted accidentally, fo that I miffed the precife degree I meant to have recorded, and do not pretend to fupply it from memory. The bath is at the head of the fountain, and the ftream runs off to a confiderable diftance. I think there were about five or fix dozen of thefe fifh in the pool. I was told likewife, that they went down into the ftream to a certain diftance in the day, and returned to the pool, or warmeft and deepeft water, at night.

From Feriana I proceeded S. E. to Gafsa, the ancient Capfa†, and thence to Tozer, formerly Tifurus ‖. I then turned nearly N. E. and entered a large lake of water called the Lake of Marks, becaufe in the paffage of it there is a row of large trunks of palm-trees fet up to guide travellers in the road which croffes it. Doctor Shaw has fettled very diftinctly the geography of this place, and thofe about it. It is the Palus Tritonidis ‡, as he juftly obferves; this was the moft barren and unpleafant part of my journey

in

---

* This fountain is called El Tarmid. Nub. Geog. p. 86.

† Sal. Bell. § 94.   ‖ Itin. Anton, p. 4.   ‡ Shaw's Travels, cap. v. p. 126.

in Africa; barren not only from the nature of its foil, but by its having no remains of antiquity in the whole courfe of it.

From this I came to Gabs, or Tacape*, after paffing El Hammah, the baths which were the Aquas Tacapitanas of antiquity, where the fmall river Triton, by the moifture which it furnifhes, moft agreeably and fuddenly changes the defert fcene, and covers the adjacent fields with all kinds of flowers and verdure.

I was now arrived upon the leffer Syrtis, and continued along the fea-coaft northward to Infhilla, without having made any addition to my obfervations. I turned again to the N. W. and came to El Gemme ‡, where there is a very large and fpacious amphitheatre, perfect as to the defolation of time, had not Mahomet Bey blown up four arches of it from the foundation, that it might not ferve as a fortrefs to the rebel Arabs. The fections, elevations, and plans, with the whole detail of its parts, are in the King's collection.

I have ftill remaining, but not finifhed, the lower or fubterraneous plan of the building, an entrance to which I forced open in my journey along the coaft to Tripoli. This was made fo as to be filled with water by means of a fluice and aqueduct, which are ftill entire. The water rofe up in the arena, through a large fquare-hole faced with hewn-ftone in the middle, when there was occafion for water-games or naumachia. Doctor Shaw † imagines this was intended

---

* Itin. Anton. p. 4. ‡ Id. Ibid. † Shaw's Travels, p. 117. cap. 5.

INTRODUCTION.

intended to contain the pillar that fupported the velum, which covered the fpectators from the influence of the fun. It might have ferved for both purpofes, but it feems to be too large for the latter, though I confefs the more I have confidered the fize and conftruction of thefe amphitheatres, the lefs I have been able to form an idea concerning this velum, or the manner in which it ferved the people, how it was fecured, and how it was removed. This was the laft ancient building I vifited in the kingdom of Tunis, and I believe I may confidently fay, there is not, either in the territories of Algiers or Tunis, a fragment of good tafte of which I have not brought a drawing to Britain.

I continued along the coaft to Sufa, through a fine country planted with olive-trees, and came again to Tunis, not only without difagreeable accident, but without any interruption from ficknefs or other caufe. I then took leave of the Bey, and, with the acknowledgments ufual on fuch occafions, again fet out from Tunis, on a very ferious journey indeed, over the defert to Tripoli, the firft part of which to Gabs was the fame road by which I had fo lately returned. From Gabs I proceeded to the ifland of Gerba, the Meninx * Infula, or Ifland of the Lotophagi.

Doctor Shaw fays, the fruit he calls the Lotus is very frequent all over that coaft. I wifh he had faid what was this Lotus. To fay it is the fruit the moft common on that coaft is no defcription, for there is there no fort of fruit whatever;

---

† Boch. Chan. lib. i. cap. 25, Shaw's Travels, cap. iv. p. 115.

whatever; no bufh, no tree, nor verdure of any kind, excepting the fhort grafs that borders thefe countries before you enter the moving fands of the defert. Doctor Shaw never was at Gerba, and has taken this particular from fome unfaithful ftory-teller. The Wargumma and Noile, two great tribes of Arabs, are mafters of thefe deferts. Sidi Ifmain, whofe grandfather, the Bey of Tunis, had been dethroned and ftrangled by the Algerines, and who was himfelf then prifoner at Algiers, in great repute for valour, and in great intimacy with me, did often ufe to fay, that he accounted his having paffed that defert on horfeback as the hardieft of all his undertakings.

About four days journey from Tripoli I met the Emir Hadje conducting the caravan of pilgrims from Fez and Sus in Morocco, all acrofs Africa to Mecca, that is, from the Weftern Ocean, to the weftern banks of the Red Sea in the kingdom of Sennaar. He was a middle-aged man, uncle to the prefent emperor, of a very uncomely, ftupid kind of countenance. His caravan confifted of about 3000 men, and, as his people faid, from 12,000 to 14,000 camels, part loaded with merchandife, part with fkins of water, flour, and other kinds of food, for the maintenance of the hadjees; they were a fcurvy, diforderly, unarmed pack, and when my horfemen, tho' but fifteen in number, came up with them in the grey of the morning, they fhewed great figns of trepidation, and were already flying in confufion. When informed who they were, their fears ceafed, and, after the ufual manner of cowards, they became extremely infolent.

INTRODUCTION.

AT Tripoli I met the Hon. Mr Frazer of Lovat, his Majefty's conful in that ftation, from whom I received every fort of kindnefs, comfort, and affiftance, which I very much needed after fo rude a journey, made with fuch diligence that two of my horfes died fome days after.

I HAD hopes of finding fomething at Lebeda, formerly Leptis Magna*, three days journey from Tripoli, where are indeed a great number of buildings, many of which are covered by the fands; but they are of a bad tafte, moftly ill-proportioned Dorics of the time of Aurelian. Seven large columns of granite were fhipped from this for France, in the reign of Louis XIV. deftined for one of the palaces he was then building. The eighth was broken on the way, and lies now upon the fhore. Though I was difappointed at Lebeda, ample amends were made me at Tripoli on my return.

FROM Tripoli I fent an Englifh fervant to Smyrna with my books, drawings, and fupernumerary inftruments, retaining only extracts from fuch authors as might be neceffary for me in the Pentapolis, or other parts of the Cyrenaicum. I then croffed the Gulf of Sidra, formerly known by the name of the Syrtis Major, and arrived at Bengazi, the ancient Berenice §, built by Ptolemy Philadelphus.

THE brother of the Bey of Tripoli commanded here, a young man, as weak in underftanding as he was in health.

---

* Itin. Anton. p. 104. § Ptol. Geog. p. 4.

INTRODUCTION.

All the province was in extreme confufion. Two tribes of Arabs, occupying the territory to the weft of the town, who in ordinary years, and in time of peace, were the fources of its wealth and plenty, had, by the mifmanagement of the Bey, entered into deadly quarrel. The tribe that lived moft to the weftward, and which was reputed the weakeft, had beat the moft numerous that was neareft the town, called Welled Abid, and driven them within its walls. The inhabitants of Bengazi had for a year before been labouring under a fevere famine, and by this accident about four thoufand perfons, of all ages and fexes, were forced in upon them, when perfectly deftitute of every neceffary. Ten or twelve people were found dead every night in the ftreets, and life was faid in many to be fupported by food that human nature fhudders at the thoughts of. Impatient to fly from thefe Thyeftean feafts, I prevailed upon the Bey to fend me out fome diftance to the fouthward, among the Arabs where famine had been lefs felt.

I encompassed a great part of the Pentapolis, vifited the ruins of Arfinoe, and, though I was much more feebly recommended than ufual, I happily received neither infult nor injury. Finding nothing at Arfinoe nor Barca, I continued my journey to Ras Sem, the petrified city, concerning which fo many monftrous lies were told by the Tripoline ambaffador, Caffem Aga, at the beginning of this century, and all believed in England, though they carried falfehood upon the very face of them*. It was not then the age of incredulity

---

* Shaw's Travels, fect. vi. p. 156.

INTRODUCTION.

incredulity, we were faft advancing to the celebrated epoch of the man in the pint-bottle, and from that time to be as abfurdly incredulous as we were then the reverfe, and with the fame degree of reafon.

Ras Sem is five long days journey fouth from Bengazi; it has no water, except a fpring very difagreeable to the tafte, that appears to be impregnated with alum, and this has given it the name it bears of Ras Sem, or the Fountain of Poifon, from its bitternefs. The whole remains here confift in the ruins of a tower or fortification, that feems to be a work full as late as the time of the Vandals. How or what ufe they made of this water I cannot poffibly guefs; they had no other at the diftance of two days journey. I was not fortunate enough to difcover the petrified men and horfes, the women at the churn, the little children, the cats, the dogs, and the mice, which his Barbarian excellency affured Sir Hans Sloane exifted there: Yet, in vindication of his Excellency, I muft fay, that though he propagated, yet he did not invent this falfehood; the Arabs who conducted me maintained the fame ftories to be true, till I was within two hours of the place, where I found them to be falfe. I faw indeed mice*, as they are called, of a very extraordinary kind, having nothing of petrifaction about them, but agile and active, fo to partake as much of the bird as the beaft.

Approaching now the fea-coaft I came to Ptolometa, the ancient Ptolemais ‡, the work of Ptolemy Philadelphus, the walls

---

* Jerboa, fee a figure of it in the Appendix.   ‡ Itin. Anton. p. 4.

walls and gates of which city are still entire. There is a prodigious number of Greek inscriptions, but there remain only a few columns of the portico, and an Ionic temple, in the first manner of executing that order; and therefore, slight as the remains are, they are treasures in the history of architecture which are worthy to be preserved. These are in the King's collection, with all the parts that could be recovered.

Here I met a small Greek junk belonging to Lampedosa, a little island near Crete, which had been unloading corn, and was now ready to sail. At the same time the Arabs of Ptolometa told me, that the Welled Ali, a powerful tribe that occupy the whole country between that place and Alexandria, were at war among themselves, and had plundered the caravan of Morocco, of which I have already spoken, and that the pilgrims composing it had mostly perished, having been scattered in the desert without water; that a great famine had been at Derna, the neighbouring town, to which I intended to go; that a plague had followed, and the town, which is divided into upper and lower, was engaged in a civil war. This torrent of ill news was irresistible, and was of a kind I did not propose to wrestle with; besides, there was nothing, as far as I knew, that merited the risk. I resolved, therefore, to fly from this inhospitable coast, and save to the public, at least, that knowledge and entertainment I had acquired for them.

I embarked on board the Greek vessel, very ill accoutred, as we afterwards found, and, though it had plenty of sail, it had not an ounce of ballast. A number of people, men, women, and children, flying from the calamities which attend

tend famine, crowded in unknown to me; but the paſſage was ſhort, the veſſel light, and the maſter, as we ſuppoſed, well accuſtomed to theſe ſeas. The contrary of this, however, was the truth, as we learned afterwards, when too late, for he was an abſolute landſman; proprietor indeed of the veſſel, but this had been his firſt voyage. We ſailed at dawn of day in as favourable and pleaſant weather as ever I ſaw at ſea. It was the beginning of September, and a light and ſteady breeze, though not properly fair, promiſed a ſhort and agreeable voyage; but it was not long before it turned freſh and cold; we then had a violent ſhower of hail, and the clouds were gathering as if for thunder. I obſerved that we gained no offing, and hoped, if the weather turned bad, to perſuade the Captain to put into Bengazi, for one inconvenience he preſently diſcovered, that they had not proviſion on board for one day.

However, the wind became contrary, and blew a violent ſtorm, ſeeming to menace both thunder and rain. The veſſel being in her trim with large latine ſails, fell violently to leeward, and they ſcarce would have weathered the Cape that makes the entrance into the harbour of Bengazi, which is a very bad one, when all at once it ſtruck upon a ſunken rock, and ſeemed to be ſet down upon it. The wind at that inſtant ſeemed providentially to calm; but I no ſooner obſerved the ſhip had ſtruck than I began to think of my own ſituation. We were not far from ſhore, but there was an exceeding great ſwell at ſea. Two boats were ſtill towed aſtern of them, and had not been hoiſted in. Roger M'Cormack, my Iriſh ſervant, had been a ſailor on board the Monarch before he deſerted to the Spaniſh ſervice. He and the other, who had likewiſe been a ſailor, preſently unlaſh-
ed

INTRODUCTION.

ed the largeſt boat, and all three got down into her, followed by a multitude of people whom we could not hinder, and there was, indeed, ſomething that bordered on cruelty, in preventing poor people from uſing the ſame means that we had done for preſerving their lives; yet, unleſs we had killed them, the prevention was impoſſible, and, had we been inclined to that meaſure, we dared not, as we were upon a Mooriſh coaſt. The moſt that could be done was, to get looſe from the ſhip as ſoon as poſſible, and two oars were prepared to row the boat aſhore. I had ſtript myſelf to a ſhort under-waiſtcoat and linen drawers; a ſilk faſh, or girdle, was wrapt round me; a pencil, ſmall pocket-book, and watch, were in the breaſt-pocket of my waiſtcoat; two Mooriſh and two Engliſh ſervants followed me; the reſt, more wiſe, remained on board.

We were not twice the length of the boat from the veſſel before a wave very nearly filled the boat. A howl of deſpair from thoſe that were in her ſhewed their helpleſs ſtate, and that they were conſcious of a danger they could not ſhun. I ſaw the fate of all was to be decided by the very next wave that was rolling in; and apprehenſive that ſome woman, child, or helpleſs man would lay hold of me, and entangle my arms or legs and weigh me down, I cried to my ſervants, both in Arabic and Engliſh, We are all loſt; if you can ſwim, follow me; I then let myſelf down in the face of the wave. Whether that, or the next, filled the boat, I know not, as I went to leeward to make my diſtance as great as poſſible. I was a good, ſtrong, and practiſed ſwimmer, in the flower of life, full of health, trained to exerciſe and fatigue of every kind. All this, however, which might have availed much in deep water, was not sufficient when I came to the surf. I received a violent blow upon my breast from the eddy wave and reflux, which seemed as given me by a large branch of a tree, thick cord, or some elastic weapon. It threw me upon my back, made me swallow a considerable quantity of water, and had then almost suffocated me.

I AVOIDED the next wave, by dipping my head and letting it pass over, but found myself breathless, exceedingly weary and exhausted. The land, however, was before me, and close at hand. A large wave floated me up. I had the prospect of escape still nearer, and endeavoured to prevent myself from going back into the surf. My heart was strong, but strength was apparently failing, by being involuntarily twisted about, and struck on the face and breast by the violence of the ebbing wave : it now seemed as if nothing remained but to give up the struggle, and resign to my destiny. Before I did this I sunk to found if I could touch the ground, and found that I reached the sand with my feet, though the water was still rather deeper than my mouth. The success of this experiment infused into me the strength of ten men, and I strove manfully, taking advantage of floating only with the influx of the wave, and preserving my strength for the struggle against the ebb, which, by sinking and touching the ground, I now made more easy. At last, finding my hands and knees upon the sands, I fixed my nails into it, and obstinately resisted being carried back at all, crawling a few feet when the sea had retired. I had perfectly lost my recollection and understanding, and after creeping so far as to be out of the reach of the sea, I suppose pofe I fainted, for from that time I was totally infenfible of any thing that paffed around me.

In the mean time the Arabs, who live two fhort miles from the fhore, came down in crowds to plunder the veffel. One of the boats was thrown afhore, and they had belonging to them fome others; there was one yet with the wreck, which fcarcely appeared with its gunnel above water. All the people were now taken on fhore, and thofe only loft who perifhed in the boat. What firft wakened me from this femblance of death was a blow with the butt-end of a lance, fhod with iron, upon the juncture of the neck with the back-bone. This produced a violent fenfation of pain; but it was a mere accident the blow was not with the point, for the fmall, fhort waiftcoat, which had been made at Algiers, the fafh and drawers, all in the Turkifh fafhion, made the Arabs believe that I was a Turk; and after many blows, kicks, and curfes, they ftript me of the little cloathing I had, and left me naked. They ufed the reft in the fame manner, then went to their boats to look for the bodies of thofe that were drowned.

After the difcipline I had received, I had walked, or crawled up among fome white, fandy hillocks, where I fat down and concealed myfelf as much as poffible. The weather was then warm, but the evening promifed to be cooler, and it was faft drawing on; there was great danger to be apprehended if I approached the tents where the women were while I was naked, for in this cafe it was very probable I would receive another baftinado fomething worfe than the firft. Still I was fo confufed that I had not recollected I could fpeak to them in their own language, and it now only

INTRODUCTION.

ly came into my mind, that by the gibberiſh, in imitation of Turkiſh, which the Arab had uttered to me while he was beating and ſtripping me, he took me for a Turk, and to this in all probability the ill-uſage was owing.

An old man and a number of young Arabs came up to me where I was ſitting. I gave them the ſalute *Salam Alicum!* which was only returned by one young man, in a tone as if he wondered at my impudence. The old man then aſked me, Whether I was a Turk, and what I had to do there? I replied, I was no Turk, but a poor Chriſtian phyſician, a Derviſh that went about the world ſecking to do good for God's ſake, was then flying from famine, and going to Greece to get bread. He then aſked me if I was a Cretan? I ſaid, I had never been in Crete, but came from Tunis, and was returning to that town, having loſt every thing I had in the ſhipwreck of that veſſel. I ſaid this in ſo deſpairing a tone, that there was no doubt left with the Arab that the fact was true. A ragged, dirty baracan was immediately thrown over me, and I was ordered up to a tent, in the end of which ſtood a long ſpear thruſt through it, a mark of ſovereignty.

I there ſaw the Shekh of the tribe, who being in peace with the Bey of Bengazi, and alſo with the Shekh of Ptolometa, after many queſtions ordered me a plentiful ſupper, of which all my ſervants partook, none of them having periſhed. A multitude of conſultations followed on their complaints, of which I freed myſelf in the beſt manner I could, alleuging the loſs of all my medicines, in order to induce ſome of them to ſeek for the ſextant at leaſt, but all to no purpoſe,

purpose, so that, after staying two days among them, the Shekh restored to us all that had been taken from us, and mounting us upon camels, and giving us a conductor, he forwarded us to Bengazi, where we arrived the second day in the evening. Thence I sent a compliment to the Shekh, and with it a man from the Bey, intreating that he would use all possible means to fish up some of my cases, for which I assured him he should not miss a handsome reward. Promises and thanks were returned, but I never heard further of my instruments; all I recovered was a silver watch of Ellicot, the work of which had been taken out and broken, some pencils, and a small port-folio, in which were sketches of Ptolemeta; my pocket-book too was found, but my pencil was lost, being in a common silver case, and with them all the astronomical observations which I had made in Barbary. I there lost a sextant, a parallactic instrument, a time-piece, a reflecting telescope, an achromatic one, with many drawings, a copy of M. de la Caille's ephemerides down to the year 1775, much to be regretted, as being full of manuscript marginal notes; a small camera obscura, some guns, pistols, a blunderbuss, and several other articles.

I FOUND at Bengazi a small French sloop, the master of which had been often at Algiers when I was consul there. I had even, as the master remembered, done him some little service, for which, contrary to the custom of that sort of people, he was very grateful. He had come there laden with corn, and was going up the Archipelago, or towards the Morea, for more. The cargo he had brought was but a mite compared to the necessities of the place; it only relieved

lieved the foldiers for a time, and many people of all ages and fexes were ftill dying every day.

The harbour of Bengazi is full of fifh, and my company caught a great quantity with a fmall net; we likewife procured a multitude with the line, enough to have maintained a larger number of perfons than the family confifted of; we got vinegar, pepper, and fome ftore of onions; we had little bread it is true, but ftill our induftry kept us very far from ftarving. We endeavoured to inftruct thefe wretches, gave them pack-thread, and fome coarfe hooks, by which they might have fubfifted with the fmalleft attention and trouble; but they would rather ftarve in multitudes, ftriving to pick up fingle grains of corn, that were fcattered upon the beach by the burfting of the facks, or the inattention of the mariners, than take the pains to watch one hour at the flowing of the tide for excellent fifh, where, after taking one, they were fure of being mafters of multitudes till it was high water.

The Captain of the fmall veffel loft no time. He had done his bufinefs well, and though he was returning for another cargo, yet he offered me what part of his funds I fhould need with great franknefs. We now failed with a fair wind, and in four or five days eafy weather landed at Canea, a confiderable fortified place at the weft end of the ifland of Crete. Here I was taken dangeroufly ill, occafioned by the bathing and extraordinary exertions in the fea of Prolometa, nor was I in the leaft the better from the beating I had received, figns of which I bore very long afterwards.

From Canea I failed for Rhodes, and there met my books; I then proceeded to Castelroffo, on the coast of Caramania, and was there credibly informed that there were very magnificent remains of ancient buildings a short way from the shore, on the opposite continent. Caramania is a part of Asia Minor yet unexplored. But my illness increasing, it was impossible to execute, or take any measures to secure protection, or do the business safely, and I was forced to relinquish this discovery to some more fortunate traveller.

Mr Peyssonel, French consul at Smyrna, a man not more distinguished for his amiable manners than for his polite taste in literature, of which he has given several elegant specimens, furnished me with letters for that part of Caramania, or Asia Minor, and there is no doubt but they would have been very efficacious. What increased the obligation for this kind attention shewn, was, that I had never seen Mr Peyssonel; and I am truly mortified, that, since my arrival in England, I have had no opportunity to return my grateful thanks for this kindness, which I therefore beg that he will now accept, together with a copy of these travels, which I have ordered my French bookseller to forward to him.

From Castelroffo I continued, without any thing remarkable, till I came to Cyprus; I staid there but half a day, and arrived at Sidon, where I was most kindly received by Mr Clerambaut, brother-in-law to Mr Peyssonel, and French consul at this place; a man in politeness, humanity, and every social quality of the mind, inferior to none I have ever known. With him, and a very flourishing, well-informed, and industrious nation, I continued for some time, then

INTRODUCTION.

in a weak state of health, but still making partial excursions from time to time into the continent of Syria, through Libanus, and Anti Libanus; but as I made these without instruments, and passed pretty much in the way of the travellers who have described these countries before, I leave the history to those gentlemen, without swelling, by entering into particular narratives, this Introduction, already too long.

WHILE at Canea I wrote by way of France, and again while at Rhodes by way of Smyrna, to particular friends both in London and France, informing them of my disastrous situation, and desiring them to send me a moveable quadrant or sextant, as near as possible to two feet radius, more or less, a time-keeper, stop-watch, a reflecting telescope, and one of Dolland's achromatic ones, as near as possible to three-feet reflectors, with several other articles which I then wanted.

I RECEIVED from Paris and London much about the same time, and as if it had been dictated by the same person, nearly the same answer, which was this, That everybody was employed in making instruments for Danish, Swedish, and other foreign astronomers; that all those which were completed had been bought up, and without waiting a considerable, indefinite time, nothing could be had that could be depended upon. At the same time I was told, to my great mortification, that no accounts of me had arrived from Africa, unless from several idle letters, which had been industriously wrote by a gentleman whose name 1 abstain from mentioning, first, because he is dead, and next, out of respect to his truly great and worthy relations,.

INTRODUCTION.

In thefe letters it was announced, that I was gone with a Ruffian caravan through the Curdiftan, where I was to obferve the tranfit of Venus in a place where it was not vifible, and that I was to proceed to China, and return by the way of the Eaft Indies :—a ftory which fome of his correfpondents, as profligate as himfelf, induftrioufly circulated at the time, and which others, perhaps weaker than wicked, though wicked enough, have affected to believe to this day.

I conceived a violent indignation at this, and finding myfelf fo treated in return for fo complete a journey as I had then actually terminated, thought it below me to facrifice the beft years of my life to daily pain and danger, when the impreffion it made in the breafts of my countrymen feemed to be fo weak, fo infinitely unworthy of them or me. One thing only detained me from returning home; it was my defire of fulfilling my promife to my Sovereign, and of adding the ruins of Palmyra to thofe of Africa, already fecured and out of danger.

In my anger I renounced all thoughts of the attempt to difcover the fources of the Nile, and I repeated my orders no more for either quadrant, telefcope, or time-keeper. I had pencils and paper; and luckily my large camera obfcura, which had efcaped the cataftrophe of Ptolometa, was arrived from Smyrna, and then ftanding before me. I therefore began to caft about, with my ufual care and anxiety, for the means of obtaining feafible and fafe methods of repeating the famous journey to Palmyra. I found it was neceffary to advance nearer the fcene of action. Mr Abbot, Britifh conful for Tripoli in Syria, kindly invited me, and

after

INTRODUCTION.

after him Mr Vernon, his succeffor, a very excellent man, to take up my refidence there From Tripoli there is a trade in kelp carried on to the falt marlhes near Palmyra. The Shekh of Cariateen, a town juft upon the edge of the defert, had a contract with the bafha of Tripoli for a quantity of this herb for the ufe of the foap-works. I loft no time in making a friendfhip with this man, but his return amounted to no more than to endeavour to lead me rafhly into real danger, where he knew he had not confequence enough to give me a moment's protection.

THERE are two tribes almoft equally powerful who inhabit the deferts round Palmyra; the one is the Annecy, remarkable for the fineft breed of horfes in the world; the other is the Mowalli, much better foldiers, but fewer in number, and very little inferior in the excellence of their horfes. The Annecy poffefs the country towards the S. W. at the back of Libanus, about Bozra down the Hawran, and fouthward towards the borders of Arabia Petrea and Mount Horeb. The Mowalli inhabit the plains caft of Damafcus to the Euphrates, and north to near Aleppo.

THESE two tribes were not at war, nor were they at peace; they were upon what is called ill-terms with each other, which is the moft dangerous time for ftrangers to have any dealings with either. I learned this as a certainty from a friend at Haffia, where a Shekh lives, to whom I was recommended by a letter, as a friend of the bafha of Damafcus. This man maintains his influence, not by a number of forces, but by conftantly marrying a relation of one or both of thefe tribes of Arabs, who for that reafon affift him in maintaining the fecurity of his road, and he has the care of

INTRODUCTION.   liii

of that part of it by which the couriers pafs from Conftantinople into Egypt, belonging to both thefe tribes, who were then at a diftance from each other, and roved in flying fquadrons all round Palmyra, by way of maintaining their right of pafture in places that neither of them chofe at that time to occupy. Thefe, I fuppofe, are what the Englifh writers call Wild Arabs, for otherwife, though they are all wild enough, I do not know one wilder than another. This is very certain, thefe young men, compofing the flying parties I fpeak of, are truly wild while at a diftance from their camp and government; and the ftranger that falls in unawares with them, and efcapes with his life, may fet himfelf down as a fortunate traveller.

RETURNING from Haffia I would have gone fouthward to Baalbec, but it was then befieged by Emir Youfef prince of the Drufes, a Pagan nation, living upon mount Libanus. Upon that I returned to Tripoli, in Syria, and after fome time fet out for Aleppo, travelling northward along the plain of Jeune betwixt mount Lebanon and the fea.

I VISITED the ancient Byblus, and bathed with pleafure in the river Adonis. All here is claffic ground. I faw feveral confiderable ruins of Grecian architecture all very much defaced. Thefe are already publifhed by Mr Drummond, and therefore I left them, being never defirous of interfering with the works of others.

I PASSED Latikea, formerly Laodicea ad Mare, and then came to Antioch, and afterwards to Aleppo. The fever and ague, which I had firft caught in my cold bath at Bengazi, had returned upon me with great violence, after paffing

one

one night encamped in the mulberry gardens behind Sidon. It had returned in very flight paroxyfms feveral times, but laid hold of me with more than ordinary violence on my arrival at Aleppo, where I came juft in time to the houfe of Mr Belville, a French merchant, to whom I was addreffed for my credit. Never was a more lucky addrefs, never was there a foul fo congenial to my own as was that of Mr Belville: to fay more after this would be praifing myfelf. To him was immediately added Doctor Patrick Ruffel, phyfician to the Britifh factory there. Without the attention and friendfhip of the one, and the fkill and anxiety of the other of thefe gentlemen, it is probable my travels would have ended at Aleppo. I recovered flowly. By the report of thefe two gentlemen, though I had yet feen nobody, I became a public care, nor did I ever pafs more agreeable hours than with Mr Thomas the French conful, his family, and the merchants eftablifhed there. From Doctor Ruffel I was fupplied with what I wanted, fome books, and much inftruction. Noboby knew the difeafes of the Eaft fo well; and perhaps my efcaping the fever at Aleppo was not the only time in which I owed him my life.

Being now reftored to health, my firft object was the journey to Palmyra. The Mowalli were encamped at no great diftance from Aleppo. It was without difficulty I found a fure way to explain my wifhes, and to fecure the affiftance of Mahomet Kerfan, the Shekh, but from him I learned, in a manner that I could not doubt, that the way I intended to go down to Palmyra from the north was tedious, troublefome, uncertain, and expenfive, and that he did not wifh me to undertake it at that time. It is quite fuperfluous in thefe
cafes

INTRODUCTION.

cafes to prefs for particular information; an Arab conductor, who proceeds with caution, furely means you well. He told me that he would leave a friend in the houfe of a certain Arab at Hamath*, about half-way to Palmyra, and if in fomething more than a month I came there, and found that Arab, I might rely upon him without fear, and he would conduct me in fafety to Palmyra.

I RETURNED to Tripoli, and at the time appointed fet out for Hamath, found my conductor, and proceeded to Haffia. Coming from Aleppo, I had not paffed the lower way again by Antioch. The river which paffes through the plains where they cultivate their beft tobacco, is the Orontes; it was fo fwollen with rain, which had fallen in the mountains, that the ford was no longer vifible. Stopping at two miferable huts inhabited by a bafe fet called Turcomans, I afked the mafter of one of them to fhew me the ford, which he very readily undertook to do, and I went, for the length of fome yards, on rough, but very hard and folid ground. The current before me was, however, fo violent, that 1 had more than once a defire to turn back, but, not fufpecting any thing, I continued, when on a fudden man and horfe fell out of their depth into the river.

I HAD a rifled gun flung acrofs my fhoulder, with a buff belt and fwivel. As long as that held, it fo embarraffed my hands and legs that I could not fwim, and muft have funk; but luckily the fwivel gave way, the gun fell to the bottom of the river, and was pickt up in dry weather by order of the

---

* The north boundary of the Holy Land.

the bafha, at the defire of the French merchants, who kept it for a relict. I and my horfe fwam feparately afhore; at a fmall diftance from thence was a caphar*, or turnpike, to which, when I came to dry myfelf, the man told me, that the place where I had croffed was the remains of a ftone bridge now entirely carried away; where I had firft entered was one of the wings of the bridge, from which I had fallen into the fpace the firft arch occupied, one of the deepeft parts of the river; that the people who had mifguided me were an infamous fet of banditti, and that I might be thankful on many accounts that I had made fuch an efcape from them, and was now on the oppofite fide. I then prevailed on the caphar-man to fhew my fervants the right ford.

From Haffia we proceeded with our conductor to Cariateen, where there is an immenfe fpring of fine water, which overflows into a large pool. Here, to our great furprife, we found about two thoufand of the Annecy encamped, who were quarrelling with Haffan our old friend, the kelp-merchant. This was nothing to us; the quarrel between the Mowalli and Annecy had it feems been made up; for an old man from each tribe on horfeback accompanied us to Palmyra: the tribes gave us camels for more commodious travelling, and we paffed the defert between Cariateen and Palmyra in a day and two nights, going conftantly without fleeping.

Just

---

* It is a poft where a party of men are kept to receive a contribution, for maintaining the fecurity of the roads, from all paffengers.

INTRODUCTION. lvii

Just before we came in fight of the ruins, we afcended a hill of white gritty ftone, in a very narrow-winding road, fuch as we call a pafs, and, when arrived at the top, there opened before us the moft aftonifhing, ftupendous fight that perhaps ever appeared to mortal eyes. The whole plain below, which was very extenfive, was covered fo thick with magnificent buildings as that the one feemed to touch the other, all of fine proportions, all of agreeable forms, all compofed of white ftones, which at that diftance appeared like marble. At the end of it ftood the palace of the fun, a building worthy to clofe fo magnificent a fcene.

It was impoffible for two perfons to think of defigning ornaments, or taking meafures, and there feemed the lefs occafion for this as Mr Wood had done this part already. I had no intention to publifh any thing concerning Palmyra; befides, it would have been a violation of my firft principle not to interfere with the labours of others; and if this was a rule I inviolably obferved as to ftrangers, every fentiment of reafon and gratitude obliged me to pay the fame refpect to the labours of Mr Wood my friend.

I divided Palmyra into fix angular views, always bringing forward to the firft ground an edifice, or principal group of columns, that deferved it. The ftate of the buildings are particularly favourable for this purpofe. The columns are all uncovered to the very bafes, the foil upon which the town is built being hard and fixed ground. Thefe views are all upon large paper; the columns in fome of them are a foot long; the figures in the fore-ground of the temple of the fun are fome of them near four inches.

INTRODUCTION.

BEFORE our departure from Palmyra I obferved its latitude with a Hadley's quadrant from reflection. The inftrument had probably warped in carriage, as the index went unpleafantly, and as it were by ftarts, fo that I will not pretend to give this for an exact obfervation; yet, after all the care I could take, I only apprehended that 33° 58' for the latitude of Palmyra, would be nearer the truth than any other. Again, that the diftance from the coaft in a ftraight line being 160 miles, and that remarkable mountainous cape on the coaft of Syria, between Byblus and Tripoli, known by the name of Theoprofopon, being nearly due weft, or under the fame parallel with Palmyra, I conceive the longitude of that city to be nearly 37° 9' from the obfervatory of Greenwich.

FROM Palmyra I proceeded to Baalbec, diftant about 130 miles, and arrived the fame day that Emir Youfef had reduced the town and fettled the government, and was decamping from it on his return home. This was the luckieft moment poffible for me, as I was the Emir's friend, and I obtained liberty to do there what I pleafed, and to this indulgence was added the great convenience of the Emir's abfence, fo that I was not troubled by the obfervance of any court-ceremony or attendance, or teazed with impertinent queftions.

BAALBEC is pleafantly fituated in a plain on the weft of Anti Libanus, is finely watered, and abounds in gardens. It is about fifty miles from Haffia, and about thirty from the neareft fea-coaft, which is the fituation of the ancient Byblus. The interior of the great temple of Baalbec, fuppofed to be that of the fun, furpaffes any thing at Palmyra,

INTRODUCTION. lix

myra, indeed any sculpture I ever remember to have seen in stone. All these views of Palmyra and Baalbec are now in the King's collection. They are the most magnificent offering in their line that ever was made by one subject to his sovereign.

Passing by Tyre, from curiosity only, I came to be a mournful witness of the truth of that prophecy, That Tyre, the queen of nations, should be a rock for fishers to dry their nets on*. Two wretched fishermen, with miserable nets, having just given over their occupation with very little success, I engaged them, at the expence of their nets, to drag in those places where they said shell-fish might be caught, in hopes to have brought out one of the famous purple-fish. I did not succeed, but in this I was, I believe, as lucky as the old fishers had ever been. The purple fish at Tyre seems to have been only a concealment of their knowledge of cochineal, as, had they depended upon the fish for their dye, if the whole city of Tyre applied to nothing else but fishing, they would not have coloured twenty yards of cloth in a year. Much fatigued, but satisfied beyond measure with what I had seen, I arrived in perfect health, and in the gayest humour possible, at the hospitable mansion of M. Clerambaut at Sidon.

I found there letters from Europe, which were in a very different style from the last. From London, my friend Mr Russel acquainted me, that he had sent me an excellent reflecting telescope of two feet focal length, moved by

rack-

---

* Ezek chap. xxvi. ver. 5.

INTRODUCTION.

rack-work, and the laft Mr Short ever made, which proved a very excellent inftrument; alfo an achromatic telefcope by Dolland, nearly equal to a three-feet reflector, with a foot, or ftand, very artificially compofed of rulers fixed together by fcrews. I think this inftrument might be improved by fhortening the three principal legs of it. If the legs of its ftand were about fix inches fhorter, this, without inconvenience, would take away the little fhake it has when ufed in the outer air. Perhaps this defect is not in all telefcopes of this conftruction. It is a pleafant inftrument, and for its fize takes very little packing, and is very manageable.

I have brought home both thefe inftruments after performing the whole journey, and they are now ftanding in my library, in the moft perfect order; which is rather to be wondered at from the accounts in which moft travellers feem to agree, that metal fpeculums, within the tropics, fpot and ruft fo much as to be ufelefs after a few obfervations made at or near the zenith. The fear of this, and the fragility of glafs of achromatic telefcopes, were the occafion of a confiderable expence to me; but from experience I found, that, if a little care be taken, one reflector would be fufficient for a very long voyage.

From Paris I received a time-piece and a ftop-watch made by M. Lepeaute, dearer than Ellicot's, and refembling his in nothing elfe but the price. The clock was a very neat, portable inftrument, made upon very ingenious, fimple principles, but fome of the parts were fo grofsly neglected in the execution, and fo unequally finifhed, that it was not difficult for the meaneft novice in the trade to point out the

caufe

INTRODUCTION. lxi

caufe of its irregularity. It remains with me in ftatu quo. It has been of very little ufe to me, and never will be of much more to any perfon elfe. The price is, I am fure, ten times more than it ought to be in any light I can confider it.

ALL thefe letters ftill left me in abfolute defpair about obtaining a quadrant, and confequently gave me very little fatisfaction, but in fome meafure confirmed me in my refolution already taken, to go from Sidon to Egypt; as I had then feen the greateft part of the good architecture in the world, in all its degrees of perfection down to its decline, I wifhed now only to fee it in its origin, and for this it was neceffary to go to Egypt.

NORDEN, Pococke, and many others, had given very ingenious accounts of Egyptian architecture in general, of the difpofition and fize of their temples, magnificence of their materials, their hieroglyphics, and the various kinds of them, of their gilding, of their painting, and their prefent ftate of prefervation. I thought fomething more might be learnt as to the firft proportions of their columns, and the conftruction of their plans. Dendera, the ancient Tentyra, feemed by their accounts to offer a fair field for this.

I HAD already collected together a great many obfervations on the progrefs of Greek and Roman architecture in different ages, drawn not from books or connected with fyftem, but from the models themfelves, which I myfelf had meafured. I had been long of the opinion, in which I am ftill further confirmed, that tafte for ancient architecture, founded ed upon the examples that Italy alone can furnifh, was not giving ancient architects fair play. What was to be learned from the firft proportions of their plans and elevations feemed to have remained untouched in Egypt; after having confidered thefe, I propofed to live in retirement on my native patrimony, with a fair ftock of unexceptionable materials upon this fubject, to ferve for a pleafant and ufeful amufement in my old age. I hope ftill thefe will not be loft to the public, unlefs the encouragement be in proportion to what my labours have already had.

I now received, however, a letter very unexpectedly by way of Alexandria, which, if it did not overturn, at leaft fhook thefe refolutions. The Comte de Buffon, Monf. Guys of Marfeilles, and feveral others well known in the literary world, had ventured to ftate to the minifter, and through him to the king of France, Louis XV. how very much it was to be lamented, that after a man had been found who was likely to fucceed in removing that opprobrium of travellers and geographers, by difcovering the fources of the Nile, one moft unlucky accident, at a moft unlucky time, fhould fruftrate the moft promifing endeavours. That prince, diftinguifhed for every good quality of the heart, for benevolence, beneficence, and a defire of promoting and protecting learning, ordered a moveable quadrant of his own military academy at Marfeilles, as the neareft and moft convenient port of embarkation, to be taken down and fent to me at Alexandria.

With this I received a letter from Mr Ruffel, which informed me that aftronomers had begun to cool in the fanguine expectations of difcovering the precife quantity of the

INTRODUCTION.   lxiii

the fun's parallax by obfervation of the tranfit of Venus, from fome apprehenfion that errors of the obfervers would probably be more than the quantity of the equation fought, and that they now ardently wifhed for a journey into Abyffinia, rather than an attempt to fettle a nicety for which the learned had now begun to think the accuracy of our inftruments was not fufficient. A letter from my correfpondent at Alexandria alfo acquainted me, that the quadrant, and all other inftruments, were in that city.

WHAT followed is the voyage itfelf, the fubject of the prefent publication. I am happy, by communicating every previous circumftance that occurred to me, to have done all in my power to remove the greateft part of the reafonable doubts and difficulties which might have perplexed the reader's mind, or biaffed his judgment in the perufal of the narrative of the journey, and in this I hope I have fucceeded

I HAVE now one remaining part of my promife to fulfil, to account for the delay in the publication. It will not be thought furprifing to any that fhall reflect on the diftant, dreary, and defert ways by which all letters were neceffarily to pafs, or the civil wars then raging in Abyffinia, the robberies and violences infeparable from a total diffolution of government, fuch as happened in my time, that no accounts for many years, one excepted, ever arrived in Europe. One letter, accompanied by a bill for a fum borrowed from a Greek at Gondar, found its way to Cairo; all the reft had mifcarried: my friends at home gave me up for dead; and, as my death muft have happened in circumftances difficult to have been proved, my property became

INTRODUCTION.

as it were an *hereditas jacens*, without an owner, abandoned in common to those whose original title extended no further than temporary possession.

A number of law-suits were the inevitable consequence of this upon my return. One carried on with a very expensive obstinacy for the space of ten years, by a very opulent and active company, was determined finally in the House of Peers, in the compass of a very few hours, by the well-known sagacity and penetration of a noble Lord, who, happily for the subjects of both countries, holds the first office in the law; and so judicious was the sentence, that harmony, mutual confidence, and good neighbourhood has ever since been the consequence of that determination.

Other suits still remained, which unfortunately were not arrived to the degree of maturity to be so cut off; they are yet depending; patience and attention, it is hoped, may bring them to an issue at some future time. No imputation of rashness can possibly fall upon the decree, since the action has depended above thirty years.

To these disagreeable avocations, which took up much time, were added others still more unfortunate. The relentless ague caught at Bengazi maintained its ground at times for a space of more than sixteen years, though every remedy had been used, but in vain; and, what was worst of all, a lingering distemper had seriously threatened the life of a most near relation, which, after nine years constant alarm, where every duty bound me to attention and attendance,

INTRODUCTION.

ance, conducted her at last, in very early life, to her grave *.

The love of solitude is the constant follower of affliction; this again naturally turns an instructed mind to study. My friends unanimously assailed me in the part most accessible when the spirits are weak, which is vanity. They represented to me how ignoble it was, after all my dangers and difficulties were over, to be conquered by a misfortune incident to all men, the indulging of which was unreasonable in itself, fruitless in its consequences, and so unlike the expectation I had given my country, by the firmness and intrepidity of my former character and behaviour. Among these, the principal and most urgent was a gentleman well known to the literary world, in which he holds a rank nearly as distinguished as that to which his virtues entitle him in civil life; this was the Hon. Daines Barrington, whose friendship, valuable on every account, had this additional merit, that it had existed uninterrupted since the days we were at school. It is to this gentleman's persuasions, assistance, protection, and friendship, that the world owes this publication, if indeed there is any merit in it; at least, they are certainly indebted to him for the opportunity of judging whether there is any merit in it or not.

No great time has passed since the work was in hand. The materials collected upon the spot were very full, and seldom deferred to be set down beyond the day wherein the events described happened, but oftner, when speeches

---

* Mrs Bruce died in 1784.

and arguments were to be mentioned, they were noted the inſtant afterwards; for, contrary I believe to what is often the caſe, I can aſſure the reader theſe ſpeeches and converſations are abſolutely real, and not the fabrication of after-hours.

It will perhaps be ſaid, this work hath faults; nay, perhaps, great ones too, and this I readily confeſs. But I muſt likewiſe beg leave to ſay, that I know no books of the kind that have not nearly as many, and as great, though perhaps not of the ſame kind with mine. To ſee diſtinctly and accurately, to deſcribe plainly, diſpaſſionately and truly, is all that ought to be expected from one in my ſituation, conſtantly ſurrounded with every ſort of difficulty and danger.

It may be ſaid, too, there are faults in the language; more pains ſhould have been taken. Perhaps it may be ſo; yet there has not been wanting a conſiderable degree of attention even to this. I have not indeed confined myſelf to a painful and ſlaviſh nicety that would have produced nothing but a diſageeable ſtiffneſs in the narrative. It will be remembered likewiſe, that one of the motives of my writing is my own amuſement, and I would much rather renounce the ſubject altogether than walk in fetters of my own forging. The language is, like the ſubject, rude and manly. My paths have not been flowery ones, nor would it have added any credit to the work, or entertainment to the reader, to employ in it a ſtile proper only to works of imagination and pleaſure. Theſe trifling faults I willingly leave as food to the malice of critics, who perhaps,

INTRODUCTION. lxvii

haps, were it not for thefe blemifhes, would find no other enjoyment in the perufal of the work.

It has been faid that parties have been formed againft this work. Whether this is really the cafe I cannot fay, nor have I ever been very anxious in the inquiry. They have been harmlefs adverfaries at leaft, for no bad effects, as far as I know, have ever as yet been the confequences; neither is it a difquifition that I fhall ever enter into, whether this is owing to the want of will or of power. I rather believe it is to the former, the want of will, for no one is fo perfectly inconfiderable, as to want the power of doing mifchief.

Having now fulfilled my promife to the reader, in giving him the motive and order of my travels, and the reafon why the publication has been delayed, I fhall proceed to the laft article promifed, the giving fome account of the work itfelf. The book is a large one, and expenfive by the number of engravings; this was not at firft intended, but the journey has proved a long one, and matter has increafed as it were infenfibly under my hands. It is now come to fill a great chafm in the hiftory of the univerfe. It is not intended to refemble the generality of modern travels, the agreeable and rational amufement of one vacant day, it is calculated to employ a greater fpace of time.

Those that are the beft acquainted with Diodorus, Herodotus, and fome other Greek hiftorians, will find fome very confiderable difficulties removed; and they that are unacquainted with thefe authors, and receive from this work the firft information of the geography, climate, and manners of thefe countries, which are little altered, will have no great occafion

INTRODUCTION.

occafion to regret they have not fearched for information in more ancient fources.

THE work begins with my voyage from Sidon to Alexandria, and up the Nile to the firft cataract. The reader will not expect that I fhould dwell long upon the particular hiftory of Egypt; every other year has furnifhed us with fome account of it, good or bad; and the two laft publications of M. Savary and Volney feem to have left the fubject thread-bare. This, however, is not the only reafon.

AFTER Mr Wood and Mr Dawkins had publifhed their Ruins of Palmyra, the late king of Denmark, at his own expence, fent out a number of men, eminent in their feveral profeffions, to make difcoveries in the eaft, of every kind, with thefe very flattering inftructions, that though they might, and ought, to vifit both Baalbec and Palmyra for their own ftudies and improvement, yet he prohibited them to fo far interfere with what the Englifh travellers had done, as to form any plan of another work fimilar to theirs. This compliment was gratefully received; and, as I was directly to follow this miffion, Mr Wood defired me to return it, and to abftain as much as poffible from writing on the fame fubjects chofen by M. Niebuhr, at leaft to abftain either from criticifing or differing from him on fuch fubjects. I have therefore paffed flightly over Egypt and Arabia; perhaps, indeed, I have faid enough of both: if any fhall be of another opinion, they may have recourfe to M. Niebuhr's more copious work; he was the only perfon of fix who lived to come home, the reft having died in different parts of Arabia, without having been able to enter Abyffinia, one of the objects of their miffion.

My

INTRODUCTION. lxix

My leaving Egypt is followed by my furvey of the Arabian gulf as far as the Indian Ocean—Arrival at Mafuah—Some account of the firft peopling of Atbara and Abyffinia—Conjectures concerning language—Firft ages of the Indian trade—Foundation of the Abyffinian monarchy, and various revolutions till the Jewifh ufurpation about the year 900. Thefe compofe the firft volume.

The fecond begins with the reftoration of the line of Solomon, compiled from their own annals, now firft tranflated from the Ethiopic; the original of which has been lodged in the Britifh Mufeum, to fatisfy the curiofity of the public.

The third comprehends my journey from Mafuah to Gondar, and the manners and cuftoms of the Abyffinians, alfo two attempts to arrive at the fountains of the Nile—Defcription of thefe fources, and of every thing relating to that river and its inundation.

The fourth contains my return from the fource of the Nile to Gondar—The campaign of Serbraxos, and revolution that followed—My return through Sennaar and Beja, or the Nubian defert, and my arrival at Marfeilles.

In overlooking the work I have found one circumftance, and I think no more, which is not fufficiently clear, and may create a momentary doubt in the reader's mind, although to thofe who have been fufficiently attentive to the narrative, I can fcarce think it will do this. The difficulty is, How did you procure funds to fupport yourfelf,

and

lxx   INTRODUCTION.

and ten men, fo long, and fo eafily, as to enable you to un-
dervalue the uſeful character of a phyſician, and feek neither to draw money nor protection from it? And how came
it, that, contrary to the uſage of other travellers, at Gondar
you maintained a character of independence and equality,
efpecially at court; inſtead of crouching, living out of fight
as much as poffible, in continual fear of prieſts, under the
patronage, or rather as fervant to fome men of power.

To this fenfible and well-founded doubt I anfwer
with great pleaſure and readineſs, as I would do to all o-
thers of the fame kind, if I could poffibly divine them:—It
is not at all extraordinary that a ſtranger like me, and a parcel
of vagabonds like thoſe that were with me, ſhould get themfelves maintained, and find at Gondar a precarious livelihood for a limited time. A mind ever fo little poliſhed and
inſtructed has infinite fuperiority over Barbarians, and it is
in circumſtances like thefe that a man fees the great advantages of education. All the Greeks in Gondar were o-
riginally criminals and vagabonds; they neither had, nor
pretended to any profeffion, except Petros the king's cham-
berlain, who had been a ſhoemaker at Rhodes, which profeffion at his arrival he carefully concealed. Yet theſe
were not only maintained, but by degrees, and without
pretending to be phyſicians, obtained property, commands,
and placer.

HOSPITALITY is the virtue of Barbarians, who are hofpi-
table in the ratio that they are barbarous, and for obvious
reafons this virtue fubfides among poliſhed nations in the
fame proportion. If on my arrival in Abyffinia I affumed
                    2   a ſpirit

a fpirit of independence, it was from policy and reflection. I had often thought that the misfortunes which had befallen other travellers in Abyssinia arofe from the bafe eftimation the people in general entertained of their rank, and the value of their perfons. From this idea I refolved to adopt a contrary behaviour. I was going to a court where there was a *king of kings*, whofe throne was furrounded by a number of high-minded, proud, hereditary, punctilious nobility. It was impoffible, therefore, too much lowlinefs and humility could pleafe there.

Mr Murray, the ambaffador at Conftantinople, in the firman obtained from the grand fignior, had qualified me with the diftinction of Bey-Adzè, which means, not an Englifh nobleman (a peer) but a noble Englifhman, and he had added likewife, that I was a fervant of the king of Great Britain. All the letters of recommendation, very many and powerful, from Cairo and Jidda, had conftantly echoed this to every part to which they were addreffed. They announced that I was not a man, fuch as ordinarily came to them, to live upon their charity, but had ample means of my own, and each profeffed himfelf guarrantee of that fact, and that they themfelves on all occafions were ready to provide for me, by anfwering my demands.

The only requeft of thefe letters was fafety and protection to my perfon. It was mentioned that I was a phyfician, to introduce a conciliatory cirumftance, that I was above practifing for gain. That all I did was from the fear of God, from charity, and the love of mankind. I was a phyfician in the city, a foldier in the field, a courtier every where, demeaning myfelf, as confcious that I was not unworthy

of

of being a companion to the firſt of their nobility, and the king's ſtranger and gueſt, which is there a character, as it was with eaſtern nations of old, to which a certain ſort of conſideration is due. It was in vain to compare myſelf with them in any kind of learning, as they have none; muſic they have as little; in eating and drinking they were indeed infinitely my ſuperiors; but in one accompliſhment that came naturally into compariſon, which was horſemanſhip, I ſtudiouſly eſtabliſhed my ſuperiority.

My long reſidence among the Arabs had given me more than ordinary facility in managing the horſe; I had brought my own ſaddle and bridle with me, and, as the reader will find, bought my horſe of the Baharnagaſh in the firſt days of my journey, ſuch a one as was neceſſary to carry me, and him I trained carefully, and ſtudied from the beginning. The Abyſſinians, as the reader will hereafter ſee, are the worſt horſemen in the world. Their horſes are bad, not equal to our Welſh or our Scotch galloways. Their furniture is worſe. They know not the uſe of fire-arms on horſeback; they had never ſeen a double-barrelled gun, nor did they know that its effect was limited to two diſcharges, but that it might have been fired on to infinity. All this gave me an evident ſuperiority.

To this I may add, that, being in the prime of life, of no ungracious figure, having an accidental knack, which is not a trifle, of putting on the dreſs, and ſpeaking the language eaſily and gracefully, I cultivated with the utmoſt aſſiduity the friendſhip of the fair ſex, by the moſt modeſt, reſpectful diſtant attendance, and obſequiouſneſs in public, abating juft as much of that in private as fuited their humour and inclinations. I foon acquired a great fupport from thefe at court; jealoufy is not a paffion of the Abyffinians, who are in the contrary extreme, even to indifference.

Besides the money I had with me, I had a credit of L.400 upon Youfef Cabil, governor of Jidda. I had another upon a Turkifh merchant there. I had ftrong and general recommendations, if I fhould want fupplies, upon Metical Aga, firft minifter to the fherriffe of Mecca. This, well managed, was enough; but when I met my countrymen, the captains of the Englifh fhips from India, they added additional ftrength to my finances; they would have poured gold upon me to facilitate a journey they fo much defired upon feveral accounts. Captain Thornhill of the Bengal Merchant, and Captain Thomas Price of the Lion, took the conduct of my money-affairs under their direction. Their Saraf, or broker, had in his hands all the commerce that produced the revenues of Abyffinia, together with great part of the correfpondence of the eaft; and, by a lucky accident for me, Captain Price ftaid all winter with the Lion at Jidda; nay, fo kind and anxious was he as to fend over a fervant from Jidda on purpofe, upon a report having been raifed that I was flain by the ufurper Socinios, though it was only one of my fervants, and the fervant of Metical Aga, who were murdered by that monfter, as is faid, with his own hand. Twice he fent over filver to me when I had plenty of gold, and wanted that metal only to apply it in furniture and workmanfhip. I do not pretend to fay but fometimes thefe fupplies failed me, often by my negligence in not applying in proper time, fometimes by the abfence of merchants, who were all Mahometans, conftantly engaged in bufinefs and in journies, and more efpecially on the king's retiring to Tigré, after the battle of Limjour, when I was abandoned during the ufurpation of the unworthy Socinios. It was then I had recourfe to Petros and the Greeks, but more for their convenience than my own, and very feldom from neceffity. This opulence enabled me to treat upon equal footing, to do favours as well as to receive them.

EVERY mountebank-trick was a great accomplifhment there, fuch as making fquibs, crackers, and rockets. There was no ftation in the country to which by thefe accomplifhments I might not have pretended, had I been mad enough to have ever directed my thoughts that way; and I am certain, that in vain I might have folicited leave to return, had not a melancholy defpondency, the *amor patriæ*, feized me, and my health fo far declined as apparently to threaten death; but I was not even then permitted to leave Abyffinia till under a very folemn oath I promifed to return.

THIS manner of conducting myfelf had likewife its difadvantages. The reader will fee the times, without their being pointed out to him, in the courfe of the narrative. It had very near occafioned me to be murdered at Mafuah, but it was the means of preferving me at Gondar, by putting me above being infulted or queftioned by priefts, the fatal rock upon which all other European travellers had fplit : It would have occafioned my death at Sennaar, had I not been fo prudent as to difguife and lay afide the independent carriage

INTRODUCTION. lxxv

riage in time. Why should I not now speak as I really think, or why be guilty of ingratitude which my heart disclaims. I escaped by the providence and protection of heaven; and so little store do I set upon the advantage of my own experience, that I am satisfied, were I to attempt the same journey again, it would not avail me a straw, or hinder me from perishing miserably, as others have done, though perhaps a different way.

I HAVE only to add, that were it probable, as in my decayed state of health it is not, that I should live to see a second edition of this work, all well-founded, judicious remarks suggested should be gratefully and carefully attended to; but I do solemnly declare to the public in general, that I never will refute or answer any cavils, captious, or idle objections, such as every new publication seems unavoidably to give birth to, nor ever reply to those witticisms and criticisms that appear in newspapers and periodical writings. What I have written I have written. My readers have before them, in the present volumes, all that I shall ever say, directly or indirectly, upon the subject; and I do, without one moment's anxiety, trust my defence to an impartial, well-informed, and judicious public.

CONTENTS

OF THE

FIRST VOLUME.

DEDICATION.

INTRODUCTION, Page i

BOOK I.

THE AUTHOR'S JOURNEY AND VOYAGE FROM SIDON TILL HIS ARRIVAL AT MASUAH.

CHAP. I.

THE Author sails from Sidon—Touches at Cyprus—Arrives at Alexandria—Sets out for Rosetto—Embarks on the Nile, and arrives at Cairo, Page 1

CONTENTS.

CHAP. II.

Author's Reception at Cairo—Procures Letters from the Bey and the Greek Patriarch—Vifits the Pyramids—Obfervations on their Conftruction, P. 24

CHAP. III.

Leaves Cairo—Embarks on the Nile for Upper Egypt—Vifits Metrahenny and Mohannan—Reafons for fuppofing this the Situation of Memphis, 43

CHAP. IV.

Leaves Metrahenny—Comes to the Ifland Halouon—Falfe Pyramid—Thefe Buildings end—Sugar Canes—Ruins of Antinopolis—Reception there, 69

CHAP. V.

Voyage to Upper Egypt continued---Afhmounein, Ruins there—Gawa Kibeer Ruins---Mr Norden miftaken---Achmim---Convent of Catholics---Dendera---Magnificent Ruins---Adventure with a Saint there, 91

CHAP.

CONTENTS.

CHAP VI.

Arrives at Furshout—Adventure of Friar Christopher—Visits Thebes—Luxor and Carnac—Large Ruins at Edfu and Esné—Proceeds on his Voyage, P. 114

CHAP. VII.

Arrives at Syene---Goes to see the Cataract---Remarkable Tombs—The Situation of Syene—The Aga proposes a visit to Deir and Ibrim—The Author returns to Kenné, 150

CHAP. VIII.

The Author sets out from Kenné—Crosses the Desert of the Thebaid—Visits the Marble Mountains—Arrives at Cosseir on the Red Sea—Transactions there, 169

CHAP. IX.

Voyage to Jibbel Zumrud—Returns to Cosseir—Sails from Cosseir—Jaffateen Islands—Arrives at Tor, 204

CHAP. X.

Sails from Tor—Passes the Elanitic Gulf—Sees Raddua—Arrives at Yambo—Incidents there—Arrives at Jidda, 239

CONTENTS.

CHAP. XI.

Occurrences at Jidda—Visit of the Vizir—Alarm of the Factory—Great Civility of the English trading from India—Polygamy—Opinion of Dr Arbuthnot ill-founded—Contrary to Reason and Experience—Leaves Jidda,   P. 269

CHAP. XII.

Sails from Jidda—Konfodah—Ras Heli, Boundary of Arabia Felix—Arrives at Loheia—Proceeds to the Straits of the Indian Ocean—Arrives there—Returns by Azab to Loheia,   294

CHAP. XIII.

Sails for Masuah---Passes a Volcano---Comes to Dahalac—Troubled with a Ghost---Arrives at Masuah,   327

BOOK

CONTENTS.

BOOK II.

ACCOUNT OF THE FIRST AGES OF THE INDIAN AND AFRICAN TRADE—THE FIRST PEOPLING OF ABYSSINIA AND ATBARA—SOME CONJECTURES CONCERNING THE ORIGIN OF LANGUAGE THERE.

CHAP. I.

Of the Indian Trade in its earliest Ages—Settlement of Ethiopia—Troglodytes—Building of the first Cities, P. 365

CHAP. II.

Saba and the South of Africa peopled—Shepherds, their particular Employment and Circumstances—Abyssinia occupied by seven Stranger Nations—Specimens of their several Languages—Conjectures concerning them, 381

CHAP. III.

Origin of Characters or Letters—Ethiopic the first Language—How and why the Hebrew Letter was formed. 411

CHAP. IV.

Some Account of the Trade-Winds and Monsoons—Application of this to the Voyage to Ophir and Tarshish P. 427

CHAP. V.

Fluctuating State of the India Trade---Hurt by military Expeditions of the Persians—Revives under the Ptolemies—Falls to Decay under the Romans, 447

CHAP. VI.

Queen of Saba visits Jerusalem---Abyssinian Tradition concerning Her—Supposed Founder of that Monarchy---Abyssinia embraces the Jewish Religion—Jewish Hierarchy still retained by the Falasha---Some Conjectures concerning their Copy of the Old Testament, 471

CHAP. VII.

Books in use in Abyssinia---Enoch—Abyssinia not converted by the Apostles---Conversion from Judaism to Christianity by Frumentius, 493

CHAP.

CHAP. VIII.

War of the Elephant—First Appearance of the Small-Pox---Jews persecute the Christians in Arabia---Defeated by the Abyssinians Mahomet pretends a Divine Mission---Opinion concerning the Koran---Revolution under Judith---Restoration of the Line of Solomon from Shoa, P. 510

TRAVELS

TO DISCOVER

THE SOURCE OF THE NILE.

BOOK I.

THE AUTHOR'S TRAVELS IN EGYPT—VOYAGE IN THE RED SEA, TILL HIS ARRIVAL AT MASUAH.

CHAP. I.

The Author sails from Sidon—Touches at Cyprus—Arrives at Alexandria—Sets out for Rosetto—Embarks on the Nile—and arrives at Cairo.

IT was on Saturday the 15th of June, 1768, I sailed in a French vessel from Sidon, once the richest and most powerful city in the world, though now there is not remaining a shadow of its ancient grandeur. We were bound for the island of Cyprus; the weather clear and exceedingly hot, the wind favourable.

This island is not in our courfe for Alexandria, but lies to the northward of it; nor had I, for my own part, any curiofity to fee it. My mind was intent upon more uncommon, more diftant, and more painful voyages. But the mafter of the veffel had bufinefs of his own which led him thither; with this I the more readily complied, as we had not yet got certain advice that the plague had ceafed in Egypt, and it ftill wanted fome days to the Feftival of St John, which is fuppofed to put a period to that cruel diftemper*.

We obferved a number of thin, white clouds, moving with great rapidity from fouth to north, in direct oppofition to the courfe of the Etefian winds; thefe were immenfely high. It was evident they came from the mountains of Abyffinia, where, having difcharged their weight of rain, and being preffed by the lower current of heavier air from the northward, they had mounted to poffefs the vacuum, and returned to reftore the equilibrium to the northward, whence they were to come back, loaded with vapour from Mount Taurus, to occafion the overflowing of the Nile, by breaking againft the high and rugged mountains of the fouth.

Nothing could be more agreeable to me than that fight, and the reafoning upon it. I already, with pleafure, anticipated the time in which I fhould be a fpectator firft, afterwards hiftorian, of this phænomenon, hitherto a myftery through all ages. I exulted in the meafures I had taken, which I flattered myfelf, from having been digefted with greater confideration than thofe adopted by others, would fecure

---

* The nucta, or dew, that falls on St John's night, is fuppofed to have the virtue to ftop the plague. I have confidered this in the fequel.

THE SOURCE OF THE NILE.

secure me from the melancholy cataftrophes that had terminated thefe hitherto-unfuccefsful attempts.

On the 16th, at dawn of day, I faw a high hill, which, from its particular form, defcribed by Strabo*, I took for Mount Olympus †. Soon after, the reft of the ifland, which feemed low, appeared in view. We fcarce faw Lernica till we anchored before it. It is built of white clay, of the fame colour as the ground, precifely as is the cafe with Damafcus, fo that you cannot, till clofe to it, diftinguifh the houfes from the earth they ftand upon.

It is very remarkable that Cyprus was fo long undifcovered‡; fhips had been ufed in the Mediterranean 1700 years before Chrift; yet, though only a day's failing from the continent of Afia on the north and eaft, and little more from that of Africa on the fouth, it was not known at the building of Tyre, a little before the Trojan war, that is 500 years after fhips had been paffing to and fro in the feas around it.

It was, at its difcovery, thick covered with wood; and what leads me to believe it was not well known, even fo late as the building of Solomon's Temple, is, that we do not find that Hiram king of Tyre, juft in its neighbourhood, ever had recourfe to it for wood, though furely the carriage would have been eafier than to have brought it down from the top of Mount Libanus.

---

* Strabo, lib. xiv. p. 781.   † It is called Mamilho.   ‡ Newton's Chronol. p. 183.

THAT there was great abundance in it, we know from Eratofthenes*, who tells us it was fo overgrown that it could not be tilled; fo that they firft cut down the timber to be ufed in the furnaces for melting filver and copper; that after this they built fleets with it, and when they could not even deftroy it this way, they gave liberty to all ftrangers to cut it down for whatever ufe they pleafed; and not only fo, but they gave them the property of the ground they cleared.

THINGS are fadly changed now. Wood is one of the wants of moft parts of the ifland, which has not become more healthly by being cleared, as is ordinarily the cafe

AT † Cacamo (Acamas) on the weft fide of the ifland, the wood remains thick and impervious as at the firft difcovery. Large ftags, and wild boars of a monftrous fize, fhelter themfelves unmolefted in thefe their native woods; and it depended only upon the portion of credulity that I was endowed with, that I did not believe that an elephant had, not many years ago, been feen alive there. Several families of Greeks declared it to me upon oath; nor were there wanting perfons of that nation at Alexandria, who laboured to confirm the affertion. Had fkeletons of that animal been there, I fhould have thought them antediluvian ones. I know none could have been at Cyprus, unlefs in the time of Darius Ochus, and I do not remember that there were elephants, even with him.

---

* Strabo, lib. xiv. p. 684. † Strabo, lib. xiv. p. 780.

THE SOURCE OF THE NILE.

In paſſing, I would fain have gone aſhore to ſee if there were any remains of the celebrated temple of Paphos; but a voyage, ſuch as I was then embarked on, ſtood in need of vows to Hercules rather than to Venus, and the maſter, fearing to loſe his paſſage, determined to proceed.

Many medals (ſcarce any of them good) are dug up in Cyprus; ſilver ones, of very excellent workmanſhip, are found near Paphos, of little value in the eyes of antiquarians, being chiefly of towns of the ſize of thoſe found at Crete and Rhodes, and all the iſlands of the Archipelago. Intaglios there are ſome few, part in very excellent Greek ſtyle, and generally upon better ſtones than uſual in the iſlands. I have ſeen ſome heads of Jupiter, remarkable for buſhy hair and beard, that were of the moſt exquiſite workmanſhip, worthy of any price. All the inhabitants of the iſland are ſubject to fevers, but more eſpecially thoſe in the neighbourhood of Paphos.

We left Lernica the 17th of June, about four o'clock in the afternoon. The day had been very cloudy, with a wind at N. E. which freſhened as we got under weigh. Our maſter, a ſeaman of experience upon that coaſt, ran before it to the weſtward with all the ſails he could ſet. Truſting to a ſign that he ſaw, which he called a bank, reſembling a dark cloud in the horizon, he gueſſed the wind was to be from that quarter the next day.

Accordingly, on the 18th, a little before twelve o'clock, a very freſh and favourable breeze came from the N. W. and we pointed our prow directly, as we thought, upon Alexandria.

The

The coast of Egypt is exceedingly low, and, if the weather is not clear, you often are close in with the land before you discover it.

A strong current sets constantly to the eastward; and the way the masters of vessels pretend to know their approach to the coast is by a black mud, which they find upon the plummet* at the end of their founding-line, about seven leagues distant from land.

Our master pretended at midnight he had found that black sand, and therefore, although the wind was very fair, he chose to lie to, till morning, as thinking himself near the coast; although his reckoning, as he said, did not agree with what he inferred from his foundings.

As I was exceedingly vexed at being so disappointed of making the best of our favourable wind, I rectified my quadrant, and found by the passages of two stars over the meridian, that we were in lat. 32° 1′ 45″, or seventeen leagues distant from Alexandria, instead of seven, and that by difference of our latitude only.

From this I inferred that part of the assertion, that it is the mud of the Nile which is supposed to shew seamen their approach to Egypt, is mere imagination; seeing that the point where we then were was really part of the sea opposite to the desert of Barca, and had no communication whatever with the Nile.

---

* This is an old prejudice. See Herodotus, lib. ii. p. 90. sect. 5.

THE SOURCE OF THE NILE.

On the contrary, the Etefian winds blowing all Summer upon that coaft, from the weftward of north, and a current fetting conftantly to the eaftward, it is impoffible that any part of the mud of the Nile can go fo high to the windward of any of the mouths of that river.

It is well known, that the action of thefe winds, and the conftancy of that current, has thrown a great quantity of mud, gravel, and fand, into all the ports on the coaft of Syria.

All veftiges of old Tyre are defaced; the ports of Sidon, *Berout, Tripoli, and †Latikea, are all filled up by the accretion of fand; and, not many days before my leaving Sidon, Mr de Clerambaut, conful of France, fhewed me the pavements of the old city of Sidon, $7\frac{1}{2}$ feet lower than the ground upon which the prefent city ftands, and confiderably farther back in the gardens nearer to Mount Libanus.

This every one in the country knows is the effect of that eafterly current fetting upon the coaft, which, as it acts perpendicularly to the courfe of the Nile when difcharging itfelf, at all or any of its mouths, into the Mediterranean, muft hurry what it is charged with on towards the coaft of Syria, and hinder it from fettling oppofite to, or making thofe additions to the land of Egypt, which ‡ Herodotus has vainly fuppofed.

The 20th of June, early in the morning, we had a diftant profpect of Alexandria rifing from the fea. Was not the ftate of

---

* Berytus.   † Laodicea ad mare.   ‡ Herod. lib. ii. p. 90.

of that city perfectly known, a traveller in search of antiquities in architecture would think here was a field for long study and employment.

It is in this point of view the town appears most to the advantage. The mixture of old monuments, such as the Column of Pompey, with the high moorish towers and steeples, raise our expectations of the consequence of the ruins we are to find.

But the moment we are in the port the illusion ends, and we distinguish the immense Herculean works of ancient times, now few in number, from the ill-imagined, ill-constructed, and imperfect buildings, of the several barbarous masters of Alexandria in later ages.

There are two ports, the Old and the New. The entrance into the latter is both difficult and dangerous, having a bar before it; it is the least of the two, though it is what is called the Great Port, by *Strabo.

Here only the European ships can lie; and, even when here, they are not in safety; as numbers of vessels are constantly lost, though at anchor.

Above forty were cast a-shore and dashed to pieces in March 1773, when I was on my return home, mostly belonging to Ragusa, and the small ports in Provence, while little harm was done to ships of any nation accustomed to the ocean.

---

* Strabo, lib. xvii. p. 922.

It was curious to obferve the different procedure of thefe different nations upon the fame accident. As foon as the fquall began to become violent, the mafters of the Ragufan veffels, and the French caravaneurs, or veffels trading in the *Mediterranean*, after having put out every anchor and cable they had, took to their boats and fled to the neareft fhore, leaving the veffels to their chance in the ftorm. They knew *the furniture* of their fhips to be too flimfy to truft their lives to it.

Many of their cables being made of a kind of grafs called Spartum, could not bear the ftrefs of the veffels or agitation of the waves, but parted with the anchors, and the fhips perifhed.

On the other hand, the Britifh, Danifh, Swedifh, and Dutch navigators of the *ocean*, no fooner faw the ftorm beginning, than they left their houfes, took to their boats, and went all hands on board. Thefe knew the fufficiency of their tackle, and provided they were prefent, to obviate unforefeen accidents, they had no apprehenfion from the weather. They knew that their cables were made of good hemp, that their anchors were heavy and ftrong. Some pointed their yards to the wind, and others lowered them upon deck. Afterwards they walked to and fro on their quarter-deck with perfect compofure, and bade defiance to the ftorm. Not one man of thefe ftirred from the fhips, till calm weather, on the morrow, called upon them to affift their feeble and more unfortunate brethren, whofe fhips were wrecked and lay fcattered on the fhore.

The other port is the *Eunoſtus of the ancients, and is to the weſtward of the Pharos. It was called alſo the Port of Africa; is much larger than the former, and lies immediately under part of the town of Alexandria. It has much deeper water, though a multitude of ſhips have every day, for ages, been throwing a quantity of ballaſt into it; and there is no doubt, but in time it will be filled up, and joined to the continent by this means. And poſterity may, probably, following the ſyſtem of Herodotus (if it ſhould be ſtill faſhionable) call this as they have done the reſt of Egypt, *the Gift of the Nile.*

Christian veſſels are not ſuffered to enter this port; the only reaſon is, leaſt the *Mooriſh women* ſhould be ſeen taking the air in the evening at open windows; and this has been thought to be of weight enough for Chriſtian powers to ſubmit to it, and to over-balance the conſtant loſs of ſhips, property, and men.

† Alexander, returning to Egypt from the Libyan ſide, was ſtruck with the beauty and ſituation of theſe two ports. ‡ Dinochares, an architect who accompanied him, traced out the plan, and Ptolemy I. built the city.

The healthy, though deſolate and bare country round it, part of the Deſert of Libya, was another inducement to prefer this ſituation to the unwholeſome black mud of Egypt; but it had no water; this Ptolemy was obliged to bring far
above

---

* Strabo, lib. xvii. p. 922. † Strabo, lib. xvii. p. 920. Q Curt. lib. iv. cap. 8.
‡ Plin. lib. v. cap. 10. p. 273.

THE SOURCE OF THE NILE.

above from the Nile, by a califh, or canal, vulgarly called the Canal of Cleopatra, though it was certainly coeval with the foundation of the city; it has no other name at this day.

This circumftance, however, remedied in the beginning, was fatal to the city's magnificence ever after, and the caufe of its being in the ftate it is at this day.

The importance of its fituation to trade and commerce, made it a principal object of attention to each party in every war. It was eafily taken, becaufe it had no water; and, as it could not be kept, it was deftroyed by the conqueror, that the temporary poffeffion of it might not turn to be a fource of advantage to an enemy.

We are not, however, to fuppofe, that the country all around it was as bare in the days of profperity as it is now. Population, we fee, produces a fwerd of grafs round ancient cities in the moft defert parts of Africa, which keeps the fand immoveable till the place is no longer inhabited.

I apprehend the numerous lakes in Egypt were all contrived as refervoirs to lay up a ftore of water for fupplying gardens and plantations in the months of the Nile's decreafe. The great effects of a very little water are feen along the califh, or canal, in a number of bufhes that it produces, and thick plantations of date-trees, all in a very luxuriant ftate; and this, no doubt, in the days of the Ptolemies, was extended further, more attended to, and better underftood.

Pompey's pillar, the obelisks, and subterraneous cisterns, are all the antiquities we find now in Alexandria; these have been described frequently, ably, and minutely.

The foliage and capital of the pillar are what seem generally to displease; the fust is thought to have merited more attention than has been bestowed upon the capital.

The whole of the pillar is granite, but the capital is of another stone; and I should suspect those rudiments of leaves were only intended to support firmly leaves of metal* of better workmanship; for the capital itself is near nine feet high, and the work, in proportionable leaves of stone, would be not only very large, but, after being finished, liable to injuries.

This magnificent monument appears, in taste, to be the work of that period, between Hadrian and Severus; but, though the former erected several large buildings in the east, it is observed of him he never put inscriptions upon them.

This has had a Greek inscription, and I think may very probably be attributed to the time of the latter, as a monument of the gratitude of the city of Alexandria for the benefits he conferred on them, especially since no ancient history mentions its existence at an earlier period.

I apprehend it to have been brought in a block from the Thebais in Upper Egypt, by the Nile; though some have imagined

---

* We see many examples of such leaves both at Palmyra and Baalbec.

THE SOURCE OF THE NILE.

imagined it was an old obelisk, hewn to that round form. It is nine feet diameter; and were it but 80 feet high, it would require a prodigious obelisk indeed, that could admit to be hewn to this circumference for such a length, so as perfectly to efface the hieroglyphics that must have been very deeply cut in the four faces of it.

THE tomb of Alexander has been talked of as one of the antiquities of this city. Marmol * says he saw it in the year 1546. It was, according to him, a small house, in form of a chapel, in the middle of the city, near the church of St Mark, and was called Escander.

THE thing itself is not probable, for all those that made themselves masters of Alexandria, in the earliest times, had too much respect for Alexander, to have reduced his tomb to so obscure a state. It would have been spared even by the Saracens; for Mahomet speaks of Alexander with great respect, both as a king and a prophet. The body was preserved in a glass coffin, in † Strabo's time, having been robbed of the golden one in which it was first deposited.

THE Greeks, for the most part, are better instructed in the history of these places than the Cophts, Turks, or Christians; and, after the Greeks, the Jews.

As I was perfectly disguised, having for many years worn the dress of the Arabs, I was under no constraint, but walked through the town in all directions, accompanied by any of
those

---

* Marmol, lib. xi. cap. 14. p. 276. tom. 3.   † Strabo, lib. xvii. p. 922.

those different nations I could induce to walk with me; and, as I constantly spoke Arabic, was taken for a * Bedowé by all sorts of people; but, notwithstanding the advantage this freedom gave me, and of which I daily availed myself, I never could hear a word of this monument from either Greek, Jew, Moor, or Christian.

ALEXANDRIA has been often taken since the time of Cæsar. It was at last destroyed by the Venetians and Cypriots, upon, or rather after the release of St Lewis, and we may say of it as of Carthage, *Periére ruinæ*, its very ruins appear no longer.

THE building of the present gates and walls, which some have thought to be antique, does not seem earlier than the last restoration in the 13th century. Some parts of the gate and walls may be of older date; (and probably were those of the last Caliphs before Salidan) but, except these, and the pieces of columns which lie horizontally in different parts of the wall, every thing else is apparently of very late times, and the work has been huddled together in great haste.

IT is in vain then to expect a plan of the city, or try to trace here the Macedonian mantle of Dinophares; the very vestiges of ancient ruins are covered, many yards deep, by rubbish, the remnant of the devastations of later times. Cleopatra, were she to return to life again, would scarcely know where her palace was situated, in this her own capital.

THERE

---

* A peasant Arab.

THE SOURCE OF THE NILE. 15

There is nothing beautiful or pleasant in the present Alexandria, but a handsome street of modern houses, where a very active and intelligent number of merchants live upon the miserable remnants of that trade, which made its glory in the first times.

It is thinly inhabited, and there is a tradition among the natives, that, more than once, it has been in agitation to abandon it all together, and retire to Rosetto, or Cairo, but that they have been withheld by the opinion of divers saints from Arabia, who have assured them, that Mecca being destroyed, (as it must be as they think by the Russians) Alexandria is then to become *the holy place*, and that Mahomet's body is to be transported thither; when that city is destroyed, the sanctified reliques are to be transported to Cairouan, in the kingdom of Tunis: lastly, from Cairouan they are to come to Rosetto, and there to remain till the consummation of all things, which is not then to be at a great distance.

Ptolemy places his Alexandria in lat. 30° 31' and in round numbers in his almagest, lat. 31° north.

Our Professor, Mr. Greaves, one of whose errands into Egypt was to ascertain the latitude of this place, seems yet, from some cause or other, to have failed in it, for though he had a brass sextant of five feet radius, he makes the latitude of Alexandria, from a mean of many observations, to be lat 31° 4' N. whereas the French astronomers from the Academy of Sciences have settled it at 31° 11' 20", so between Mr Greaves and the French there is a difference of 7' 20", which is too much. There is not any thing, in point of
situation,

situation, that can account for this variance, as in the case of Ptolemy; for the new town of Alexandria is built from east to west; and as all christian travellers necessarily make their observations now on the same line, there cannot possibly be any difference from situation.

Mr NIEBUHR, whether from one or more observations he does not say, makes the latitude to be 31° 12'. From a mean of thirty-three observations, taken by the three-feet quadrant I have spoken of, I found it to be 31° 11' 16": So that, taking a medium of these three results, you will have the latitude of Alexandria 31° 11' 32", or, in round number, 31° 11' 30", nor do I think there possibly can be 5" difference.

By an eclipse, moreover, of the first satellite of Jupiter, observed on the 23d day of June 1769, I found its longitude to be 30° 17' 30" east, from the meridian of Greenwich.

WE arrived at Alexandria the 20th of June, and found that the plague had raged in that city and neighbourhood from the beginning of March, and that two days only before our arrival people had begun to open their houses and communicate with each other; but it was no matter, St John's day was *past*, the miraculous nucta, or dew, had fallen, and every body went about their ordinary business in safety, and without fear.

WITH very great pleasure I had received my instruments at Alexandria. I examined them, and, by the perfect state in which they arrived, knew the obligations I was under

to

THE SOURCE OF THE NILE. 17

to my correspondents and friends. Prepared now for any enterprise, I left with eagerness the thread-bare inquiries into the meagre remains, of this once-famous capital of Egypt.

The journey to Rosetto is always performed by land, as the mouth of the branch of the Nile leading to Rosetto, called the Bogaz*, is very shallow and dangerous to pass, and often tedious; besides, nobody wishes to be a partner for any time in a voyage with Egyptian sailors, if he can possibly avoid it.

The journey by land is also reputed dangerous, and people travel burdened with arms, which they are determined never to use.

For my part, I placed my safety, in my disguise, and my behaviour. We had all of us pistols at our girdles, against an extremity; but our fire-arms of a larger sort, of which we had great store, were sent with our baggage, and other instruments, by the Bogaz to Rosetto. I had a small lance, called a Jerid, in my hand, my servants were without any visible arms.

We left Alexandria in the afternoon, and about three miles before arriving at Aboukeer, we met a man, in appearance of some consequence, going to Alexandria.

Vol. I.   C   As

---

* Means a narrow or shallow entrance of a river from the ocean.

As we had no fear of him or his party, we neither court- ed nor avoided them. We paffed near enough, however, to give them the ufual falute, *Salam Alicum;* to which the leader of the troop gave no anfwer, but faid to one of his fervants, as in contempt, Bedowé! they are peafants, or coun- try Arabs. I was much better pleafed with this token that we had deceived them, than if they had returned the falute twenty times.

Some inconfiderable ruins are at Aboukeer, and feem to denote, that it was the former fituation of an ancient city. There is here alfo an inlet of the fea; and the diftance, fome- thing lefs than four leagues from Alexandria, warrants us to fay that it is Canopus, one of the moft ancient cities in the world; its ruins, notwithftanding the neighbourhood of the branch of the Nile, which goes by that name, have not yet been covered by the increafe of the land of Egypt.

At Medea, which we fuppofe, by its diftance of near feven leagues, to be the ancient Heraclium, is the paffage or ferry which terminates the fear of danger from the Arabs of Libya; and it is here *fuppofed the Delta, or Egypt, be- gins.

Dr Shaw† is obliged to confefs, that between Alexandria and the Canopic branch of the Nile, few or no *vefliges* are feen of the increafe of the land by the inundation of the river; indeed it would have been a wonder if there had.

Alexandria,

---

*Herod. p. 108.   † Shaw's Travels p. 293.

THE SOURCE OF THE NILE.

Alexandria, and its environs, are part of the defert of Barca, too high to have ever been overflowed by the Nile, from any part of its lower branches; or elfe there would have been no neceffity for going fo high up as above Rofetto, to get level enough, to bring water down to Alexandria by the canal.

Dr Shaw adds, that the ground hereabout may have been an ifland; and fo it may, and fo may almoft any other place in the world; but there is no fort of indication that it was fo, nor vifible means by which it was formed.

We faw no vegetable from Alexandria to Medea, excepting fome fcattered roots of Abfinthium; nor were thefe luxuriant, or promifing to thrive, but though they had not a very ftrong fmell, they were abundantly bitter; and their leaves feemed to have imbibed a quantity of faline particles, with which the foil of the whole defert of Barca is ftrongly impregnated.

We faw two or three gazels, or antelopes, walking one by one, at feveral times, in nothing differing from the fpecies of that animal, in the defert of Barca and Cyrenaicum; and the * jerboa, another inhabitant of thefe deferts; but from the multitude of holes in the ground, which we faw at the root of almoft every plant of Abfinthium, we were very certain its companion, the † Ceraftes, or horned viper, was an inhabitant of that country alfo.

---

* See a figure of this animal in the Appendix.   † See Appendix.

From Medea, or the Paſſage, our road lay through very dry ſand; to avoid which, and ſeek firmer footing, we were obliged to ride up to the bellies of our horſes in the ſea. If the wind blows this quantity of duſt or ſand into the Mediterranean, it is no wonder the mouths of the branches of the Nile are choked up.

All Egypt is like to this part of it, full of deep duſt and ſand, from the beginning of March till the firſt of the inundation. It is this fine powder and ſand, raiſed and looſened by the heat of the ſun, and want of dew, and not being tied faſt, as it were, by any root or vegetation, which the Nile carries off with it, and buries in the ſea, and which many ignorantly ſuppoſe comes from Abyſſinia, where every river runs in a bed of rock.

When you leave the ſea, you ſtrike off nearly at right angles, and purſue your journey to the eaſtward of north. Here heaps of ſtone and trunks of pillars, are ſet up to guide you in your road, through moving ſands, which ſtand in hillocks in proper directions, and which conduct you ſafely to Roſetto, ſurrounded on one ſide by theſe hills of ſand, which ſeem ready to cover it.

Rosetto is upon that branch of the Nile which was called the Bolbuttic Branch, and is about four miles from the ſea. It probably obtained its preſent name from the Venetians, or Genoeſe, who monopolized the trade of this country, before the Cape of Good Hope was diſcovered; for it is known to the natives by the name of Raſhid, by which is meant the Orthodox.

The

THE SOURCE OF THE NILE.

THE reason of this I have already explained, it is some time or other to be a substitute to Mecca, and to be blessed with all that holiness, that the possession of the reliques, of their prophet can give it.

Dr SHAW* having always in his mind the strengthening of Herodotus's hypothesis, *that Egypt is created by the Nile*, says, that perhaps this was once a Cape, because Rashid has that meaning. But as Dr Shaw understood Arabic perfectly well, he must therefore have known, that Rashid has no such signification in any of the Oriental Languages. Ras, indeed, is a head land, or cape; but Rassit has no such signification, and Rashid a very different one, as I have already mentioned.

RASHID then, or Rosetto, is a large, clean, neat town, or village, upon the eastern side of the Nile. It is about three miles long, much frequented by studious and religious Mahometans; among these too are a considerable number of merchants, it being the entrepot between Cairo and Alexandria, and *vice versa;* here too the merchants have their factors, who superintend and watch over the merchandise which passes the Bogaz to and from Cairo.

THERE are many gardens, and much verdure, about Rosetto; the ground is low, and retains long the moisture it imbibes from the overflowing of the Nile. Here also are many curious plants and flowers, brought from different countries, by *Fakirs*, and merchants. Without this, Egypt, subject

---

*Shaw's Travels, p. 294.

subject to such long inundation, however it may abound in necessaries, could not boast of many beautiful productions of its own gardens, though flowers, trees, and plants, were very much in vogue in this neighbourhood, two hundred years ago, as we find by the observations of Prosper Alpinus.

The study and search after every thing useful or beautiful, which for some time had been declining gradually, fell at last into total contempt and oblivion, under the brutal reign of these last slaves*, the most infamous reproach to the name of Sovereign.

Rosetto is a favourite halting-place of the Christian travellers entering Egypt, and merchants established there. There they draw their breaths, in an imaginary increase of freedom, between the two great sinks of tyranny, oppression, and injustice, Alexandria and Cairo.

Rosetto has this good reputation, that the people are milder, more tractable, and less avaricious, than those of the two last-mentioned capitals; but I must say, that, in my time, I could not discern much difference.

The merchants, who trade at all hours of the day with Christians, are indeed more civilized, and less insolent, than the soldiery and the rest of the common people, which is the case every where, as it is for their own interest; but their

---

* The Mamaluke Beys.

THE SOURCE OF THE NILE.   23

their priests, and moullahs, their foldiers, and people living in the country, are, in point of manners, juſt as bad as the others.

ROSETTO is in lat. 31° 24′ 15″ N.; it is the place where we embark for Cairo, which we accordingly did on June the 30th.

THERE is a wonderful deal of talk at Alexandria of the danger of paſſing over the defert to Rofetto. The fame converſation is held here. After you embark on the Nile in your way to Cairo, you hear of pilots, and maſters of veſſels, who land you among robbers to ſhare your plunder, and twenty ſuch like ſtories, all of them of old date, and which perhaps happened long ago, or never happened at all.

BUT provided the government of Cairo is ſettled, and you do not land at villages in ſtrife with each other, (in which circumſtances no perſon of any nation is ſafe) you muſt be very unfortunate indeed, if any great accident befal you between Alexandria and Cairo.

FOR, from the conſtant intercourſe between theſe two cities, and the valuable charge confided to theſe maſters of veſſels, they are all as well known, and at the leaſt as much under authority, as the boatmen on the river Thames; and, if they ſhould have either killed, or robbed any perſon, it muſt be with a view to leave the country immediately; elſe either at Cairo, Rofetto, Fuè, or Alexandria, wherever they were firſt caught, they would infallibly be hanged.

CHAP. II.

Author's Reception at Cairo—Procures Letters from the Bey and the Greek Patriarch—Visits the Pyramids—Observations on their Construction.

IT was in the beginning of July we arrived at Cairo, recommended to the very hospitable house of Julian and Bertran, to whom I imparted my resolution of pursuing my journey into Abyssinia.

The wildness of the intention seemed to strike them greatly, on which account they endeavoured all they could to persuade me against it, but, upon seeing me resolved, offered kindly their most effectual services.

As the government of Cairo hath always been jealous of this enterprise I had undertaken, and a regular prohibition had been often made by the Porte, among indifferent people, I pretended that my destination was to India, and no one conceived any thing wrong in that.

This intention was not long kept secret, (nothing can be concealed at Cairo:) All nations, Jews, Turks, Moors, Cophts, and Franks, are constantly upon the inquiry, as much after things that concern other people's business as their own.

The plan I adopted was to appear in public as seldom as possible, unless disguised; and I soon was considered as a
Fakir,

Fakir, or *Dervich*, moderately skilled in magic, and who cared for nothing but study and books.

This reputation opened me, privately, a channel for purchasing many Arabic manuscripts, which the knowledge of the language enabled me to chuse, free from the load of trash that is generally imposed upon Christian purchasers

The part of Cairo where the French are settled is exceedingly commodious, and fit for retirement. It consists of one long street, where all the merchants of that nation live together. It is shut at one end, by large gates, where there is a guard, and these are kept constantly close in the time of the plague.

At the other end is a large garden tolerably kept, in which there are several pleasant walks, and seats; all the enjoyment that Christians can hope for, among this vile people, reduces itself to peace, and quiet; nobody seeks for more. There are, however, wicked emissaries who are constantly employed, by threats, lies, and extravagant demands, to torment them, and keep them from enjoying that repose, which would content them instead of freedom, and more solid happiness, in their own country.

I have always confidered the French at Cairo, as a number of honest, polished, and industrious men, by some fatality condemned to the gallies; and I must own, never did a set of people bear their continual vexations with more fortitude and manliness.

Their own affairs they keep to themselves, and, notwithstanding the bad profpect always before them, they never fail to put on a chearful face to a ftranger, and protect and help him to the utmoft of their power; as if his little concerns, often ridiculous, always very troublefome ones, were the only charge they had in hand.

But a more brutal, unjuft, tyrannical, oppreffive, avaricious fet of infernal mifcreants, there is not on earth, than are the members of the government of Cairo.

There is alfo at Cairo a Venetian conful, and a houfe of that nation called *Pini*, all excellent people.

The government of Cairo is much praifed by fome. It may perhaps have merit when explained, but I never could underftand it, and therefore cannot explain it.

It is faid to confift of twenty-four Beys; yet its admirers could never fix upon one year in which there was that number. There were but feven when I was at Cairo, and one who commanded the whole.

The Beys are underftood to be vefted with the fovereign power of the country; yet fometimes a Kaya commands abfolutely, and, though of an inferior rank, he makes his fervants, Beys or Sovereigns.

At a time of peace, when Beys are contented to be on an equality, and no ambitious one attempts to govern the whole, there is a number of inferior officers depending upon each of the Beys, fuch as Kayas, Schourbatchies, and the

THE SOURCE OF THE NILE.

the like, who are but fubjects in refpect to the Beys, yet exercife unlimited jurifdiction over the people in the city, and appoint others to do the fame over villages in the country.

There are perhaps four hundred inhabitants in Cairo, who have abfolute power, and adminifter what they call juftice, in their own way, and according to their own views.

Fortunately in my time this many-headed monfter was no more, there was but one Ali Bey, and there was neither inferior nor fuperior jurifdiction exercifed, but by his officers only. This happy ftate did not laft long. In order to be a Bey, the perfon muft have been a flave, and bought for money, at a market. Every Bey has a great number of fervants, flaves to him, as he was to others before; thefe are his guards, and thefe he promotes to places in his houfehold, according as they are qualified.

The firft of thefe domeftic charges is that of hafnadar, or treafurer, who governs his whole houfehold; and whenever his mafter the Bey dies, whatever number of children he may have, they never fucceed him; but this man marries his wife, and inherits his dignity and fortune.

The Bey is old, the wife is young, fo is the hafnadar, upon whom fhe depends for every thing, and whom fhe muft look upon as the prefumptive hufband; and thofe people who conceal, or confine their women, and are jealous, upon the moft remote occafion, never feel any jealoufy for the probable confequences of this paffion, from the exiftence of fuch connection.

It is very extraordinary, to find a race of men in power, all agree to leave their succeſſion to ſtrangers, in preference to their own children, for a number of ages; and that no one ſhould ever have attempted to make his ſon ſucceed him, either in dignity or eſtate, in preference to a ſlave, whom he has bought for money like a beaſt.

The Beys themſelves have ſeldom children, and thoſe they have, ſeldom live. I have heard it as a common obſervation, that Cairo is very unwholeſome for young children in general; the proſtitution of the Beys from early youth probably give their progeny a worſe chance than thoſe of others.

The inſtant that I arrived at Cairo was perhaps the only one in which I ever could have been allowed, ſingle and unprotected as I was, to have made my intended journey.

Ali Bey, lately known in Europe by various narratives of the laſt tranſactions of his life, after having undergone many changes of fortune, and been baniſhed by his rivals from his capital, at laſt had enjoyed the ſatisfaction of a return, and of making himſelf abſolute in Cairo.

The Port had conſtantly been adverſe to him, and he cheriſhed the ſtrongeſt reſentment in his heart. He wiſhed nothing ſo much as to contribute his part to rend the Ottoman empire to pieces.

A favourable opportunity preſented itſelf in the Ruſſian war, and Ali Bey was prepared to go all lengths in ſupport of that power. But never was there an expedition ſo

ſuccefsful

successful and so distant, where the officers were less instructed from the cabinet, more ignorant of the countries, more given to useless parade, or more intoxicated with pleasure, than the Russians on the Mediterranean then were.

AFTER the defeat, and burning of the Turkish squadron, upon the coast of Asia Minor, there was not a sail appeared that did not do them homage. They were prope ly and advantageously situated at Paros, or rather, I mean, a squadron of ships of one half their number, would have been properly placed there.

THE number of Bashas and Governors in Caramania, very seldom in their allegiance to the Port, were then in actual rebellion; great part of Syria was in the same situation, down to Tripoli and Sidon; and thence Shekh Daher, from Acre to the plains of Esdraelon, and to the very frontiers of Egypt.

WITH circumstances so favourable, and a force so triumphant, Egypt and Syria would probably have fallen dismembered from the Ottoman empire. But it was very plain, that the Russian commanders were not provided with instructions, and had no idea how far their victory might have carried them, or how to manage those they had conquered.

They had no confidential correspondence with Ali Bey, though they might have safely trusted him as he would have trusted them; but neither of them were provided with proper negotiators, nor did they ever understand one another till it was too late, and till their enemies, taking advantage

vantage of their tardinefs, had rendered the firft and great fcheme impoffible.

Carlo Rozetti, a Venetian merchant, a young man of capacity and intrigue, had for fome years governed the Bey abfolutely. Had fuch a man been on board the fleet with a commiffion, after receiving inftructions from Peterfburgh, the Ottoman empire in Egypt was at an end.

The Bey, with all his good fenfe and underftanding, was ftill a mamaluke, and had the principles of a flave. Three men of different religions poffeffed his confidence and governed his councils all at a time. The one was a Greek, the other a Jew, and the third an Egyptian Copht, his feeretary. It would have required a great deal of difcernment and penetration to have determined which of thefe was the moft worthlefs, or moft likely to betray him.

The fecretary, whofe name was Rifk, had the addrefs to fupplant the other two at the time they thought themfelves at the pinnacle of their glory; over-awing every Turk, and robbing every Chriftian, the Greek was banifhed from Egypt, and the Jew baftinadoed to death. Such is the tenure of Egyptian minifters.

Risk profeffed aftrology, and the Bey, like all other Turks, believed in it implicitely, and to this folly he facrificed his own good underftanding; and Rifk, probably in pay to Conftantinople, led him from one wild fcheme to another, till he undid him—by the ftars.

THE SOURCE OF THE NILE.

THE apparatus of inftruments that were opened at the cuftom-houfe of Alexandria, prepoffeffed Rifk in favour of my fuperior knowledge in aftrology.

THE Jew, who was mafter of the cuftom-houfe, was not only ordered to refrain from touching or taking them out of their places (a great mortification to a Turkifh cuftom-houfe, where every thing is handed about and fhewn) but an order from the Bey alfo arrived that they fhould be fent to me without duty or fees, becaufe they were not merchandife.

I WAS very thankful for that favour, not for the fake of faving the dues at the cuftom-houfe, but becaufe I was excufed from having them taken out of their cafes by rough and violent hands, which certainly would have broken fomething.

RISK waited upon me next day, and let me know from whom the favour came; on which we all thought this was a hint for a prefent; and accordingly, as I had other bufinefs with the Bey, I had prepared a very handfome one.

BUT I was exceedingly aftonifhed when defiring to know the time when it was to be offered; it not only was refufed, but fome few trifles were fent as a prefent from the fecretary with this meffage: "That, when I had repofed, he
" would vifit me, defire to fee me make ufe of thefe inftru-
" ments; and, in the mean time, that I might reft confident,
" that nobody durft any way moleft me while in Cairo, for
" I was under the immediate protection of the Bey"

HE

He added also, "That if I wanted any thing I should send "my Armenian servant, Arab Keer, to him, without trou- "bling myself to communicate my necessities to the French, "or trust my concerns to their Dragomen."

Although I had lived for many years in friendship and in constant good understanding with both Turks and Moors, there was something more polite and considerate in this than I could account for.

I had not seen the Bey, it was not therefore any particular address, or any prepossession in my favour, with which these people are very apt to be taken at first sight, that could account for this; I was an absolute stranger; I therefore opened myself entirely to my landlord, Mr Bertran.

I told him my apprehension of too much fair weather in the beginning, which, in these climates, generally leads to a storm in the end; on which account, I suspected some design; Mr Bertran kindly promised to found Risk for me.

At the same time, he cautioned me equally against offending him, or trusting myself in his hands, as being a man capable of the blackest designs, and merciless in the execution of them.

It was not long before Risk's curiosity gave him a fair opportunity. He inquired of Bertran as to my knowledge of the stars; and my friend, who then saw perfectly the drift of all his conduct, so prepossessed him in favour of my superior science, that he communicated to him in the instant the great expectations he had formed, to be enabled

by

by me, to forefee the deftiny of the Bey; the fuccefs of the war; and, in particular, whether or not he fhould make himfelf mafter of Mecca; to conquer which place, he was about to difpatch his flave and fon-in-law, Mahomet Bey Abou Dahab, at the head of an army conducting the pilgrims.

BERTRAN communicated this to me with great tokens of joy: for my own part, I did not greatly like the profeffion of fortune-telling, where baftinado or impaling might be the reward of being miftaken.

BUT I was told I had moft credulous people to deal with, and that there was nothing for it but efcaping as long as poffible, before the iffue of any of my prophecies arrived, and as foon as I had done my own bufinefs.

THIS was my own idea likewife; I never faw a place I liked worfe, or which afforded lefs pleafure or inftruction than Cairo, or antiquities which lefs anfwered their defcriptions.

IN a few days I received a letter from Rifk, defiring me to go out to the Convent of St George, about three miles from Cairo, where the Greek patriarch had ordered an apartment for me; that I fhould pretend to the French merchants that it was for the fake of health, and that there I fhould receive the Bey's orders.

PROVIDENCE feemed to teach me the way I was to go. I went accordingly to St George, a very folitary manfion, but large and quiet, very proper for ftudy, and ftill more for executing a plan which I thought moſt neceſſary for my undertaking.

During my ſtay at Algiers, the Rev. Mr Tonyn, the king's chaplain to that factory, was abſent upon leave. The bigotted catholic prieſts there neither marry, baptize, nor bury the dead of thoſe that are Proteſtants.

There was a Greek prieſt, *Father Chriſtopher, who conſtantly had offered gratuitouſly to perform theſe functions. The civility, humanity, and good character of the man, led me to take him to reſide at my country houſe, where I lived the greateſt part of the year; beſides that he was of a chearful diſpoſition, I had practiſed much with him both in ſpeaking and reading Greek with the accent, not in uſe in our ſchools, but without which that language, in the mouth of a ſtranger, is perfectly unintelligible all over the Archipelago.

Upon my leaving Algiers to go on my voyage to Barbary, being tired of the place, he embarked on board a veſſel, and landed at Alexandria, from which ſoon after he was called to Cairo by the Greek patriarch Mark, and made *Archimandrites*, which is the ſecond dignity in the Greek church under the patriarch. He too was well acquainted in the houſe of Ali Bey, where all were Georgian and Greek ſlaves; and it was at his ſolicitation that Riſk had deſired the patriarch to furniſh me with an apartment in the Convent of St George.

The

---

* Vid. Introduction.

THE SOURCE OF THE NILE.

The next day after my arrival I was furprifed by the vifit of my old friend Father Chriftopher; and, not to detain the reader with ufelefs circumftances, the intelligence of many vifits, which I fhall comprehend in one, was, that there were many Greeks then in Abyffinia, all of them in great power, and fome of them in the firft places of the empire; that they correfponded with the patriarch when occafion offered, and, at all times, held him in fuch refpect, that his will, when fignified to them, was of the greateft authority, and that obedience was paid to it as to holy writ.

Father Christopher took upon him, with the greateft readinefs, to manage the letters, and we digefted the plan of them; three copies were made to fend feparate ways, and an admonitory letter to the whole of the Greeks then in Abyffinia, in form of a bull.

By this the patriarch enjoined them as a penance, upon which a kind of jubilee was to follow, that, laying afide their pride and vanity, great fins with which he knew them much *infected*, and, inftead of pretending to put themfelves on a footing with me when I fhould arrive at the court of Abyffinia, they fhould concur, heart and hand, in ferving me; and that, before it could be fuppofed they had received inftructions from *me*, they fhould make a declaration before the king, that they were not in condition equal to me, that I was a free citizen of a *powerful nation*, and fervant of a great king; that *they* were born flaves of the Turk, and, at beft, ranked but as would my fervants; and that, in fact, one of their countrymen was in that ftation then with me.

AFTER

AFTER having made that declaration publicly, and *bona fide*, in prefence of their prieft, he thereupon declared to them, that all their paft fins were forgiven.

ALL this the patriarch moft willingly and chearfully performed. I faw him frequently when I was in Cairo; and we had already commenced a great friendfhip and intimacy.

IN the mean while, Rifk fent to me, one night about nine o'clock, to come to the Bey. I faw him then for the firft time. He was a much younger man than I conceived him to be; he was fitting upon a large fofa, covered with crimfon-cloth of gold; his turban, his girdle, and the head of his dagger, all thick covered with fine brilliants; one in his turban, that ferved to fupport a fprig of brilliants alfo, was among the largeft I had ever feen.

HE entered abruptly into difcourfe upon the war between Ruffia and the Turk, and afked me if I had calculated what would be the confequence of that war? I faid, the Turks would be beaten by fea and land wherever they prefented themfelves.

AGAIN, Whether Conftantinople would be burned or taken? —I fa'd, Neither; but peace would be made, after much bloodfhed, with little advantage to either party.

HE clapped his hands together, and fwore an oath in Turkifh, then turned to Rifk, who ftood before him, and faid, That will be fad indeed! but truth is truth, and God is merciful.

HE

THE SOURCE OF THE NILE.

He offered me coffee and sweatmeats, promised me his protection, bade me fear nothing, but, if any body wronged me, to acquaint him by Risk.

Two or three nights afterwards the Bey sent for me again. It was near eleven o'clock before I got admittance to him.

I met the janiffary Aga going out from him, and a number of soldiers at the door. As I did not know him, I passed him without ceremony, which is not usual for any person to do. Whenever he mounts on horseback, as he was then just going to do, he has absolute power of life and death, without appeal, all over Cairo and its neighbourhood.

He stopt me just at the threshold, and asked one of the Bey's people who I was? and was answered, " It is Hakim Englese," the English philosopher, or physician.

He asked me in Turkish, in a very polite manner, if I would come and see him, for he was not well? I answered him in Arabic, " Yes, whenever he pleased, but could not then stay, as I had received a message that the Bey was waiting." He replied in Arabic, " No, no; go, for God's sake go; any time will do for me."

The Bey was sitting, leaning forward, with a wax taper in one hand, and reading a small slip of paper, which he held close to his face. He seemed to have little light, or weak eyes; nobody was near him: his people had been all dismissed, or were following the janiffary Aga out.

He

He did not seem to observe me till I was close upon him, and started when I said, "*Salam.*" I told him I came upon his message. He said, I thank you, did I send for you? and without giving me leave to reply, went on, "O true, I did so," and fell to reading his paper again.

After this was over, he complained that he had been ill, that he vomited immediately after dinner, though he eat moderately; that his stomach was not yet settled, and was afraid something had been given him to do him mischief.

I felt his pulse, which was low, a d weak; but very little feverish. I desired he would order his people to look if his meat was dressed in copper properly tinned; I assured him he was in no danger, and insinuated that I thought he had been guilty of some excess before dinner; at which he smiled, and said to Risk, who was standing by, "Afrite! Afrite"! he is a devil! he is a devil! I said, If your stomach is really uneasy from what you may have ate, warm some water, and, if you please, put a little green tea into it, and drink it till it makes you vomit gently, and that will give you ease; after which you may take a dish of strong coffee, and go to bed, or a glass of spirits, if you have any that are good.

He looked surprised at this proposal, and said very calmly, "Spirits! do you know I am a Mussulman?" But I, Sir, said I, am none. I tell you what is good for your body, and have nothing to do with your religion, or your soul. He seemed vastly diverted, and pleased with my frankness, and only said, "He speaks like a man." There was no word of the war, nor of the Russians that night. I went home desperately

perately tired, and peevish at being dragged out, on so foolish an errand.

Next morning, his secretary Risk came to me to the convent. The Bey was not yet well; and the idea still remained that he had been poisoned. Risk told me the Bey had great confidence in me. I asked him how the water had operated? He said he had not yet taken any of it, that he did not know how to make it, therefore he was come at the desire of the Bey, to see how it was made.

I immediately shewed him this, by infusing some green tea in some warm water. But this was not all, he modestly insinuated that I was to drink it, and so vomit myself, in order to shew him how to do with the Bey

I excused myself from being patient and physician at the same time, and told him, I would vomit *him*, which would answer the same purpose of instruction; neither was this proposal accepted.

The old Greek priest, Father Christopher, coming at the same time, we both agreed to vomit the Father, who would not consent, but produced a Caloyeros, or young monk, and we forced *him* to take the water whether he would or not.

As my favour with the Bey was now established by my midnight interviews, I thought of leaving my solitary mansion at the convent. I desired Mr Risk to procure me peremptory letters of recommendation to Shekh Haman, to the governor of Syene, Ibrim, and Deir, in Upper Egypt. I procured also the same from the janissaries, to these three
last

laſt places, as their garriſons are from that body at Cairo, which they call their Port. I had alſo letters from Ali Bey, to the Bey of Suez, to the Sherriffe of Mecca, to the Naybe (ſo they call the Sovereign) of Maſuah, and to the king of Sennaar, and his miniſter for the time being.

Having obtained all my letters and diſpatches, as well from the patriarch as from the Bey, I ſet about preparing for my journey.

Cairo is ſuppoſed to be the ancient Babylon*, at leaſt part of it. It is in lat. 30° 2′ 30″ north, and in long. 31° 16′ eaſt, from Greenwich. I cannot aſſent to what is ſaid of it, that it is built in form of a creſcent. You ride round it, gardens and all, in three hours and a quarter, upon an aſs, at an ordinary pace, which will be above three miles an hour.

The Caliſh †, or Amnis Trajanus, paſſes through the length of it, and fills the lake called Birket el Hadje, the firſt ſupply of water the pilgrims get in their tireſome journey to Mecca.

On the other ſide of the Nile, from Cairo, is Geeza, ſo called, as ſome Arabian authors ſay, from there having been a bridge there; Geeza ſignifies the Paſſage.

About eleven miles beyond this are the Pyramids, called the Pyramids of Geeza, the deſcription of which is in every

---

* Ptol. Geograph. lib. 4 Cap. 5.   † Shaw's travels p. 294.

every body's hands. Engravings of them had been publifh-ed in England, with plans of them upon a large fcale, two years before I came into Egypt, and were fhewn me by Mr Davidfon conful of Nice, whofe drawings they were.

He it was too that difcovered the fmall chamber above the landing-place, after you afcend through the long gallery of the great Pyramid on your left hand, and he left the ladder by which he afcended, for the fatisfaction of other travellers. But there is nothing in the chamber further worthy of notice, than its having efcaped difcovery fo many ages.

I think it more extraordinary ftill, that, for fuch a time as thefe Pyramids have been known, travellers were content rather to follow the report of the ancients, than to make ufe of their own eyes.

Yet it has been a conftant belief, that the ftones compofing thefe Pyramids have been brought from the *Libyan mountains, though any one who will take the pains to remove the fand on the fouth fide, will find the folid rock there hewn into fteps.

And in the roof of the large chamber, where the Sarcophagus ftands, as alfo in the top of the roof of the gallery, as you go up into that chamber, you fee large fragments of

---

* Herod. lib. 2. cap. 8.

of the rock, affording an unanfwerable proof, that thofe Pyramids were once huge rocks, ftanding where they now are; that fome of them, the moft proper from their form, were chofen for the body of the Pyramid, and the others hewn into fteps, to ferve for the fuperftructure, and the exterior parts of them.

CHAP.

CHAP. III.

Leaves Cairo—Embarks on the Nile for Upper Egypt—Visits Metrahenny and Mohannan—Reasons for supposing this the situation of Memphis.

HAVING now provided every thing necessary, and taken a rather melancholy leave of our very indulgent friends, who had great apprehensions that we should never return; and fearing that our stay till the very excessive heats were past, might involve us in another difficulty, that of missing the Etesian winds, we secured a boat to carry us to Furshout, the residence of Hamam, the Shekh of Upper Egypt.

This sort of vessel is called a Canja, and is one of the most commodious used on any river, being safe, and expeditious at the same time, though at first sight it has a strong appearance of danger.

That on which we embarked was about 100 feet from stern to stem, with two masts, main and foremast, and two monstrous *Latine* sails; the main-sail yard being about 200 feet in length.

The structure of this vessel is easily conceived, from the draught, plan, and section. It is about 30 feet in the beam, and about 90 feet in keel.

The keel is not straight, but a portion of a parabola whose curve is almost insensible to the eye. But it has this good effect

effect in failing, that whereas the bed of the Nile, when the water grows low, is full of fand banks under water, the keel under the ftem, where the curve is greateft, firft ftrikes upon thefe banks, and is faft, but the reft of the fhip is afloat; fo that by the help of oars, and affiftance of the ftream, furling the fails, you get eafily off; whereas, was the keel ftraight, and the veffel going with the preffure of that immenfe mam-fail, you would be fo faft upon the bank as to lie there like a wreck for ever.

This yard and fail is never lowered. The failors climb and furl it as it ftands. When they fhift the fail, they do it with a thick ftick like a quarter ftaff, which they call a *noboot*, put between the lafhing of the yard and the fail; they then twift this ftick round till the fail and yard turn over to the fide required.

When I fay the yard and fail are never lowered, I mean while we are getting up the ftream, before the wind; for, otherwife, when the veffel returns, they take out the maft, lay down the yards, and put by their fails, fo that the boat defcends like a wreck broadfide forwards; otherwife, being fo heavy a-loft, were fhe to touch with her ftem going down the ftream, fhe could not fail to carry away her mafts, and perhaps be ftaved to pieces.

The cabin has a very decent and agreeable dining-room, about twenty feet fquare, with windows that have clofe and latticed fhutters, fo that you may open them at will in the day-time, and enjoy the frefhnefs of the air; but great care muft be taken to keep thefe fhut at night.

A CERTAIN

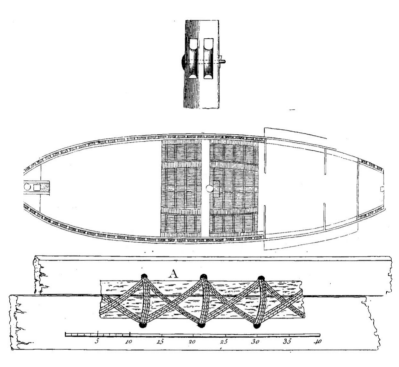

Section of the Canja.

nailing.

London Published Dec.r 1.st 1789 by G. Robinson & Co.

A certain kind of robber, peculiar to the Nile, is conſtantly on the watch to rob boats, in which they ſuppoſe the crew are off their guard. They generally approach the boat when it is calm, either ſwimming under water, or when it is dark, upon goats ſkins; after which, they mount with the utmoſt ſilence, and take away whatever they can lay their hands on.

They are not very fond, I am told, of meddling with veſſels whereon they ſee Franks, or Europeans, becauſe by them ſome have been wounded with fire-arms.

The attempts are generally made when you are at anchor, or under weigh, at night, in very moderate weather; but ofteneſt when you are falling down the ſtream without maſts; for it requires, ſtrength, vigour, and ſkill, to get aboard a veſſel going before a briſk wind; though indeed they are abundantly provided with all theſe requiſites.

Behind the dining-room (that is, nearer the ſtern,) you have a bed-chamber ten feet long, and a place for putting your books and arms. With the latter we were plentifully ſupplied, both with thoſe of the uſeful kind, and thoſe (ſuch as large blunderbuſſes,) meant to ſtrike terror. We had great abundance of ammunition likewiſe, both for our defence and ſport.

With books we were leſs furniſhed, yet our library was *choſen*, and a very *dear* one; for, finding how much my baggage was increaſed by the acceſſion of the large quadrant and its foot, and Dolland's large achromatic teleſcope, I began to think it folly to load myſelf more with things to be

carried

carried on mens shoulders through a country full of mountains, which it was very doubtful whether I should get liberty to enter, much more be able to induce savages to carry these incumbrances for me.

To reduce the bulk as much as possible, after considering in my mind what were likeliest to be of service to me in the countries through which I was passing, and the several inquiries I was to make, I fell, with some remorse, upon garbling my library, tore out all the leaves which I had marked for my purpose, destroyed some editions of very rare books, rolling up the needful, and tying them by themselves. I thus reduced my library to a more compact form.

It was December 12th when I embarked on the Nile at Bulac, on board the Canja already mentioned, the remaining part of which needs no description, but will be understood immediately upon inspection.

At first we had the precaution to apply to our friend Risk concerning our captain Hagi Hassan Abou Cuffi, and we obliged him to give his son Mahomet in security for his behaviour towards us. Our hire to Furshout was twenty-seven patakas, or about L. 6 : 15 : 0 Sterling.

There was nothing so much we desired as to be at some distance from Cairo on our voyage. Bad affairs and extortions always overtake you in this detestable country, at the very time when you are about to leave it.

The wind was contrary, so we were obliged to advance against the stream, by having the boat drawn with a rope.

WE were furprifed to fee the alacrity with which two young Moors beftirred themfelves in the boat, they fupplied the place of mafters, companions, pilots, and feamen to us.

OUR Rais had not appeared, and I did not augur much good from the alacrity of thefe Moors, fo willing to proceed without him.

HOWEVER, as it was conformable to our own wifhes, we encouraged and cajoled them all we could. We advanced a few miles to two convents of Cophts, called Deireteen*

HERE we ftopped to pafs the night, having had a fine view of the Pyramids of Geeza and Saccara, and being then in fight of a prodigious number of others built of white clay, and ftretching far into the defert to the fouth-weft.

Two of thefe feemed full as large as thofe that are called the Pyramids of Geeza. One of them was of a very extraordinary form, it feemed as if it had been intended at firft to be a very large one, but that the builder's heart or means had failed him, and that he had brought it to a very mif-fhapen difproportioned head at laft

WE were not a little difpleafed to find, that, in the firft promife of punctuality our Rais had made, he had difappointed us by abfenting himfelf from the boat. The fear of a complaint, if we remained near the town, was the reafon why his fervants had hurried us away; but being now out

---

* This has been thought to mean the Convent of Figs, but it only fignifies the Two Convents.

out of reach, as they thought, their behaviour was entirely changed; they fcarce deigned to fpeak to us, but fmoked their pipes, and kept up a converfation bordering upon ridicule and infolence.

On the fide of the Nile, oppofite to our boat, a little farther to the fouth, was a tribe of Arabs encamped.

These are fubject to Cairo, or were then at peace with its government. They are called Howadat, being a part of the Atouni, a large tribe that poffeffes the Ifthmus of Suez, and from that go up between the Red Sea and the mountains that bound the eaft part of the Valley of Egypt. They reach to the length of Coffeir, where they border upon another large tribe called Ababdé, which extends from thence up into Nubia.

Both thefe are what were anciently called *Shepherds*, and are now conftantly at war with each other.

The Howadat are the fame that fell in with Mr Irvine* in thefe very mountains, and conducted him fo generoufly and fafely to Cairo. Though little acquainted with the manners, and totally ignorant of the language of his conductors, he imagined them to be, and calls them by no other name, than "*the Thieves.*"

One or two of thefe ftraggled down to my boat to feek tobacco and coffee, when I told them, if a few decent men
among

---

* See Mr Irvine's Letters.

among them would come on board, I fhould make them partakers of the coffee and tobacco I had. Two of them accepted the invitation, and we prefently became great friends.

I REMEMBERED, when in Barbary, living with the tribes of Noile and Wargumma (two numerous and powerful clans of Arabs in the kingdom of Tunis) that the Howadat, or Atouni, the Arabs of the Ifthmus of Suez, were of the fame family and race with one of them.

I EVEN had marked this down in my memorandum-book, but it happened not to be at hand; and I did not really remember whether it was to the Noile or Wargumma they were friends, for thefe two are rivals, and enemies, fo in a miftake there was danger. I, however, caft about a little to difcover this if poffible; and foon, from difcourfe and circumftances that came into my mind, I found it was the Noile to whom thefe people belonged; fo we foon were familiar, and as our converfation tallied fo that we found we were *true men*, they got up and infifted on fetching one of their Shekhs.

I TOLD them they might do fo if they pleafed; but they were firft bound to perform me a piece of fervice, to which they willingly and readily offered themfelves. I defired, that, early next morning, they would have a boy and horfe ready to carry a letter to Rifk, Ali Bey's fecretary, and I would give him a piafter upon bringing back the anfwer.

THIS they inftantly engaged to perform, but no fooner were they gone a-fhore, than, after a fhort council held together,

gether, one of our laughing boat-companions ſtole off on foot, and, before day, I was awakened by the arrival of our Rais Abou Cuffi, and his ſon Mahomet.

Abou Cuffi was *drunk*, though a *Sherriffe*, a *Hagi*, and half a *Saint* beſides, who never taſted *fermented* liquor, as he told me when I hired him.—The ſon was terrified out of his wits. He ſaid he ſhould have been impaled, had the meſſenger arrived; and, ſeeing that I fell upon means to keep open a correſpondence with Cairo, he told me he would not run the riſk of being ſurety, and of going back to Cairo to anſwer for his father's faults, leaſt, one day or another, upon ſome complaint of that kind, he might be taken out of his bed and baſtinadoed to death, without knowing what his offence was.

An altercation enſued; the father declined ſtaying upon pretty much the ſame reaſons, and I was very happy to find that Riſk had dealt roundly with them, and that I was maſter of the ſtring upon which I could touch their fears.

They then both agreed to go the voyage, for none of them thought it very ſafe to ſtay; and I was glad to get men of ſome ſubſtance along with me, rather than truſt to hired vagabond ſervants, which I eſteemed the two Moors to be.

As the Shekh of the Howadat and I had vowed friendſhip, he offered to carry me to Coſſeir by land, without any expence, and in perfect ſafety, thinking me diffident of my boatmen, from what had paſſed.

I thanked

THE SOURCE OF THE NILE.

I THANKED him for this friendly offer, which I am perfuaded I might have accepted very fafely, but I contented myfelf with defiring, that one of the Moor fervants in the boat fhould go to Cairo to fetch Mahomet Abou Cuffi's fon's cloaths, and agreed that I fhould give five patakas additional hire for the boat, on condition that Mahomet fhould go with us in place of the Moor fervant, and that Abou Cuffi, the father and faint (that never drank fermented liquors) fhould be allowed to fleep himfelf fober, till his fervant the Moor returned from Cairo with his fon's cloaths.

IN the mean time, I bargained with the Shekh of the Howadat to furnifh me with horfes to go to Metrahenny or Mohannan, where once he faid Mimf had ftood, a large city, the capital of all Egypt.

ALL this was executed with great fuccefs. Early in the morning the Shekh of the Howadat had paffed at Miniel, where there is a ferry, the Nile being very deep, and attended me with five horfemen and a fpare horfe for myfelf, at Metrahenny, fouth of Miniel, where there is a great plantation of palm-trees.

THE 13th, in the morning about eight o'clock, we let out our vaft fails, and paffed a very confiderable village called Turra, on the eaft fide of the river, and Shekh Atman, a fmall village, confifting of about thirty houfes, on the weft.

THE mountains which run from the caftle to the eaftward of fouth-eaft, till they are about five miles diftant from the Nile eaft and by north of this ftation, approach again the banks of the river, running in a direction fouth and by weft,

weft, till they end clofe on the banks of the Nile about Turra.

The Nile here is about a quarter of a mile broad ; and there cannot be the fmalleft doubt, in any perfon difpofed to be convinced, that this is by very far * the narroweft part of Egypt yet feen. For it certainly wants of half-a-mile between the foot of the mountain and the Libyan fhore, which cannot be faid of any other part of Egypt we had yet come to ; and it cannot be better defcribed than it is by † Herodotus ; and " again, *oppofite* to the Arabian fide, is another " ftony mountain of Egypt towards Libya, covered with " fand, where are the Pyramids."

As this, and many other circumftances to be repeated in the fequel, muft naturally awaken the attention of the traveller to look for the ancient city of Memphis here, I left our boat at Shekh Atman, accompanied by the Arabs, pointing nearly fouth. We entered a large and thick wood of palm-trees, whofe greateft extenfion feemed to be fouth by eaft. We continued in this courfe till we came to one, and then to feveral large villages, all built among the plantation of date-trees, fo as fcarce to be feen from the fhore.

These villages are called Metrahenny, a word from the etymology of which I can derive no information, and leaving the river, we continued due weft to the plantation that is called Mohannan, which, as far as I know, has no fignification either.

All

---

*Herod. lib. ii. p. 99.   †Herod. lib. ii. cap. 8.

THE SOURCE OF THE NILE.

All to the fouth, in this defert, are vaft numbers of Pyramids; as far as I could difcern, all of clay, fome fo diftant as to appear juft in the horizon.

Having gained the weftern edge of the palm-trees at Mohannan, we have a fair view of the Pyramids at Geeza, which lie in a direction nearly S. W. As far as I can compute the diftance, I think about nine miles, and as near as it was poffible to judge by fight, Metrahenny, Geeza, and the center of the three Pyramids, made an Ifofceles triangle, or nearly fo.

I asked the Arab what he thought of the diftance? whether it was fartheft to Geeza, or the Pyramids? He faid, they were *fowah, fowah*, juft alike, he believed; from Metrahenny to the Pyramids perhaps might be fartheft, but he would much fooner go it, than along the coaft to Geeza, becaufe he fhould be interrupted by meeting with water.

All to the weft and fouth of Mohannan, we faw great mounds and heaps of rubbifh, and califhes that were not of any length, but were lined with ftone, covered and choked up in many places with earth.

We faw three large granite pillars S. W. of Mohannan, and a piece of a broken cheft or ciftern of granite; but no obelifks, or ftones with hieroglyphics, and we thought the greateft part of the ruins feemed to point that way, or more foutherly.

These, our conductor faid, were the ruins of Mimf, the ancient feat of the Pharaohs kings of Egypt, that there was

v. i. g another

another Mimf, far down in the Delta, by which he meant Menouf, below Terrane and Batn el Baccara*.

Perceiving now that I could get no further intelligence, I returned with my kind guide, whom I gratified for his pains, and we parted content with each other.

In the fands I faw a number of hares. He faid, if I would go with him to a place near Faioume, I fhould kill half a boat-load of them in a day, and antelopes likewife, for he knew where to get dogs; mean-while he invited me to fhoot at them there, which I did not choofe; for, paffing very quietly among the date-trees, I wifhed not to invite further curiofity.

All the people in the date villages feemed to be of a yellower and more fick-like colour, than any I had ever feen; befides, they had an inanimate, dejected, grave countenance, and feemed rather to avoid, than wifh any converfation.

It was near four o'clock in the afternoon when we returned to our boatmen. By the way we met one of our Moors, who told us they had drawn up the boat oppofite to the northern point of the palm-trees of Metrahenny.

My Arab infifted to attend me thither, and, upon his arrival, I made him fome trifling prefents, and then took my leave.

In the evening I received a prefent of dry dates, and fome fugar cane, which does not grow here, but had been brought

to,

---

* See the Chart of the Nile.

THE SOURCE OF THE NILE. 55

to the Shekh by some of his friends, from some of the villages up the river.

The learned Dr Pococke, as far as I know, is the first European traveller that ventured to go out of the beaten path, and look for Memphis, at Metrahenny and Mohannan.

Dr Shaw, who in judgment, learning, and candour, is equal to Dr Pococke, or any of those that have travelled into Egypt, contends warmly for placing it at Geeza.

Mr Niebuhr, the Danish traveller, agrees with Dr Pococke. I believe neither Shaw nor Niebuhr were ever at Metrahenny, which Dr Pococke and myself visited; though all of us have been often enough at Geeza, and I must confess, strongly as Dr Shaw has urged his arguments, I cannot consider any of the reasons for placing Memphis at Geeza as convincing, and very few of them that do not go to prove just the contrary in favour of Metrahenny.

Before I enter into the argument, I must premise, that Ptolemy, if he is good for any thing, if he merits the hundredth part of the pains that have been taken with him by his commentators, must surely be received as a competent authority in this case.

The inquiry is into the position of the old capital of Egypt, not fourscore miles from the place where he was writing, and immediately in dependence upon it. And therefore, in dubious cases, I shall have no doubt to refer to him as deserving the greatest credit.

Dr

Dr Pococke * says, that the situation of Memphis was at Mohannan, or Metrahenny, because Pliny says the † Pyramids were between Memphis and the Delta, as they certainly are, if Dr Pococke is right as to the situation of Memphis.

Dr Shaw does not undertake to answer this direct evidence, but thinks to avoid its force by alledging a contrary sentiment of the same Pliny, " that the Pyramids ‡ lay between Memphis and the Arsinoite nome, and consequently, as Dr Shaw thinks, they must be to the westward of Memphis."

Memphis, if situated at Metrahenny, was in the middle of the Pyramids, three of them to the N. W. and above threescore of them to the south.

When Pliny said that the Pyramids were between Memphis and the Delta, he meant the three large Pyramids, commonly called the Pyramids of Geeza.

But in the last instance, when he spoke of the Pyramids of Saccara, or that great multitude of Pyramids southward, he said they were between Memphis and the Arsinoite nome; and so they are, placing Memphis at Metrahenny.

For Ptolemy gives Memphis 29° 50′ in latitude, and the Arsinoite nome 29° 30′ and there is 8′ of longitude betwixt them. Therefore the Arsinoite nome cannot be to the west, either of Geeza or Metrahenny; the Memphitic nome extends

---

* Pococke, vol. I. cap v. p. 39.   † Plin. lib. 5, cap. 9.   ‡ Plin. lib. 36. cap. 12.

THE SOURCE OF THE NILE.

tends to the westward, to that part of Libya called the Scythian Region; and south of the Memphitic nome is the Arsinoite nome, which is bounded on the westward by the same part of Libya.

To prove that the latter opinion of Pliny should outweigh the former one, Dr Shaw cites *Diodorus Siculus, who says Memphis was most commodiously situated in the very key, or inlet of the country, where the river begins to divide itself into several branches, and forms the Delta.

I cannot conceive a greater proof of a man being blinded by attachment to his own opinion, than this quotation. For Memphis was in lat. 29° 50', and the point of the Delta was in 30°, and this being the latitude of Geeza, it cannot be that of Memphis. That city must be sought for ten or eleven miles farther south.

If, as Dr Shaw supposes, it was nineteen miles round, and that it was five or six miles in breadth, its greatest breadth would probably be to the river. Then 10 and 6 make 16, which will be the latitude of Metrahenny, according to † Dr Shaw's method of computation.

But then it cannot be said that Geeza is either in the key or inlet of the country; all to the westward of Geeza is plain, and desert, and no mountain nearer it on the other side than the castle of Cairo.

---

* Diod. Sic. p. 45. § 50.   † Shaw's Travels, p. 296. in the latitude quoted.

Dr Shaw* thinks that this is further confirmed by Pliny's saying that Memphis was within fifteen miles of the Delta. Now if this was really the case, he suggests a plain reason, if he relies on ancient measures, why Geeza, that is only ten miles, cannot be Memphis.

If a person, arguing from measures, thinks he is intitled to throw away or add, the third part of the quantity that he is contending for, he will not be at a great stress to place these ancient cities in what situation he pleases.

Nor is it fair for Dr Shaw to suppose quantities that never did exist; for Metrahenny, instead of † forty, is not quite twenty-seven miles from the Delta; such liberties would confound any question.

The Doctor proceeds by saying, that heaps of ruins ‡ alone are not proof of any particular place; but the agreeing of the distances between Memphis and the Delta, which is a fixed and standing boundary, lying at a determinate distance from Memphis, must be a proof beyond all exception ‖.

If I could have attempted to advise Dr Shaw, or have had an opportunity of doing it, I would have suggested to him, as one who has maintained that all Egypt is the gift of the Nile, not to say that the point of the Delta is a standing and determined boundary that cannot alter. The inconsistency is apparent, and I am of a very contrary opinion.

BABYLON

---

* Shaw's Travels, cap. 4. p. 298.   † Id. ibid. 299.   ‡ Id ibid.   ‖ Id. ibid.

THE SOURCE OF THE NILE. 59

BABYLON, or Cairo, as it is now called, is fixed by the Calish or Amnis Trajanus paffing through it. Ptolemy * fays fo, and Dr Shaw fays that Geeza was oppofite to Cairo, or in a line eaft and weft from it, and is the ancient Memphis.

Now, if Babylon is lat. 30°, and fo is Geeza, they may be oppofite to one another in a line of eaft and weft. But if the latitude of Memphis is 29° 50', it cannot be at Geeza, which is oppofite to Babylon, but ten miles farther fouth, in which cafe it cannot be oppofite to Babylon or Cairo. Again, if the point of the Delta be in lat. 30°, Babylon, or Cairo, 30°, and Geeza be 30°, then the point of the Delta cannot be ten miles from Cairo or Babylon, or ten miles from Geeza

It is ten miles from Geeza, and ten miles from Babylon, or Cairo, and therefore the diftances do not agree as Dr Shaw fays they do; nor can the point of the Delta, as he fays, be a permanent boundary confiftently with his own figures and thofe of Ptolemy, but it muft have been wafhed away, or gone 10' northward; for Babylon, as he fays, is a certain boundary fixed by the Amnis Trajanus, and, fuppofing the Delta had been a fixed boundary, and in lat. 30°, then the diftance of fifteen miles would juft have made up the fpace that Pliny fays was between that point and Memphis, if we fuppofe that great city was at Metrahenny.

I SHALL fay nothing as to his next argument in relation to the diftance of Geeza from the Pyramids; becaufe, making

---

* Ptol. Geograph. lib. iv. cap. 5.

king the same suppositions, it is just as much in favour of one as of the other.

His next argument is from *Herodotus, who says, that Memphis lay under the sandy mountain of Libya, and that this mountain is a stony mountain covered with sand, and is opposite to the Arabian mountain.

Now this surely cannot be called Geeza; for Geeza is under no mountain, and the Arabian mountain spoken of here is that which comes close to the shore at Turra.

Diodorus says, it was placed in the straits or narrowest part of Egypt; and this Geeza cannot be so placed, for, by Dr Shaw's own confession, it is at least twelve miles from Geeza to the sandy mountain where the Pyramids stand on the Libyan side; and, on the Arabian side, there is no mountain but that on which the castle of Cairo stands, which chain begins there, and runs a considerable way into the desert, afterwards pointing south-west, till they come so near to the eastern shore as to leave no room but for the river at Turra; so that, if the cause is to be tried by this point only, I am very confident that Dr Shaw's candour and love of truth would have made him give up his opinion if he had visited Turra.

The last authority I shall examine as quoted by Dr Shaw, is to me so decisive of the point in question, that, were I writing to those only who are acquainted with Egypt, and the navigation of the Nile, I would not rely upon another.

HERODOTUS

---

*Herod. lib. ii. p. 141. Ibid. p. 168. Ibid. p. 105. Ibid. p. 103. Edit. Steph.

THE SOURCE OF THE NILE. 61

HERODOTUS* says, "At the time of the inundation, the Egyptians do not sail from Naucratis to Memphis by the common channel of the river, that is Cercasora, and the point of the Delta, but over the plain country, along the very side of the Pyramids."

NAUCRATIS was on the west side of the Nile, about lat. 30° 30'. let us say about Terrane in my map. They then sailed along the plain, out of the course of the river, upon the inundation, close by the Pyramids, whatever side they pleased, till they came to Metrahenny, the ancient Memphis.

THE Etesian wind, fair as it could blow, forwarded their course whilst in this line. They went directly before the wind, and, if we may suppose, accomplished the navigation in a very few hours; having been provided with those barks, or canjas, with their powerful sails, which I have already described, and, by means of which, they shortened their passage greatly, as well as added pleasure to it.

BUT very different was the case if the canja was going to Geeza.

THEY had nothing to do with the Pyramids, nor to come within three leagues of the Pyramids; and nothing can be more contrary, both to fact and experience, than that they would shorten their voyage by sailing along the side of them; for the wind being at north and north-west as fair as possible for Geeza, they had nothing to do but to keep

as

---

*Herod. lib. ii. § 97 p. 123

as direct upon it as they could lie. But if, as Dr Shaw thinks, they made the Pyramids first, I would wish to know in what manner they conducted their navigation to come down upon Geeza.

Their veffels go only before the wind, and they had a ftrong fteady gale almoft directly in their teeth.

They had no current to help them; for they were in ftill water; and if they did not take down their large yards and fails, they were fo top-heavy, the wind had fo much purchafe upon them above, that there was no alternative, but, either with fails or without, they muft make for Upper Egypt; and there, entering into the firft practicable califh that was full, get into the main ftream.

But their dangers were not ftill over, for, going down with a violent current, and with their ftanding rigging up, the moment they touched the banks, their mafts and yards would go overboard, and, perhaps, the veffel ftave to pieces.

Nothing would then remain, but for fafety's fake to ftrike their mafts and yards, as they always do when they go down the river; they muft lie broadfide foremoft, the ftrong wind blowing perpendicular on one fide of the veffel, and the violent current pufhing it in a contrary direction on the other; while a man, with a long oar, balances the advantage the wind has of the ftream, by the hold it has of the cabin and upper works.

This would moft infallibly be the cafe of the voyage from Naucratis, unlefs in ftriving to fail by tacking, (a manœuvre

of

of which their veffel is not capable) their canja fhould overfet, and then they muft all perifh.

If Memphis was Metrahenny, I believe moft people who had leifure would have tried the voyage from Naucratis by the plain. They would have been carried ftraight from north to fouth. But Dr Shaw is exceedingly miftaken, if he thinks there is any way fo expeditious as going up the current of the river. As far as I can guefs, from ten to four o'clock, we feldom went lefs than eight miles in the hour, againft a current that furely ran more than fix. This current kept our veffel ftiff, whilft the monftrous fail forced us through with a facility not to be imagined.

Dr Shaw, to put Geeza and Memphis perfectly upon a footing, fays*, that there were no traces of the city now to be found, from which he imagines it began to decay foon after the building of Alexandria, that the mounds and ramparts which kept the river from it were in procefs of time neglected, and that Memphis, which he fuppofes was in the old bed of the river about the time of the Ptolemies, was fo far abandoned, that the Nile at laft got in upon it, and overflowing its old ruins, great part of the beft of which had been carried firft to build the city of Alexandria, that the mud covered the reft, fo that no body knew what was its true fituation. This is the opinion of Dr Pococke, and likewife of M. de Maillet.

The opinion of thefe two laft-mentioned authors, that the ruins and fituation of Memphis are now become obfcure,

is

---

* Shaw's Travels, cap. 4.

is certainly true; the foregoing difpute is a fufficient evidence of this.

But I will not fuffer it to be faid, that, foon after the building of Alexandria, or in the time of the Ptolemies, this was the cafe, becaufe Strabo * fays, that when he was in Egypt, Memphis, next to Alexandria, was the moft magnificent city in Egypt.

It was called the Capital † of Egypt, and there was entire a temple of Ofiris; the Apis (or facred ox) was kept and worfhipped there. There was likewife an apartment for the mother of that ox ftill ftanding, a temple of Vulcan of great magnificence, a large ‡ circus, or fpace for fighting bulls; and a great coloffus in the front of the city thrown down; there was alfo a temple of Venus, and a ferapium; in a very fandy place, where the wind heaps up hills of moving fand very dangerous to travellers, and a number of § fphinxes, (of fome only their heads being vifible) the others covered up to the middle of their body.

In the ‖ front of the city were a number of palaces then in ruins, and likewife lakes. Thefe buildings, he fays, ftood formerly upon an eminence; they lay along the fide of the hill, ftretching down to the lakes and the groves, and forty ftadia from the city; there was a mountainous height, that had many Pyramids ftanding upon it, the fepulchres of the kings, among which there are three remarkable, and two the wonders of the world.

This

---

* Strabo. lib. vii. . 914.   † Id. ibid.   ‡ Id. ibid.   § Strabo, ibid.   ‖ Id. ibid.

THE SOURCE OF THE NILE.

THIS is the account of an eye-witnefs, an hiftorian of the firft credit, who mentions Memphis, and this ftate of it, fo late as the reign of Nero; and therefore I fhall conclude this argument with three obfervations, which, I am very forry to fay, could never have efcaped a man of Dr Shaw's learning and penetration.

1*ft*, THAT by this defcription of Strabo, who was in it, it is plain that the city was not deferted in the time of the Ptolemies.

2*dly*, THAT no time, between the building of Alexandria and the time of the Ptolemies, could it be fwallowed up by the river, or its fituation unknown.

3*dly*, THAT great part of it having been built upon an eminence on the fide of a hill, efpecially the large and magnificent edifices I have fpoken of, it could not be fituated, as he fays, low in the bed of the river; for, upon the giving way of the Memphitic rampart, it would be fwallowed up by it.

IF it was fwallowed up by the river, it was not Geeza; and this accident muft have been fince Strabo's time, which Dr Shaw will not aver; and it is by much too loofe arguing to fay, firft, that the place was deftroyed by the violent overflowing of the river, and then pretend its fituation to be Geeza, where a river never came.

THE defcent of the hill to where the Pyramids were, and the number of Pyramids that were there around it, of which three are remarkable; the very fandy fituation, and the quantity of loose flying hillocks that were there (dangerous in windy weather to travellers) are very ſtrong pictures of the Saccara, the neighbourhood of Metrahenny and Mohannan, but they have not the ſmalleſt or moſt diſtant reſemblance to any part in the neighbourhood of Geeza

It will be aſked, Where are all thoſe temples, the Serapium, the Temple of Vulcan, the Circus, and Temple of Venus? Are they found near Metrahenny?

To this I anſwer, Are they found at Geeza? No, but had they been at Geeza, they would have ſtill been viſible, as they are at Thebes, Diofpolis, and Syene, becauſe they are ſurrounded with black earth not moveable by the wind. Vaſt quantities of theſe ruins, however, are in every ſtreet of Cairo: every wall, every Bey's ſtable, every ciſtern for horſes to drink at, preſerve part of the magnificent remains that have been brought from Memphis or Metrahenny.—The reſt are covered with the moving ſands of the Saccara; as, the ſphinxes and buildings that had been deſerted were in Strabo's time for want of graſs and roots, which always ſpread and keep the ſoil firm in populous inhabited places, the ſands of the deſerts are let looſe upon them, and have covered them *probably for ever.*

A man's heart fails him in looking to the ſouth and ſouthweſt of Metrahenny. He is loſt in the immenſe expanſe of deſert, which he ſees full of Pyramids before him. Struck with terror from the unuſual ſcene of vaſtneſs opened all at once upon leaving the palm-trees, he becomes diſpirited from the effects of ſultry climates.

FROM

THE SOURCE OF THE NILE.

From habits of idlenefs contracted at Cairo, from the ftories he has heard of the bad government and ferocity of the people, from want of language and want of plan, he fhrinks from the attempting any difcovery in the moving fands of the Saccara, embraces in fafety and in quiet the reports of others, whom he thinks have been more inquifitive and more adventurous than himfelf.

Thus, although he has created no new error of his own he is acceffary to the having corroborated and confirmed the ancient errors of others; and, though people travel in the fame numbers as ever, phyfics and geography continue at a ftand.

In the morning of the 14th of December, after having made our peace with Abou Cuffi, and received a multitude of apologies and vows of amendment and fidelity for the future, we were drinking coffee preparatory to our leaving Metrahenny, and beginning our voyage in earneft, when an Arab arrived from my friend the Howadat, with a letter, and a few dates, not amounting to a hundred.

The Arab was one of his people that had been fick, and wanted to go to Kenné in Upper Egypt. The Shekh expreffed his defire that I would take him with me this trifle of about two hundred and fifty miles, that I would give him medicines, cure his difeafe, and maintain him all the way.

On thefe occafions there is nothing like ready compliance. He had offered to carry me the fame journey with all my people and baggage without hire; he conducted me with fafety and great politenefs to the Saccara; I therefore

fore anfwered inftantly, " You fhall be very welcome, upon my head be it." Upon this the miferable wretch, half naked, laid down a dirty clout containing about ten dates, and the Shekh's fervant that had attended him returned in triumph.

I mention this trifling circumftance, to fhew how effential to humane and civil intercourfe prefents are confidered to be in the eaft; whether it be dates, or whether it be diamonds, they are fo much a part of their manners, that, without them an inferior will never be at peace in his own mind, or think that he has a hold of his fuperior for his favour or protection.

CHAP. IV.

Leave Metrahenny—Come to the Island Halouan—False Pyramid—These buildings end—Sugar Canes—Ruins of Antinopolis—Reception there.

OUR wind was fair and fresh, rather a little on our beam; when, in great spirits, we hoisted our main and fore-sails, leaving the point of Metrahenny, where our reader may think we have too long detained him. We saw the Pyramids of Saccara still S. W. of us; several villages on both sides of the river, but very poor and miserable; part of the ground on the east side had been overflowed, yet was not sown; a proof of the oppression and distress the husbandman suffers in the neighbourhood of Cairo, by the avarice and disagreement of the different officers of that motely incomprehensible government.

AFTER sailing about two miles, we saw three men fishing in a very extraordinary manner and situation. They were on a raft of palm branches, supported on a float of clay jars, made fast together. The form was like an Isosceles triangle, or face of a Pyramid; two men, each provided with a casting net, stood at the two corners, and threw their net into the stream together; the third stood at the apex of the triangle, or third corner, which was foremost, and threw his net the moment the other two drew theirs out of the water. And this they repeated, in perfect time, and with furprifing regularity. Our Rais thought we wanted to buy fifh; and letting go his main-fail, ordered them on board with a great tone of fuperiority.

They were in a moment alongfide of us; and one of them came on board, lafhing his miferable raft to a rope at our ftern. In recompence for their trouble, we gave them fome large pieces of tobacco, and this tranfported them fo much, that they brought us a bafket, of feveral different kinds of fifh, all fmall; excepting one laid on the top of the bafket, which was a clear falmon-coloured fifh, filvered upon its fides, with a fhade of blue upon its back*. It weighed about 10 lib. and was moft excellent, being perfectly firm and white like a perch. There are fome of this kind 70 lib. weight. I examined their nets, they were rather of a fmaller circumference than our cafting nets in England; the weight, as far as I could guefs, rather heavier in proportion than ours, the thread that compofed them being fmaller. I could not fufficiently admire their fuccefs, in a violent ftream of deep water, fuch as the Nile; for the river was at leaft twelve feet deep where they were fifhing, and the current very ftrong.

These fifhers offered willingly to take me upon the raft to teach me; but I cannot fay my curiofity went fo far. They faid their fifhing was merely accidental, and in courfe of their trade, which was felling thefe potter earthen jars, which they got near Afhmounein; and after having carried the

---

* Named *Binny*. See Appendix.

THE SOURCE OF THE NILE. 71

the raft with them to Cairo, they untie, fell them at the market, and carry the produce home in money, or in neceſſaries upon their back. A very poor œconomical trade, but ſufficent, as they ſaid, from the carriage of crude materials, the moulding, making, and ſending them to market, to Cairo and to different places in the Delta, to afford occupation to two thouſand men; this is nearly four times the number of people employed in the largeſt iron foundery in England. But the reader will not underſtand, that I warrant this fact from any authority but what I have given him.

About two o'clock in the afternoon, we came to the point of an iſland; there were ſeveral villages with date trees on both ſides of us; the ground is overflowed by the Nile, and cultivated. The current is very ſtrong here. We paſſed a village called Regnagiè, and another named Zaragara, on the eaſt ſide of the Nile. We then came to Caphar el Hay at, or the Toll of the Tailor; a village with great plantations of dates, and the largeſt we had yet ſeen.

We paſſed the night on the S. W. point of the iſland be tween Caphar el Hayat, and Gizier Azali, the wind failing us about four o'clock. This place is the beginning of the Heracleotic nome, and its ſituation a ſufficient evidence that Metrahenny was Memphis; its name is Halouan.

This iſland is now divided into a number of ſmall ones, by caliſhes being cut through and through it, and, under different Arabic names, they ſtill reach very far up the ſtream. I landed to ſee if there were remains of the olive tree which
Strabo

Strabo* fays grew here, but without fuccefs. We may imagine, however, that there was fome fuch like thing; becaufe oppofite to one of the divifions into which this large ifland is broken, there is a village called Zeitoon, or the Olive Tree.

On the 15th of December, the weather being nearly calm, we left the north end of the ifland, or Heracleotic nome; our courfe was due fouth, the line of the river; and three miles farther we paffed Woodan, and a collection of villages, all going by that name, upon the eaft: to the weft, or right, were fmall iflands, part of the ancient nome of which I have already fpoken.

The ground is all cultivated about this village, to the foot of the mountains, which is not above four miles; but it is full eight on the weft, all overflowed and fown. The Nile is here but fhallow, and narrow, not exceeding a quarter of a mile broad, and three feet deep; owing, I fuppofe, to the refiftance made by the ifland in the middle of the current, and by a bend it makes, thus intercepting the fand brought down by the ftream.

The mountains here come down till within two miles of Suf el Woodan, for fo the village is called. We were told there were fome ruins to the weftward of this, but only rubbifh, neither arch nor column ftanding. I fuppofe it is the Aphroditopolis, or the city of Venus, which we are to look for

---

* Strabo, lib. xvii. p. 936.

for here, and the nome of that name, all to the eastward of it.

The wind still freshening, we passed by several villages on each side, all surrounded with palm-trees, verdant and pleasant, but conveying an idea of sameness and want of variety, such as every traveller must have felt who has sailed in the placid, muddy, green-banked rivers in Holland.

The Nile, however, is here fully a mile broad, the water deep, and the current strong. The wind seemed to be exasperated by the resistance of the stream, and blew fresh and steadily, as indeed it generally does where the current is violent.

We passed Nizelet Embarak, which means the Blessed Landing-place. Mr Norden * calls it Giesiret Barrakaed, which he says is the *watering-place of the crofs*. Was this even the proper name here given it, it should be translated the Blessed Island; but, without understanding the language, it is in vain to keep a register of names.

The boatmen, living either in the Delta, Cairo, or one of the great towns in Upper Egypt, and coming constantly loaded with merchandise, or strangers from these great places, make swift passages by the villages, either down the river with a rapid current, or up with a strong, fair, and steady wind: And, when the season of the Nile's inundation is over, and the wind turns southward, they repair all to the Delta,

---

* Norden's travels, vol ii. p. 19.

the river being no longer navigable above, and there they are employed till the next feafon.

They know little, therefore, and care lefs about the names or inhabitants of thefe villages, who have each of them barks of their own to carry on their own trade. There are fome indeed employed by the Coptic and Turkifh merchants, who are better verfed in the names of villages than others; but, if they are not, and find you do not underftand the language, they will never confefs ignorance; they will tell you the firft name that comes uppermoft, fometimes very ridiculous, often very indecent, which we fee afterwards pafs into books, and wonder that fuch names were ever given to towns.

The reader will obferve this in comparing Mr Norden's voyage and mine, where he will feldom fee the fame village pafs by the fame name. My Rais, Abou Cuffi, when he did not know a village, fometimes tried this with me. But when he faw me going to write, he ufed then to tell me the truth, that he did not know the village; but that fuch was the cuftom of him, and his brethren, to people that did not underftand the language, efpecially if they were priefts, meaning Catholic Monks.

We paffed with great velocity Nizelet Embarak, Cubabac, Nizelet Omar, Racca Kibeer, then Racca Seguier, and came in fight of Atfia, a large village at fome diftance from the Nile; all the valley here is green, the palm-groves beautiful, and the Nile deep.

Still

STILL it is not the profpect that pleafes, for the whole ground that is fown to the fandy afcent of the mountains, is but a narrow ftripe of three quarters of a mile broad, and the mountains themfelves, which here begin to have a moderate degree of elevation, and which bound this narrow valley, are white, gritty, fandy, and uneven, and perfectly deftitute of all manner of verdure.

AT the fmall village of Racca Seguier there was this remarkable, that it was thick, furrounded with trees of a different nature and figure from palms; what they were I know not, I believe they were pomegranate-trees; I thought, that with my glafs I difcerned fome reddifh fruit upon them; and we had paffed a village called Rhoda, a name they give in Egypt to pomegranates; Salcah is on the oppofite, or eaft-fide of the river. The Nile divides above the village; it fell very calm, and here we paffed the night of the fifteenth.

OUR Rais Abou Cuffi begged leave to go to Comadreedy, a fmall village on the weft of the Nile, with a few palm-trees about it; he faid that his wife was there. As I never heard any thing of this till now, I fancied he was going to divert himfelf in the manner he had done the night before he left Cairo; for he had put on his black furtout, or great coat, his fcarlet turban, and a new fcarlet fhaul, both of which he faid he had brought, to do me honour in my voyage.

I THANKED him much for his confideration, but afked him why, as he was a Sherriffe, he did not wear the *green turban* of Mahomet? He anfwered, Poh! that was a trick put upon ſtrangers; there were many men who wore green turbans, he ſaid, that were very great raſcals; but he was a *Saint*, which was better than a Sherriffe, and was known as ſuch all over the world, whatever colour of a turban he wore, or whether a turban at all, and he only dreſſed for my honour; would be back early in the morning, and bring me a fair wind.

"HASSAN, ſaid I, I fancy it is much more likely that you "bring me ſome aquavitæ, if you do not drink it all." He promiſed that he would ſee and procure ſome, for mine was now at an end. He ſaid, the Prophet never forbade aquavitæ, only the drinking of wine; and the prohibition could not be intended for Egypt, for there was no wine in it. But Bouza, ſays he, Bouza I will drink, as long as I can walk from ſtem to ſtern of a veſſel, and away he went. I had indeed no doubt he would keep his reſolution of drinking whether he returned or not.

WE kept, as uſual, a very good watch all night, which paſſed without diſturbance. Next day, the 17th, was exceedingly hazy in the morning, though it cleared about ten o'clock. It was, however, ſufficient to ſhew the falſity of the obſervation of the author, who ſays that the Nile* emits no fogs, and in courſe of the voyage we often ſaw other examples of the fallacy of this aſſertion.

IN the afternoon, the people went aſhore to ſhoot pigeons; they were very bad, and black, as it was not the ſeaſon of grain.

---

* Herod. lib. ii. cap. 19.

grain. I remained arranging my journal, when, with fome furprize, I faw the Howadat Arab come in, and fit down clofe to me; however, I was not afraid of any evil intention, having a crooked knife at my girdle, and two piftols lying by me.

WHAT's this? How now, friend? faid I; Who fent for you? He would have kiffed my hand, faying *Fiardue*, I am under your protection: he then pulled out a rag from within his girdle, and faid he was going to Mecca, and had taken that with him; that he was afraid my boatmen would rob him, and throw him into the Nile, or get fomebody to rob and murder him by the way; and that one of the Moors, Haffan's fervant, had been feeling for his money the night before, when he thought him afleep.

I MADE him count his fum, which amounted to $7\frac{1}{2}$ fequins, and a piece of filver, value about half-a-crown, which in Syria they call Abou Kelb, Father Dog. It is the Dutch Lion rampant, which the Arabs, who never call a thing by its right name, term *a dog*.—In fhort, this treafure amounted to fomething more than three guineas; and this he defired me to keep till we feparated. Do not you tell them, faid he, and I will throw off my cloaths and girdle, and leave them on board, while I go to fwim, and when they find I have nothing upon me they will not hurt me.

BUT what fecurity, faid I, have you that I do not rob you of this, and get you thrown into the Nile fome night? No, no, fays he, that I know is impoffible. I have never been able to fleep till I fpoke to you; do with me what you pleafe, and my money too, only keep me out of the hands of thofe murderers. " Well, well, faid I, now you have got rid of your money, you are fafe, and you fhall be my fervant; lye before the door of my dining-room all night, they dare not hurt a hair of your head while I am alive."

The Pyramids, which had been on our right hand at different diſtances fince we paſſed the Saccara, terminated here in one of a very fingular conſtruction. About two miles from the Nile, between Suf and Woodan, there is a Pyramid, which at firſt fight appears all of a piece; it is of unbaked bricks, and perfectly entire; the inhabitants call it the * Falfe Pyramid. The lower part is a hill exactly fhaped like a Pyramid for a confiderable height. Upon this is continued the fuperſtructure in proportion till it terminates like a Pyramid above; and, at a diftance, it would require a good eye to difcern the difference, for the face of the ſtone has a great refemblance to clay, of which the Pyramids of the Saccara are compofed.

Hassan Abou Cuffi was as good as his word in one refpect; he came in the night, and had not drunk much fermented liquors; but he could find no fpirits, he faid, and that, to be fure, was one of the reafons of his return; I had fat up a great part of the night waiting a feafon for obfervation, but it was very cloudy, as all the nights had been fince we left Cairo.

The 18th, about eight o'clock in the morning, we prepared to get on our way; the wind was calm, and fouth. I afked

---

* Dagjour.

I afked our Rais where his fair wind was which he promifed to bring? He faid, his wife had quarrelled with him all night, and would not give him time to pray; and therefore, fays he with a very droll face, you fhall fee me do all that a Saint can do for you on this occafion. I afked him what that was? He made another droll face, "Why, it is to draw " the boat by the rope till the wind *turns fair*." I commended very much this wife alternative, and immediately the veffel began to move, but very flowly, the wind being ftill unfavourable.

On looking into Mr Norden's voyage, I was ftruck at firft fight with this paragraph*· "We faw this day abundance of " camels, but they did not come near enough for us to fhoot " them."—I thought with myfelf, to *fhoot* camels in Egypt would be very little better than to *fhoot* men, and that it was very lucky for him the camels did not come near, if that was the only thing that prevented him. Upon looking at the note, I fee it is a fmall miftake of the tranflator †, who fays, " that in the original it is Chameaux d'eau, *water-* " *camels;* but whether they are a particular fpecies of camels, " or a different kind of animal, he does not know.

But

---

* Norden's Travels, vol. ii. p. 17.

† I cannot here omit to rectify another fmall miftake of the tranflator, which involves him in a difference with this Author which he did not mean.—

Mr Norden, in the French, fays, that the mafter of his veffel being much frightened, " avoit perdu la tramontane;" the true meaning of which is, That he had loft his judgment, not loft the north wind, as it is tranflated, which is really nonfenfe.

Norden's Travels, vol. ii. p. 59.

But this is no species of camel, it is a bird called a Pelican, and the proper name in Arabic, is Jimmel el Bahar, the Camel of the River. The other bird like a partridge, which Mr Norden's people shot, and did not know its name, and which was better than a pigeon, is called Gooto, very common in all the desert parts of Africa. I have drawn them of many different colours. That of the Deserts of Tripoli, and Cyrenaicum, is very beautiful; that of Egypt is spotted white like the Guinea-fowl, but upon a brown ground, not a blue one, as that latter bird is. However, they are all very bad to eat, but they are not of the same kind with the partridge. Its legs and feet are all covered with feathers, and it has but two toes before. The Arabs imagine it feeds on stones, but its food is insects.

After Comadreedy, the Nile is again divided by another fragment of the island, and inclines a little to the westward. On the east is the village Sidi Ali el Courani. It has only two palm-trees belonging to it, and on that account hath a deserted appearance; but the wheat upon the banks was five inches high, and more advanced than any we had seen. The mountains on the east-side come down to the banks of the Nile, are bare, white, and sandy, and there is on this side no appearance of villages.

The river here is about a quarter of a mile broad, or something more. It should seem it was the Angyrorum Civitas of Ptolemy, but neither night nor day could I get an instant for observation, on account of thin white clouds, which confused (for they scarce can be said to cover) the heavens continually.

We

THE SOURCE OF THE NILE. 81

We paffed now a convent of cophts, with a fmall plantation of palms. It is a miferable building, with a dome like to a faint's or marabout's, and ftands quite alone.

About four miles from this is the village of Nizelet el Arab, confifting of miferable huts. Here begin large plantations of fugar canes, the firft we had yet feen ; they were then loading boats with thefe to carry them to Cairo. I procured from them as many as I defired. The canes are about an inch and a quarter in diameter, they are cut in round pieces about three inches long, and, after having been flit, they are fteeped in a wooden bowl of water. They give a very agreeable tafte and flavour to it, and make it the moft refrefhing drink in the world, whilft by imbibing the water, the canes become more juicy, and lofe a part of their heavy clammy fweetnefs, which would occafion thirft. I was furprized at finding this plant in fuch a ftate of perfection fo far to the northward. We were now fcarcely arrived in lat. 29°, and nothing could be more beautiful and perfect than the canes were.

I apprehend they were originally a plant of the old continent, and tranfported to the new, upon its firft difcovery, becaufe here in Egypt they grow from feed. I do not know if they do fo in Brazil, but they have been in all times the produce of Egypt. Whether they have been found elfewhere, I have not had an opportunity of being informed, but it is time that fome fkilful perfon, verfed in the hiftory of plants, fhould feparate fome of the capital productions of the old, and new continent, from the adventitious, before, from length of time, that which we now know of their hiftory be loft.

Vol. I.   L   Sugar,

Sugar, tobacco, red podded or Cayenne pepper, cotton some species of Solanum, Indigo, and a multitude of others, have not as yet their origin well ascertained.

Prince Henry of Portugal put his discoveries to immediate profit, and communicated what he found new in each part in Europe, Asia, Africa, and America, to where it was wanting. It will be soon difficult to ascertain to each quarter of the world the articles that belong to it, and fix upon those few that are common to all.

Even wheat, the early produce of Egypt, is not a native of it. It grows under the Line, within the Tropics, and as far north and south as we know. Severe northern winters seem to be necessary to it, and it vegetates vigorously in frost and snow. But whence it came, and in what shape, is yet left to conjecture.

Though the stripe of green wheat was continued all along the Nile, it was interrupted for about half a mile on each side of the coptish convent. These poor wretches know, that though they may sow, yet, from the violence of the Arabs, they shall never reap, and therefore leave the ground desolate.

On the side opposite to Sment, the stripe begins again, and continues from Sment to Mey-Moom, about two miles, and from Mey-Moom to Shenuiah, one mile further. In this small stripe, not above a quarter of a mile broad, besides wheat, clover is sown, which they call Berfine. I don't think it equals what I have seen in England, but it is sown and cultivated in the same manner.

Immediately

THE SOURCE OF THE NILE.

IMMEDIATELY behind this narrow stripe, the white mountains appear again, square and flat on the top like tables. They seem to be laid upon the surface of the earth, not inserted into it, for the several strata that are divided lye as level as it is possible to place them with a rule; they are of no considerable height.

WE next passed Boush, a village on the west-side of the Nile, two miles south of Shenuiah; and, a little further, Beni Ali, where we see for a minute the mountains on the right or west-side of the Nile, running in a line nearly south, and very high. About five miles from Boush is the village of Maniareish on the east-side of the river, and here the mountains on that side end.

BOUSH is about two miles and a quarter from the river. Beni Ali is a large village, and its neighbour, Zeytoom, still larger, both on the western shore. I suppose this last was part of the Heracleotic nome, where * Strabo says the olive-tree grew, and no where else in Egypt, but we saw no appearance of the great works once said to have been in that nome. A little farther south is Baiad, where was an engagement between Hussein Bey, and Ali Bey then in exile, in which the former was defeated, and the latter restored to the government of Cairo.

FROM Maniareish to Beni Suef is two miles and a half, and opposite to this the mountains appear again of considerable height, about twelve miles distant. Although Beni Suef

---

* Strabo, lib. xvii. p. 936.

is no better built than any other town or village that we had paſſed, yet it intereſts by its extent; it is the moſt conſiderable place we had yet ſeen ſince our leaving Cairo. It has a cacheff and a moſque, with three large ſteeples, and is a market-town.

The country all around is well cultivated, and ſeems to be of the utmoſt fertility; the inhabitants are better cloathed, and ſeemingly leſs miſerable, and oppreſſed, than thoſe we had left behind in the places nearer Cairo.

The Nile is very ſhallow at Beni Suef, and the current ſtrong. We touched ſeveral times in the middle of the ſtream, and came to an anchor at Baha, about a quarter of a mile above Beni Suef, where we paſſed the night.

We were told to keep good watch here all night, that there were troops of robbers on the eaſt-ſide of the water, who had lately plundered ſome boats, and that the cacheff either dared not, or would not give them any aſſiſtance. We did indeed keep ſtrict watch, but ſaw no robbers, and were no other way moleſted.

The 18th we had fine weather and a fair wind. Still I thought the villages were beggarly, and the conſtant groves of palm-trees ſo perfectly verdant, did not compenſate for the penury of ſown land, the narrowneſs of the valley, and barrenneſs of the mountains.

We paſſed Manfura, Gadami, Magaga, Malatiah, and other ſmall villages, ſome of them not conſiſting of fifteen houſes. Then follow Gundiah and Kerm on the weſt-ſide of the river,

river, with a large plantation of dates, and four miles further Sharuni. All the way from Boufh there appeared no mountains on the weft fide, but large plantations of dates, which extended from Gundiah four miles.

From this to Abou Azeeze, frequent plantations of fugar canes were now cutting. All about Kafoor is fandy and barren on both fides of the river. Etfa is on the weft fide of the Nile, which here again makes an ifland. All the houfes have now receptacles for pigeons on their tops, from which is derived a confiderable profit. They are made of earthen pots one above the other, occupying the upper ftory, and giving the walls of the turrets a lighter and more ornamented appearance.

We arrived in the evening at Zohora, about a mile fouth of Etfa. It confifts of three plantations of dates, and is five miles from Miniet, and there we paffed the night of the 18th of December.

There was nothing remarkable till we came to Barkaras, a village on the fide of a hill, planted with thick groves of palm-trees.

The wind was fo high we fcarcely could carry our fails; the current was ftrong at Shekh Temine, and the violence with which we went through the water was terrible. My Rais told me we fhould have flackened our fails, if it had not been, that, feeing me curious about the conftruction of the veffel and her parts, and as we were in no danger of ftriking, though the water was low, he wanted to fhew me what fhe could do.

I THANKED

I thanked him for his kindnefs. We had all along preferved ftrict friendfhip. Never fear the banks, faid I; for I know if there is one in the way, you have nothing to do but to bid him begone, and he will hurry to one fide directly "I have had paffengers, fays he, who would believe " that, and more than that, when I told them; but there is " no occafion I fee to wafte much time with you in fpeak- " ing of miracles."

" You are miftaken, Rais, I replied, very much miftaken; " I love to hear modern miracles vaftly, there is always fome " amufement in them."—" Aboard your Chriftian fhips, fays " he, you always have a prayer at twelve o'clock, and drink " a glafs of brandy; fince you won't be a Turk like me, I " wifh at leaft you would be a Chriftian."—Very fairly put, faid I, Haffan, let your veffel keep her wind if there is no danger, and I fhall take care to lay in a flock for the whole voyage at the firft town in which we can purchafe it.

We paffed by a number of villages on the weftern fhore, the eaftern feeming to be perfectly unpeopled: Firft, Fefhné, a confiderable place; then *Miniet, or the ancient Phylæ, a large town which had been fortified towards the water, at leaft there were fome guns there. A rebel Bey had taken poffeffion of it, and it was ufual to ftop here, the river being both narrow and rapid; but the Rais was in great fpirits, and refolved to hold his wind, as I had defired him, and nobody made us any fignal from fhore.

We

---

* Signifies the Narrow Faffage, and is meant what *Phylæ* is in Latin.

THE SOURCE OF THE NILE.

WE came to a village called Rhoda, whence we faw the magnificent ruins of the ancient city of Antinous, built by Adrian. Unluckily I knew nothing of thefe ruins when I left Cairo, and had taken no pains to provide myfelf with letters of recommendation as I could eafily have done. Perhaps I might have found it difficult to avail myfelf of them, and it was, upon the whole, better as it was.

I ASKED the Rais what fort of people they were? He faid that the town was compofed of very bad Turks, very bad Moors, and very bad Chriftians; that feveral devils had been feen among them lately, who had been difcovered by being better and quieter than any of the reft.—The Nubian geographer informs us, that it was from this town Pharaoh brought his magicians, to compare their powers with thofe of Mofes; an anecdote worthy that great hiftorian.

I TOLD the Rais, that I muft, of neceffity, go afhore, and afked him, if the people of this place had no regard for faints? that I imagined, if he would put on his red turban as he did at Comadreedy for my honour, it would then appear that he was a faint, as he before faid he was known to be all the world over. He did not feem to be fond of the expedition; but hauling in his main-fail, and with his forefail full, ftood S. S. E. directly under the Ruins. In a fhort time we arrived at the landing-place; the banks are low, and we brought up in a kind of bight or fmall bay, where there was a ftake, fo our veffel touched very little, or rather fwung clear.

ABOU CUFFI's fon Mahomet, and the Arab, went on fhore, under pretence of buying fome provifion, and to fee how
the

the land lay, but after the character we had of the inhabitants, all our fire-arms were brought to the door of the cabin. In the mean time, partly with my naked eye and partly with my glafs, I obferved the ruins fo attentively as to be perfectly in love with them.

These columns of the angle of the portico were ftanding fronting to the north, part of the tympanum, cornice, frize, and architrave, all entire, and very much ornamented; thick trees hid what was behind. The columns were of the largeft fize and fluted; the capitals Corinthian, and in all appearance entire. They were of white Parian marble probably, but had loft the extreme whitenefs, or polifh, of the Antinous at Rome, and were changed to the colour of the fighting gladiator, or rather to a brighter yellow. I faw indiftinctly, alfo, a triumphal arch, or gate of the town, in the very fame ftyle; and fome blocks of very white fhining ftone, which feemed to be alabafter, but for what employed I do not know.

No perfon had yet ftirred, when all on a fudden we heard the noife of Mahomet and the Moor in ftrong difpute. Upon this the Rais ftripping off his coat, leaped afhore, and flipped off the rope from the flake, and another of the Moors ftuck a ftrong perch or pole into the river, and twifted the rope round it. We were in a bight, or calm place, fo that the ftream did not move the boat.

Mahomet and the Moor came prefently in fight; the people had taken Mahomet's turban from him, and they were apparently on the very worft terms. Mahomet cried to us, that the whole town was coming, and getting near

THE SOURCE OF THE NILE.

the boat, he and the Moor jumped in with great agility. A number of people was affembled, and three fhots were fired at us, very quickly, the one after the other.

I cried out in Arabic, "Infidels, thieves, and robbers! come " on, or we fhall prefently attack you:" upon which I immediately fired a fhip-blunderbufs with piftol fmall bullets, but with little elevation, among the bufhes, fo as not to touch them. The three or four men that were neareft fell flat upon their faces, and flid away among the bufhes on their bellies, like eels, and we faw no more of them.

We now put our veffel into the ftream, filled our forefail, and ftood off, Mahomet crying, Be upon your guard, if you are men, we are the Sanjack's foldiers, and will come for the turban to-night. More we neither heard nor faw.

We were no fooner out of their reach, than our Rais, filling his pipe, and looking very grave, told me to thank God that I was in the veffel with fuch a man as he was, as it was owing to that only I efcaped from being murdered a-fhore " Certainly, faid I, Haffan, under God, the way of " efcaping from being murdered on land, is never to go " out of the boat, but don't you think that my blunderbufs " was as effectual a mean as your holinefs? Tell me, Maho- " met, What did they do to you?" He faid, They had not feen us come in, but had heard of us ever fince we were at Metrahenny, and had waited to rob or murder us; that upon now hearing we were come, they had all ran to their houfes for their arms, and were coming down, immediately, to plunder the boat; upon which he and the Moor ran off, and being met by thefe three people, and the boy, on the road, who had nothing in their hands, one of them fnatched the turban off. He likewife added, that there were two parties in the town; one in favour of Ali Bey, the other friends to a rebel Bey who had taken Miniet; that they had fought, two or three days ago, among themfelves, and were going to fight again, each of them having called A- rabs to their affiftance. "Mahomet Bey, fays my Howadat " Arab, will come one of thefe days with the foldiers, " and bring our Shekh and people with him, who will " burn their houfes, and deftroy their corn, that they will " be all ftarved to death next year."

HASSAN and his fon Mahomet were violently exafperated, and nothing would ferve them but to go in again near the fhore, and fire all the guns and blunderbuffes among the people. But, befides that I had no inclination of that kind, I was very loth to fruftrate the attempts of fome future traveller, who may add this to the great remains of archi- tecture we have preferved already.

IT would be a fine outfet for fome engraver; the elegance and importance of the work are certain. From Cairo the diftance is but four days pleafant and fafe navigation, and in quiet times, protection might, by proper means, be eafily enough obtained at little expence.

CHAP.

CHAP. V.

Voyage to Upper Egypt continued—Ashmounein, Ruins there—Gawa Kibeer Ruins—Mr Norden mistaken—Achmim—Convent of Catholics—Dendera—Magnificent Ruins—Adventure with a Saint there.

THE Rais's curiosity made him attempt to prevail with me to land at Reremont, three miles and a half off, just a-head of us; this I understood was a Coptic Christian town, and many of Shekh Abadé's people were Christians also. I thought them too near to have any thing to do with either of them. At Reremont there are a great number of Persian wheels, to draw the water for the sugar canes, which belong to Christians. The water thus brought up from the river runs down to the plantations, below or behind the town, after being emptied on the banks above; a proof that here the descent from the mountains is not an optic fallacy, as Dr Shaw says.

We passed Ashmounein, probably the ancient Latopolis, a large town, which gives the name to the province, where there are magnificent ruins of Egyptian architecture; and after that we came to Melawé, larger, better built, and better inhabited than Ashmounein, the residence of the Cacheff. Mahomet Aga was there at that time with troops from Cairo, he had taken Miniet, and, by the friendship of Shekh Hamam, the great Arab, governor of Upper Egypt, he kept all the people on that side of the river in their allegiance to Ali Bey.

I had seen him at Cairo, and Risk had spoken to him to do me service if he met with me, which he promised. I called at Melawé to complain of our treatment at Shekh Abadé, and see if I could engage him, as he had nothing else to employ him, to pay a visit to my friends at that inhospitable place. This I was told he would do upon the slightest intimation. He, unfortunately, however, happened to be out upon some party; but I was lucky in getting an old Greek, a servant of his, who knew I was a friend, both to the Bey and to his Patriarch.

He brought me about a gallon of brandy, and a jar of lemons and oranges, preserved in honey; both very agreeable. He brought likewise a lamb, and some garden-stuffs. Among the sweetmeats was some horse-raddish preserved like ginger, which certainly, though it might be wholesome, was the very worst stuff ever I tasted. I gave a good square piece of it, well wrapt in honey, to the Rais, who coughed and spit half an hour after, crying he was poisoned.

I saw he did not wish me to stay at Melawé, as he was afraid of the Bev's troops, that they might engage him in their service to carry them down, so went away with great good will, happy in the acquisition of the brandy, declaring he would carry sail as long as the wind held.

We paffed Mollé, a fmall village with a great number of acacia trees intermixed with the plantations of palms. Thefe occafion a pleafing variety, not only from the difference of the fhape of the tree, but alfo from the colour and diverfity of the green.

As the fycamore in Lower Egypt, fo this tree feems to be the only indigenous one in the Thebaid. It is the Acacia Vera, or the Spina Egyptiaca, with a round yellow flower. The male is called the Saiel; from it proceeds the gum arabic, upon incifion with an ax. This gum chiefly comes from Arabia Petrea, where thefe trees are moft numerous. But it is the tree of all deferts, from the northmoft part of Arabia, to the extremity of Ethiopia, and its leaves the only food for camels travelling in thofe defert parts. This gum is called Sumach in the weft of Africa, and is a principal article of trade on the Senega among the Ialofes.

A LARGE plantation of Dates reaches all along the weft fide, and ends in a village called Mafara. Here the river, though broad, happened to be very fhallow; and by the violence with which we went, we ftuck upon a fand bank fo faft, that it was after fun-fet before we could get off; we came to an anchor oppofite to Mafara the night of the 19th of December.

On the 20th, early in the morning, we again fet fail and paffed two villages, the firft called Welled Behi, the next Salem, about a mile and a half diftant from each other on the weft fide of the Nile. The mountains on the weft fide of the valley are about fixteen miles off, in a high even ridge, running in a direction fouth-eaft; while the mountains,

tains on the east run in a parellel direction with the river, and are not three miles distant.

We passed Deirout on the east side, and another called Zohor, in the same quarter, surrounded with palms; then Siradé on the east side also, where is a wood of the Acacia, which seems very luxuriant; and, though it was now December, and the mornings especially very cold, the trees were in full flower. We passed Monfalout, a large town on the western shore. It was once an old Egyptian town, and place of great trade; it was ruined by the Romans, but re-established by the Arabs.

An Arabian * author says, that, digging under the foundation of an old Egyptian temple here, they found a crocodile made of lead, with hieroglyphics upon it, which they imagine to be a talisman, to prevent crocodiles from passing further. Indeed, as yet, we had not seen any; that animal delights in heat, and, as the mornings were very cold, he keeps himself to the southward. The valley of Egypt here is about eight miles from mountain to mountain.

We passed Siout, another large town built with the remains of the ancient city † Isiu. It is some miles in land, upon the side of a large calish, over which there is an ancient bridge. This was formerly the station of the caravan for Sennaar. They assembled at Monfalout and Siout, under the protection of a Bey residing there. They then passed nearly south-west, into the sandy desert of Libya, to El Wah,

---

* Messoudi. † Itin. Anton. p. 14.

Wah, the Oasis Magna of antiquity, and so into the great Desert of Selima.

Three miles beyond Siout, the wind turned directly south, so we were obliged to stay at Tima the rest of the 20th. I was wearied with continuing in the boat, and went on shore at Tima. It is a small town, surrounded like the rest with groves of palm-trees. Below Tima is Bandini, three miles on the east side. The Nile is here full of sandy islands. Those that the inundation has first left are all sown, these are chiefly on the east. The others on the west were barren and uncultivated; all of them mostly composed of sand.

I walked into the desert behind the village, and shot a considerable number of the bird called Gooto, and several hares likewise, so that I sent one of my servants loaded to the boat. I then walked down past a small village called Nizelet el Himma, and returned by a still smaller one called Shuka, about a quarter of a mile from Tima. I was exceedingly fatigued with the heat by the south wind *blowing, and the deep sand on the side of the mountain. I was then beginning my apprenticeship, which I fully compleated.

The people in these villages were in appearance little less miserable than those of the villages we had passed. They seemed shy and surly at first, but, upon conversation, became placid enough. I bought some medals from them of no value, and my servants telling them I was a physician, I gave my advice to several of the sick. This reconciled them

---

* It is called Hamseen, because it is expected to blow all Pentecost.

them perfectly, they brought me fresh water and some sugar-canes, which they split and steeped in it. If they were satisfied, I was very much so. They told me of a large scene of ruins that was about four miles distant, and offered to send a person to conduct me, but I did not accept their offer, as I was to pass there next day.

THE 21st, in the morning, we came to Gawa, where is the second scene of ruins of Egyptian architecture, after leaving Cairo. I immediately went on shore, and found a small temple of three columns in front, with the capitals entire, and the columns in several separate pieces. They seemed by that, and their slight proportions, to be of the most modern of that species of building; but the whole were covered with hieroglyphics, the old story over again, the hawk and the serpent, the man sitting with the dog's head, with the perch, or measuring-rod; in one hand, the hemisphere and globes with wings, and leaves of the banana-tree, as is supposed, in his other. The temple is filled with rubbish and dung of cattle, which the Arabs bring in here to shelter them from the heat.

Mr NORDEN says, that these are the remains of the ancient Diospolis Parva, but, though very loth to differ from him, and without the least desire of criticising, I cannot here be of his opinion. For Ptolemy, I think, makes Diospolis Parva about lat. 26° 40', and Gawa is 27° 20', which is by much too great a difference. Besides, Diospolis and its nome were far to the southward of Panopolis; but we shall shew, by undoubted evidence, that Gawa is to the northward.

THERE

THE SOURCE OF THE NILE.

There are two villages of this name oppofite to each other; the one Gawa Shergieh, which means the Eaftern Gawa, and this is by much the largeft; the other Gawa Garbieh. Several authors, not knowing the meaning of thefe terms, call it Gawa Gebery; a word that has no fignification whatever, but Garbieh means the Weftern.

I was very well pleafed to fee here, for the firft time, two fhepherd dogs lapping up the water from the ftream, then lying down in it with great feeming leifure and fatisfaction. It refuted the old fable, that the dogs living on the banks of the Nile run as they drink, for fear of the crocodile.

All around the villages of Gawa Garbieh, and the plantations belonging to them, Mefhta and Raany, with theirs alfo joining them (that is, all the weft fide of the river) are cultivated and fown from the very foot of the mountains to the water's edge, the grain being thrown upon the mud as foon as ever the water has left it. The wheat was at this time about four inches in length.

We paffed three villages, Shaftour, Commawhaia, and Zinedi; we anchored off Shaftour, and within fight of Taahta. Taahta is a large village, and in it are feveral mofques. On the eaft is a mountain called Jibbel Heredy, from a Turkifh faint, who was turned into a fnake, has lived feveral hundred years, and is to live for ever. As Chriftians, Moors, and Turks, all faithfully believe in this, the confequence is, that abundance of nonfenfe is daily writ and told concerning it. Mr Norden difcuffes it at large, and afterwards gravely tells us, he does not believe it; in which I certainly muſt heartily join him, and recommend to my readers to do the ſame, without reading any thing about it.

On the 22d, at night, we arrived at Achmim. I landed my quadrant and inſtruments, with a view of obſerving an eclipſe of the moon; but, immediately after her riſing, clouds and miſt ſo effectually covered the whole heavens, that it was not even poſſible to catch a ſtar of any ſize paſſing the meridian.

Achmim is a very conſiderable place. It belonged once to an Arab prince of that name, who poſſeſſed it by a grant from the Grand Signior, for a certain revenue to be paid yearly. That family is now extinct; and another Arab prince, Hamam Shekh of Furſhout, now rents it for his life-time, from the Grand Signior, with all the country (except Girgé) from Siout to Luxor

The inhabitants of Achmim are of a very yellow, unhealthy appearance, probably owing to the bad air, occaſioned by a very dirty califh that paſſes through the town. There are, likewiſe, a great many trees, buſhes, and gardens, about the ſtagnated water, all which increaſe the bad quality of the air.

There is here what is called a Hoſpice, or Convent of religious Franciſcans, for the entertainment of the converts, or perſecuted Chriſtians in Nubia, *when they can find them*. This inſtitution I ſpeak of at large in the ſequel. One of the laſt princes of the houſe of Medicis, all patrons of learning, propoſed to furniſh them with a compleat obſervatory, with the moſt perfect and expenſive inſtruments; but they refuſed

refused them, from a scruple least it would give umbrage to the natives. The fear that it should expose their own ignorance and idleness, I must think, entered a little into the consideration.

They received us civilly, and that was just all. I think I never knew a number of priests met together, who differed so little in capacity and knowledge, having barely a rotine of scholastic disputation, on every other subject inconceivably ignorant. But I understood afterwards, that they were low men, all Italians; some of them had been barbers, and some of them tailors at Milan; they affected to be all Anti-Copernicans, upon scripture principles, for they knew no other astronomy.

These priests lived in great ease and safety, were much protected and favoured by this Arab prince Hamam; and their acting as physicians reconciled them to the people. They told me there were about eight hundred catholics in the town, but I believe the fifth part of that number would never have been found, even such catholics as they are. The rest of them were Cophts, and Moors, but a very few of the latter, so that the missionaries live perfectly unmolested.

There was a manufactory of coarse cotton cloth in the town, to considerable extent; and great quantity of poultry, esteemed the best in Egypt, was bred here, and sent down to Cairo. The reason is plain, the great export from Achmim is wheat; all the country about it is sown with that grain, and the crops are superior to any in Egypt. Thirty-two grains pulled from the ear was equal to forty-nine of the best Barbary wheat gathered in the fame feafon; a prodigious difproportion, if it holds throughout. The wheat, however, was not much more forward in Upper Egypt, than that lower down the country, or farther northward. It was little more than four inches high, and fown down to the very edge of the water.

THE people *here* wifely purfuing agriculture, fo as to produce wheat in the greateft quantity, have dates only about their houfes, and a few plantations of fugar cane near their gardens. As foon as they have reaped their wheat, they fow for another crop, before the fun has drained the moifture from the ground. Great plenty of excellent fifh is caught here at Achmim, particularly a large one called the Binny, a figure of which I have given in the Appendix. I have feen them about four feet long, and one foot and a half broad.

THE people feemed to be very peaceable, and well difpofed, but of little curiofity. They expreffed not the leaft furprife at feeing my large quadrant and telefcopes mounted. We paffed the night in our tent upon the river fide, without any fort of moleftation, though the men are reproached with being very great thieves. But feeing, I fuppofe, by our lights, that we were awake, they were afraid.

THE women feldom marry after fixteen; we faw feveral with child, who they faid were not eleven years old. Yet I did not obferve that the men were lefs in fize, lefs vigorous and active in body, than in other places. This, one would not imagine from the appearance thefe young wives make. They are little better coloured than a corpfe, and

look

look older at fixteen, than many Englifh women at fixty, fo that you are to look for beauty here in childhood only.

ACHMIM appears to be the Panopolis of the ancients, not only by its latitude, but alfo by an infcription of a very large triumphal arch, a few hundred yards fouth of the convent. It is built with marble by the Emperor Nero, and is dedicated in a Greek infcription, ΠΑΝΙ ΘΕΩ. The columns that were in its front are broken and thrown away; the arch itfelf is either funk into the ground, or overturned on the fide, with little feparation of the feveral pieces.

THE 24th of December we left Achmim, and came to the village Shekh Ali on the weft, two miles and a quarter diftant. We then paffed Hamdi, about the fame diftance farther fouth; Aboudarac and Salladi on the caft; then Salladi Garbieh, and Salladi Shergieh on the eaft and weft, as the names import; and a number of villages, almoft oppofite, on each fide of the river.

AT three o'clock in the afternoon we arrived at Girgé, the largeft town we had feen fince we left Cairo; which, by the latitude Ptolemy has very rightly placed it in, fhould be the Diofpolis Parva, and not Gawa, as Mr Norden makes it. For this we know is the beginning of the Diofpolitan nome, and is near a remarkable crook of the Nile, as it fhould be. It is alfo on the weftern fide of the river, as Diofpolis was, and at a proper diftance from Dendera, the ancient Tentyra, a mark which cannot be miftaken.

THE Nile makes a kind of loop here; is very broad, and the current ftrong. We paffed it with a wind at north; but the

the waves ran high as in the ocean. All the country, on both fides of the Nile, to Girgé, is but one continued grove of palm-trees, in which are feveral villages a fmall diftance from each other, Doulani, Confaed, Deirout, and Berdis, on the weft fide; Welled Hallifi, and Beni Haled, on the eaft.

The villages have all a very picturefque appearance among the trees, from the many pigeon-houfes that are on the tops of them. The mountains on the eaft begin to depart from the river, and thofe on the weft to approach nearer it. It feems to me, that, foon, the greateft part of Egypt on the eaft fide of the Nile, between Achmim and Cairo, will be defert; not from the rifing of the ground by the mud, as is fuppofed, but from the quantity of fand from the mountains, which covers the mould or earth feveral feet deep. This 24th of December, at night, we anchored between two villages, Beliani and Mobanniny.

Next morning, the 25th, impatient to vifit the greateft, and moft magnificent fcene of ruins that are in Upper Egypt, we fet out from Beliani, and, about ten o'clock in the forenoon, arrived at Dendera. Although we had heard that the people of this place were the very worft in Egypt, we were not very apprehenfive. We had two letters from the Bey, to the two principal men there, commanding them, as they would anfwer with their lives and fortunes, to have a fpecial care that no mifchief befel us; and likewife a very preffing letter to Shekh Hamam at Furfhout, in whofe territory we were.

I pitched my tent by the river fide, juft above our bark, and fent a meffage to the two principal people, firft to the one,

THE SOURCE OF THE NILE. 103

one, then to the other, defiring them to fend a proper perfon, for I had to deliver to them the commands of the Bey. I did not choofe to truft thefe letters with our boatman; and Dendera is near half a mile from the river. The two men came after fome delay, and brought each of them a fheep; received the letters, went back with great fpeed, and, foon after, returned with a horfe and three affes, to carry me to the ruins

DENDERA is a confiderable town at this day, all covered with thick groves of palm-trees, the fame that Juvenal defcribes it to have been in his time. Juvenal himfelf muft have feen it, at leaft once, in paffing, as he himfelf died in a kind of honourable exile at Syene, whilft in command there.

Terga fugæ celeri, præftantibus omnibus inftant,
Qui vicina colunt umbrofæ Tentyra palmæ.

JUV. Sat. 15. v. 75.

THIS place is governed by a cacheff appointed by Shekh Hamam. A mile fouth of the town, are the ruins of two temples, one of which is fo much buried under ground, that little of it is to be feen; but the other, which is by far the moft magnificent, is entire, and acceffible on every fide. It is alfo covered with hieroglyphics, both within and without, all in relief; and of every figure, fimple and compound, that ever has been publifhed, or called an hieroglyphic.

THE form of the building is an oblong fquare, the ends of which are occupied by two large apartments, or veftibules, fupported by monftrous columns, all covered with hieroglyphics,

hieroglyphics likewife. Some are in form of men and beafts; fome feem to be the figures of inftruments of facrifice, while others, in a fmaller fize, and lefs diftinct form, feem to be infcriptions in the current hand of hieroglyphics, of which I fhall fpeak at large afterwards. They are all finifhed with great care.

THE capitals are of one piece, and confift of four huge human heads, placed back to back againft one another, with bat's ears, and an ill-imagined, and worfe-executed, fold of drapery between them.

ABOVE thefe is a large oblong fquare block, ftill larger than the capitals, with four flat fronts, difpofed like pannels, that is, with a kind of fquare border round the edges, while the faces and fronts are filled with hieroglyphics; as are the walls and cielings of every part of the temple. Between thefe two apartments in the extremities, there are three other apartments, refembling the firft, in every refpect, only that they are fmaller.

THE whole building is of common white ftone, from the neighbouring mountains, only thofe two in which have been funk the pirns for hanging the outer doors, (for it feems they had doors even in thofe days) are of granite, or black and blue porphyry.

THE top of the temple is flat, the fpouts to carry off the water are monftrous heads of fphinxes; the globes with wings, and the two ferpents, with a kind of fhield or breaftplate between them, are here frequently repeated, fuch as we fee them on the Carthaginian medals.

THE

THE SOURCE OF THE NILE.

The hieroglyphics have been painted over, and great part of the colouring yet remains upon the stones, red, in all its shades, especially that dark dusky colour called Tyrian Purple; yellow, very fresh; sky-blue (that is, near the blue of an eastern sky, several shades lighter than ours; green of different shades; these are all the colours preserved.

I could discover no vestiges of common houses in Dendera more than in any other of the great towns in Egypt. I suppose the common houses of the ancients, in these warm countries, were constructed of very slight materials, after they left their caves in the mountains. There was indeed no need for any other. Not knowing the regularity of the Nile's inundation, they never could be perfectly secure in their own minds against the deluge; and this slight structure of private buildings seems to be the reason so few ruins are found in the many cities once built in Egypt. If there ever were any other buildings, they must be now covered with the white sand from the mountains, for the whole plain to the foot of these is overflowed, and in cultivation. It was no part, either of my plan or inclination, to enter into the detail of this extraordinary architecture. Quantity, and solidity, are two principal circumstances that are seen there, with a vengeance.

It strikes and imposes on you, at first sight, but the impressions are like those made by the size of mountains, which the mind does not retain for any considerable time after seeing them; I think, a very ready hand might spend six months, from morning to night, before he could copy the hieroglyphics in the inside of the temple. They are, however, in several combinations, which have not appeared in the collection of hieroglyphics. I wonder that, being in the neighbourhood, as we are, of Lycopolis, we never fee a wolf as an hieroglyphic; and nothing, indeed, but what has fome affinity to water; yet the wolf is upon all the medals, from which I apprehend that the worſhip of the wolf was but a modern fuperſtition.

DENDERA ſtands on the edge of a fmall, but fruitful plain; the wheat was thirteen inches high, now at Chriſtmas; their harveſt is in the end of March. The valley is not above five miles wide, from mountain to mountain. Here we firſt faw the Doom-tree in great profuſion growing among the palms, from which it fcarcely is diſtinguiſhable at a diſtance. It is the * Palma Thebaica Cuciofera. Its ſtone is like that of a peach covered with a black bitter pulp, which refembles a walnut over ripe.

A LITTLE before we came to Dendera we faw the firſt crocodile, and afterwards hundreds, lying upon every iſland, like large flocks of cattle, yet the inhabitants of Dendera drive their beaſts of every kind into the river, and they ſtand there for hours. The girls and women too, that come to fetch water in jars, ſtand up to their knees in the water for a confiderable time; and if we guefs by what happens, their danger is full as little as their fear, for none of them, that ever I heard of, had been bit by a crocodile. However, if the Denderites were as keen and expert hunters of Crocodiles, as fome † hiſtorians tell us they were formerly, there is furely no part in the Nile where they would have better ſport than here, immediately before their own city.

HAVING

---

* Theophraſt. Hiſt. Plan. lib. iii. cap. 8—lib. iv. cap. 2.   † Strabo lib. vii. p. 941.

Having made some little acknowledgment to those who had conducted me through the ruins in great safety, I returned to the Canja, or rather to my tent, which I placed in the first firm ground. I saw, at some distance, a well-dressed man, with a white turban, and yellow shawl covering it, and a number of ill-looking people about him. As I thought this was some quarrel among the natives, I took no notice of it, but went to my tent, in order to rectify my quadrant for observation.

As soon as our Rais saw me enter my tent, he came with expressions of very great indignation. " What signifies it, said he, that you are a friend to the Bey, have letters to every body, and are at the door of Furshout, if yet here is a man that will take your boat away from you?"

" Softly, softly, I answered, Hassan, he may be in the right. If Ali Bey, Shekh Hamam, or any body want a boat for public service, I must yield mine. Let us hear."

Shekh Hamam and Ali Bey! says he; why it is a fool, an idiot, and an ass; a fellow that goes begging about, and says he is a saint; but he is a natural fool, full as much knave as fool however; he is a thief, I know him to be a thief."

If he is a saint, said I, Hagi Hassan, as you are another, known to be so all the world over, I don't see why I should interfere; saint against saint is a fair battle."—" It is the Cadi, replies he, and no one else."

" Come away with me, said I, Hassan, and let us see this cadi; if it is the cadi, it is not the fool, it may be the knave."

He was sitting upon the ground on a carpet, moving his head backwards and forwards, and saying prayers with beads in his hand. I had no good opinion of him from his first appearance, but said, *Salam alicum,* boldy; this seemed to offend him, as he looked at me with great contempt, and gave me no answer, though he appeared a little disconcerted by my confidence.

"Are you the *Cafr,* said he, to whom that boat belongs?"

" No, Sir, said I, it belongs to Hagi Haffan."

" Do you think, says he, I call Hagi Haffan, who is a Sher-
" riffe, *Cafr?*"

"That depends upon the measure of your prudence, said
" I, of which as yet I have no proof that can enable me to
" judge or decide."

"Are you the *Christian* that was at the ruins in the morn-
" ing? says he."

"I was at the ruins in the morning, replied I, and *I am*
" *a Christian.* Ali Bey calls that denomination of people
" *Nazarani,* that is the Arabic of Cairo and Constantinople,
" and I understand no other "

"I am, said he, going to Girgé, and this holy saint is with
" me, and there is no boat but your's bound that way, for
" which reason I have promised to take him with me."

By

By this time the *faint* had got into the boat, and fat forward; he was an ill-favoured, low, fick-like man, and feemed to be almoft blind.

You fhould not make rafh promifes, faid I to the cadi, for this one you made you never can perform; I am not going to Girgé. Ali Bey, *whofe flave you are*, gave me this boat, but told me, I was not to fhip either faints or cadies. There is my boat, go a-board if you dare; and you, Hagi Haffan, let me fee you lift an oar, or loofe a fail, either for the cadi or the faint, if I am not with them.

I went to my tent, and the Rais followed me. "Hagi
" Haffan, faid I, there is a proverb in my country, It is bet-
" ter to flatter fools than to fight them: Cannot you go to
" the fool, and give him half-a-crown? will he take it, do
" you think, and abandon his journey to Girgé? after-
" wards leave me to fettle with the cadi for his voyage thi-
" ther.'

" He will take it with all his heart, he will kifs your hand
" for half-a-crown, fays Haffan."

" Let him have half-a-crown from me, faid I, and defire
" him to go about his bufinefs, and intimate that I give him
" it in charity; at fame time expect compliance with the
" condition."

In the interim, a Chriftian Copht came into the tent:
" Sir, faid he, you don't know what you are doing; the cadi
" is a great man, give him his prefent, and have done with
" him."

"When

" When he behaves better, it will be time enough for that,
" said I?—If you are a friend of his, advife him to be quiet,
" before an order comes from Cairo by a Serach, and car-
" ries him thither. Your countryman Rifk would not give
" me the advice you do?"

Risk! fays he; Do you know Rifk? Is not that Rifk's writing, faid I, fhewing him a letter from the Bey? Wallah!
(by God) it is, fays he, and away he went without fpeaking
a word farther.

The faint had taken his half-crown, and had gone away
finging, it being now near dark.—The cadi went away, and
the mob difperfed, and we directed a Moor to cry, That all
people fhould, in the night-time, keep away from the tent,
or they would be fired at; a ftone or two were afterwards
thrown, but did not reach us.

I finished my obfervation, and afcertained the latitude
of Dendera, then packed up my inftruments, and fent them
on board.

Mr Norden feems greatly to have miftaken the pofition
of this town, which, confpicuous and celebrated as it is by
ancient authors, and juftly a principal point of attention to
modern travellers, he does not fo much as defcribe; and, in
his map, he places Dendera twenty or thirty miles to the
fouthward of Badjoura; whereas it is about nine miles to
the northward. For Badjoura is in lat. 26° 3', and Dendera
is in 26° 10'.

THE SOURCE OF THE NILE.

It is a great pity, that he who had a taste for this very remarkable kind of architecture, should have passed it, both in going up and coming down; as it is, beyond comparison, a place that would have given more satisfaction than all Upper Egypt.

While we were striking our tent, a great mob came down, but without the cadi. As I ordered all my people to take their arms in their hands, they kept at a very considerable distance; but the fool, or saint, got into the boat with a yellow flag in his hand, and sat down at the foot of the main-mast, saying, with an idiot smile, That we should fire, for he was out of the reach of the shot; some stones were thrown, but did not reach us.

I ordered two of my servants with large brass ship-blunderbusses, very bright and glittering, to get upon the top of the cabbin. I then pointed a wide-mouthed Swedish blunderbuss from one of the windows, and cried out, Have a care;—the next stone that is thrown I fire my cannon amongst you, which will sweep away 300 of you instantly from the face of the earth; though I believe there were not above two hundred then present.

I ordered Hagi Hassan to cast off his cord immediately, and, as soon as the blunderbuss appeared, away ran every one of them, and, before they could collect themselves to return, our vessel was in the middle of the stream. The wind was fair, though not very fresh, on which we set both our sails, and made great way.

THE faint, who had been finging all the time we were difputing, began now to fhew fome apprehenfions for his own fafety: He afked Hagi Haffan, if this was the way to Girgé? and had for anfwer, "Yes, it is the fool's way to "Girgé."

WE carried him about a mile, or more, up the river; then a convenient landing-place offering, I afked him whether he got my money, or not, laft night? He faid, he had for yefterday, but he had got none for to-day.—" Now, the next thing I have to afk you, faid I, is, Will you go afhore of your own accord, or will you be thrown into the Nile? He anfwered with great confidence, Do you know, that, at my word, I can fix your boat to the bottom of the Nile, and make it grow a tree there for ever?" " Aye, fays Hagi Haffan, and make oranges and lemons grow on it likewife, can't you? You are a cheat." " Come, Sirs, faid I, lofe no time, put him out." I thought he had been blind and weak; and the boat was not within three feet of the fhore, when placing one foot upon the gunnel, he leaped clean upon land.

WE flacked our veffel down the ftream a few yards, filling our fails, and ftretching away. Upon feeing this, our faint fell into a defperate paflion, curfing, blafpheming, and ftamping with his feet, at every word crying " Shar Ullah!" *i. e.* may God fend, and do juftice. Our people began to taunt and gibe him, afking him if he would have a pipe of tobacco to warm him, as the morning was very cold; but I bade them be content. It was curious to fee him, as far as we could difcern, fometimes fitting down, fometimes jumping and fkipping about, and waving his flag, then running

about

about a hundred yards, as if it were after us; but always returning, though at a flower pace.

None of the reft followed. He was indeed apparently the tool of that rafcal the cadi, and, after his defigns were fruftrated, nobody cared what became of him. He was left in the lurch, as thofe of his character generally are, after ferving the purpofe of *knaves*.

CHAP. VI.

Arrive at Furſhout—Adventure of Friar Chriſtopher—Viſit Thebes—Luxor and Carnac—Large Ruins at Edfu and Eſné   Proceed on our Voyage.

WE arrived happily at Furſhout that ſame forenoon, and went to the convent of Italian Friars, who, like thoſe of Achmim, are of the order of the reformed Franciſcans, of whoſe miſſion I ſhall ſpeak at large in the ſequel.

We were received more kindly here than at Achmim; but Padre Antonio, ſuperior of that laſt convent, upon which this of Furſhout alſo depends, following us, our good reception ſuffered a ſmall abatement. In ſhort, the good Friars would not let us *buy* meat, becauſe they ſaid it would be a *ſhame* and *reproach* to them; and they would not *give* us any, for fear that ſhould be a reproach to them likewiſe, if it was told in Europe they *lived well*.

After ſome time I took the liberty of providing for myſelf, to which they ſubmitted with chriſtian patience. Yet theſe convents were founded expreſsly with a view, and from a neceſſity of providing for travellers between Egypt and Ethiopia, and we were ſtrictly intitled to that entertainment.

tainment. Indeed there is very little ufe for this inftitution in Upper Egypt, as long as rich Arabs are there, much more charitable and humane to ftranger Chriftians than the Monks.

FURSHOUT is in a large and cultivated plain. It is nine miles over to the foot of the mountains, all fown with wheat. There are, likewife, plantions of fugar canes. The town, as they faid, contains above 10,000 people, but I have no doubt this computation is rather exaggerated.

WE waited upon the Shekh Hamam; who was a big, tall, handfome man; I apprehend not far from fixty. He was dreffed in a large fox-fkin peliffe over the reft of his cloaths, and had a yellow India fhawl wrapt about his head, like a turban. He received me with great politenefs and condefenfion, made me fit down by him, and afked me more about Cairo than about Europe.

THE Rais had told him our adventure with the faint, at which he laughed very heartily, faying, I was a wife man. and a man of conduct. To me he only faid, " they are bad people at Dendera;" to which I anfwered, " there were very few places in the world in which there were not fome bad." He replied, " Your obfervation is true, but there they are all bad; reft yourfelves however here, it is a quiet place; though there are ftill fome even in this place not quite fo good as they *ought* to be."

THE Shekh was a man of immenfe riches, and, little by little, had united in his own perfon, all the feparate diftricts of Upper Egypt, each of which formerly had its particular prince. But his interest was great at Constantinople, where he applied directly for what he wanted, infomuch as to give a jealoufy to the Beys of Cairo. He had in farm from the Grand Signior almoft the whole country, between Siout and Syene, or Affouan. I believe this is the Shekh of Upper Egypt, whom Mr Irvine fpeaks of fo gratefully. He was betrayed, and murdered fome time after, by one of the Beys whom he had protected in his own country.

While we were at Furfhout, there happened a very extraordinary phænomenon. It rained the whole night, and till about nine o'clock next morning; and the people began to be very apprehenfive leaft the whole town fhould be deftroyed. It is a perfect prodigy to fee rain here; and the prophets faid it portended a diffolution of government, which was juftly verified foon afterwards, and at that time indeed was extremely probable.

Furshout is in lat 26° 3' 30"; above that, to the fouth ward, on the fame plain, is another large village, belonging to Shekh Ifmael, a nephew of Shekh Hamam. It is *a large town*, built with clay like Furfhout, and furrounded with groves of palm trees, and very large plantations of fugar canes. Here they make fugar.

Shekh Ismael was a very pleafant and agreeable man, but in bad health, having a violent afthma, and fometimes pleuretic complaints, to be removed by bleeding only. He had given thefe friars a houfe for a convent in Badjoura; but as they had not yet taken poffeffion of it, he defired me to come and ftay there.

Friar

FRIAR CHRISTOPHER, whom I underftood to have been a Milanefe barber, was his phyfician, but he had not the fcience of an Englifh barber in furgery. He could not bleed, but with a fort of inftrument refembling that which is ufed in cupping, only that it had but a fingle lancet; with this he had been lucky enough as yet to efcape laming his patients. This bleeding inftrument they call the Tabange, or the Piftol, as they do the cupping inftrument likewife. I never could help fhuddering at feeing the confidence with which this man placed a fmall brafs box upon all forts of arms, and drew the trigger for the point to go where fortune pleafed

SHEKH ISMAEL was very fond of this furgeon, and the furgeon of his patron; all would have gone well, had not friar Chriftopher aimed likewife at being an Aftronomer. Above all he gloried in being a violent enemy to the Copernican fyftem, which unluckily he had miftaken for a herefy in the church; and partly from his own flight ideas and ftock of knowledge, partly from fome Milanefe almanacs he had got, he attempted, the weather being cloudy, to foretel the time when the moon was to change, it being that of the month Ramadan, when the Mahometans' lent, or fafting, was to begin.

IT happened that the Badjoura people, and their Shekh Ifmael, were upon indifferent terms with Hamam, and his men of Furfhout, and being defirous to get a triumph over their neighbours by the help of their friar Chriftopher, they continued to eat, drink, and fmoke, two days after the conjunction.

THE

THE moon had been seen the second night, by a Fakir*, in the desert, who had sent word to Shekh Hamam, and he had begun his fast. But Ismael, assured by friar Christopher that it was impossible, had continued eating.

THE people of Furshout, meeting their neighbours singing and dancing, and with pipes of tobacco in their mouths, *all cried out* with astonishment, and asked, "Whether they had "abjured their religion or not?"—From words they came to blows; seven or eight were wounded on each side, luckily none of them mortally.—Hamam next day came to inquire at his nephew Shekh Ismael, what had been the occasion of all this, and to consult what was to be done, for the two villages had declared one another infidels

I WAS then with my servants in Badjoura, in great quiet and tranquillity, under the protection, and very much in the confidence of Ismael; but hearing the hooping, and noise in the streets, I had barricadoed my outer-doors. A high wall surrounded the house and court-yard, and there I kept quiet, satisfied with being in perfect safety.

IN the interim, I heard it was a quarrel about the keeping of Ramadan, and, as I had provisions, water, and employment enough in the house, I resolved to stay at home till they fought it out; being very little interested which of them should be victorious.—About noon, I was sent for to Ismael's house, and found his uncle Hamam with him.

HE

---

* A poor saint.

THE SOURCE OF THE NILE.

He told me, there were several wounded in a quarrel about the Ramadan, and recommended them to my care. " About Ramadan, said I! what, your principal fast! have " you not settled that yet?"—Without answering me as to this, he asked, " When does the moon change?" As I knew nothing of friar Christopher's operations, I answered, in hours, minutes, and seconds, as I found them in the ephemerides.

"Look you there, says Hamam, this is fine work!" and, directing his discourse to me, " When shall we see it?" Sir, said I, that is impossible for me to tell, as it depends on the state of the heavens; but, if the sky is clear, you must see her to-night; if you had looked for her, probably you would have seen her last night low in the horizon, thin like a thread; she is now three days old.—He started at this, then told me friar Christopher's operation, and the consequences of it.

Ismael was ashamed, cursed him, and threatned revenge. It was too late to retract, the moon appeared, and spoke for herself; and the unfortunate friar was disgraced, and banished from Badjoura. Luckily the pleuretic stitch came again, and I was called to bleed him, which I did with a lancet; but he was so terrified at its brightness, at the ceremony of the towel and the bason, and at my preparation, that it did not please him, and therefore he was obliged to be reconciled to Christopher and his tabange.—Badjoura is in lat. 26° 3' 16"; and is situated on the western shore of the Nile, as Furshout is likewise.

We left Furſhout the 7th of January 1769, early in the morning. We had not hired our boat farther than Furſhout; but the good terms which ſubſiſted between me and the ſaint, my Rais, made an accommodation very eaſy to carry us farther. He now agreed for L. 4 to carry us to Syene and down again; but, if he behaved well, he expected a trifling premium. "And, if you behave ill, Haſſan," ſaid I, what do you think you deſerve?"—"To be hanged," ſaid he, I deſerve, and deſire no better."

Our wind at firſt was but ſcant. The Rais ſaid, that he thought his boat did not go as it uſed to do, and that it was growing into a tree. The wind, however, freſhened up towards noon, and eaſed him of his fears. We paſſed a large town called How, on the weſt ſide of the Nile. About four o'clock in the afternoon we arrived at El Gourni, a ſmall village, a quarter of a mile diſtant from the Nile. It has in it a temple of old Egyptian architecture. I think that this, and the two adjoining heaps of ruins, which are at the ſame diſtance from the Nile, probably might have been part of the ancient Thebes.

Shaamy and Taamy are two coloſſal ſtatues in a ſitting poſture covered with hieroglyphics. The ſouthmoſt is of one ſtone, and perfectly entire. The northmoſt is a good deal more mutilated. It was probably broken by Cambyſes; and they have ſince endeavoured to repair it. The other has a very remarkable head-dreſs, which can be compared to nothing but a tye-wig, ſuch as worn in the preſent day. Theſe two, ſituated in a very fertile ſpot belonging to Thebes, were apparently the Nilometers of that town, as the marks which the water has left upon the baſes ſufficiently ſhew.

shew. The bases of both of them are bare, and uncovered, to the bottom of the plinth, or lowest member of their pedestal; so that there is not the eighth of an inch of the lowest part of them covered with mud, though they stand in the middle of a plain, and have stood there certainly above 3000 years; since which time, if the fanciful rise of the land of Egypt by the Nile had been true, the earth should have been raised so as fully to conceal half of them both.

These statues are covered with inscriptions of Greek and Latin; the import of which seems to be, that there were certain travellers, or particular people, who heard Memnon's statue utter the sound it was said to do, upon being struck with the rays of the sun.

It may be very reasonably expected, that I should here say something of the building and fall of the first Thebes; but as this would carry me to very early ages, and interrupt for a long time my voyage upon the Nile; as this is, besides, connected with the history of several nations which I am about to describe, and more proper for the work of an historian, than the cursory descriptions of a traveller, I shall defer saying any thing upon the subject, till I come to treat of it in the first of these characters, and more especially till I shall speak of the origin of the *shepherds*, and the calamities brought upon Egypt by that powerful nation, a people often mentioned by different writers, but whose history hitherto has been but imperfectly known.

Nothing remains of the ancient Thebes but four prodigious temples, all of them in appearance more ancient, but neither so entire, nor so magnificent, as those of Dendera.

The temples at Medinet Tabu are the moſt elegant of theſe. The hieroglyphics are cut to the depth of half-a-foot, in ſome places, but we have ſtill the ſame figures, or rather a leſs variety, than at Dendera.

The hieroglyphics are of four ſorts; firſt, ſuch as have only the contour marked, and, as it were, ſcratched only in the ſtone. The ſecond are hollowed; and in the middle of that ſpace riſes the figure in relief, ſo that the prominent part of the figure is equal to the flat, unwrought ſurface of the ſtone, and ſeems to have a frame round it, deſigned to defend the hieroglyphic from mutilation. The third ſort is in relief, or baſſo relievo, as it is called, where the figure is left bare and expoſed, without being ſunk in, or defended, by any compartment cut round it in the ſtone. The fourth are thoſe mentioned in the beginning of this deſcription, the outlines of the figure being cut very deep in the ſtone.

All the hieroglyphics, but the laſt mentioned, which do not admit it, are painted red, blue, and green, as at Dendera, and with no other colours.

Notwithstanding all this variety in the manner of executing the hieroglyphical figures, and the prodigious multitude which I have ſeen in the ſeveral buildings, I never could make the number of different hieroglyphics amount to more than five hundred and fourteen, and of theſe there were certainly many, which were not really different, but from the ill execution of the ſculpture only appeared ſo. From this I conclude, certainly, that it can be no entire language which hieroglyphics are meant to contain, for no

language

THE SOURCE OF THE NILE.

language could be comprehended in five hundred words, and it is probable that these hieroglyphics are not *alphabetical*, or *single letters* only; for five hundred letters would make *too large* an alphabet. The Chinese indeed have many more letters in use, but have no alphabet, but *who is it that understands the Chinese?*

THERE are three different characters which, I observe, have been in use at the same time in Egypt, Hieroglyphics, the Mummy character, and the Ethiopic. These are all three found, as I have seen, on the same mummy, and therefore were certainly used at the same time. The last only I believe was a *language*.

THE mountains immediately above or behind Thebes, are hollowed out into numberless caverns, the first habitations of the Ethiopian colony which built the city. I imagine they continued long in these habitations, for I do not think the temples were ever intended but for *public* and *solemn* uses, and in none of these ancient cities did I ever see a wall or foundation, or any thing like a private house; all are temples and tombs, if temples and tombs in those times were not the same thing. But vestiges of houses there are none, whatever * Diodorus Siculus may say, building with stone was too expensive for individuals; the houses probably were all of clay, thatched with palm branches, as they are at this day. This is one reason why so few ruins of the immense number of cities we hear of remain.

* Diod. Sic. lib. 1.

THEBES, according to Homer, had a *hundred gates*. We cannot, however, discover yet the foundation of any wall that it had; and as for the horsemen and chariots it is said to have sent out, all the Thebaid sown with wheat would not have maintained *one-half* of them.

THEBES, at least the ruins of the temples, called Medinet Tabu, are built in a long stretch of about a mile broad, most parsimoniously chosen at the sandy foot of the mountains. The Horti* Pensiles, or hanging gardens, were surely formed upon the sides of these hills, then supplied with water by mechanical devices. The utmost is done to spare the plain, and with great reason; for all the space of ground this ancient city has had to maintain its myriads of horses and men, is a plain of three quarters of a mile broad, between the town and the river, upon which plain the water rises to the height of four, and five feet, as we may judge by the marks on the statues Shaamy and Taamy. All this pretended populousness of ancient Thebes I therefore believe fabulous.

IT is a circumstance very remarkable, in building the first temples, that, where the side-walls are solid, that is, not supported by pillars, some of these have their angles and faces perpendicular, others inclined in a very considerable angle to the horizon. Those temples, whose walls are inclined, you may judge by the many hieroglyphics and ornaments, are of the first ages, or the greatest antiquity. From which, I am disposed to think, that singular construction was a remnant

---

* Plin. lib. 26. cap. 14.

THE SOURCE OF THE NILE.

nant of the partiality of the builders for their firſt domiciles; an imitation of the ſlope*, or inclination of the ſides of mountains, and that this inclination of flat ſurfaces to each other in building, gave afterwards the firſt idea of Pyramids †

A NUMBER of robbers, who much reſemble our gypſies, live in the holes of the mountains above Thebes. They are all out-laws, puniſhed with death if elſewhere found. Oſman Bey, an ancient governor of Girgé, unable to ſuffer any longer the diſorders committed by theſe people, ordered a quantity of dried faggots to be brought together, and, with his ſoldiers, took poſſeſſion of the face of the mountain, where the greateſt number of theſe wretches were: He then ordered all their caves to be filled with this dry bruſhwood, to which he ſet fire, ſo that moſt of them were deſtroyed; but they have ſince recruited their numbers, without changing their manners.

ABOUT half a mile north of El Gourni, are the magnificent, ſtupendous ſepulchres, of Thebes. The mountains of the Thebaid come cloſe behind the town; they are not run in upon one another like ridges, but ſtand inſulated upon their baſes; ſo that you can get round each of them. A hundred of theſe, it is ſaid, are excavated into ſepulchral, and a variety of other apartments. I went through ſeven of them with a great deal of fatigue. It is a ſolitary place; and

---

* See Norden's views of the Temples at Efné and Edfu. Vol. ii. plate 6. p. 80.

† This inclined figure of the ſides, is frequently found in the ſmall boxes within the mummy-cheſts.

and my guides, either from a natural impatience and diftafte that thefe people have at fuch employments, or, that their fears of the banditti that live in the caverns of the mountains were real, importuned me to return to the boat, even before I had begun my fearch, or got into the mountains where are the many large apartments of which I was in queſt.

In the firſt one of thefe I entered is the prodigious farcophagus, fome fay of Menes, others of Ofimandyas; poffibly of neither. It is fixteen feet high, ten long, and fix broad, of one piece of red-granite; and, as fuch, is, I fuppofe, the fineſt vafe in the world. Its cover is ftill upon it, (broken on one fide,) and it has a figure in relief on the outfide. It is not probably the tomb of Ofimandyas, becaufe, Diodorus * fays, that it was ten ftadia from the tomb of the kings; whereas this is one among them.

There have been fome ornaments at the outer-pillars, or outer-entry, which have been broken and thrown down. Thence you defcend through an inclined paffage, I fuppofe, about twenty feet broad; I fpeak only by guefs, for I did not meafure. The fide-walls, as well as the roof of this paffage, are covered with a coat of ftucco, of a finer and more equal grain, or furface, than any I ever faw in Europe. I found my black-lead pencil little more worn by it than by writing upon paper.

Upon

---

* Diod. Sic. lib. 1.

Upon the left-hand side is the crocodile seizing upon the apis, and plunging him into the water. On the right-hand is the * scarabæus thebaicus, or the thebaic beetle, the first animal that is seen alive after the Nile retires from the land; and therefore thought to be an emblem of the resurrection. My own conjecture is, that the apis was the emblem of the arable land of Egypt; the crocodile, the typhon, or cacodæmon, the type of an over-abundant Nile; that the scarabæus was the land which had been overflowed, and from which the water had soon retired, and has nothing to do with the resurrection or immortality, neither of which at that time were in contemplation.

Farther forward on the right-hand of the entry, the pannels, or compartments, were still formed in stucco, but, in place of figures in relief, they were painted in fresco. I dare say this was the case on the left-hand of the passage, as well as the right. But the first discovery was so unexpected, and I had flattered myself that I should be so far master of my own time, as to see the whole at my leisure, that I was rivetted, as it were, to the spot by the first sight of these paintings, and I could proceed no further.

In one pannel were several musical instruments strowed upon the ground, chiefly of the hautboy kind, with a mouthpiece of reed. There were also some simple pipes or flutes. With them were several jars apparently of potter-ware, which, having their mouths covered with parchment or
skin,

---

* See the figure of this Insect in Paul Lucas.

skin, and being braced on their sides like a drum, were probably the instrument called the *tabor*, or *tabret, beat upon by the hands, coupled in earliest ages with the harp, and preserved still in Abyssinia, though its companion, the last mentioned instrument, is no longer known *there*.

In three following pannels were painted, in fresco, three harps, which merited the utmost attention, whether we consider the elegance of these instruments in their form, and the detail of their parts as they are here clearly expressed, or confine ourselves to the reflection that necessarily follows, to how great perfection music must have arrived, before an artist could have produced so complete an instrument as either of these.

As the first harp seemed to be the most perfect, and least spoiled, I immediately attached myself to this, and desired my clerk to take upon him the charge of the second. In this way, by sketching exactly, and loosely, I hoped to have made myself master of all the paintings in that cave, perhaps to have extended my researches to others, though, in the sequel, I found myself miserably deceived.

My first drawing was that of a man playing upon a harp; he was standing, and the instrument being broad, and flat at the base, probably for that purpose, supported itself easily with a very little inclination upon his arm; his head is close shaved, his eye-brows black, without beard or mustachoes.

---

* Gen. xxxi. 27. Isa. chap. xxx. ver. 32.

Painting in Fresco, in the Sepulchres of Thebes.

London Publish'd Decr 1st 1789 by G. Robinson & Co

tachoes. He has on him a loofe fhirt, like what they wear at this day in Nubia (only it is not blue) with loofe fleeves, and arms and neck bare. It feemed to be thick muflin, or cotton cloth, and long-ways through it is a crimfon ftripe about one-eighth of an inch broad; a proof, if this is Egyptian manufacture, that they underftood at that time how to dye cotton, crimfon, an art found out in Britain only a very few years ago. If this is the fabric of India, ftill it proves the antiquity of the commerce between the two countries, and the introduction of Indian manufactures into Egypt.

It reached down to his ancle; his feet are without fandals; he feems to be a corpulent man, of about fixty years of age, and of a complexion rather dark for an Egyptian. To guefs by the detail of the figure, the painter feems to have had the fame degree of merit with a good fign-painter in Europe, at this day.—If we allow this harper's ftature to be five feet ten inches, then we may compute the harp, in its extreme length, to be fomething lefs than fix feet and a half.

This inftrument is of a much more advantageous form than the triangular Grecian harp. It has thirteen ftrings, but wants the forepiece of the frame oppofite to the longeft ftring. The back part is the founding-board, compofed of four thin pieces of wood, joined together in form of a cone, that is, growing wider towards the bottom; fo that, as the length of the ftring increafes, the fquare of the correfponding fpace in the founding-board, in which the found was to undulate, always increafes in proportion. The whole principles, on which this harp is conftructed, are rational and ingenious,

ingenious, and the ornamented parts are executed in the very beft manner.

The bottom and fides of the frame feem to be fineered, and inlaid, probably with ivory, tortoife-fhell, and mother-of-pearl, the ordinary produce of the neighbouring feas and deferts. It would be even now impoffible, either to conftruct or to finifh a harp of any form with more tafte and elegance. Befides the proportions of its outward form, we muft obferve likewife how near it approached to a perfect inftrument, for it wanted only two ftrings of having two complete octaves; that thefe were purpofely omitted, not from defect of tafte or fcience, muft appear beyond contradiction, when we confider the harp that follows.

I had no fooner finifhed the harp which I had taken in hand, than I went to my affiftant, to fee what progrefs he had made in the drawing in which he was engaged. I found, to my very great furprife, that this harp differed effentially, in form and diftribution of its parts, from the one I had drawn, without having loft any of its elegance; on the contrary, that it was finifhed with full more attention than the other. It feemed to be fineered with the fame materials, ivory and tortoife-fhell, but the ftrings were differently difpofed, the ends of the three longeft, where they joined to the founding-board below, were defaced by a hole dug in the wall. Several of the ftrings in different parts had been fcraped as with a knife, for the reft, it was very perfect. It had eighteen ftrings. A man, who feemed to be ftill older than the former, but in habit perfectly the fame, bare-footed, clofe fhaved, and of the fame complexion with him, ftood
playing

Paintings in Fresco, in the Sepulchres of Thebes.

playing with both his hands near the middle of the harp, in a manner seemingly less agitated than in the other

I WENT back to my first harp, verified, and examined my drawing in all its parts; it is with great pleasure I now give a figure of this second harp to the reader, it was mislaid among a multitude of other papers, at the time when I was solicited to communicate the former drawing to a gentleman then writing the History of Music, which he has already submitted to the public; it is very lately and unexpectedly this last harp has been found; I am only sorry this accident has deprived the public of Dr Burney's remarks upon it. I hope he will yet favour us with them, and therefore abstain from anticipating his reflections, as I consider this as his province; I never knew any one so capable of affording the public, new, and at the same time just lights on this subject.

THERE still remained a third harp of ten strings, its precise form I do not well remember, for I had seen it but once when I first entered the cave, and was now preparing to copy that likewise. I do not recollect that there was any man playing upon this one, I think it was rather resting upon a wall, with some kind of drapery upon one end of it, and was the smallest of the three. But I am not at all so certain of particulars concerning this, as to venture any description of it; what I have said of the other two may be absolutely depended upon.

I LOOK upon these harps then as the Theban harps in use in the time of Sesostris, who did not rebuild, but decorate ancient Thebes; I consider them as affording an incontestible

contestible proof, were they the only monuments remaining; that every art necessary to the construction, ornament, and use of this instrument, was in the highest perfection, and if so, all the others must have probably attained to the same degree.

We see in particular the ancients then possessed an art relative to architecture, that of hewing the hardest stones with the greatest ease, of which we are at this day utterly ignorant and incapable. We have no instrument that could do it, no composition that could make tools of temper sufficient to cut bass reliefs in granite or porphyry so readily; and our ignorance in this is the more completely shewn, in that we have all the reasons to believe, the cutting instrument with which they did these surprising feats was composed of brass; a metal of which, after a thousand experiments, no tool has ever been made that could serve the purpose of a common knife, though we are at the same time certain, it was of brass the ancients made their razors.

These harps, in my opinion, overturn all the accounts hitherto given of the earliest state of music and musical instruments in the east; and are altogether in their form, ornaments, and compass, an incontestible proof, stronger than a thousand Greek quotations, that geometry, drawing, mechanics, and music, were at the greatest perfection when this instrument was made, and that the period from which we date the invention of these arts, was only the beginning of the æra of their restoration. This was the sentiment of Solomon, a writer who lived at the time when this harp was painted: " Is there (says Solomon) any thing whereof it may be said,

" See,

"See, this is new! it hath been already of old time which was before us*."

We find, in thefe very countries, how a later calamity, of the fame public nature, the conqueft of the Saracens, occafioned a fimilar downfal of literature, by the burning the Alexandrian library under the fanatical caliph Omar. We fee how foon after, they flourifhed, planted by the fame hands that before had rooted them out.

The effects of a revolution occafioned, at the period I am now fpeaking of, by the univerfal inundation of the *Shepherds*, were the deftruction of Thebes, the ruin of architecture, and the downfal of aftronomy in Egypt. Still a remnant was left in the colonies and correfpondents of Thebes, though fallen. Ezekiel† celebrates Tyre as being, from her beginning, famous for the tabret and harp, and it is probably to Tyre the tafte for mufic fled from the contempt and perfecution of the barbarous Shepherds; who, though a numerous nation, to this day never have yet poffeffed any fpecies of mufic, or any kind of mufical inftruments capable of improvement.

Although it is a curious fubject for reflection, it fhould not furprife us to find here the harp, in fuch variety of form. Old Thebes, as we prefently fhall fee, had been deftroyed, and was foon after decorated and adorned, but not rebuilt by Sefoftris. It was fome time between the reign of Menes, the firft king of the Thebaid, and the firft general war of

the

---

* Eccles. chap. i. ver. 10.   † Ezek. chap. xxviii. ver. 13.

the Shepherds, that these decorations and paintings were made. This gives it a prodigious antiquity; but supposing it was a favourite instrument, consequently well understood at the building of Tyre * in the year 1320 before Christ, and Sesostris had lived in the time of Solomon, as Sir Isaac Newton imagines; still there were 320 years since that instrument had already attained to great perfection, a sufficient time to have varied it into every form.

Upon seeing the preparations I was making to proceed farther in my researches, my conductors lost all sort of subordination. They were afraid my intention was to sit in this cave all night, (as it really was,) and to visit the others next morning. With great clamour and marks of discontent, they dashed their torches against the largest harp, and made the best of their way out of the cave, leaving me and my people in the dark; and all the way as they went, they made dreadful denunciations of tragical events that were immediately to follow, upon their departure from the cave.

There was no possibility of doing more. I offered them money, much beyond the utmost of their expectations; but the fear of the Troglodytes, above Medinet Tabu, had fallen upon them; and seeing at last this was real, I was not myself without apprehensions, for they were banditti, and outlaws, and no reparation was to be expected, whatever they should do to hurt us.

Very

---

* Nay, prior to this, the harp is mentioned as a common instrument in Abraham's time 1370 years before Christ, Gen. chap. xxxii. ver. 27.

Very much vexed, I mounted my horfe to return to the boat. The road lay through a very narrow valley, the fides of which were covered with bare loofe ftones. I had no fooner got down to the bottom, than I heard a great deal of loud fpeaking on both fides of the valley; and, in an inftant, a number of large ftones were rolled down upon me, which, though I heard in motion, I could not fee, on account of the darknefs; this increafed my terror.

Finding, by the impatience of the horfe, that feveral of thefe ftones had come near him, and that it probably was the noife of his feet which guided thofe that threw them, I difmounted, and ordered the Moor to get on horfeback; which he did, and in a moment galloped out of danger. This, if I had been wife, I certainly might have done before him, but my mind was occupied by the paintings. Neverthelefs, I was refolved upon revenge before leaving thefe banditti, and liftened till I heard voices, on the right fide of the hill. I accordingly levelled my gun as near as poffible, by the ear, and fired one barrel among them. A moment's filence enfued, and then a loud howl, which feemed to have come from thirty or forty perfons. I took my fervant's blunderbufs, and difcharged it where I heard the howl, and a violent confufion of tongues followed, but no more ftones. As I found this was the time to efcape, I kept along the dark fide of the hill, as expeditioufly as poffible, till I came to the mouth of the plain, when we reloaded our firelocks, expecting fome interruption before we reached the boat; and then we made the beft of our way to the river.

We found our Rais full of fears for us. He had been told, that, as foon as day light fhould appear, the whole Troglodytes were to come down to the river, in order to plunder and deftroy our boat.

This night expedition at the mountains was but partial, the general attack was referved for next day. Upon holding council, we were unanimous in opinion, as indeed we had been during the whole courfe of this voyage. We thought, fince our enemy had left us to-night, it would be our fault if they found us in the morning. Therefore, without noife, we caft off our rope that faftened us, and let ourfelves over to the other fide. About twelve at night a gentle breeze began to blow, which wafted us up to Luxor, where there was a governor, for whom I had letters.

From being convinced by the fight of Thebes, which had not the appearance of ever having had walls, that the fable of the hundred gates, mentioned by Homer, was mere invention, I was led to conjecture what could be the origin of that fable.

That the old inhabitants of Thebes lived in caves in the mountains, is, I think, without doubt, and that the hundred mountains I have fpoken of, excavated, and adorned, were the greateft wonders at that time, feems equally probable. Now, the name of thefe to this day is Beeban el Meluke, the ports or gates of the kings, and hence, perhaps, come the hundred gates of Thebes upon which the Greeks have dwelt fo much. Homer never faw Thebes, it was demolifhed before the days of any profane writer, either in profe or verfe. What he added to its hiftory muft have been from imagination.

THE SOURCE OF THE NILE. 137

All that is said of Thebes, by poets or historians, after the days of Homer, is meant of Diospolis; which was built by the Greeks long after Thebes was destroyed, as its name testifies; though Diodorus *says it was built by Busiris. It was on the east side of the Nile, whereas ancient Thebes was on the west, though both are considered as one city; and † Strabo says, that the river ‡ runs through the middle of Thebes, by which he means between old Thebes and Diospolis, or Luxor and Medinet Tabu.

While in the boat, I could not help regretting the time I had spent in the morning, in looking for the place in the narrow valley where the mark of the famous golden circle was visible, which Norden says he saw, but I could discern no traces of it any where, and indeed it does not follow that the mark left was that of a circle. This magnificent instrument was probably fixed perpendicular to the horizon in the plane of the meridian; so that the appearance of the place where it stood, would very probably not partake of the circular form at all, or any precise shape whereby to know it. Besides, as I have before said, it was not among these tombs or excavated mountains, but ten stades from them, so the vestiges of this famous instrument § could not be found here. Indeed, being omitted in the latest edition of Norden, it would seem that traveller himself was not perfectly well assured of its existence.

Vol. I.   S   We

---

* Diod. Sic. Bib. lib. i. p. 42. § d.   † Strabo, lib. 17. p. 943.   ‡ Nah. ch. 3. ver. 8, & 9.

§ A similar instrument, erected by Eratosthenes at Alexandria, cut of copper, was used by Hipparchus and Ptolemy.—Alm. lib. I. cap. 11. 3. cap. 2.   Vide his remarks on Mr Greave's Pyramidographia, p. 134.

We were well received by the governor of Luxor, who was alfo a believer in judicial aftrology. Having made him a fmall prefent, he furnifhed us with provifions, and, among feveral other articles, fome brown fugar; and as we had feen limes and lemons in great perfection at Thebes, we were refolved to refrefh ourfelves with fome punch, in remembrance of Old England. But, after what had happened the night before, none of our people chofe to run the rifk of meeting the Troglodytes. We therefore procured a fervant of the governor's of the town, to mount upon his goatfkin filled with wind, and float down the ftream from Luxor to El Gournie, to bring us a fupply of thefe, which he foon after did.

He informed us, that the people in the caves had, early in the morning, made a defcent upon the townfmen, with a view to plunder our boat; that feveral of them had been wounded the night before, and they threatened to purfue us to Syene. The fervant did all he could to frighten them, by faying that his mafter's intention was to pafs over with troops, and exterminate them, as Ofman Bey of Girgé had before done, and *we* were to affift him with our fire-arms.— After this we heard no more of them.

Luxor, and Carnac, which is a mile and a quarter below it, are by far the largeft and moft magnificent fcenes of ruins in Egypt, much more extenfive and ftupendous than thofe of Thebes and Dendera put together.

There are two obelifks here of great beauty, and in good prefervation, they are lefs than thofe at Rome, but not at all mutilated. The pavement, which is made to receive

the

THE SOURCE OF THE NILE.

the shadow, is to this day so horizontal, that it might still be used in obfervation. The top of the obelifk is femicircular, an experiment, I fuppofe, made at the inftance of the obferver, by varying the shape of the point of the obelifk to get rid of the penumbra.

At Carnac we faw the remains of two vaft rows of fphinxes, one on the right-hand, the other on the left, (their heads were moftly broken) and, a little lower, a number of termini as it fhould feem. They were compofed of bafaltes, with a dog or lion's head, of Egyptian fculpture. They ftood in lines likewife, as if to conduct or ferve as an avenue to fome principal building.

They had been covered with earth, till very lately a *Venetian phyfician and antiquary bought one of them at a very confiderable price, as he faid, for the king of Sardinia. This has caufed feveral others to be uncovered, though no purchafer hath yet offered.

Upon the outfide of the walls at Carnac and Luxor there feems to be an hiftorical engraving inftead of hieroglyphics; this we had not met with before. It is a reprefentation of men, horfes, chariots, and battles; fome of the attitudes are freely and well drawn, they are rudely fcratched upon the furface of the ftone, as fome of the hieroglyphics at Thebes are. The weapons the men make ufe of are fhort javelins, fuch as are common at this day among the inhabitants of Egypt,

---

*Signior Donati.

Egypt, only they have feathered wings like arrows. There is also diftinguifhed among the reft, the figure of a man on horfeback, with a lion fighting furioufly by him, and Diodorus * fays, Ofimandyas was fo reprefented at Thebes. This whole compofition merits great attention.

I HAVE faid, that Luxor is Diofpolis, and fhould think, that that place, and Carnac together, made the Jovis Civitas Magna of Ptolemy, though there is 9ʹ difference of the latitude by my obfervation compared with his. But as mine was made on the fouth of Luxor, if his was made on the north of Carnac, the difference will be greatly diminifhed.

THE 17th we took leave of our friendly Shekh of Luxor, and failed with a very fair wind, and in great fpirits. The liberality of the Shekh of Luxor had extended as far as even to my Rais, whom he engaged to land me here upon my return.—I had procured him confiderable cafe in fome complaints he had; and he faw our departure with as much regret as in other places they commonly did our arrival.

On the eaftern fhore are Hambdé, Mafchergarona, Tot, Senimi, and Gibeg. Mr Norden feems to have very much confufed the places in this neighbourhood, as he puts Erment oppofite to Carnac, and Thebes farther fouth than Erment, and on the eaft fide of the Nile, whilft he places Luxor farther fouth than Erment. But Erment is fourteen miles farther fouth than Thebes, and Luxor about a quarter

---

* Diod. Sic. Bib. lib. 1. p. 45. § c.

ter of a mile (as I have already said) farther south on the East side of the river, whereas Thebes is on the West.

He has fixed a village (which he calls *Demegeit) in the situation where Thebes stands, and he calls it Crocodilopolis, from what authority I know not; but the whole geography is here exceedingly confused, and out of its proper position.

In the evening we came to an anchor on the eastern shore nearly opposite to Efné. Some of our people had landed to shoot, trusting to a turn of the river that is here, which would enable them to keep up with us; but they did not arrive till the sun was setting, loaded with hares, pigeons, gootos, all very bad game. I had, on my part, staid on board, and had shot two geese, as bad eating as the others, but very beautiful in their plumage.

We passed over to Efné next morning. It is the ancient Latopolis, and has very great remains, particularly a large temple, which, though the whole of it is of the remotest antiquity, seems to have been built at different times, or rather out of the ruins of different ancient buildings. The hieroglyphics upon this are very ill executed, and are not painted. The town is the residence of an Arab Shekh, and the inhabitants are a very greedy, bad sort of people; but as I was dressed like an Arab, they did not molest, because they did not know me

The 18th, we left Efné, and passed the town of Edfu, where there is likewise considerable remains of Egyptian architecture. It is the Appollinis Civitas Magna

THE

---

* Vide Norden's map of the Nile.

The wind failing, we were obliged to stop in a very poor, desolate, and dangerous part of the Nile, called Jibbel el Silfelly, where a boom, or chain, was drawn across the river, to hinder, as is supposed, the Nubian boats from committing piratical practices in Egypt lower down the stream. The stones on both sides, to which the chain was fixed, are very visible; but I imagine that it was for fiscal rather than for warlike purposes, for Syene being garrisoned, there is no possibility of boats passing from Nubia by that city into Egypt. There is indeed another purpose to which it might be designed; to prevent war upon the Nile between any two states.

We know from Juvenal*, who lived some time at Syene, that there was a tribe in that neighbourhood called Ombi, who had violent contentions with the people of Dendera about the crocodile; it is remarkable these two parties were Anthropophagi so late as Juvenal's time, yet no historian speaks of this extraordinary fact, which cannot be called in question, as he was an eye-witness and resided at Syene.

Now these two nations who were at war had above a hundred miles of neutral territory between them, and therefore they could never meet except on the Nile. But either one or the other possessing this chain, could hinder his adversary from coming nearer him. As the chain is in the hermonthic nome, as well as the capital of the Ombi, I suppose this chain to be the barrier of this

last

---

* Juven. Sat. 15. ver. 76.

last state, to hinder those of Dendera from coming up the river *to eat* them.

About noon we passed Coom Ombo, a round building like a castle, where is supposed to have been the metropolis of Ombi, the people last spoken of. We then arrived at Daroo*, a miserable mansion, unconscious that, some years after, we were to be indebted to that paltry village for the man who was to guide us through the desert, and restore us to our native country and our friends.

We next came to Shekh Ammer, the encampment of the Arabs † Ababdé, I suppose the same that Mr Norden calls Ababuda, who reach from near Cosseir far into the desert. As I had been acquainted with one of them at Badjoura, who desired medicines for his father, I promised to call upon him, and see their effect, when I should pass Shekh Ammer, which I now accordingly did; and by the reception I met with, I found they did not expect I would ever have been as good as my word. Indeed they would probably have been in the right, but as I was about to engage myself in extensive deserts, and this was a very considerable nation in these tracts, I thought it was worth my while to put myself under their protection.

Shekh Ammer is not one, but a collection of villages, composed of miserable huts, containing, at this time, about a thousand effective men: they possess few horse, and are mostly

---

* Idris Welled Hamran, our guide through the great desert, dwelt in this village.
† The ancient Adei.

moftly mounted on camels. Thefe were friends to Shekh Hamam, governor of Upper Egypt for the time, and confequently to the Turkifh government at Syene, as alfo to the janiffaries there at Deir and Ibrim. They were the barrier, or bulwark, againft the prodigious number of Arabs, the Bifhareen, and others, depending upon the kingdom of Sennaar.

Ibrahim, the fon, who had feen me at Furfhout and Badjoura, knew me as foon as I arrived, and, after acquainting his father, came with about a dozen of naked attendants, with lances in their hands to efcort me. I was fcarce got into the door of the tent, before a great dinner was brought after their cuftom; and, that being difpatched, it was a thoufand times repeated, how little they expected that I would have thought or inquired about them.

We were introduced to their Shekh, who was fick, in a corner of a hut, where he lay upon a carpet, with a cufhion under his head. This chief of the Ababdé, called Nimmer, *i. e. the Tiger* (though his furious qualities were at this time in great meafure allayed by ficknefs) afked me much about the ftate of Lower Egypt. I fatisfied him as far as poffible, but recommended to him to confine his thoughts nearer home, and not to be over anxious about thefe diftant countries, as he himfelf feemed, at that time, to be in a declining ftate of health.

Nimmer was a man about fixty years of age, exceedingly tormented with the gravel, which was more extraordinary as he dwelt near the Nile; for it is, univerfally, the difeafe with

---

* The Bifhareen are the Arabs who live in the frontier between the two nations. They are the nominal fubjects of Sennaar, but, in fact, indifcreet banditti, at leaft as to ftrangers.

with those who use water from draw-wells, as in the desert. But he told me, that, for the first twenty-seven years of his life, he never had seen the Nile, unless upon some plundering party; that he had been constantly at war with the people of the cultivated part of Egypt, and reduced them often to the state of starving; but now that he was old, a friend to Shekh Hamam, and was resident near the Nile, he drank of its water, and was little better, for he was already a martyr to the disease. I had sent him soap pills from Badjoura, which had done him a great deal of good, and now gave him lime-water, and promised him, on my return, to shew his people how to make it.

A very friendly conversation ensued, in which was repeated often, how little they expected I would have visited them! As this implied two things; the first, that I paid no regard to my promise when given; the other, that I did not esteem them of consequence enough to give myself the trouble, I thought it right to clear myself from these suspicions.

" Shekh Nimmer, said I, this frequent repetition that you
" thought I would not keep my word is *grievous* to me. I am
" a Christian, and have lived now many years among you
" Arabs. Why did you imagine that I would not keep my
" word, since it is a principle among all the Arabs I have
" lived with, inviolably to keep theirs? When your son Ibra-
" him came to me at Badjoura, and told me the pain that
" you was in, night and day, fear of God, and desire to do
" good, even to them I had never seen, made me give you
" those medicines that have eased you. After this proof of
" my humanity, what was there extraordinary in my com-
" ing to see you in the way? I knew you not before; but
" my

" my religion teaches me to do good to all men, even to
" enemies, without reward, or without confidering whether
" I ever fhould fee them again."

" Now, after the drugs I fent you by Ibrahim, tell me,
" and tell me truly, upon the *faith* of an *Arab*, would your
" people, if they met me in the *defert*, do me any wrong,
" more than *now*, as I have eat and drank with you to-day?"

The old man Nimmer, on this rofe from his carpet, and
fat upright, a more ghaftly and more horrid figure I never faw. " No, faid he, Shekh, curfed be thofe men of *my people*, or *others*, that ever fhall lift up their hand againft you, either in the *Defert* or the *Tell*, *i. e.* the part of Egypt which is cultivated. As long as you are in this country, or between this and Coffeir, my fon fhall ferve you with heart and hand; one night of pain that your medicines freed me from, would not be repaid, if I was to follow you on foot to Meffir, that is Cairo."

I then thought it a proper time to enter into converfation about penetrating into Abyffinia that way, and they difcuffed it among themfelves in a very friendly, and at the fame time in a very fagacious and fenfible manner.

" We could carry you to *El Haïmer*, (which I underftood to be a well in the defert, and which I afterwards was much better acquainted with to my forrow.) We could conduct you fo far, fays old Nimmer, under God, without fear of harm, all that country was Chriftian once, and *we* Chriftians

THE SOURCE OF THE NILE.

Chriftians like yourfelf *. The *Saracens* having nothing in their power there, we could carry you fafely to Suakem, but the Bifhary are men not to be trufted, and we could go no farther than to land you among them, and they would put you to death, and laugh at you all the time they were tormenting you †. Now, if you want to vifit Abyffinia, go by Coffeir and Jidda, there *you Chriftians* command the country."

"I TOLD him, I apprehended, the *Kennoufs*, about the fecond cataract, above Ibrim, were bad people. He faid the Kennoufs were, he believed, bad enough in their hearts, but they were wretched flaves, and fervants, had no power in their hands, would not wrong any body that was with his people; if they did, he would extirpate them in a day."

"I TOLD him, I was fatisfied of the truth of what was faid, and afked him the beft way to Coffeir. He faid, the beft way for me to go, was from Kenné, or Cuft, and that he was carrying a quantity of wheat from Upper Egypt, while Shekh Hamam was fending another cargo from his country, both which would be delivered at Coffeir, and loaded there for Jidda."

" ALL that is right, Shekh, faid I, but fuppofe your people meet us in the defert, in going to Coffeir, or otherwife, how fhould we fare in that cafe? Should we fight?" "I have

---

* They were *Shepherds* Indigenæ, not Arabs.
† *Qui Ludit in Hofpite fixo.*—Was a character long ago given to the Moors.
HORACE ODE.

told you Shekh already, says he, Cursed be the man who lifts his hand against you, or even does not defend and befriend you, to his own loss, were it Ibrahim my own son."

I THEN told him I was bound to Cosseir, and that if I found myself in any difficulty, I hoped, upon applying to his people, they would protect me, and that he would give them the word, that I was *yagoube*, a physician, seeking no harm, but doing good; bound by a vow, for a certain time, to wander through deserts, from fear of God, and that they should not have it in their power to do me harm.

THE old man muttered something to his sons in a dialect I did not then understand; it was that of the *Shepherds* of Suakem. As that was the first word he spoke, which I did not comprehend, I took no notice, but mixed some limewater in a large Venetian bottle that was given me when at Cairo full of *liqueur*, and which would hold about four quarts; and a little after I had done this the whole hut was filled with people.

THERE were *priests* and *monks* of their religion, and the heads of families, so that the house could not contain half of them. The great people among them came, and, after joining hands, repeated a kind of * prayer, of about two minutes long, by which they declared themselves, and their children, accursed, if ever they lifted their hands against me in the *Tell*, or Field in the *desert*, or on the river; or, in case that I, or mine should fly

to

---

* This kind of oath was in use among the Arabs, or *Shepherds*, early as the time of Abraham, Gen. xxi. 22, 23. xxvi. 28.

to them for refuge, if they did not protect us at the risk of their lives, their families, and their fortunes, or, as they emphatically expressed it, to the death of the last male child among them.

MEDICINES and advice being given on my part, faith and protection pledged on theirs, two bushels of wheat and seven sheep were carried down to the boat, nor could we decline their kindness, as refusing a present in that country (however it is understood in ours,) is just as great an affront, as coming into the presence of a superior without a present at all.

I TOLD them, however, that I was going up among Turks who were *obliged* to maintain me, the consequence therefore will be, to save their own, that they will take your sheep, and make my dinner of them; you and I are *Arabs*, and know what *Turks* are. They all muttered curses between their teeth at the name of Turk, and we agreed they should keep the sheep till I came back, provided they should be then at liberty to add as many more.

THIS was all understood between us, and we parted perfectly content with one another. But our Rais was very far from being satisfied, having heard something of the seven sheep; and as we were to be next day at Syene, where he knew we were to get meat enough, he reckoned that they would have been his property. To stifle all cause of discontent, however, I told him he was to take no notice of my visit to Shekh Ammer, and that I would make him amends when I returned.

CHAP.-

CHAP. VII.

Arrives at Syene—Goes to see the Cataract—Remarkable Tombs—the situation of Syene—The Aga proposes a Visit to Deir and Ibrim—The Author returns to Kenné.

WE failed on the 20th, with the wind favouring us, till about an hour before sun-rise, and about nine o'clock came to an anchor on the south end of the palm groves, and north end of the town of Syene, nearly opposite to an island in which there is a small handsome Egyptian temple, pretty entire. It is the temple of * *Cnuphis*, where formerly was the Nilometer.

ADJOINING to the palm trees was a very good comfortable house, belonging to Hussein Schourbatchie, the man that used to be sent from that place to Cairo, to receive the pay of the janissaries in garrison at Syene, upon whom too I had credit for a very small sum.

THE reasons of a credit in such a place are three: First, in case of sickness, or purchase of any antiquities: Secondly, that you give the people an idea (a very useful one) that you carry no money about with you: Thirdly, that your money

---

* Strabo, lib. xvii. p. 944.

money changes its value, and is not even current beyond Efné.

HUSSEIN was not at home, but was gone fomewhere up on bufinefs, but I had hopes to find him in the courfe of the day. Hofpitality is never refufed, in thefe countries, upon the flighteft pretence. Having therefore letters to him, and hearing his houfe was empty, we fent our people and baggage to it.

I WAS not well arrived before a janiffary came, in long Turkifh cloaths, without arms, and a white wand in his hand, to tell me that Syene was a garrifon town, and that the Aga was at the caftle ready to give me audience.

I RETURNED him for anfwer, that I was very fenfible it was my firft duty, as a ftranger, to wait upon the Aga in a *garrifoned* town of which he had the command, but, being bearer of the Grand Signior's Firman, having letters from the Bey of Cairo, and from the Port of Janiffaries *to him in particular*, and, at prefent being indifpofed and fatigued, I hoped he would indulge me till the arrival of my landlord; in which interim I fhould take a little reft, change my cloaths, and be more in the fituation in which I would wifh to pay my refpects to him.

I RECEIVED immediately an anfwer by two janiffaries, who infifted to fee me, and were accordingly introduced while I was lying down to reft. They faid that Mahomet Aga had received my meffage, that the reafon of fending to me was

not

not either to hurry or disturb me; but the earlier to know in what he could be of service to me; that he had *a particular letter* from the Bey of Cairo, in consequence of which, he had dispatched orders to receive me at Efné, but as I had not waited on the Cacheff there, he had not been apprised.

AFTER giving coffee to these very civil messengers, and taking two hours rest, our landlord the Schourbatchie arrived; and, about four o'clock in the afternoon, we went to the Aga.

THE fort is built of clay, with some small guns mounted on it; it is of strength sufficient to keep people of the country in awe.

I FOUND the Aga sitting in a small kioosk, or closet, upon a stone-bench covered with carpets. As I was in no fear of him, I was resolved to walk according to my privileges; and, as the meanest Turk would do before the greatest man in England, I sat down upon a cushion below him, after laying my hand on my breast, and saying in an audible voice, with great marks of respect, however, *Salam alicum!* to which he answered, without any of the usual difficulty, *Alicum salam!* *Peace be between us* is the salutation; *There is peace between us* is the return.

AFTER sitting down about two minutes, I again got up, and stood in the middle of the room before him, saying, I am bearer of a hatésherriffe, or royal mandate, to you, Mahomet Aga! and took the firman out of my bosom, and presented it to him. Upon this he stood upright, and all the rest of the people, before sitting with him likewise; he bowed his head upon the carpet, then put the firman to his forehead, opened it, and pretended to read it; but he knew well the contents, and I believe, besides, he could neither read nor write any language. I then gave him the other letters from Cairo, which he ordered his secretary to read in his ear.

ALL this ceremony being finished, he called for a pipe, and coffee. I refused the first, as never using it; but I drank a dish of coffee, and told him, that I was bearer of a *confidential message* from Ali Bey of Cairo, and wished to deliver it to him without witnesses, whenever he pleased. The room was accordingly cleared without delay, excepting his secretary, who was also going away, when I pulled him back by the cloaths, saying, " Stay, if you please, we shall need you " to write the answer." We were no sooner left alone, than I told the Aga, that, being a stranger, and not knowing the disposition of his people, or what footing they were on together, and being desired to address myself only to him by the Bey, and our mutual friends at Cairo, I wished to put it in his power (as he pleased or not) to have witnesses of delivering the small *present* I had brought him from Cairo. The Aga seemed very sensible of this delicacy; and particularly desired me to take no notice to my landlord, the Schourbatchie, of any thing I had brought him.

ALL this being over, and a *confidence* established with *government*, I sent his present by his own servant that night, under pretence of desiring horses to go to the cataract next day. The message was returned, that the horses were to be ready by six o'clock next morning. On the 21st, the Aga sent me his own horse, with mules and asses for my servants, to go to the cataract.

We paſſed out at the ſouth gate of the town, into the firſt ſmall ſandy plain. A very little to our left, there are a number of tomb-ſtones with inſcriptions in the Cufic character, which travellers erroneouſly have called *unknown* language, and letters, although it was the only letter and language known to Mahomet, and the moſt learned of his ſect in the firſt ages.

The Cufic characters ſeem to be all written in capitals, which one might learn to read much more eaſily than the modern Arabic, and they more reſemble the Samaritan. We read there—Abdullah el Hejazi el Anſari—Mahomet Abdel Shems el Taiefy el Anſari. The firſt of theſe, Abdullah el Hejazi, is Abdullah born in Arabia Petrea. The other is, Mahomet the ſlave of the ſun, born in Taief. Now, both of theſe are called *Anſari*, which many writers, upon Arabian hiſtory, think, means, *born in Medina;* becauſe, when Mahomet fled from Mecca, the night of the hegira, the people of Medina received him willingly, and thenceforward got the name of * Anſari, or Helpers. But this honourable name was extended afterwards to all thoſe who fought under Mahomet in his wars, and after, even to thoſe who had been born in his lifetime.

These of whoſe tombs we are now ſpeaking, were of the army of Haled Ibn el Waalid, whom Mahomet named, Saif-Ullah, the ' Sword of God,' and who, in the califat of Omar, took and deſtroyed Syene, after loſing great part of his army before

---

* This word, improperly uſed and ſpelled by M. de Volney, has nothing to do with theſe Anſaris.

THE SOURCE OF THE NILE.

before it. It was afterwards rebuilt by the *Shepherds* of Beja, then Chriſtians, and again taken in the time of Salidan, and, with the reſt of Egypt, *ever ſince* hath belonged to Cairo. It was conquered by, or rather ſurrendered to, Selim Emperor of the Turks, in 1516, who planted two advanced poſts (Deir and Ibrim) beyond the cataract in Nubia, with ſmall garriſons of janiſſaries likewiſe, where they continue to this day.

THEIR pay is iſſued from Cairo; ſometimes they marry each others daughters, rarely marry the women of the country, and the ſon, or nephew, or neareſt relation of each deceaſed, ſucceeds as janiſſary in room of his father. They have loſt their native language, and have indeed nothing of the Turk in them, but a propenſity to violence, rapine, and injuſtice; to which they have joined the perfidy of the Arab, which, as I have ſaid, they ſometimes inherit from their mother. An Aga commands theſe troops in the caſtle. They have about two hundred horſemen armed with firelocks; with which, by the help of the Ababdé, encamped at Shekh Ammer, they keep the Biſhareen, and all theſe numerous tribes of Arabs, that inhabit the Deſert of Sennaar, in tolerable order.

THE inhabitants, merchants, and common people of the town, are commanded by a cacheff. There is neither butter nor milk at Syene (the latter comes from Lower Egypt) the ſame may be ſaid of fowls. Dates do not ripen at Syene, thoſe that are ſold at Cairo come from Ibrim and Dongola. There are good fiſh in the Nile, and they are eaſily caught, eſpecially at the cataract, or in broken water; there are only two kinds of large ones which I have happened to ſee, the

binny

binny and the boulti. The binny I have defcribed in its proper place.

After paffing the tomb-ftones without the gate, we come to a plain about five miles long, bordered on the left by a hill of no confiderable height, and fandy like the plain, upon which are feen fome ruins, more modern than thofe Egyptian buildings we have defcribed. They feem indeed to be a mixture of all kinds and ages.

The diftance from the gate of the town to Termiffi, or Marada, the fmall villages on the cataract, is exactly fix Englifh miles. After the defcription already given of this cataract in fome authors, a traveller has reafon to be furprifed, when arrived on its banks, to find that veffels fail up the cataract, and confequently the fall cannot be fo violent as to deprive people of their hearing.*

The bed of the river, occupied by the water, was not then half a mile broad. It is divided into a number of fmall channels, by large blocks of granite, from thirty to forty feet high. The current, confined for a long courfe between the rocky mountains of Nubia, tries to expand itfelf with great violence. Finding, in every part before it, oppofition from the rocks of granite, and forced back by thefe, it meets the oppofite currents. The chafing of the water againft thefe huge obftacles, the meeting of the contrary currents one with another, creates fuch a violent ebullition, and

makes

---

* Cicero de Somnio Scipronis.

THE SOURCE OF THE NILE.

makes such a noise and disturbed appearance, that it fills the mind with confusion rather than with terror.

We saw the miserable Kennoufs (who inhabit the banks of the river up into Nubia, to above the second cataract) to procure their daily food, lying behind rocks, with lines in their hands, and catching fish; they did not seem to be either dexterous or successful in the sport. They are not black, but of the darkest brown; are not woolly-headed, but have hair. They are small, light, agile people, and seem to be more than half-starved. I made a sign that I wanted to speak with one of them; but seeing me surrounded with a number of horse and fire-arms, they did not choose to trust themselves. I left my people behind with my firelock, and went alone to see if I could engage them in a conversation. At first they walked off; finding I persisted in following them, they ran at full speed, and hid themselves among the rocks.

Pliny* says, that, in his time, the city of Syene was situated so directly under the tropic of Cancer, that there was a well, into which the sun shone so perpendicular, that it was enlightened by its rays down to the bottom. Strabo † had said the same. The ignorance, or negligence, in the Geodesique measure in this observation, is extraordinary; Egypt had been measured yearly, from early ages, and the distance between Syene and Alexandria should have been known to an ell. From this inaccuracy, I do very much suspect the other measure Eratosthenes is said to have made, by which he fixed the sun's parallax at 10 seconds and a half,

---

* Pliny, lib. ii. cap. 73.   † Strabo, lib. xvii. p. 944.

half, was not really made by him, but was some old Chaldaic, or Egyptian obfervation, made by more inftructed aftronomers which he had fallen upon.

The Arabs call it Affouan, which they fay fignifies *enlightened;* in allufion, I fuppofe, to the circumftance of the well, enlightened within by the fun's being ftationary over it in June; in the language of Beja its name fignifies a circle, or portion of a circle.

Syene, among other things, is famous for the firft attempt made by Greek aftronomers to afcertain the meafure of the circumference of the earth. Eratofthenes, born at Cyrene about 276 years before Chrift, was invited from Athens to Alexandria by Ptolemy Evergetes, who made him keeper of the Royal Library in that city. In this experiment two pofitions were affumed, that Alexandria and Syene were exactly 5000 ftades diftant from each other, and that they were precifely under the fame meridian. Again, it was verified by the experiment of the well, that, in the fummer folftice at mid-day, when the fun was in the tropic of Cancer, in its greateft northern declination, the well* at that inftant was totally and equally illuminated; and that no ftyle, or gnomon, erected on a perfect plane, did caft, or project, any manner of fhadow for 150 ftades round, from which it was juftly concluded, that the fun, on that day, was fo exactly vertical to Syene, that the center of its difk immediately correfponded to the center of the bottom of the well. Thefe preliminaries being fixed, Eratofthenes fet about his obfervation thus:—

On

---

* Strabo, lib. ii. p. 133.

THE SOURCE OF THE NILE.

ON the day of the summer solstice, at the moment the sun was stationary in the meridian of Syene, he placed a style perpendicularly in the bottom of a half-concave sphere, which he exposed in open air to the sun at Alexandria. Now, if that style had cast no shade at Alexandria, it would have been precisely in the same circumstance with a style in the well in Syene; and the reason of its not casting the shade would have been, that the sun was directly vertical to it. But he found, on the contrary, this style at Alexandria did cast a shadow; and by measuring the distance of the top of this shadow from the foot of the style, he found, that, when the sun cast no shadow at Syene, by being in the zenith, at Alexandria he projected a shadow; which shewed he was distant from the vertical point, or zenith, $7\frac{1}{5}° = 7° \ 12'$, which was $\frac{1}{50}$th of the circumference of the whole heavens, or of a great circle.

THIS being settled, the conclusion was, that Alexandria and Syene must be distant from each other by the 50th part of the circumference of the whole earth.

Now 5000 stades was the distance already assumed between Alexandria and the well of Syene; and all that was to be done was to repeat 5000 stades fifty times, or multiply 5000 stades by 50, and the answer was 250,000 stades, which was the total of the earth's circumference. This, admitting the French contents of the Egyptian stadium to be just, will amount to 11,403 leagues for the circumference of the earth sought; and as our present account fixes it to be 9000, the error will be 2403 leagues in excess, or more than one-fourth of the whole sum required.

THIS

This obfervation furely therefore is not worth recording, unlefs to fhew the infufficiency or imperfection of the method; it cannot deferve the encomiums * that have been beftowed upon it, if juftice has been done to Eratofthenes' geodefique meafures, which I do not, by any manner of means, warrant to be the cafe, becaufe the meafure of his arch of the meridian feems to have been conducted with a much greater degree of fuccefs and precifion than that of his bafe.

On the 22d, 23d, and 24th of January, being at Syene, in a houfe immediately eaft of the fmall ifland in the Nile (where the temple of Cnuphis is ftill ftanding, very little injured, and which †Strabo, who was himfelf there, fays was in the ancient town, and near the well built for the obfervation of the folftice) with a three-foot brafs quadrant, made by Langlois, and defcribed by ‡ Monfieur de la Lande, by a mean of three obfervations of the fun in the meridian, I concluded the latitude of Syene to be 24° 0′ 45″ north.

And, as the latitude of Alexandria, by a medium of many obfervations made by the French academicians, and more recently by Mr Niebuhr and myfelf, is beyond poffibility of contradiction 31° 11′ 33″, the arch of the meridian contained between Syene and Alexandria, muft be 7° 10′ 48″, or 1′ 12″ lefs than Eratofthenes made it. And this is a wonderful precifion, if we confider the imperfection of his inftrument, in the probable fhortnefs of his radius, and difficulty

(almoft

---

* Spectacle de la Nature.
[† Strabo, lib. 17. p. 944.   ‡ L'hiftoire d'aftronomie, de M. de la Lande, vol. i. lib. 2.

(almoſt infurmountable) in diſtinguiſhing the diviſion of the penumbra.

There certainly is one error very apparent, in meaſuring the baſe betwixt Syene and Alexandria; that is, they were not (as ſuppoſed) under the ſame meridian; for though, to my very great concern afterwards, I had no opportunity of fixing the longitude at this firſt viſit to Syene, as I had done the latitude, yet on my return, in the year 1772, from an eclipſe of the firſt ſatellite of Jupiter, I found its longitude to be 33° 30'; and the longitude of Alexandria, being 30° 16' 7", there is 3° 14' that Syene is to the eaſtward of the meridian of Alexandria, or ſo far from their being under the ſame meridian as ſuppoſed.

It is impoſſible to fix the time of the building of Syene; upon the moſt critical examination of its hieroglyphics and proportions, I ſhould imagine it to have been founded ſome time after Thebes, but before Dendera, Luxor, or Carnac.

It would be no leſs curious to know, whether the well, which Eratoſthenes made uſe of for one of the terms of the geodeſique baſe, and his arch of the meridian, between Alexandria and Syene, was coeval with the building of that city, or whether it was made for the experiment. I ſhould be inclined to think the former was the caſe; and the placing this city firſt, then the well under the tropic, were with a view of aſcertaining the length of the ſolar year. In ſhort, this point, ſo material to be ſettled, was the conſtant object of attention of the firſt aſtronomers, and this was the uſe of the dial of Oſimandyas; this inquiry was the occaſion of the number of obeliſks raiſed in every ancient city in Egypt.

We cannot miſtake this, if we obſerve how anxiouſly they have varied the figure of the top, or point of each obeliſk; ſometimes it is a very ſharp one; ſometimes a portion of a circle, to try to get rid of the great impediment that perplexed them, the penumbra.

The projection of the pavements, conſtantly to the northward, ſo diligently levelled, and made into exact planes by large flabs of granite, moſt artificially joined, have been ſo ſubſtantially ſecured, that they might ſerve for the obſervation to this day; and it is probable, the poſition of this city and the well were coeval, the reſult of intention, and both the works of theſe firſt aſtronomers, immediately after the building of Thebes. If this was the caſe, we may conclude, that the fact of the ſun illuminating the bottom of the well in Eratoſthenes's time was a ſuppoſed one, from the uniform tradition, that once it had been ſo, the periodical change of the quantity of the angle, made by the equator and ecliptic, not being then known, and therefore that the quantity of the celeſtial arch, comprehended between Alexandria and Syene, might be as erroneous from another cauſe, as the baſe had been by aſſuming a wrong diſtance on the earth, in place of one exactly meaſured.

There is at Axum an obeliſk erected by Ptolemy Evergetes, the very prince who was patron to Eratoſthenes, without hieroglyphics, directly facing the ſouth, with its top firſt cut into a narrow neck, then ſpread out like a fan in a ſemicircular form, with a pavement curiouſly levelled to receive the ſhade, and make the ſeparation of the true ſhadow from the penumbra as diſtinct as poſſible.

This

This was probably intended for verifying the experiment of Eratosthenes with a larger radius, for, by this obelisk, we must not imagine Ptolemy intended to observe the obliquity of the ecliptic at Axum. Though it was true, that Axum, by its situation, was a very proper place, the sun passing over that city and obelisk twice a-year, yet it was equally true, that, from another circumstance, which he might have been acquainted with, at less expence of time than building the obelisk would have cost him, that he himself could not make any use of the sun's being twice vertical to Axum; for the sun is vertical at Axum about the 25th of April, and again about the 20th of August; and, at both these seasons, the heaven is so overcast with clouds, and the rain so continual, especially at mid-day, that it would be a wonder indeed, if Ptolemy had once seen the sun during the months he staid there.

Though Syene, by its situation should be healthy, the general complaint is a weakness and soreness in the eyes; and this not a temporary one only, but generally ending in blindness of one, or both eyes; you scarce ever see a person in the street that sees with both eyes. They say it is owing to the hot wind from the desert; and this I apprehend to be true, by the violent soreness and inflammation we were troubled with in our return home, through the great Desert, to Syene.

We had now finished every thing we had to do at Syene, and prepared to descend the Nile. After having been quiet, and well used so long, we did not expect any altercation at parting; we thought we had contented every body, and we were perfectly content with them. But, unluckily for us, our landlord, the Schourbatchie, upon whom I had my credit, and who had diftinguifhed himfelf by being very ferviceable and obliging to us, happened to be the *proprietor* of a boat, for which, at that time, he had *little* employment; nothing would fatisfy him but my hiring that boat, inftead of returning in that which brought us up.

THIS could by no means be done, without breaking faith with our Rais, Abou Cuffi, which I was refolved not to do on any account whatever, as the man had behaved honeftly and well in every refpect. The janiffaries took the part of their brother againft the ftranger, and threatened to cut Abou Cuffi to pieces, and throw him to the crocodiles.

ON the other part, he was very far from being terrified. He told them roundly, that he was a fervant of Ali Bey, that, if they attempted to take his fare from him, their pay fhould be ftopped at Cairo, till they furrendered the guilty perfon to do him juftice. He laughed moft unaffectedly at the notion of cutting him to pieces; and declared, that, if he was to complain of the ufage he met when he went down to Lower Egypt, there would not be a janiffary from Syene who would not be in much greater danger of crocodiles than he.

I WENT in the evening to the Aga, and complained of my landlord's behaviour. I told him pofitively, but with great fhew of refpect, I would rather go down the Nile upon a *raft*, than fet my foot in any other boat but the one that brought me up. I begged him to be cautious how he proceeded, as it would be *my ftory*, and not *his*, that would go

to

to the Bey. This grave and refolute appearance had the effect. The Schourbatchie was fent for, and reprimanded, as were all thofe that fided with him; while privately, to calm all animofities againſt my Rais, I promifed him a piece of green cloth, which was his wiſh; and fo heartily were we reconciled, that, the next day, he made his fervants help Abou Cuffi to put our baggage on board the boat.

The Aga hinted to me, in converfation, that he wondered at my departure, as he heard my intention was to go to Ibrim and Deir. I told him, thofe garrifons had a bad name; that a Daniſh gentleman, fome years ago, going up thither, with orders from the government of Cairo, was plundered, and very nearly affaffinated, by Ibrahim, Cacheff of Deir. He looked furprifed, fhook his head, and feemed not to give me credit; but I perfifted, in the terms of Mr Norden's * Narrative; and told him, the brother of the Aga of Syene was along with him at the time. " Will any perfon, faid he, tell me, that a man who is in my hands once a month, who has not an ounce of bread but what I furniſh him from this garrifon, and whofe pay would be ſtopt (as your Rais truly faid) on the firſt complaint tranfmitted to Cairo, could affaffinate a man with Ali Bey's orders, and my brother along with him? Why, what do you think he is? I ſhall fend a fervant to the Cacheff of Deir to-morrow, who ſhall bring him down by the beard, if he refufes to come willingly." I faid, " Then times were very much changed for the better; it was not always fo, there was not always at Cairo a fovereign like

---

* Vide Mr Norden's Voyage up the Nile.

like Ali Bey, nor at Syene a man of his prudence, and capacity in commanding; but having no bufinefs at Deir and Ibrim, I fhould not rifk finding them in another humour, exercifing other powers than thofe he allowed them to have."

The 26th we embarked at the north end of the town, in the very fpot where I again took boat above three years afterwards. We now no longer enjoyed the advantage of our prodigious main-fail; not only our yards were lowered, but our mafts were taken out; and we floated down the current, making the figure of a wreck. The current, pufhing againft one of our fides, the wind directly contrary, prefling us on the other, we went down *broad fide foremoft*; but fo fteadily, as fcarce to be fenfible the veffel was in motion.

In the evening I ftopt at Shekh Ammer, and faw my patient Nimmer, Shekh of the Ababdé. I found him greatly better, and as thankful as ever; I renewed my prefcriptions, and he his offers of fervice.

I was vifited, however, with a pretty fmart degree of fever by hunting crocodiles on the Nile as I went down, without any poffibility of getting near them.

On the 31ft of January we arrived at Negadé, the fourth fettlement of the Francifcan friars in Upper Egypt, for the pretended miffion of Ethiopia. I found it to be in lat. 25° 53' 30". It is a fmall neat village, covered with palm-trees, and mofily inhabited by Cophts, none of whom the friars have yet converted, nor ever will, unlefs by fmall penfions,

penfions, which they give to the pooreft of them, to be decoy-ducks to the reft.

OPPOSITE to Negadé, on the other fide of the river about three miles, is Cus, a large town, the Appollonis Civitas Parva of the ancients. There are no antiquities at this place; but the caravan, which was to carry the corn for Mecca, acrofs the defert to Coffeir, was to affemble there. I found they were not near ready; and that the Arabs Atouni had threatened they would be in their way, and would not fuffer them to pafs, at any rate, and that the guard commanded to efcort them acrofs the defert, would come from Furfhout, and therefore I fhould have early warning,

IT was the 2d of February I returned to Badjoura, and took up my quarters in the houfe formerly affigned me, greatly to the joy of Shekh Ifmael, who, though he was in the main reconciled to his friend, friar Chriftopher, had not yet forgot the wounding of the five men by his mifcalculating ramadan; and was not without fears that the fame inadvertence might, fome day or other, be fatal to him, in his pleurify and afthma, or, what is ftill more likely, by the operation of the tabange.

As I was now about to launch into that part of my expedition, in which I was to have no further intercoufe with Europe I fet myfelf to work to examine all my obfervations, and put my journal in fuch forwardnefs by explanations, where needful, that the labours and pains I had hitherto been at, might not be totally loft to the public, if I fhould perifh in the journey I had undertaken, which, every day, from

from all information I could procure, appeared to be more and more desperate.

Having finished these, at least so far as to make them intelligible to others, I conveyed them to my friends Messrs Julian and Rosa at Cairo, to remain in their custody till I should return, or news come that I was otherwise disposed of.

CHAP

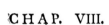

CHAP. VIII.

The Author sets out from Kenné—Crosses the Desert of the Thebaid—Visits the Marble Mountains—Arrives at Cosseir, on the Red Sea—Transactions there.

IT was Thursday, the 16th of February 1769, we heard the caravan was ready to set out from Kenné, the Cæne Emporium of antiquity. From Kenné our road was first East, for half an hour, to the foot of the hills, which here bound the cultivated land; then S. E. when, at 11 o'clock in the forenoon, we passed a very dirty small village called Sheraffa. All the way from Kenné, close on our left, were desert hills, on which not the least verdure grew, but a few plants of a large species of Solanum, called Burrumbuc.

At half past two we came to a well, called Bir Ambar, the well of spices, and a dirty village of the same name, belonging to the Azaizy, a poor inconsiderable tribe of Arabs. They live by letting out their cattle for hire to the caravans that go to Cosseir, and attending themselves, when necessary. It got its name, I suppose, from its having formerly been a station of the caravans from the Red Sea, loaded with this kind of merchandise from India. The houses of the Azaizy are of a very particular construction, if they can be called houses.

houfes. They are all made of potter-clay, in one piece, in fhape of a bee-hive; the largeſt is not above ten feet high, and the greateſt diameter fix.

THERE are no veſtiges here of any canal, mentioned to have been cut between the Nile and the Red Sea. The cultivated land here is not above half a mile in extent from the river, but the inundation of the Nile reaches much higher, nor has it left behind it any appearance of foil. After paffing Bir Ambar, we pitched our tent about four o'clock at Gabba*, a fhort mile from Cuft, on the borders of the defert—here we paffed the night.

ON the 17th, at eight o clock in the morning, having mounted my fervants all on horfeback, and taken the charge of our own camels, (for there was a confufion in our caravan not to be defcribed, and our guards we knew were but a fet of thieves) we advanced flowly into the defert. There were about two hundred men on horfeback, armed with firelocks; all of them lions, if you believed their word or appearance; but we were credibly informed, that fifty of the Arabs, at firſt fight, would have made thefe heroes fly without any bloodfhed.

I HAD not gone two miles before I was joined by the Howadat Arab, whom I had brought with me in the boat from Cairo. He offered me his fervice with great profeffions of gratitude, and told me, that he hoped I would again take charge of his money, as I had before done from Cairo.

It

---

* It is no town, but fome fand and a few buſhes, fo called.

It was now for the firft time he told me his name, which was Mahomet Abdel Gin, "the Slave of the Devil, or the "Spirit." There is a large tribe of that name, many of which come to Cairo from the kingdom of Sennaar; but he had been born among the Howadat, oppofite to Metrahenny, where I found him.

Our road was all the way in an open plain, bounded by hillocks of fand, and fine gravel, perfectly hard, and not perceptibly above the level of the plain country of Egypt. About twelve miles diftant there is a ridge of mountains of no confiderable height, perhaps the moft barren in the world. Between thefe our road lay through plains, never three miles broad, but without trees, fhrubs, or herbs. There are not even the traces of any living creature, neither ferpent nor lizard, antelope nor oftrich, the ufual inhabitants of the moft dreary deferts. There is no fort of water on the furface, brackifh or fweet. Even the birds feem to avoid the place as peftilential, not having feen one of any kind fo much as flying over. The fun was burning hot, and, upon rubbing two fticks together, in half a minute they both took fire, and flamed; a mark how near the country was reduced to a general conflagration!

At half paft three, we pitched our tent near fome drawwells, which, upon tafting, we found bitterer than foot. We had, indeed, other water carried by the camels in fkins. This well-water had only one needful quality, it was cold, and therefore very comfortable for refrefhing us outwardly. This unpleafant ftation is called Legeta; here we were obliged to pafs the night, and all next day, to wait the arrival of the caravans of Cus, Efné, and part of thofe of Kenné, and Ebanout.

WHILE at the wells of Legeta, my Arab, Abdel Gin, came to me with his money, which had increafed now to nineteen fequins and a half. "What! faid I, Mahomet, are you never fafe among your countrymen, neither by fea nor land?" "Oh, no, replied Mahomet; the difference, when we were on board the boat, was, we had three thieves only; but, when *affembled, here*, we fhall have above three thoufand.—But I have an advice to give you."—"And my ears," faid I, "Mahomet, are always open to advice, efpecially in ftrange countries."—" Thefe people," continued Mahomet, "are all afraid of the Atouni Arabs; and, when attacked, they will run away, and leave you in the hands of thefe Atouni, who will carry off your baggage. Therefore, as you have nothing to do with their corn, do not kill any of the Atouni if they come, for that will be a bad affair, but go afide, and let me manage. I will anfwer with my life, though all the caravan fhould be ftripped ftark-naked, and you loaded with gold, not one article belonging to you fhall be touched." I queftioned him very particularly about this intimation, as it was an affair of much confequence, and I was fo well fatisfied, that I refolved to conform ftrictly to it.

IN the evening came twenty Turks from Caramania which is that part of Afia Minor immediately on the fide of the Mediterranean oppofite to the coaft of Egypt; all of them neatly and cleanly dreffed like Turks, all on camels, armed with fwords, a pair of piftols at their girdle, and a fhort neat gun; their arms were in very good order, with their flints and

and ammunition ſtowed in cartridge-boxes, in a very ſoldier-like manner. A few of theſe ſpoke Arabic, and my Greek ſervant, Michael, interpreted for the reſt. Having been informed, that the large tent belonged to an Engliſhman, they came into it without ceremony. They told me, that they were a number of neighbours and companions, who had ſet out together to go to Mecca, to the Hadje; and not knowing the language, or cuſtoms of the people, they had been but indifferently uſed ſince they landed at Alexandria, particularly ſomewhere (as I gueſſed) about Achmim; that one of the Owani, or ſwimming thieves, had been on board of them in the night, and had carried off a ſmall portmanteau with about 200 ſequins in gold; that, though a complaint had been made to the Bey of Girgé, yet no ſatisfaction had been obtained; and that now they had heard an Engliſhman was here, whom they reckoned their *countryman*, they had come to propoſe, that we ſhould make a common cauſe to defend each other againſt all enemies.—What they meaned by *countryman* was this:—

THERE is in Aſia Minor, ſomewhere between Anatolia and Caramania, a diſtrict which they call Caz Dagli, corruptly Caz Dangli, and this the Turks believe was the country from which the Engliſh firſt drew their origin; and on this account they never fail to claim kindred with the Engliſh wherever they meet, eſpecially if they ſtand in need of their aſſiſtance.

I TOLD them the arrangement I had taken with the Arab. At firſt, they thought it was too much confidence to place in him, but I convinced them, that it was greatly diminiſhing our riſk, and, let the worſt come to the worſt, I was

I was well satisfied that, armed as we were, on foot, we were more than sufficient to beat the Atouni, after they had defeated the clownish caravan of Egypt, from whose courage we certainly had nothing to expect.

I cannot conceal the secret pleasure I had in finding the character of my country so firmly established among nations so distant, enemies to our religion, and strangers to our government. Turks from Mount Taurus, and Arabs from the desert of Libya, thought themselves unsafe among their own countrymen, but trusted their lives and their little fortunes implicitly to the direction and word of an Englishman whom they had never before seen.

These Turks seemed to be above the middling rank of people; each of them had his little cloak-bag very neatly packed up; and they gave me to understand that there was money in it. These they placed in my servants tent, and chained them all together, round the middle pillar of it; for it was easy to see the Arabs of the caravan had those packages in view, from the first moment of the Turk's arrival.

We staid all the 18th at Legeta, waiting for the junction of the caravans, and departed the 19th at six o'clock in the morning. Our journey, all that day, was through a plain, never less than a mile broad, and never broader than three; the hills, on our right and left, were higher than the former, and of a brownish calcined colour, like the stones on the sides of Mount Vesuvius, but without any herb or tree upon them.

At half paſt ten, we paſſed a mountain of green and red marble, and at twelve we entered a plain called Hamra, where we firſt obſerved the ſand red, with a purple caſt, of the colour of porphyry, and this is the ſignification of Hamra, the name of the valley. I diſmounted here, to examine of what the rocks were compoſed; and found, with the greateſt pleaſure, that here began the quarries of porphyry, without the mixture of any other ſtone; but it was imperfect, brittle, and ſoft. I had not been engaged in this purſuit an hour, before we were alarmed with a report that the Atouni had attacked the rear of the caravan; we were at the head of it. The Turks and my ſervants were all drawn together, at the foot of the mountain, and poſted as advantageouſly as poſſible. But it ſoon appeared that they were ſome thieves only, who had attempted to ſteal ſome loads of corn from camels that were weak, or fallen lame, perhaps in intelligence with thoſe of our own caravans.

All the reſt of the afternoon, we ſaw mountains of a perfectly purple colour, all of them porphyry; nor has Ptolemy † much erred in the poſition of them. About four o'clock, we pitched our tent at a place called Main el Mafarek. The colour of the valley El Hamra continued to this ſtation; and it was very ſingular to obſerve, that the ants, or piſmires, the only living creatures I had yet obſerved, were all of a beautiful red colour like the ſand.

The 20th, at ſix oclock in the morning, we left Main el Mafarek,

---

† Ptol. Almag. lib. 4. Geograph. pag. 104.

Mafarek, and, at ten, came to the mouth of the defiles. At eleven we began to defcend, having had a very imperceptible afcent from Kenné all the way.

We were now indemnified for the famenefs of our natural productions yefterday; for, on each fide of the plain, we found different forts of marble, twelve kinds of which I felected, and took with me.

At noon, we came to a plain planted with acacia-trees, at equal diftances; fingle trees, fpreading broader than ufual, as if on purpofe to proportion the refrefhment they gave to the number of travellers who ftood in need of it. This is a ftation of the Atouni Arabs after rain. From our leaving Legeta, we had no water that, nor the following day.

On the right-hand fide of this plain we found porphyry and granite, of very beautiful kinds. All the way, on both fides of the valley, this day, the mountains were of porphyry, and a very few of ftone.

At a quarter paft four, we encamped at Koraim, a fmall plain, perfectly barren, confifting of fine gravel, fand, and ftones, with a few acacia-trees, interfperfed throughout.

The 21ft, we departed early in the morning from Koraim, and, at ten o'clock, we paffed feveral defiles, perpetually alarmed by a report, that the Arabs were approaching; none of whom we ever faw. We then proceeded through feveral defiles, into a long plain that turns to the eaft, then north-eaft, and north, fo as to make a portion of a circle. At the end of this plain we came to a mountain, the greateft part of which was of the marble, *verde antico*, as it is called in Rome, but by far the moft beautiful of the kind I had ever feen.

HAVING paffed this, we had mountains on both fides of us, but particularly on our right. The only ones that I myfelf examined were of a kind of granite, with reddifh veins throughout, with triangular and fquare black fpots. Thefe mountains continued to Mefag el Terfowey, where we encamped at twelve o'clock; we were obliged to bring our water from about five miles to the fouth-eaft. This water does not appear to be from fprings, it lies in cavities and grottos in the rock, of which there are twelve in number, whether hollowed by nature or art, or partly by both, is more than I can folve. Great and abundant rains fall here in February. The clouds, breaking on the tops of thefe mountains, in their way to Abyffinia, fill thefe cifterns with large fupplies, which the impending rocks fecure from evaporation.

IT was the firft frefh water we tafted fince we left the Nile; and the only water of any kind fince we left Legeta. But fuch had been the forefight of our caravan, that very few reforted thither, having all laid in abundant ftore from the Nile; and fome of them a quantity fufficient to ferve them till their return. This was not our cafe. We had water, it is true, from the Nile; but we never thought we could have too much, as long as there was room in our water-fkins to hold more; I therefore went early with my camel-drivers, expecting to have feen fome antelopes, which every night come to drink from the well, having no opportunity to do it throughout the day.

I HAD not concealed myfelf half an hour, above a narrow path leading to the principal cave, before I faw, firft one antelope walking very flately alone; then four others, clofely following him. Although I was wholly hid as long as I lay ftill, he feemed to have difcerned me from the inftant that I faw him. I fhould have thought it had been the fmell that had difcovered me, had not I ufed the precaution of carrying a piece of burnt turf along with me, and left one with my horfe likewife; perhaps it was this unufual fmell that terrified him. Whatever was the caufe, he advanced apparently in fear, and feemed to be trufted with the care of the flock, as the others teftified no apprehenfion, but were rather fporting or fighting with each other. Still he advanced flower, and with greater caution; but, being perfectly within reach, I did not think proper any longer to rifk the whole from a defire to acquire a greater number. I fhot him fo juftly, that, giving one leap five or fix feet high, he fell dead upon his head. I fired at the others, retiring all in a croud; killed one likewife, and lamed another, who fled among the mountains, where darknefs protected him. We were perfectly content with our acquifition, and the nature of the place did not prompt us to look after the wounded. We continued at the well to affift our companions who came in want of water, a duty with which neceffity binds us all to comply.

WE returned near midnight with our game and our water. We found our tents all lighted, which, at that time of night, was unufual. I thought, however, it was on account of my abfence, and to guide me the furer home. We were however furprifed, when, coming within a moderate diftance of our tent, we heard *the word* called for; I anfwered immediately,

diately, *Charlotte;* and, upon our arrival, we perceived the Turks were parading round the tents in arms, and soon after our Howadat Arab came to us, and with him a messenger from Sidi Haffan, desiring me to come instantly to his tent, while my servants advised me first to hear what they had to say to me in mine.

I soon, therefore, perceived that all was not well, and I returned my compliments to Haffan, adding, that, if he had any thing to say to me so late, he would do well to come, or send, as it was past my hour of visiting in the desert, especially as I had not eat, and was tired with having the charge of the water. I gave orders to my servants to put out all the extraordinary lights, as that seemed to be a mark of fear; but forbade any one to sleep, excepting those who had the charge of our beasts, and had been fetching the water.

I found that, while our people had been asleep, two persons had got into the tent and attempted to steal one of the portmanteaus; but, as they were chained together, and the tent-pole in the middle, the noise had awakened my servants, who had seized one of the men; and that the Turks had intended instantly to have dispatched him with their knives, and with great difficulty had been prevented by my servants, according to my constant orders, for I wished to avoid all extremities, upon such occasions, when possible. They had indeed leave to deal with their sticks as freely as their prudence suggested to them; and they had gone, in this case, fully beyond the ordinary limits of *discretion*, especially Abdel Gin, who was the first to seize the robber. In short, they had dealt so liberally with their sticks, that the thief was only known to be living by his groans, and they had thrown him at a small distance, for any person to own him that pleased. It appeared, that he was a servant of Sidi Hassan, an Egyptian slave, or servant to Shekh Hamam, who conducted or commanded the caravan, if there was any *conduct* or *command* in it.

There were with me ten servants, all completely armed, twenty-five Turks, who seemed worthy to be depended upon, and four janissaries, who had joined us from Cairo, so that there were of us forty men perfectly armed, besides attendants on the cattle. As we had people with us who knew the wells, and also a friend who was acquainted with the Atouni, nothing, even in a desert, could reasonably alarm us.

With great difficulty we pulled down an old acacia-tree, and procured some old-dried camels dung, with which we roasted our two antelopes: very ill-roasted they were; and execrable meat, though they had been ever so well dressed, and had had the best sauce of Christendom. However, we were in the desert, and every thing was acceptable. We had some spirits, which finished our repast that night: it was exceedingly cold, and we sat thick about the fire.

Five men with firelocks, and a number of Arabs with lances, having come towards us, and being challenged by the centinel for not giving *the word*, were then desired to stand, or they would be fired upon. They all cried out, *Salam Alicum!* and I intimated that any three of them might come forward, but desired them to keep away the Arabs. Three of them accordingly came, and then two more. They delivered

delivered a meſſage from Sidi Haſſan, that my people had killed a man; they deſired that the murderer might be delivered to them, and that I ſhould come to his tent, and ſee juſtice done. " I told them, that none of my people, however pro-
" voked, would put a man to death in my abſence, unleſs
" in defence of their own lives; that, if I had been there, I
" ſhould certainly have ordered them to fire upon a thief
" catched in the act of ſtealing within my tent; but, ſince
" he was dead, I was ſatisfied as to him, only expected that
" Sidi Haſſan would give me up his companion, who had
" fled; that, as it was near morning, I ſhould meet him
" when the caravan decamped, and hear what he had to ſay
" in his defence. In the mean time I forbade any perſon
" to come near my tent, or quarters, on any pretence whatever, till day light." Away they went murmuring, but what they ſaid I did not underſtand. We heard no more of them, and none of us ſlept. All of us, however, repeated our vows of ſtanding by each other; and we ſince found, that we had ſtood in the way of a common practice, of ſtripping theſe poor ſtrangers, the Turks, who come every year this road to Mecca.

At dawn of day, the caravan was all in motion. They had got intelligence, that two days before, about 300 Atouni had watered at Terfowey; and, indeed, there were marks of great reſort at the well, where we filled the water. We had agreed not to load one of our camels, but let the caravan go on before us, and meet the Atouni firſt; that I only ſhould go on horſeback, about two hundred yards into the plain from the tent, and all the reſt follow me on foot with arms in their hands.

HASSAN

HASSAN, too, was mounted on horfeback, with about a hundred of his myrmidons, and a number of Arabs on foot. He fent me word that I was to advance, with only two fervants; but I returned for anfwer, that I had no intention to advance at all; that if he had any bufinefs, he fhould fay fo, and that I would meet him one to one, or three to fix, juft as he pleafed. He fent me again word, that he wanted to communicate the intelligence he had of the Atouni, to put me on my guard. I returned for anfwer, that I was already upon my guard, againft all thieves, and did not make any diftinction, if people were thieves themfelves, or encouraged others to be fo, or whether they were Atouni or Ababdé. He then fent me a meffage, that it was a cold morning, and wifhed I would give him a difh of coffee, and keep thofe ftrangers away. I therefore defired one of my fervants to bring the coffee-pot, and directing my people to fit down, I rode up to him, and difmounted, as he did alfo, when twenty or thirty of his vagabonds came, and fat down likewife. He faid he was exceedingly furprifed, after fending to me laft night, that I did not come to him; that the whole camp was in murmur at beating the man, and that it was all that he could do to hinder his foldiers from falling upon us, and extirpating us all at once; that I did wrong to protect thofe Turks, who carried always money to Mecca for merchandife, and defrauded them of their dues.

My fervant having juft poured out a difh of coffee to give him, I faid, Stay, Sir, till we know whether we are in peace. Sidi Haffan, if that is the way of levying dues upon the Turks, to fend thieves to rob them in my tent, you fhould advife me firft of it, and then we fhould have fettled the bufinefs. With regard to your preventing people from
murdering

murdering me, it is a boaſt ſo ridiculous that I laugh at it. Thoſe pale-faced fellows who are about you muffled up in burnooſes for fear of cold in the morning, are they capable to look janiſſaries in the face like mine? Speak lowly, and in Arabic, when you talk at this rate, or perhaps it will not be in my power to return you the compliment you did me laſt night, or hinder them from killing you on the ſpot. Were ever ſuch words ſpoken! ſaid a man behind; tell me, maſter, are you a king? If Sidi Haſſan, anſwered I, is your maſter, and you ſpeak to me on this occaſion, you are a wretch; get out of my ſight; I ſwear I will not drink a diſh of coffee while you are here, and will mount my horſe directly.

I THEN roſe, and the ſervant took back the coffee-pot; upon which Haſſan ordered his ſervant out of his preſence, ſaying, "No, no; give me the coffee if we are in peace;" and he drank it accordingly. Now, ſays he, paſt is paſt; the Atouni are to meet us at the *mouth of Beder; your people are better armed than mine, are Turks, and uſed to fighting. I would wiſh you to go foremoſt, and we will take charge of your camels, though my people have 4000 of their own, and they have enough to do to take charge of the corn. "And I," ſaid I, "if I wanted water or proviſion, would go to meet the Atouni, who would uſe me well. Why, you don't know to whom you are ſpeaking, nor that the Atouni are Arabs of Ali Bey, and that I am his man of confidence, going to the Sherriffe of Mecca? The Atouni will not hurt *us*; but, as you ſay, you are commander of the caravan, we have

all

---

* The Arabs call theſe narrow paſſes in the mountains Fum, as the Hebrews did Pi, the mouth. Fum el Beder, is the mouth of Beder; Fum el Teifowey, the mouth or paſſage of Terfowey; Piha Hhiroth, the mouth of the valley cut through with ravines.

all fworn we will not fire a fhot, till we fee you heartily engaged; and then we will do our beft to hinder the Arabs from ftealing the Sherriffe of Mecca's corn, tor *his fake only.*" They all cried out El Fedtah! El Fedtah! fo I faid the prayer of peace as a proxy; for none of the Turks would come near him.

OPPOSITE to where we were encamped is Terfowey, a large mountain, partly green-marble, partly granite, with a red blufh upon a grey ground, with fquare oblong fpots. About forty yards within the narrow valley, which fcparates this mountain from its neighbour, we faw a part of the fuft or fhaft of a monftrous obelifk of marble, very nearly fquare, broken at the end, and towards the top. It was nearly thirty feet long, and nineteen feet in the face; about two feet of the bottom were perfectly infulated, and one whole fide feparated from the mountain. The gully had been widened and levelled, and the road made quite up to underneath the block.

WE faw likewife, throughout the plain, fmall pieces of jafper, having green, white, and red fpots, called in Italy, " Diafpo Sanguineo." All the mountains on both fides of the plain feemed to be of the fame fort, whether they really were fo or not, I will not fay, having had no time to examine them.

THE 22d, at half paft one in the morning, we fet out full of terror about the Atouni. We continued in a direction nearly caft, till at three we came to the defiles; but it was fo dark, that it was impoffible to difcern of what the country on each fide confifted. At day-break, we found ourfelves

THE SOURCE OF THE NILE.

selves at the bottom of a mountain of granite, bare like the former.

We saw quantities of small pieces of various sorts of granite, and porphyry scattered over the plain, which had been carried down by a torrent, probably from quarries of ancient ages; these were white, mixed with black spots; red, with green veins, and black spots. After this, all the mountains on the right hand were of red marble in prodigious abundance, but of no great beauty. They continued, as the granite did, for several miles along the road, while the opposite side was all of dead-green, supposed serpentine marble.

It was one of the most extraordinary sights I ever saw. The former mountains were of considerable height, without a tree, or shrub, or blade of grass upon them; but these now before us had all the appearance, the one of having been sprinkled over with Havannah, the other with Brazil snuff. I wondered, that, as the red is nearest the sea, and the ships going down the Abyssinian coast observe this appearance within lat. 26°, writers have not imagined this was called the *Red Sea* upon that account, rather than for the many weak reasons they have relied upon.

About eight o'clock we began to descend smartly, and, half an hour after, entered into another defile like those before described, having mountains of green marble on every side of us. At nine, on our left, we saw the highest mountain we had yet passed. We found it, upon examination, to be composed of serpentine marble; and, thro' about one-third of the thickness, ran a large vein of jasper, green, spotted with red. Its exceeding hardness was such as not to yield to the blows of a hammer; but the works of old times were more apparent in it, than in any mountain we had seen. Ducts, or channels, for carrying water tranfverfely, were obferved evidently to terminate in this quarry of jafper: a proof that water was one of the means ufed in cutting thefe hard ftones.

About ten o'clock, defcending very rapidly, with green marble and jafper on each fide of us, but no other green thing whatever, we had the firft profpect of the Red Sea, and, at a quarter paft eleven, we arrived at Coffeir. It has been a wonder with all travellers, and with myfelf among the reft, where the ancients procured that prodigious quantity of fine marble, with which all their buildings abound. That wonder, however, among many others, now ceafes, after having paffed, in four days, more granite, porphyry, marble, and jafper, than would build Rome, Athens, Corinth, Syracufe, Memphis, Alexandria, and half a dozen fuch cities. It feemed to be very vifible, that thofe openings in the hills, which I call Defiles, were not natural, but artificial; and that whole mountains had been cut out at thefe places, to preferve a flope towards the Nile as gentle as poffible: this, I fuppofe, might be a defcent of about one foot in fifty at moft; fo that, from the mountains to the Nile, thofe heavy carriages muft have moved with as little draught as poffible, and, at the fame time, been fufficiently impeded by friction, fo as not to run amain, or acquire an increafed velocity, againft which, alfo, there muft have been other provifions contrived. As I made another excurfion to thefe marble mountains from Coffeir, I will, once for all, here fet down what I obferved concerning their natural appearance.

THE

THE porphyry fhews itfelf by a fine purple fand, without any glofs or glitter on it, and is exceedingly agreeable to the eye. It is mixed with the native white fand, and fixed gravel of the plains. Green unvariegated marble, is generally feen in the fame mountain with the porphyry. Where the two veins meet, the marble is for fome inches brittle, but the porphyry of the fame hardnefs as in other places.

THE granite is covered with fand, and looks like ftone of a dirty, brown colour. But this is only the change and impreffion the fun and weather have made upon it; for, upon breaking it, you fee it is grey granite, with black fpots, with a reddifh caft, or blufh over it. This red feems to fade and fuffer from the outward air, but, upon working or polifhing the furface, this colour again appears. It is in greater quantity than the porphyry, and nearer the Red Sea. Pompey's pillar feems to have been from this quarry.

NEXT to the granite, but never, as I obferved, joined with it in the fame mountain, is the red marble. It is covered with fand of the fame colour, and looks as if the whole mountain were fpread over with brick duft. There is alfo a red marble with white veins, which I have often feen at Rome, but not in principal fubjects, I have alfo feen it in Britain. The common green (called Serpentine) looks as if covered over with Brazil fnuff. Joined with this green, I faw two famples of that beautiful marble they call Ifabella; one of them with a yellowifh caft, which we call Quaker-colour; the other with a blueifh, which is commonly termed Dove-colour. Thefe two feem to divide the refpective mountains with the ferpentine. In this green, likewife, it was we faw the vein of jafper; but whether it was abfolutely the fame with this which is the bloody jafper, or bloodftone, is what we had not time to fettle.

I should firſt have made mention of the verde antico, the dark green with white irregular fpots, becauſe it is of the greateſt value, and neareſt the Nile. This is produced in the mountains of the plain green, or ſerpentine, as is the jafper, and is not difcoverable by the duſt, or any particular colour upon it. Firſt, there is a blue fleaky ſtone, exceedingly even and ſmooth in the grain, folid, and without fparks or colour. When broken, it is fomething lighter than a ſlate, and more beautiful than moſt marble; it is like the lava of volcanoes, when poliſhed. After lifting this, we come to the beds of verde antico; and here the quarrying is very obvious, for it has been uncovered in patches, not above twenty feet fquare. Then, in another part, the green ſtone has been removed, and another pit of it wrought.

I saw, in feveral places in the plain, fmall pieces of African marble fcattered about, but no rocks or mountains of it. I fuppoſe it is found in the heart of fome other coloured marble, and in ſtrata, like the jafper and verde antico, and, I fufpect, in the mountains of Iſabella marble, eſpecially of the yelloweſt fort of it, but this is mere conjecture. This prodigious ſtore of marble is placed upon a ridge, whence there is a defcent to the eaſt or weſt, either to the Nile or Red Sea. The level ground and hard-fixed gravel are proper for the heavieſt carriages, and will eaſily and fmoothly convey any weight whatever to its place of embarkation on the Nile; fo that another wonder ceaſed, how the ancients tranſported thoſe vaſt blocks to Thebes, Memphis, and Alexandria.

Cosseir

THE SOURCE OF THE NILE.

Cosseir is a small mud-walled village, built upon the shore, among hillocks of floating sand. It is defended by a square fort of hewn stone, with square towers in the angles, which have in them three small cannon of iron, and one of brass, all in very bad condition; of no other use but to terrify the Arabs, and hinder them from plundering the town when full of corn, going to Mecca in time of famine. The walls are not high; nor was it necessary, if the great guns were in order. But as this is not the case, the ramparts are heightened by clay, or by mud-walls, to screen the soldiers from the fire-arms of the Arabs, that might otherwise command them from the sandy hills in the neighbourhood.

There are several wells of brackish water on the N. W. of the castle, which, for experiment's sake, I made drinkable, by filtering it through sand; but the water in use is brought from Terfowey, a good day's journey off.

The port, if we may call it so, is on the south-east of the town. It is nothing but a rock which runs out about four hundred yards into the sea, and defends the vessels, which ride to the west of it, from the north and north-east winds as the houses of the town cover them from the north-west.

There is a large inclosure with a high mud-wall, and, within, every merchant has a shop or magazine for his corn and merchandise: little of this last is imported, unless coarse India goods, for the consumption of Upper Egypt itself, since the trade to Dongola and Sennaar has been interrupted.

I HAD

I HAD orders from Shekh Hamam to-lodge in the caftle. But a few hours before my arrival, Huffein Bey Abou Kerfh landed from Mecca, and Jidda, and he had taken up the apartments which were deftined for me. He was one of thofe Beys whom Ali Bey had defeated, and driven from Cairo. He was called *Abou Kerſh*, i. e. Father Belly, from being immoderately fat; his adverfity had brought him a little into fhapes. My fervants, who had gone before, thinking that a friend of the Bey in power was better than an enemy outlawed, and banifhed by him, had inadvertently put fome of my baggage into the caftle juft when this potentate was taking poffeffion. Swords were immediately drawn, death and deftruction threatened to my poor fervants, who fled and hid themfelves till I arrived.

UPON their complaint, I told them they had acted improperly; that a fovereign was a fovereign all the world over; and it was not my bufinefs to make a difference, whether he was in power or not. I eafily procured a houfe, and fent a janiffary of the four that had joined us from Cairo, with my compliments to the Bey, defiring reftitution of my baggage, and that he would excufe the ignorance of my fervants, who did not know that he was at Coffeir; but only, having the firman of the Grand Signior, and letters from the Bey and Port of janiffaries of Cairo, they prefumed that I had a right to lodge there, if he had not taken up the quarters.

IT happened, that an intimate friend of mine, Mahomet Topal, captain of one of the large Cairo fhips, trading to Arabia, was a companion of this Huffein Bey, and had carried him to fee Captain Thornhill, and fome of our Englifh captains at Jidda, who, as their very laudable cuſtom is, always ſhew ſuch people ſome civilities. He queſtioned the janiſſary about me, who told him I was Engliſh; that I had the protection I had mentioned, and that, from kindneſs and charity, I had furniſhed the ſtranger Turks with water, and proviſion at my own expence, when croſſing the deſert. He profeſſed himſelf exceedingly aſhamed at the behaviour of his ſervants, who had drawn their ſabres upon mine, and had cut my carpet and ſome cords. After which, of his own accord, he ordered his kaya, or next in command, to remove from the lodging he occupied, and inſtead of ſending back my baggage by my ſervant, he directed it to be carried into the apartment from which the kaya had removed. This I abſolutely refuſed, and ſent word, I underſtood he was to be there for a few days only; and as I might ſtay for a longer time, I ſhould only deſire to ſucceed him after his departure, in order to put my baggage in ſafety from the Arabs; but for the preſent they were in no danger, as long *as he was in the town*. I told him, I would pay my reſpects to him in the evening, when the weather cooled. I did ſo, and, contrary to his expectations, brought him a ſmall preſent. Great intercourſe of civility paſſed, my fellow-travellers, the Turks, were all ſeated there, and he gave me, repeatedly, very honourable teſtimonials of my charity, generoſity, and kindneſs to them.

These Turks, finding themſelves in a ſituation to be heard, had not omitted the opportunity of complaining to Huſſein Bey of the attempt of the Arab to rob them in the deſert. The Bey aſked me, If it happened in my tent? I ſaid, It was in that of my ſervants. "What is the reaſon, says he, that, when you English people know so well what good government is, you did not order his head to be struck off, when you had him in your hands, before the door of the tent?" "Sir," said I, "I know well what good government is; but being a stranger, and a Christian, I have no sort of title to exercise the power of life and death in this country; only in this one case, when a man attempts my life, then I think I am warranted to defend myself, whatever may be the consequence to him. My men took him in the fact, and they had my orders, in such cases, to beat the offenders so that they should not steal these two months again: They did so; that was punishment enough in cold blood."—" But my blood," says he, "never cools with regard to such rascals as these: Go (and he called one of his attendants) tell Haffan, the head of the caravan, from me, that unless he hangs that Arab before sun-rise to-morrow, I will carry him in irons to Furshout."

Upon this message I took my leave; saying only, "Huffein Bey, take my advice; procure a vessel and send these Turks over to Mecca before you leave this town, or, be assured they will all be made responsible for the death of this Arab; will be stripped naked, and perhaps murdered, as soon as your back is turned." It was all I could do to get them protected thus far. This measure was already provided for, and the poor Turks joyfully embarked next morning. The thief was not at all molested: he was sent out of the way, under pretence that he had fled.

Cosseir has been mistaken by different authors. Mr Huet, Bishop of Avranches, says, It is the Myos Hormos of antiquity; others, the Philoteras Portus of Ptolemy.
The

THE SOURCE OF THE NILE. 193

The fact is, that neither one nor other is the port, both being considerably farther to the northward. Nay, more, the present town of Cosseir was no ancient port at all; old Cosseir was five or six miles to the northward. There can be no sort of doubt, that it was the Portus Albus, or the White Harbour; for we find the steep descent from Terfowey, and the marble mountains, called, to this day, the Accaba, which, in Arabic, signifies a steep ascent or descent, is placed here by Ptolemy with the same name, though in Greek that name has no signification. Again, Ptolemy places *Aias Mons, or the mountain Aias, just over Cosseir, and this mountain, by the same name, is found there at this day. And, upon this mountain, and the one next it, (both over the port) are two very remarkable chalky cliffs; which, being conspicuous and seen far at sea, have given the name of the White Port, which Cosseir bore in all antiquity.

I found, by many meridian altitudes of the sun, taken at the castle, that Cosseir is in lat. 26° 7' 51" north; and, by three observations of Jupiter's satellites, I found its longitude to be 34° 4' 15" east of the meridian of Greenwich.

The caravan from Syené arrived at this time, escorted by four hundred Ababdé, all upon camels, each armed with two short javelins. The manner of their riding was very whimsical; they had two small saddles on each camel, and sat back to back, which might be, in their practice, convenient enough; but I am sure, that, if they had been to fight with us, every ball would have killed two of them, what *their advantage* would have been, I know not.

---

* Ptolem. Geograph. lib. 4. p. 103.

THE whole town was in terror at the influx of so many barbarians, who knew no law whatever. They brought a thousand camels loaded with wheat to transport to Mecca. Every body shut their doors, and I among the rest, whilst the Bey sent to me to remove into the castle. But I had no fear, and resolved to make an experiment, after hearing these were people of *Nimmer*, whether I could trust them in the desert or not. However, I sent all my instruments, my money, and the best of my baggage, my medicines and memorandums, into a chamber in the castle: after the door was locked, and the key brought to me, the Bey ordered to nail up pieces of wood across it, and set a centinel to watch it all day, and two in the night.

I WAS next morning down at the port looking for shells in the sea, when a servant of mine came to me in apparent fright and hurry. He told me the Ababdé had found out that Abdel Gin, my Arab, was an *Atouni, their enemy*, and that they had either cut his throat, or were about to do it; but, by the fury with which they seized him, in his fight, he could not believe they would spare him a minute.

HE very providently brought me a horse, upon which I mounted immediately, seeing there was no time to be lost; and in the fishing-dress, in which I was, with a red turban about my head, I galloped as hard as the horse could carry me through the town. If I was alarmed myself, I did not fail to alarm many others. They all thought it was something behind, not any thing before me, that occasioned this speed. I only told my servant at passing, to send two of my people on horseback after me, and that the Bey would lend them horses.

I WAS

I was not got above a mile into the fands, when I began to reflect on the folly of the undertaking. I was going into the defert among a band of favages, whofe only trade was robbery and murder, where, in all probability, I fhould be as ill treated as the man I was attempting to fave. But, feeing a crowd of people about half a mile before me, and thinking they might be at that time murdering that poor, honeft, and fimple fellow, all confideration of my own fafety for the time vanifhed.

Upon my coming near them, fix or eight of them furrounded me on horfeback, and began to gabble in their own language. I was not very fond of my fituation. It would have coft them nothing to have thruft a lance through my back, and taken the horfe away; and, after ftripping me, to have buried me in a hillock of fand, if they were fo kind as give themfelves that laft trouble. However, I picked up courage, and putting on the beft appearance I could, faid to them fteadily, without trepidation, "What men are thefe before?" The anfwer, after fome paufe, was, *they are men;* and they looked very queerly, as if they meant to afk each other, What fort of a fpark is this? "Are thofe before us Ababdé, faid I; are they from Shekh Ammer?" One of them nodded, and grunted fullenly, rather than faid "Aye, Ababdé from Shekh Ammer." "Then Salam Alicum! faid I, we are brethren. How does the Nimmer? Who commands you here? Where is Ibrahim?

At the mention of Nimmer, and Ibrahim, their countenance changed, not to any thing fweeter or gentler than before, but to a look of great furprife. They had not returned my falutation, *peace be between us;* but one of them afked me who I was?—"Tell me firſt, ſaid I, who that is you have before?"—"It is an Arab, our enemy, ſays he, guilty of our blood."—"He is, replied I, my ſervant. He is a Howadat Arab, his tribe lives in peace at the gates of Cairo, in the ſame manner your's at Shekh Ammer does at thoſe of Aſſouan." "I aſk you, Where is Ibrahim your Shekh's ſon?"— "Ibrahim, ſays he, is at our head, he commands us here. But who are you?"—"Come with me, and ſhew me Ibrahim, ſaid I, and I will ſhew you who I am."

I PASSED by theſe, and by another party of them. They had thrown a hair rope about the neck of Abdel Gin, who was almoſt ſtrangled already, and cried out moſt miſerably, for me not to leave him. I went directly to the black tent which I ſaw had a long ſpear thruſt up in the end of it, and met at the door Ibrahim and his brother, and ſeven or eight Ababdé. He did not recollect me, but I diſmounted cloſe to the tent-door, and had ſcarce taken hold of the pillar of the tent, and ſaid *Fiarduc**, when Ibrahim, and his brother both knew me "What! ſaid they, are you *Yagoube* our phyſician, and our friend?"—"Let me aſk you, replied I, if you are the Ababdé of Shekh Ammer, that curſed yourſelves, and your children, if you ever lifted a hand againſt me, or mine, in the deſert, or in the plowed field: If you have repented of that oath, or ſworn falſely on purpoſe to deceive me, here I am come to you in the *deſert*." "What is the matter, ſays Ibrahim, we are the Ababdé of Shekh Ammer, there are no other, and we ſtill ſay, Curſed be he, whether

---

* That is, I am under your protection.

ther our father, or children, that lifts his hand againſt you, in the deſert, or in the plowed field." " Then, ſaid I, you are all accurſed in the deſert, and in the field, for a number of your people are going to murder my ſervant. They took him indeed from my houſe *in the town*, perhaps that is not included in your curſe, as it is neither in the *deſert* nor the *plowed field*."—I was very angry. "Whew! ſays Ibrahim with a kind of whiſtle, that is downright nonſenſe. Who are thoſe of my people that have authority to murder, and take priſoners while I am here? Here one of you, get upon Yagoube's horſe, and bring that man to me." Then turning to me, he deſired I would go into the tent and ſit down: " For God renounce me and mine, (ſays he), if it is " as you ſay, and one of them hath touched the hair of his " head, if ever *he* drinks of the Nile again."

A NUMBER of people who had ſeen me at Shekh Ammer, now came all around me; ſome with complaints of ſickneſs, ſome with compliments; more with impertinent queſtions, that had no relation to either. At laſt came in the culprit Abdel Gin, with forty or fifty of the Ababdé who had gathered round him, but no rope about his neck. There began a violent altercation between Ibrahim, and his men, in their own language. All that I could gueſs was, that the men had the worſt of it; for every one preſent ſaid ſomething harſh to them, as diſapproving the action.

I HEARD the name of Haſſan Sidi Haſſan often in the diſpute. I began to ſuſpect ſomething, and deſired in Arabic to know what that Sidi Haſſan was, ſo often mentioned in diſcourſe, and then the whole ſecret came out.

THE

The reader will remember, that this Arab, Abdel Gin, was the perfon that feized the fervant of Haffan, the Captain of the Caravan, when he was attempting to fteal the Turk's portmanteau out of my tent; that my people had beat him till he lay upon the ground like dead, and that Huffein Bey, at the complaint of the Caramaniots, had ordered him to be hanged. Now, in order to revenge this, Haffan had told the Ababdé that Abdel Gin was an Atouni fpy, that he had detected him in the Caravan, and that he was come to learn the number of the Ababdé, in order to bring his companions to furprife them. He did not fay one word that he was my fervant, nor that I was at Coffeir; fo the people thought they had a very meritorious facrifice to make, in the perfon of poor Abdel Gin

ALL paffed now in kindnefs, frefh medicines were afked for the Nimmer, great thankfulnefs, and profeffions, for what they had received, and a prodigious quantity of meat on wooden platters very excellently dreffed, and moft agreeably diluted with frefh water, from the coldeft rock of Terfowey, was fet before me.

IN the mean time, two of my fervants, attended by three of Huffein Bey, came in great anxiety to know what was the matter; and, as neither they nor the Arabs chofe much each others company, I fent them with a fhort account of the whole to the Bey; and foon after took my leave, carrying Abdel Gin along with me, who had been clothed by Ibrahim from head to foot. We were accompanied by two Ababdé, in cafe of accident.

I CANNOT

THE SOURCE OF THE NILE.

I cannot help here accusing myself of what, doubtless, may be well reputed a very great sin. I was so enraged at the traitorous part which Haffan had acted, that, at parting, I could not help saying to Ibrahim, "Now, Shekh, I have done every thing you have desired, without ever expecting fee, or reward; the only thing I now ask you, and it is probably the last, is, that you revenge me upon this Haffan, who is every day in your power." Upon this, he gave me his hand, saying, "He shall not die in his bed, or I shall never see old age."

We now returned all in great spirits to Coffeir, and I observed that my unexpected connection with the Ababdé had given me an influence in that place, that put me above all fear of personal danger, especially as they had seen in the desert, that the Atouni were my friends also, as reclaiming this Arab shewed they really were.

The Bey insisted on my supping with him. At his desire I told him the whole story, at which he seemed to be much surprised, saying, several times, "Menullah! Menullah! Mucktoub!" It is God's doing, it is God's doing, it was written so. And, when I had finished, he said to me, "I will not leave this traitor with you to trouble you further; I will oblige him, as it is his duty, to attend me to Furshout." This he accordingly did; and, to my very great surprise, though he might be assured I had complained of him to Shekh Hamam, meeting me the next day, when they were all ready to depart, and were drinking coffee with the Bey, he gave me a slip of paper, and desired me, by that direction, to buy him a sabre, which might be procured in Mecca. It seems it is the manufacture of Persia, and, though I do not understand in the leaft, the import of the terms, I give it to the reader that he may know by what defcription he is to buy an excellent fabre. It is called Suggaro Tabanne Harefanne A-gemmi, *for Sidi Haffan of Furfhout.*

ALTHOUGH pretty much ufed to ftifle my refentment upon impertinences of this kind, I could not, after the trick he had played me with the Ababdé, carry it indifferently; I threw the billet before the Bey, faying to Haffan, "A fword of that value would be ufelefs and mifemployed in the hand of a coward and a traitor, fuch as furely you muft be fenfible I know you to be." He looked to the Bey as if appealing to him, from the incivility of the obfervation; but the Bey, without fcruple, anfwered, " It is true, it is true what he fays, Haffan; if I was in Ali Bey's place, when you dared ufe a ftranger of mine, or any ftranger, as you have done him, I would plant you upon a fharp ftake in the marketplace, till the boys in the town ftoned you to death; but he has complained of you in a letter, and I will be a witnefs againft you before Hamam, for your conduct is not that of a *Muffulman*."

WHILE I was engaged with the Ababdé, a veffel was feen in diftrefs in the offing, and all the boats went out and towed her in. It was the veffel in which the twenty-five Turks had embarked, which had been heavily loaded. Nothing is fo dreadful as the embarkation in that fea; for the boats have no decks; the whole, from ftern to ftem, being filled choak-full of wheat, the wafte, that is the flope of the veffel, between the height of her ftem and ftern, is filled up by one plank on each fide, which is all that is above the furface of the waves. Sacks, tarpaulins, or mats, are ftrowed along the furface of the wheat upon which all the paffengers lye. On the leaft agitation of the waves, the fea getting in upon the wheat, increafes its weight fo prodigioufly, that, falling below the level of the gunnel, the water rufhes in between the plank and that part of the veffel, and down it goes to the bottom.

Though every day produces an accident of this kind from the fame caufe, yet fuch is the defire of gaining money in that feafon, which offers but once a-year, that every fhip fails, loaded in the fame manner as the laft which perifhed. This was juft the cafe with the veffel that had carried the Turks. Anxious to go away, they would not wait the figns of the weather being rightly fettled. *Ullah Kerim!* they cry, ' God is great and is merciful'; and upon that they embark in a navigation, where it needs indeed a miracle to fave them.

The Turks all came afhore but one; the youngeft, and, according to all appearance, the beft, had fallen over board, and perifhed. The Bey received them, and with great charity entertained them all at his own expence, but they were fo terrified with the fea, as almoft to refolve never to make another attempt.

The Bey had brought with him from Jidda, a fmall, but tight veffel belonging to * Sheher; which came from that country loaded with frankincenfe, the commodity of that port.

---

* On the eaft coaft of Arabia Felix, Syagrum Promontorium.

port. The Rais had bufinefs down the Gulf at Tor, and he had fpoken to the Bey, to recommend him to me. I had no bufinefs at Tor, but as we had grown into a kind of friendſhip, from frequent converfation, and as he was, according to his own word, a great faint, like my laſt boatman, a character that I thought I could perfectly manage, I propofed to the Bey, that he and I ſhould contribute fomething to make it worth this Captain's pains, to take our friends the Turks on board, and carry them to Yambo, that they might not be deprived of that bleſſing which would refult from their vifit to the Prophet's tomb, and which they had toiled fo much to earn. I promifed, in that cafe, to hire his veſſel at fo much a month upon its return from Yambo; and, as I had then formed a refolution of making a furvey of the Red Sea to the Straits of Babelmandeb, the Rais was to take his directions from me, till I pleafed to difmifs him.

NOTHING was more agreeable to the views of all parties than this. The Bey promifed to ſtay till they failed, and I engaged to take him after he returned; and as the captain, in quality of a faint, aſſured us, that any rock that ſtood in our way in the voyage, would either jump afide, or become foft like a fpunge, as it had often happened before, both the Turks and we were now aſſured of a voyage without danger.

ALL was fettled to our mutual fatisfaction, when, unluckily, the Turks going down to their boat, met Sidi Haſſan, whom, with reafon, they thought the author of all their misfortunes. The whole twenty-four drew their fwords, and, without feeking fabres from Perfia, as he had done,

they

they would have cut Sidi Haſſan in pieces, but, fortunately for him, the Turks had great cloth trowſers, like Dutchmen, and they could not run, whilſt he ran very nimbly in his. Several piſtols, however, were fired, one of which ſhot him in the back part of the ear; on which he fled for refuge to the Bey, and we never ſaw him more.

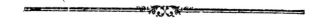

CHAP. IX.

Voyage to Jibbel Zumrud—Return to Coffeir—Sails from Coffeir—Jaffateen Iflands—Arrive at Tor.

THE Turks and the Bey departed, and with the Turks I difpatched my Arab, Abdel Gin, not only giving him fomething myfelf, but recommending him to my beneficent countrymen at Jidda, if he fhould go there.

I now took up my quarters in the caftle, and as the Ababdé had told ftrange ftories about the Mountain of Emeralds, I determined, till my captain fhould return, to make a voyage thither. There was no poffibility of knowing the diftance by report; fometimes it was twenty-five miles, fometimes it was fifty, fometimes it was a hundred, and God knows how much more.

I chose a man who had been twice at thefe mountains of emeralds; with the beft boat then in the harbour, and on Tuefday the 14th of March, we failed, with the wind at North Eaft, from the harbour of Coffeir, about an hour before the dawn of day. We kept coafting along, with a very moderate wind, much diverted with the red and green appearances

pearances of the marble mountains upon the coaſt. Our veſſel had one ſail, like a ſtraw mattreſs, made of the leaves of a kind of palm-tree, which they call *Doom*. It was fixed above, and drew up like a curtain, but did not lower with a yard like a ſail; ſo that upon ſtreſs of weather, if the ſail was furled, it was ſo top-heavy, that the ſhip muſt founder, or the maſt be carried away. But, by way of indemnification, the planks of the veſſel were ſewed together, and there was not a nail, nor a piece of iron, in the whole ſhip; ſo that, when you ſtruck upon a rock, ſeldom any damage enſued. For my own part, from an abſolute deteſtation of her whole conſtruction, I inſiſted upon keeping cloſe along ſhore, at an eaſy ſail.

The Continent, to the leeward of us, belonged to our friends the Ababdé. There was great plenty of ſhell-fiſh to be picked up on every ſhoal. I had loaded the veſſel with four ſkins of freſh water, equal to four hogſheads, with cords, and buoys fixed to the end of each of them, ſo that, if we had been ſhipwrecked near land, as rubbing two ſticks together made us fire, I was not afraid of receiving ſuccour, before we were driven to the laſt extremity, provided we did not periſh in the ſea, of which I was not very apprehenſive.

On the 15th, about nine o'clock, I ſaw a large high rock, like a pillar, riſing out of the ſea. At firſt, I took it for a part of the Continent; but, as we advanced nearer it, the ſun being very clear, and the ſea calm, I took an obſervation, and as our ſituation was lat. 25° 6', and the iſland about a league diſtant, to the S. S. W. of us, I concluded its latitude to be pretty exactly 25° 3' North. This iſland is about three miles from the shore, of an oval form, rising in the middle. It seems to me to be of granite; and is called, in the language of the country, Jibbel Siberget, which has been translated *the Mountain of Emeralds*. Siberget, however, is a word in the language of the *Shepherds*, who, I doubt, never in their lives saw an emerald; and though the Arabic translation is *Jibbel Zumrud*, and that word has been transferred to the emerald, a very fine stone, oftener seen since the discovery of the new world, yet I very much doubt, that either *Siberget* or *Zumrud* ever meant Emerald in old times. My reason is this, that we found, both here and in the Continent, splinters, and pieces of green pellucid chrystaline substance; yet, though green, they were veiny, clouded, and not at all so hard as rock-crystal; a mineral production certainly, but a little harder than glass, and this, I apprehend, was what the *Shepherds*, or people of Beja, called *Siberget*, the Latins *Smaragdus*, and the Moors *Zumrud*.

The 16th, at day-break in the morning, I took the Arab of Cosseir with me, who knew the place. We landed on a point perfectly desert; at first, sandy like Cosseir, afterwards, where the soil was fixed, producing some few plants of rue or absinthium. We advanced above three miles farther in a perfectly desert country, with only a few acacia-trees scattered here and there, and came to the foot of the mountains. I asked my guide the name of that place; he said it was Saiel. They are never at a loss for a name, and those who do not understand the language, always believe them. This would have been the case in the present conjuncture. He knew not the name of the place, and perhaps it had no name, but he called it *Saiel*, which signifies a male acacia-tree; merely because he saw an acacia growing there; and, with

THE SOURCE OF THE NILE.

with equal reason, he might have called every mile Saiel, from the Gulf of Suez to the line.

We see this abuse in the old Itineraries, especially in the *Antonine, from such a town to such a town, so many miles; and what is the next station? *(el seggera)* ten miles. This el seggera †, the Latin readers take to be the name of a town, as Harduin, and all commentators on the classics, have done. But so far from Seggera signifying a town, it imports just the contrary, that there is no town there, but the traveller must be obliged to take up his quarters under a tree that night, for such is the meaning of Seggera as a station, and so likewise of Saiel.

At the foot of the mountain, or about seven yards up from the base of it, are five pits or shafts, none of them four feet in diameter, called the *Zumrud Wells*, from which the ancients are said to have drawn the emeralds. We were not provided with materials, and little endowed with inclination, to descend into any one of them, where the air was probably bad. I picked up the nozzels, and some fragments of lamps, like those of which we find millions in Italy: and some worn fragments, but very small ones, of that brittle green chrystal, which is the siberget and bilur of Ethiopia, perhaps the zumrud, the smaragdus described by Pliny, but by no means the emerald, known since the discovery of the new world, whose first character absolute-

ly

---

* Itin. Anton. a Caith. p. 4.
† So the next stage from Syené is called Hiera Sycaminos, a sycamore-tree, Ptol. lib. 4. p. 108.

ly defeats its pretenfion, the true Peruvian emerald being equal in hardnefs to the ruby.

Pliny* reckons up twelve kind of emeralds, and names them all by the country where they are found. Many have thought the fmaragdus to be but a finer kind of jafper. Pomet affures us it is a mineral, formed in iron, and fays he had one to which iron-ore was fticking. If this was the cafe, the fineft emeralds fhould not come from Peru, where, as far as ever has been yet difcovered, there is no iron.

With regard to the Oriental emeralds, which they fay come from the Eaft Indies, they are now fufficiently known, and the value of each ftone pretty well afcertained; but all our induftry and avarice have not yet difcovered a mine of emeralds there, as far as I have heard. That there were emeralds in the Eaft Indies, upon the firft difcovery of it by the Cape, there is no fort of doubt; that there came emeralds from that quarter in the time of the Romans, feems to admit of as little; but few antique emeralds have ever been feen; and fo greatly in efteem, and rare were they in thofe times, that it was made a crime for any artift to engrave upon an emerald †.

It is very natural to fuppofe, that fome people of the Eaft had a communication and trade with the new world, before we attempted to fhare it with them; and that the emeralds, they had brought from that quarter, were thofe which came afterwards

---

* Plin. lib. xxxvii. cap. 5.   † Ditto.

THE SOURCE OF THE NILE.

afterwards into Europe, and were called the *Oriental*, till they were confounded with the * Peruvian, by the quantity of that kind brought into the East Indies, by the Jews and Moors, after the discovery of the new Continent.

BUT what invincibly proves, that the ancients and we are not agreed as to the same stone, is, that † Theophrastus says, that in the Egyptian commentaries he saw mention made of an emerald four cubits, (six feet long,) which was sent as a present to one of their kings; and in one of the temples of Jupiter in Egypt he saw an obelisk 60 feet high, made of four emeralds: and Roderick of Toledo informs us, that, when the Saracens took that city, Tarik, their chief, had a table of an emerald 365 cubits, or $547\frac{1}{2}$ feet long. The Moorish histories of the invasion of Spain are full of such emeralds.

HAVING satisfied my curiosity as to these mountains, without having seen a living creature, I returned to my boat, where I found all well, and an excellent dinner of fish prepared. These were of three kinds, called Bisser, Surrumbac, and Nhoude el Benaat. The first of these seems to be of the Oyster-kind, but the shells are both equally curved and hollow, and open with a hinge on the side like a muffel. It has a large beard, like an oyster, which is not eatable, but which should be stript off. We found some of these two feet long, but the largest I believe ever seen composes the baptismal font in the church of Notre Dame in Paris‡. The second is the Concha Veneris, with large projecting points

---

* Tavernier vol. II. Voyag.   † Theophrastus Περιλιθων.   ‡ Clamps.

points like fingers. The third, called the Breasts of the Virgin, is a beautiful shell, perfectly pyramidal, generally about four inches in height, and beautifully variegated with mother-of-pearl, and green. All these fishes have a peppery taste, but are not therefore reckoned the less wholesome, and they are so much the more convenient, that they carry that ingredient of spice along with them for sauce, with which travellers, like me, very seldom burden themselves.

BESIDES a number of very fine shells, we picked up several branches of coral, coralines, yuffer*, and many other articles of natural history. We were abundantly provided with every thing; the weather was fair; and we never doubted it was to continue, so we were in great spirits, and only regretted that we had not, once for all, taken leave of Coffeir, and stood over for Jidda

IN this disposition we failed about three o'clock in the afternoon, and the wind flattered us so much, that next day, the 17th, about eleven o'clock, we found ourselves about two leagues a-stern of a small island, known to the Pilot by the name of Jibbel Macouar. This island is at least four miles from the shore, and is a high land, so that it may be seen, I suppose, eight leagues at sea, but is generally confounded with the Continent. I computed myself to be about 4′ of the meridian distant when I made the observation, and take its latitude to be about 24° 2′ on the centre of the island.

THE

---

* It is a Keratophyte, growing at the bottom of the sea.

The land here, after running from Jibbel Siberget to Macouar, in a direction nearly N. W. and S. E. turns round in shape of a large promontory, and changes its direction to N. E. and S. W. and ends in a small bay or inlet; so that, by fanciful people, it has been thought to resemble the nose of a man, and is called by the Arabs, *Ras el Anf*, the Cape of the Nose. The mountains, within land, are of a dusky burnt colour; broken into points, as if interfected by torrents.

The coasting vessels from Masuah and Suakem which are bound to Jidda, in the strength of the Summer monsoon, stand close in shore down the coast of Abyssinia, where they find a gentle steady east wind blowing all night, and a west wind very often during the day, if they are near enough the shore, for which purpose their vessels are built.

Besides this, the violent North-East monsoon raking in the direction of the Gulf, blows the water out of the Straits of Babelmandeb into the Indian Ocean, where, being accumulated, it presses itself backwards; and, unable to find way in the middle of the Channel, creeps up among the shallows on each coast of the Red Sea. However long the voyage from Masuah to Jibbel Macouar may seem, yet these gentle winds and favourable currents, if I may so call those in the sea, soon ran us down the length of that mountain.

A large vessel, however, does not dare to try this, whilst constantly among shoals, and close on a lee-shore; but those sewed together, and yielding without damage to the stress, slide over the banks of white coral, and even sometimes the rocks. Arrived at this island, they set their prow towards

the

the oppofite fhore, and crofs the Channel in one night, to the coaft of Arabia, being nearly before the wind. The track of this extraordinary navigation is marked upon* the map, and it is fo well verified, that no fhip-mafter need doubt it.

About three o'clock in the afternoon, with a favourable wind and fine weather, we continued along the coaft, with an eafy fail. We faw no appearance of any inhabitants; the mountains were broken and pointed, as before taking the direction of the coaft; advancing and receding as the fhore itfelf did. This coaft is a very bold one, nor was there in any of the iflands we had feen, fhoals or anchoring places, unlefs upon the rock itfelf; fo that, when we landed, we could run our boltfprit home over the land.

This ifland, Jibbel Macouar, has breakers running off from it at all points; but, though we hauled clofe to thefe, we had no foundings. We then went betwixt it and the fmall ifland, that lies S. S. E. from it about three miles, and tried for foundings to the leeward, but we had none, although almoft touching the land. About fun-fet, I faw a fmall fandy ifland, which we left about a league to the weftward of us. It had no fhrubs, nor trees, nor height, that could diftinguifh it. My defign was to pufh on to the river Frat, which is reprefented in the charts as very large and deep, coming from the Continent; though, confidering by its latitude that it is above the tropical rains, (for it is laid down

---

* Vide the track of this Navigation laid down on the Chart.

down about lat. 21° 25′), I never did believe that any fuch river exifted.

In fact, we know no river, north of the fources of the Nile, that does not fall into the Nile. Nay, I may fay, that not one river, in all Abyffinia, empties itfelf into the Red Sea. The tropical rains are bounded, and finifh, in lat. 16°, and there is no river, from the mountains, that falls into the defert of Nubia; nor do we know of any river which is tributary to the Nile, but what has its rife under the tropical rains. It would be a very fingular circumftance, then, that the Frat fhould rife in one of the dryeft places in the globe, that it fhould be a river at leaft equal to the Nile; and fhould maintain itfelf full in all feafons, which the Nile does not; laft of all, in a country where water is fo fcarce and precious, that it fhould not have a town or fettlement upon it, either ancient or modern, nor that it fhould be reforted to by any encampment of Arabs, who might crofs over and traffic with Jidda, which place is immediately oppofite.

On the 18th, at day-break, I was alarmed at feeing no land, as I had no fort of confidence in the fkill of my pilot, however fure I was of my latitude. About an hour after fun-fet, I obferved a high rugged rock, which the pilot told me, upon inquiry, was Jibbel, (viz. a *Rock)*, and this was all the fatisfaction I could get. We bore down upon it with a wind, fcant enough; and, about four, we came to an anchor. As we had no name for that ifland, and I did not know that any traveller had been there before me, I ufed the privilege by giving it my own, in memory of having been there. The fouth of this ifland feems to be high and rocky,

rocky, the north is low and ends in a tail, or sloping bank, but is exceedingly steep to, and at the length of your bark any way from it, you have no foundings.

All this morning since before day, our pilot had begged us to go no farther. He said the wind had changed; that, by infallible signs he had seen to the southward, he was confident (without any chance of being mistaken) that in twenty-four hours we should have a storm, which would put us in danger of shipwreck; that Frat, which I wanted to see, was immediately opposite to Jidda, so that either a country, or English boat would run me over in a night and a day, when I might procure people who had connections in the country, so as to be under no apprehension of any accident; but that, in the present track I was going, every man that I should meet was my enemy. Although not very susceptible of fear, my ears were never shut against reason, and to what the pilot stated, I added in my own breast, that we might be blown out to sea, and want both water and provision. We, therefore, dined as quickly as possible, and encouraged one another all we could. A little safter six the wind came easterly, and changeable, with a thick haze over the land. This cleared about nine in the evening, and one of the finest and steadiest gales that ever blew, carried us swiftly on, directly for Cosseir. The sky was full of dappled clouds, so that, though I, several times, tried to catch a star in the meridian, I was always frustrated. The wind became fresher, but still very fair.

The 19th, at day-break, we saw the land stretching all the way northward, and, soon after, distinctly discerned
Jibbel

Jibbel Siberget upon our lee-bow. We had seen it indeed before, but had taken it for the main-land.

AFTER passing such an agreeable night, we could not be quiet, and laughed at our pilot about his perfect knowledge of the weather. The fellow shook his head, and said, he had been mistaken before now, and was always glad when it happened so; but still we were not arrived at Cosseir, though he hoped and believed we should get there in safety. In a very little time the vane on the mast-head began to turn, first north, then east, then south, and back again to all the points in the compass; the sky was quite dark, with thick rain to the southward of us; then followed a most violent clap of thunder, but no lightning; and back again came the wind fair at south-east. We all looked rather downcast at each other, and a general silence followed. This, however, I saw availed us nothing, we were in the scrape, and were to endeavour to get out of it the best way we could. The vessel went at a prodigious rate. The sail that was made of mat happened to be new, and, filled with a strong wind, weighed prodigiously. What made this worse, was, the masts were placed a little forward. The first thing I asked, was, if the pilot could not lower his main-sail? But that we found impossible, the yard being fixed to the mast-head. The next step was to reef it, by hauling it in part up like a curtain: this our pilot desired us not to attempt; for it would endanger our foundering. Notwithstanding which, I desired my servant to help me with the haulyards; and to hold them in his hand, only giving them a turn round the bench. This increasing the vessel's weight above and before, as she already had too much pressure, made her give

two

two pitches, the one after the other, so that I thought she was buried under the waves, and a considerable deal of water came in upon us. I am fully satisfied, had she not been in good order, very buoyant, and in her trim, she would have gone to the bottom, as the wind continued to blow a hurricane.

I began now to throw off my upper coat and trowsers, that I might endeavour to make shore, if the vessel should founder, whilst the servants seemed to have given themselves up, and made no preparation. The pilot kept in close by the land, to see if no bight, or inlet, offered to bring up in; but we were going with such violence, that I was satisfied we should overset if we attempted this. Every ten minutes we ran over the white coral banks, which we broke in pieces with the grating of a file, upon iron, and, what was the most terrible of all, a large wave followed higher than our stern, curling over it, and seemed to be the instrument destined by Providence to bury us in the abyss.

Our pilot began apparently to lose his understanding with fright. I begged him to be steady, persuading him to take a glass of spirits, and desired him not to dispute or doubt any thing that I should do or order, for that I had seen much more terrible nights in the ocean; I assured him, that all harm done to his vessel should be repaired when we should get to Cosseir, or even a new one bought for him, if his own was much damaged. He answered me nothing, but that *Mahomet was the prophet of God.*—Let him prophecy, said I, as long as he pleases, but what I order you is to keep steady to the helm; mind the vane on the top of the mast, and steer straight before the wind, for I am resolved to cut that main-fail to pieces, and prevent the maft from going a-way, and your veffel from finking to the bottom. I got no anfwer to this which I could hear, the wind was fo high, except fomething about the mercy and the merit of Sidi Ali el Genowi. I now became violently angry. "D—n Sidi Ali el Genowi, faid I, you beaft, cannot you give me a rational anfwer? Stand to your helm, look at the vane; keep the veffel ftraight before the wind, or, by the great G—d who fits in heaven, (another kind of oath than by *Sidi Ali el Genowi*), I will fhoot you dead the firft yaw the fhip gives, or the firft time that you leave the fteerage where you are ftanding." He anfwered only, Maloom, *i. e.* very well.—All this was fooner done than faid; I got the main-fail in my arms, and, with a large knife, cut it all to fhreds, which eafed the veffel greatly, though we were ftill going at a prodigious rate.

About two o'clock the wind feemed to fail, but, half an hour after, was more violent than ever. At three, it fell calm. I then encouraged my pilot, who had been very attentive, and, I believe, had pretty well got through the whole lift of faints in his calendar, and I affured him that he fhould receive ample reparation for the lofs of his mainfail. We now faw diftinctly the white cliffs of the two mountains above Old Coffeir, and on the 19th, a little before fun fet, we arrived fafely at the New.

We, afterwards, heard how much more fortunate we had been than fome of our fellow-failors that fame night; three of the veffels belonging to Coffeir, loaded with wheat for Yambo, perifhed, with all on board of them, in the gale; among thefe was the veffel that firft had the Turks on board.

This account was brought by Sidi Ali el Meymoum el Shehrie, which fignifies ' Ali, the ape or monkey, from Sheher.' For though he was a faint, yet being in figure liker to a monkey, they thought it proper to diftinguifh him by that to which he bore the greateft refemblance.

We were all heartily fick of Coffeir embarkations, but the veffel of Sidi Ali el Meymoum, tho' fmall, was tight and well-rigged; had fails of canvas, and had navigated in the Indian Ocean; the Rais had four ftout men on board, apparently good failors; he himfelf, though near fixty, was a very active, vigorous little man, and to the full as good a failor as he was a faint. It was on the 5th of April, after having made my laft obfervation of longitude at Coffeir, that I embarked on board this veffel, and failed from that port. It was neceffary to conceal from fome of my fervants our intention of proceeding to the bottom of the Gulf, leaft, finding themfelves among Chriftians fo near Cairo, they might defert a voyage of which they were fick, before it was well begun.

For the firft two days we had hazy weather, with little wind. In the evening, the wind fell calm. We faw a high land to the fouth-weft of us, very rugged and broken, which feemed parallel to the coaft, and higher in the middle than at either end. This, we conceived, was the mountain that divides the coaft of the Red Sea from the eaftern part of the Valley of Egypt, correfponding to Monfalout and Siout. We brought to, in the night, behind a fmall low Cape, tho' the wind was fair, our Rais being afraid of the Jaffateen Iflands, which we knew were not far a-head.

THE SOURCE OF THE NILE.

We caught a great quantity of fine fish this night with a line, some of them weighing 14 pounds. The best were blue in the back, like a salmon, but their belly red, and marked with blue round spots. They resembled a salmon in shape, but the fish was white, and not so firm.

In the morning of the 6th we made the Jaffateen Islands. They are four in number, joined by shoals and sunken rocks. They are crooked, or bent, like half a bow, and are dangerous for ships sailing in the night, because there seems to be a passage between them, to which, when pilots are attending, they neglect two small dangerous sunk rocks, that lie almost in the middle of the entrance, in deep water.

I understood, afterwards, from the Rais, that, had it not been from some marks he saw of blowing weather, he would not have come in to the Jaffateen Islands, but stood directly for Tor, running between the island Sheduan, and a rock which is in the middle of the channel, after you pass Ras Mahomet. But we lay so perfectly quiet, the whole night, that we could not but be grateful to the Rais for his care, although we had seen no apparent reason for it.

Next morning, the 7th, we left our very quiet birth in the bay, and stood close, nearly south-east, along-side of the two southermost Jaffateen Islands, our head upon the center of Sheduan, till we had cleared the eastermost of those islands about three miles. We then passed Sheduan, leaving it to the eastward about three leagues, and keeping nearly a N. N. W. course, to range the west side of Jibbel Zeit. This is a large desert island, or rock, that is about four miles from the main.

The paffage between them is practicable by fmall craft only, whofe planks are fewed together, and are not affected by a ftroke upon hard ground; for it is not for want of water that this navigation is dangerous. All the weft coaft is very bold, and has more depth of water than the eaft; but on this fide there is no anchoring ground, nor fhoals. It is a rocky fhore, and there is depth of water every where, yet that part is full of funken rocks; which, though not vifible, are near enough the furface to take up a large fhip, whofe deftruction thereupon becomes inevitable. This I prefume arifes from one caufe. The mountains on the fide of Egypt and Abyffinia are all (as we have ftated) hard ftone, Porphyry, Granite, Alabafter, Bafaltes, and many forts of Marble. Thefe are all therefore fixed, and even to the northward of lat 16°, where there is no rain, very fmail quantities of duft or fand can ever be blown from them into the fea. On the oppofite, or Arabian fide, the feacoaft of the Hejaz, and that of the Tehama, are all moving fands; and the dry winter-monfoon from the fouth-eaft blows a large quantity from the deferts, which is lodged among the rocks on the Arabian fide of the Gulf, and confined there by the north-caft or fummer-monfoon, which is in a contrary direction, and hinders them from coming over, or circulating towards the Egyptian fide.

From this it happens, that the weft, or Abyffinian fide, is full of deep water, interfperfed with funken rocks, unmafked, or uncovered with fand, with which they would otherwife become iflands. Thefe are naked and bare all round, and fharp like points of fpears; while on the eaft-fide there are rocks, indeed, as in the other, but being between the fouth-caft monfoon, which drives the fand into its coaft, and the

north-weft

north-west monsoon which repels it, and keeps it in there, every rock on the Arabian shore becomes an *sland*, and every two or three islands become a harbour.

Upon the ends of the principal of these harbours large heaps of stones have been piled up, to serve as signals, or marks, how to enter; and it is in these that the large vessels from Cairo to Jidda, equal in size to our 74 gun ships, (but from the cisterns of mason-work built within for holding water, I suppose double their weight) after navigating their portion of the channel in the day, come safely and quietly to, at four o'clock in the afternoon, and in these little harbours pass the night, to sail into the channel again, next morning at sun-rise.

Therefore, though in the track of my voyage to Tor, I am seen running from the west side of Jibbel Zeit a W. N. W. course (for I had no place for a compass) into the harbour of Tor, I do not mean to do so bad a service to humanity as to persuade large ships to follow my track. There are two ways of instructing men usefully, in things absolutely unknown to them. The first is, to teach them what they can do safely. The next is, to teach them what they cannot do at all, or, warranted by a pressing occasion, attempt with more or less danger, which should be explained and placed before their eyes, for without this last no man knows the extent of his own powers. With this view, I will venture, without fear of contradiction, to say, that my course from Cosseir, or even from Jibbel Siberget, to Tor, is impossible to a great ship. My voyage, painful, full of care, and dangerous as it was, is not to be accounted a surety for the lives of thousands. It may be regarded as a foundation for surveys hereafter to be made by persons more capable, and better

protected;

protected; and in this case will, I hope, be found a valuable fragment, because, whatever have been my conscientious fears of running servants, who work for pay, into danger of losing their lives by peril of the sea, yet I can safely say, that never did the face of man, or fear of danger to myself, deter me from verifying with my eyes, what my own hands have put upon paper.

In the days of the Ptolemies, and, as I shall shew, long before, the west coast of the Red Sea, where the deepest water, and most dangerous rocks are, was the track which the Indian and African ships chose, when loaded with the richest merchandise that ever vessels since carried. The Ptolemies built a number of large cities on this coast; nor do we hear that ships were obliged to abandon that track, from the disasters that befel them in the navigation. On the contrary, they avoided the coast of Arabia; and one reason, among others, is plain why they should;—they were loaded with the most valuable commodities, gold, ivory, gums, and precious stones; room for stowage on board therefore was very valuable.

Part of this trade, when at its greatest perfection, was carried on in vessels with oars. We know from the prophet Ezekiel*, 700 years before Christ, or 300 after Solomon had finished his trade with Africa and India, that they did not always make use of sails in the track of the monsoons; and consequently a great number of men must have been necessary

---

* Ezek. chap. xxvii. 6th and 29th verses.

fary for fo tedious a voyage. A number of men being necessary, a quantity of water was equally so; and this must have taken up a great deal of stowage. Now, no where on the coast of Abyssinia could they want water two days; and scarce any where, on the coast of Arabia, could they be sure of it once in fifteen, and from this the western coast was called *Ber el Ajam**, corruptly Azamia, *the country of water*, in opposition to the eastern shore, called *Ber il Arab*, where there was none.

A DELIBERATE survey became absolutely necessary, and as in proportion to the danger of the coast pilots became more skilful, when once they had obtained more complete knowledge of the rocks and dangers, they preferred the boldest shore, because they could stand on all night, and provide themselves with water every day. Whereas, on the Arabian side, they could not sail but half the day, would be obliged to lie to all night, and to load themselves with water, equal to half their cargo.

I NOW shall undertake to point out to large ships, the way by which they can safely enter the Gulf of Suez, so as that they may be competent judges of their own course, in case of accident, without implicitly surrendering themselves, and property, into the hands of pilots.

IN the first place, then, I am very confident, that, taking their departure from Jibbel el Ourée, ships may safely stand

on

---

* Ajan, in the language of Shepherds, signifies *rain-water*.

on all night mid-channel, until they are in the latitude of Yambo.

The Red Sea may be divided into four parts, of which the Channel occupies two, till about lat. 26°, or nearly that of Coffeir. On the weft fide it is deep water, with many rocks, as I have already faid. On the eaft fide, that quarter is occupied by iflands, that is, fand gathered about the rocks, the caufes whereof I have before mentioned; between which there are channels of very deep water, and harbours, that protect the largeft fhips in any winds. But among thefe, from Mocha down to Suez, you muft fail with a pilot, and during part of the day only.

To a perfon ufed to more civilized countries, it appears no great hardfhip to fail with a pilot, if you can get one, and in the Red Sea there are plenty; but thefe are creatures without any fort of fcience, who decide upon a manœuvre in a moment, without forethought, or any warning given. Such pilots often, in a large fhip deeply loaded, with every fail out which fhe can carry, in a very inftant cry out to let go your anchors, and bring you to, all ftanding, in the face of a rock, or fand. Were not our feamen's vigour, and celerity in execution, infinitely beyond the fkill and forefight of thofe pilots, I believe very few fhips, coming the inward paffage among the iflands, would ever reach the port in fafety.

If you are, however, going to Suez, without the confent of the Sherriffe of Mecca, that is, not intending to fell your cargo at Jidda, or pay your cuftom there, then you fhould

take

take in your water at Mocha; or, if any reafon fhould hinder you from touching that fhore, a few hours will carry you to Azab, or Saba, on the Abyffinian coaft, whofe latitude I found to be 13° 5' north. It is not a port, but a very tolerable road, where you have very fafe riding, under the fhelter of a low defert ifland called Crab Ifland, with a few rocks at the end of it. But it muft be remembered, the people are *Galla*, the moft treacherous and villanous wretches upon the earth. They are *Shepherds*, who fometimes are on the coaft in great numbers, or in the back of the hills that run clofe along the fhore, or in miferable villages compofed of huts, that run nearly in an eaft and weft direction from Azab to Raheeta, the largeft of all their villages. You will there, at Azab, get plenty of water, fheep, and goats, as alfo fome myrrh and incenfe, if you are in the proper feafon, or will ftay for it.

I AGAIN repeat it, that no confidence is to be had in the people. Thofe of Mocha, who even are abfolutely neceffary to them in their commercial tranfactions, cannot truft them without furety or hoftages. And it was but a few years before I was there, the furgeon and mate of the Elgin Eaft-India man, with feveral other failors, were cut off, going on fhore with a letter of fafe conduct from their Shekh to purchafe myrrh. Thofe that were in the boat efcaped, but moft of them were wounded. A fhip, on its guard, does not fear banditti like thefe, and you will get plenty of water and provifion, though I am only fpeaking of it as a ftation of neceffity.

IF you are not afraid of being known, there is a low black ifland on the Arabian coaft called Camaran, it is in lat

lat. 15° 39′, and is diftinguifhed by a white houfe, or fortrefs, on the weft end of it, where you will procure excellent water, in greater plenty than at Azab; but no provifions, or only fuch as are very bad. If you fhould not wifh to be feen, however, on the coaft at all, among the chain of iflands that reaches almoft acrofs the Gulf from Loheia to Mafuah, there is one called Foofht, where there is good anchorage; it is laid down in my map in lat. 15° 59′ 43″ N. and long. 42° 27′ E. from actual obfervation taken upon the ifland. There is here a quantity of excellent water, with a faint or monk to take care of it, and keep the wells clean. This poor creature was fo terrified at feeing us come afhore with fire-arms, that he lay down upon his face on the fand; nor would he rife, or lift up his head, till the Rais had explained to me the caufe of his fear, and till, knowing I was not in any danger of furprife, I had fent my guns on board.

From this to Yambo there is no fafe watering place. Indeed if the river Frat were to be found, there is no need of any other watering place in the Gulf; but it is abfolutely neceffary to have a pilot on board before you make Ras Mahomet; becaufe, over the mountains of Auche, the Elanitic Gulf, and the Cape itfelf, there is often a great haze, which lafts for many days together, and many fhips are conftantly loft, by miftaking the Eaftern Bay, or Elanitic Gulf, for the entrance of the Gulf of Suez; the former has a reef of rocks nearly acrofs it.

After you have made Sheduan, a large ifland three leagues farther, in a direction nearly north and by weft, is a bare rock, which, according to their ufual carelefsnefs and indifference, they are not at the pains to call by any other name.

name but *Jibbel*, the rock, island, or mountain, in general. You should not come within three full leagues of that rock, but leave it at a distance to the westward. You will then see shoals, which form a pretty broad channel, where you have soundings from fifteen to thirty fathoms. And again, standing on directly upon Tor, you have two other oval sands with sunken rocks, in the channel, between which you are to steer. All your danger is here in sight, for you might go in the inside, or to the eastward, of the many small islands you see toward the shore; and there are the anchoring places of the Cairo vessels, which are marked with the black anchor in the draught. This is the course best known and practised by pilots for ships of all sizes. But by a draught of Mr Niebuhr, who went from Suez with Mahomet Rais Tobal, his track with that large ship was through the channels, till he arrived at the point, where Tor bore a little to the northward of east of him.

Tor may be known at a distance by two hills that stand near the water side, which, in clear weather, may be seen six leagues off. Just to the south-east of these is the town and harbour, where there are some palm-trees about the houses, the more remarkable, that they are the first you see on the coast. There is no danger in going into Tor harbour, the soundings in the way are clean and regular; and by giving the beacon a small birth on the larboard hand, you may haul in a little to the northward, and anchor in five or six fathom. The bottom of the bay is not a mile from the beacon, and about the same distance from the opposite shore. There is no sensible tide in the middle of the Gulf, but, by the sides, it runs full two knots an hour. At springs, it is high water at Tor nearly at twelve o'clock.

On the 9th we arrived at Tor, a small straggling village, with a convent of Greek Monks, belonging to Mount Sinai. Don John de Castro * took this town when it was walled, and fortified, soon after the discovery of the Indies by the Portuguese; it has never since been of any consideration. It serves now, only as a watering-place for ships going to, and from Suez. From this we have a distinct view of the points of the mountains Horeb and Sinai, which appear behind and above the others, their tops being often covered with snow in winter.

There are three things, (now I am at the north end of the Arabian Gulf,) of which the reader will expect some account, and I am heartily sorry to say, that I fear I shall be obliged to disappoint him in all, by the unsatisfactory relation I am forced to give

The first is, Whether the Red Sea is not higher than the Mediterranean, by several feet or inches? To this I answer, That the fact has been supposed to be so by antiquity, and alledged as a reason why Ptolemy's canal was made from the bottom of the Heroopolitic Gulf, rather than brought due north across the Isthmus of Suez; in which last case, it was feared it would submerge a great part of Asia Minor. But who has ever attempted to verify this by experiment? or who is capable of settling the difference of levels, amounting, as supposed, to some feet and inches, between two points 120 miles distant from each other, over a desert that has no settled surface, but is changing its height every day?

---

* Vide his Journal published by Abbé Vertot.

day? Befides, fince all feas are, in fact, but one, what is it that hinders the Indian Ocean to flow to its level? What is it that keeps the Indian Ocean up?

TILL this laft branch of the queftion is refolved, I fhall take it for granted that no fuch difference of level exifts, whatever Ptolemy's engineers might have pretended to him; becaufe, to fuppofe it fact, is to fuppofe the violation of one very material law of nature.

THE next thing I have to take notice of, for the fatisfaction of my reader, is, the way by which the children of Ifrael paffed the Red Sea at the time of their deliverance from the land of Egypt.

As fcripture teaches us, that this paffage, wherever it might be, was under the influence of a miraculous power, no particular circumftance of breadth, or depth, makes one place likelier than another. It is a matter of mere curiofity, and can only promote an illuftration of the fcripture, for which reafon, I do not decline the confideration of it.

I SHALL fuppofe, that my reader has been fufficiently convinced, by other authors, that the land of Gofhen, where the Ifraelites dwelt in Egypt, was that country lying eaft of the Nile, and not overflowed by it, bounded by the mountains of the Thebaid on the fouth, by the Nile and Mediterranean on the weft and north, and the Red Sea and defert of Arabia on the eaft. It was the Heliopolitan nome; its capital was *On*; from predilection of the letter O, common to the Hebrews, they called it Gofhen; but its proper name was *Gefhen*, the country of Grafs, or Pafturage; or of

the

the *Shepherds;* in oppofition to the reft of the land which was fown, after having been overflowed by the Nile.

THERE were three ways by which the children of Ifrael, flying from Pharaoh, could have entered Paleftine. The firft was by the fea-coaft by Gaza, Afkelon, and Joppa. This was the plaineft and neareft way; and, therefore, fitteft for people incumbered with kneading troughs, dough, cattle, and children. The fea-coaft was full of rich commercial cities, the mid-land was cultivated and fown with grain. The eaftern part, neareft the mountains, was full of cattle and fhepherds, as rich a country, and more powerful than the cities themfelves.

THIS narrow valley, between the mountains and the fea, ran all along the eaftern fhore of the Mediterranean, from Gaza northward, comprehending the low part of Paleftine and Syria. Now, here a fmall number of men might have paffed, under the laws of hofpitality; nay, they did conftantly pafs, it being the high road between Egypt, and Tyre, and Sidon. But the cafe was different with a multitude, fuch as fix hundred thoufand men having their cattle along with them. Thefe muft have occupied the whole land of the Philiftines, deftroyed all private property, and undoubtedly have occafioned fome revolution; and as they were not now intended to be put in poffeffion of the land of promife, the meafure of the iniquity of the nations being not yet full, God turned them afide from going that way, though the neareft, leaft they " fhould fee war*," that is,

---

* Gen. chap. xiii. ver. 17th.

is, leaft the people fhould rife againft them, and deftroy them.

THERE was another way which led fouth-weft, upon Beerfheba and Hebron, in the middle, between the Dead Sea and the Mediterranean. This was the direction in which Abraham, Lot, and Jacob, are fuppofed to have reached Egypt. But there was neither food nor water there to fuftain the Ifraelites. When Abraham and Lot returned out of Egypt, they were obliged to feparate by confent, becaufe Abraham faid to his brother, " The land will not bear us both * "

THE third way was ftraight eaft into Arabia, pretty much the road by which the Pilgrims go at this day to Mecca, and the caravans from Suez to Cairo. In this track they would have gone round by the mountains of Moab, eaft of the Dead Sea, and paffed Jordan in the plain oppofite to Jericho, as they did forty years afterwards. But it is plain from fcripture, that God's counfels were to make Pharaoh and his Egyptians an example of his vengeance; and, as none of thefe roads led to the fea, they did not anfwer the Divine intention.

ABOUT twelve leagues from the fea, there was a narrow road which turned to the right, between the mountains, through a valley called *Badeah*, where their courfe was nearly fouth-eaft; this valley ended in a pafs, between two confiderable mountains, called *Gewoube* on the fouth; and Jibbel Attakah on the north, and opened into the low ftripe of country

---

* Gen. chap. xiii. ver. 6th. Exod. chap. xiii. ver. 17th.

country which runs all along the Red Sea; and the Israelites were ordered to encamp at Pihahiroth, oppofite to Baal-zephon, between Migdol and that fea.

It will be neceffary to explain thefe names. *Badeah*, Dr Shaw interprets, *the Valley of the Miracle*, but this is forcing an etymology, for there was yet no miracle wrought, nor was there ever any in the valley. But *Badeah*, means *barren, bare*, and *uninhabited;* fuch as we may imagine a valley between ftony mountains, a defert valley. *Jibbel Attakah*, he tranflates alfo, *the Mountain of Deliverance*. But fo far were the Ifraelites from being delivered on their arrival at this mountain, that they were then in the greateft diftrefs and danger. *Attakah*, means, however, to *arrive* or *come up with*, either becaufe there they arrived within fight of the Red Sea; or, as I am rather inclined to think, this place took its name from the arrival of Pharaoh, or his coming in fight of the Ifraelites, when encamped between Migdol and the Red Sea.

Pihahiroth is the mouth of the valley, opening to the flat country and the fea, as I have already faid, fuch are called *Mouths;* in the Arabic, *Fum;* as I have obferved in my journey to Coffeir, where the opening of the valley is called Fum el Beder, *the mouth of Beder;* Fum el Terfowey, *the mouth of Terfowey*. Hhoreth, the flat country along the Red Sea, is fo called from *Hhor*, a narrow valley where torrents run, occafioned by fudden irregular fhowers. Such we have already defcribed on the eaft fide of the mountains, bordering upon that narrow flat country along the Red Sea, where temporary fhowers fall in great abundance, while none of them touch the weft fide of the mountains or valley of
Egypt.

Egypt. Pihahiroth then is the mouth of the valley Badeah; which opens to Hhoreth, the narrow ſtripe of land where ſhowers fall.

BAAL-ZEPHON, the God of the watch-tower, was, probably, ſome idol's temple, which ſerved for a ſignal-houſe upon the Cape which forms the north entrance of the bay oppolite to Jibbel Attakah, where there is ſtill a moſque, or ſaint's tomb. It was probably a light-houſe, for the direction of ſhips going to the bottom of the Gulf, to prevent miſtaking it for another foul bay, under the high land, where there is alſo a tomb of a ſaint called Abou Derage.

THE laſt rebuke God gave to Pharaoh, by ſlaying all the firſt-born, ſeems to have made a ſtrong impreſſion upon the Egyptians. Scripture ſays, that the people were now urgent with the Iſraelites to be gone, for they ſaid, " We be all dead men *." And we need not doubt, it was in order to keep up in their hearts a motive of reſentment, ſtrong enough to make them purſue the Iſraelites, that God cauſed the Iſraelites to borrow, and take away the jewels of the Egyptians; without ſome new cauſe of anger, the late terrible chaſtiſement might have deterred them. While, therefore, they journeyed eaſtward towards the deſert, the Egyptians had no motive to attack them, becauſe they went with permiſſion there to ſacrifice, and were on their return to reſtore them their moveables. But when the Iſraelites were obſerved turning to the ſouth, among the mountains, they were

---

* Exod. ch. xii. 33.

were then supposed to flee without a view of returning, because they had left the way of the desert; and therefore Pharaoh, that he might induce the Egyptians to follow them, tells them that the Israelites were now entangled among the mountains, and the wilderness behind them, which was really the case, when they encamped at Pihahiroth, before, or south of Baal-Zephon, between Migdol and the sea. Here, then, before Migdol, the sea was divided, and they passed over dry shod to the wilderness of Shur, which was immediately opposite to them; a space something less than four leagues, and so easily accomplished in one night, without any miraculous interposition.

Three days they were without water, which would bring them to Korondel, where is a spring of brackish, or bitter water, to this day, which probably were the *waters of Marah* *

The natives still call this part of the sea Bahar Kolzum, or the Sea of Destruction; and just opposite to Pihahiroth is a bay, where the North Cape is called Ras Musa, or the Cape of Moses, even now. These are the reasons why I believe the passage of the Israelites to have been in this direction. There is about fourteen fathom of water in the channel, and about nine in the sides, and good anchorage every where; the farthest side is a low sandy coast, and a very easy landing-place. The draught of the bottom of the Gulf given by Doctor Pococke is very erroneous, in every part of it.

It was proposed to Mr Niebuhr, when in Egypt, to inquire, upon the spot, Whether there were not some ridges
of

---

* Such is the tradition among the Natives.

of rocks, where the water was shallow, so that an army at particular times might pass over? Secondly, Whether the Etesian winds, which blow strongly all Summer from the north west, could not blow so violently against the sea, as to keep it back on a heap, so that the Israelites might have passed without a miracle? And a copy of these queries was left for me, to join my inquiries likewise.

But I must confess, however learned the gentlemen were who proposed these doubts, I did not think they merited any attention to solve them. This passage is told us, by scripture, to be a miraculous one; and, if so, we have nothing to do with natural causes. If we do not believe Moses, we need not believe the transaction at all, seeing that it is from his authority alone we derive it. If we believe in God that he made the sea, we must believe he could divide it when he sees proper reason, and of that he must be the only judge. It is no greater miracle to divide the Red Sea, than to divide the river of Jordan.

If the Etesian wind blowing from the north-west in summer, could heap up the sea as a wall, on the right, or to the south, of fifty feet high, still the difficulty would remain, of building the wall on the left hand, or to the north. Besides, water standing in that position for a day, must have lost the nature of fluid. Whence came that cohesion of particles, that hindered that wall to escape at the sides? This is as great a miracle as that of Moses. If the Etesian winds had done this once, they must have repeated it many a time before and since, from the same causes. Yet, * Diodorus

---

* Diod. Sic. Lib. 3. p. 122.

dorus Siculus fays, the Troglodytes, the indigenous inhabitants of that very fpot, had a tradition from father to fon, from their very earlieſt and remoteſt ages, that once this diviſion of the fea did happen there, and that after leaving its bottom fometimes dry, the fea again came back, and covered it with great fury. The words of this author are of the moſt remarkable kind. We cannot think this heathen is writing in favour of revelation. He knew not Mofes, nor fays a word about Pharaoh, and his hoſt; but records the miracle of the diviſion of the fea, in words nearly as ſtrong as thofe of Mofes, from the mouths of unbiaſſed, undefigning Pagans.

WERE all thefe difficulties furmounted, what could we do with the pillar of fire? The anfwer is, We ſhould not believe it. Why then believe the paſſage at all? We have no authority for the one, but what is for the other; it is altogether contrary to the ordinary nature of things, and if not a miracle, it muſt be a fable.

THE caufe of the feveral names of the Red Sea, is a fubject of more liberal inquiry. I am of opinion, that it certainly derived its name from Edom, long and early its powerful maſter, that word fignifying Red in Hebrew. It formerly went by the name of Sea of Edom, or Idumea; fince, by that of the Red Sea.

IT has been obferved, indeed, that not only the Arabian Gulf, but part of the Indian Ocean *, went by this name,
though

---

* Dionyſii Periegeſis, v. 38. et Comment. Euſtathii in eundem. Strabo, lib. xvi. p. 765. Agathemeri Geographia, lib. ii. cap. 11.

THE SOURCE OF THE NILE. 237

though far diftant from Idumea. This is true, but when we confider, as we fhall do in the courfe of this hiftory, that the mafters of that fea were ftill the Edomites, who went from the one fea directly in the fame voyage to the other, we fhall not difpute the propriety of extending the name to part of the Indian Ocean alfo. As for what fanciful people* have faid of any rednefs in the fea itfelf, or colour in the bottom, the reader may affure himfelf all this is fiction, the Red Sea being in colour nothing different from the Indian, or any other Ocean.

There is greater difficulty in affigning a reafon for the Hebrew name, Yam Suph; properly fo called, fay learned authors, from the quantity of weeds in it. But I muft confefs, in contradiction to this, that I never in my life, (and I have feen the whole extent of it) faw a weed of any fort in it; and, indeed, upon the flighteft confideration, it will occur to any one, that a narrow gulf, under the immediate influence of monfoons, blowing from contrary points fix months each year, would have too much agitation to produce fuch vegetables, feldom found, but in ftagnant waters, and feldomer, if ever, found in falt ones. My opinion then is, that it is from the † large trees, or plants of white coral, fpread every where over the bottom of the Red Sea, perfectly in imitation of plants on land, that the fea has obtained this name. If not, I fairly confefs I have not any other conjecture to make.

No

---

* *Jerome Lobo*, the greateft liar of the Jefuits, ch. iv. p. 46. Englifh tranflation.

† I faw one of thefe, which, from a root nearly central, threw out ramifications in a nearly circular form, meafuring twenty-fix feet diameter every way.

No sea, or shores, I believe, in the world, abound more in subjects of Natural History than the Red Sea. I suppose I have drawings and subjects of this kind, equal in bulk to the journal of the whole voyage itself. But the vast expence in engraving, as well as other considerations, will probably hinder for ever the perfection of this work in this particular.

CHAP.

CHAP. X.

Sail from Tor—Pass the Elanitic Gulf—See Raddua—Arrive at Yambo —Incidents there—Arrive at Jidda.

OUR Rais, having dispatched his business, was eager to depart; and, accordingly, on the 11th of April, at day-break, we stood out of the harbour of Tor. At first, we were becalmed in, at the point of the Bay south of Tor town, but the wind freshening about eight o'clock, we stood through the channels of the first four shoals, and then between a smaller one. We made the mouth of a small Bay, formed by Cape Mahomet, and a low sandy point to the east-ward of it. Our vessel seemed to be a capital one for sailing, and I did every thing in my power to keep our Rais in good humour.

About half a mile from the sandy point, we struck upon a coral bank, which, though it was not of any great consistence or solidity, did not fail to make our mast nod. As I was looking out forward when the vessel touched, and the Rais by me, I cried out in Arabic, " Get out of the way you dog!" the Rais, thinking my discourse directed to him, seemed very much surprised, and asked, " what I meant?" " Why

"Why did you not tell me, said I, when I hired you, that all the rocks in the sea would get out of the way of your vessel? This ill-mannered fellow here did not *know his duty*, he was sleeping I suppose, and has given us a hearty jolt, and I was abusing him for it, till you should chastise him some other way." He shook his head, and said, "Well! you do not believe, but God knows the truth; well now where is the rock? Why he is gone." However, very prudently, he anchored soon afterwards, though we had received no damage.

At night, by an observation of two stars in the meridian I concluded the latitude of Cape Mahomet to be 27° 54′, N. It must be understood of the mountain, or high land, which forms the Cape, not the low point. The ridge of rocks that run along behind Tor, bound that low sandy country, called the Desert of Sin, to the eastward, and end in this Cape, which is the high land observed at sea; but the lower part, or southermost extreme of the Cape, runs about three leagues off from the high land, and is so low, that it cannot be seen from deck above three leagues. It was called, by the ancients, Pharan Promontorium; not because there was a light-house * upon the end of it, (though this may have perhaps been the case, and a very necessary and proper situation it is) but from the Egyptian and Arabic word Farek †, which signifies to divide, as being the point, or high land that divides the Gulf of Suez from the Elanitic Gulf.

I WENT

---

* Anciently called Pharos.

† The Koran is, therefore, called *El Farkan*, or the Divider, or Distinguisher between true faith and heresy.

THE SOURCE OF THE NILE.

I went ashore here to gather shells, and shot a small animal among the rocks, called Daman Israel, or Israel's Lamb; I do not know why, for it has no resemblance to the sheep kind. I take it to be the saphan of the Hebrew Scripture, which we translate by the coney. I have given a drawing, and description of it, in its proper place *. I shot, likewise, several dozens of gooto, the least beautiful of the kind I had seen, being very small, and coloured like the back of a partridge, but very indifferent food.

The 12th, we sailed from Cape Mahomet, just as the sun appeared. We passed the island of Tyrone, in the mouth of the Elanitic Gulf, which divides it near equally into two; or, rather the north-west side is narrowest. The direction of the Gulf is nearly north and south. I judge it to be about six leagues over. Many of the Cairo ships are lost in mistaking the entry of the Elanitic for that of the Heroopolitic Gulf, or Gulf of Suez; for, from the island of Tyrone, which is not above two leagues from the Main, there runs a string of islands, which seem to make a semicircular bar across the entry from the point, where a ship, going with a south wind, would take its departure; and this range of islands ends in a shoal with sunken rocks, which reaches near five leagues from the Main. It is probable, that, upon these islands, the fleet of Rehoboam perished, when sailing for the expedition of Ophir †.

---

* See the article Ashkoko in the Appendix.   † 2 Chron. chap. xx. ver. 37th.

I take Tyrone to be the ifland of Safpirene of Ptolemy, though this geographer has erred a little, both in its latitude and longitude.

We paffed the fecond of thefe iflands, called Senaffer, about three leagues to the northward, fteering with a frefh gale at fouth-eaft, upon a triangular ifland that has three pointed eminences upon its fouth-fide. We paffed another fmall ifland which has no name, about the fame diftance as the former; and ranged along three black rocks, the fouth-weft of the ifland, called *Sufange el Bahar*, or the *Sea-Spunge*. As our veffel made fome water, and the wind had been very ftrong all the afternoon, the Rais wanted to bring up to the leeward of this ifland, or between this, and a cape of land called *Ras Selah*; but, not being able to find foundings here, he fet fail again, doubled the point, and came to anchor under the fouth cape of a fine bay, which is a ftation of the Emir Hadje, called *Kalaat el Moilah*, the Caftle, or Station of Water.

We had failed this day about twenty-one leagues; and, as we had very fair and fine weather, and were under no fort of concern whatever, I could not neglect attending to the difpofition of thefe iflands, in a very fplendid map lately publifhed. They are carried too far into the Gulf.

The 13th, the Rais having, in the night, remedied what was faulty in his veffel, fet fail about feven o'clock in the morning. We paffed a conical hill on the land, called Abou Jubbé, where is the fepulchre of a faint of that name. The mountains here are at a confiderable diftance; and nothing can be more defolate and bare than the coaft. In

the

the afternoon, we came to an anchor at a place called Kella Clarega, after having paffed an ifland called Jibbel Numan, about a league from the fhore. By the fide of this fhoal we caught a quantity of good fifh, and a great number alfo very beautiful, and perfectly unknown, but which, when roafted, fhrank away to nothing except fkin, and when boiled, diffolved into a kind of blueifh glue.

On the 14th, the wind was variable till near ten o'clock, after which it became a little fair. At twelve it was as favourable as we could wifh; it blew however but faintly. We paffed firft by one ifland furrounded by breakers, and then by three more, and anchored clofe to the fhore, at a place called Jibbel Shekh, or the Mountain of the Saint. Here I refolved to take a walk on fhore to ftretch my limbs, and fee if I could procure any game, to afford us fome variety of food. I had my gun loaded with ball, when a vaft flock of gooto got up before me, not five hundred yards from the fhore. As they lighted very near me, I lay down among the bent grafs, to draw the charge, and load with fmall fhot. While I was doing this, I faw two antelopes, which, by their manner of walking and feeding, did not feem to be frightened. I returned my balls into the gun, and refolved to be clofe among the bent, till they fhould appear before me.

I had been quiet for fome minutes, when I heard behind me fomething like a perfon breathing, on which I turned about, and, not without great furprife, and fome little fear, faw a man, ftanding juft over me. I ftarted up, while the man, who had a little ftick only in his hand, ran two or three fteps backwards, and then ftood. He was almoft perfectly

fectly naked: he had half a yard of coarse rag only wrapt round his middle, and a crooked knife stuck in it. I asked him who he was? He said he was an Arab belonging to Shekh Abd el Macaber. I then desired to know where his master was? He replied, he was at the hill a little above, with camels that were going to Yambo. He then, in his turn, asked who I was? I told him I was an Abyssinian slave of the Sherriffe of Mecca, was going to Cairo by sea, but wished much to speak to his master, if he would go and bring him. The savage went away with great willingness, and he no sooner disappeared, than I set out as quickly as possible to the boat, and we got her hauled out beyond the shoals, where we passed the night. We saw afterwards distinctly about fifty men, and three or four camels; the men made several signs to us, but we were perfectly content with the distance that was between us, and sought no more to kill antelopes in the neighbourhood of Sidi Abd el Macaber.

I would not have it imagined, that my case was absolutely desperate, even if I had been known as a Christian, and fallen into the hands of these Arabs, of Arabia Deserta, or Arabia Petrea, supposed to be the most barbarous people in the world, as indeed they probably are. Hospitality, and attention to one's word, seem in these countries to be in proportion to the degree in which the people are savage. A very easy method is known, and followed with constant success, by all the Christians trading to the Red Sea from Suez to Jidda, to save themselves if thrown on the coast of Arabia. Any man of consideration from any tribe among the Arabs, comes to Cairo, gives his name and designation to the Christian sailor, and receives a very small present, which is repeated

THE SOURCE OF THE NILE. 245

peated annually if he performs so often the voyage. And for this the Arab promises the Christian his protection, should he ever be so unfortunate as to be shipwrecked on their coast.

The Turks are very bad seamen, and lose many ships, the greatest part of the crew are therefore Christians; when a vessel strikes, or is ashore, the Turks are all massacred if they cannot make their way good by force; but the Christians present themselves to the Arab, crying *Fiarduc*, which means, 'we are under immediate protection.' If they are asked, who is their Gaffeer, or Arab, with whom they are in friendship? They answer, Mahomet Abdelcader is our Gaffeer, or any other. If he is not there, you are told he is absent so many days journey off, or any distance. This acquaintance or neighbour, then helps you, to save what you have from the wreck, and one of them with his lance draws a circle, large enough to hold you and yours. He then sticks his lance in the sand, bids you abide within that circle, and goes and brings your Gaffeer, with what camels you want, and this Gaffeer is obliged, by rules known only to themselves, to carry you for nothing, or very little, wherever you go, and to furnish you with provisions all the way. Within that circle you are as safe on the desert coast of Arabia, as in a citadel; there is no example or exception to the contrary that has ever yet been known. There are many Arabs, who, from situation, near dangerous shoals or places, where ships often perish (as between Ras Mahomet and Ras Selah, * Dar el Hamra, and some others) have perhaps fifty

or

---

* See the Map.

or a hundred Chriftians, who have been fo protected: So that when this Arab marries a daughter, he gives perhaps his revenue from four or five protected Chriftians, as part of his daughter's portion. I had, at that very time, a Gafeer, called Ibn Talil, an Arab of Harb tribe, and I fhould have been detained perhaps three days till he came from near Medina, and carried me (had I been fhipwrecked) to Yambo, where I was going.

On the 15th we came to an anchor at El Har*, where we faw high, craggy, and broken mountains, called the Mountains of Ruddua. Thefe abound with fprings of water; all fort of Arabian and African fruits grow here in perfection, and every kind of vegetable that they will take the pains to cultivate. It is the paradife of the people of Yambo; thofe of any fubftance have country houfes there; but, ftrange to tell, they ftay there but for a fhort time, and prefer the bare, dry, and burning fands about Yambo, to one of the fineft climates, and moft verdant pleafant countries, that exifts in the world. The people of the place have told me, that water freezes there in winter, and that there are fome of the inhabitants who have red hair, and blue eyes, a thing fcarcely ever feen but in the coldeft mountains in the Eaft.

The 16th, about ten o'clock, we paffed a mofque, or Shekh's tomb on the main land, on our left hand, called Kubbet Yambo, and before eleven we anchored in the mouth
of

---

* El Har fignifies extreme heat.

of the port in deep water. Yambo, corruptly called Imbo, is an ancient city, now dwindled to a paultry village. Ptolemy calls it Iambia Vicus, or the village Yambia; a proof it was of no great importance in his time. But after the conqueſt of Egypt under Sultan Selim, it became a valuable ſtation, for ſupplying their conqueſts in Arabia, with warlike ſtores, from Suez, and for the importation of wheat from Egypt to their garriſons, and the holy places of Mecca and Medina. On this account, a large caſtle was built there by Sinan Baſha; for the ancient Yambo of Ptolemy is not that which is called ſo at this day. It is ſix miles farther ſouth; and is called Yambo el Nachel, or, Yambo among the palm-trees,' a great quantity of ground being there covered with this ſort of plantation.

Yambo, in the language of the country, ſignifies a fountain or ſpring, a very copious one of excellent water being found there among the date trees, and it is one of the ſtations of the Emir Hadje in going to, and coming from Mecca. The advantage of the port, however, which the other has not, and the protection of the caſtle, have carried trading veſſels to the modern Yambo, where there is no water, but what is brought from pools dug on purpoſe to receive the rain when it falls.

There are two hundred janiſſaries in the caſtle, the deſcendents of thoſe brought thither by Sinan Baſha; who have ſucceeded their fathers, in the way I have obſerved they did at Syené, and, indeed, in all the conqueſts in Arabia, and Egypt. The inhabitants of Yambo are deſervedly reckoned

oned * the moſt barbarous of any upon the Red Sea, and the janiſſaries keep pace with them, in every kind of malice and violence. We did not go aſhore all that day, becauſe we had heard a number of ſhots, and had received intelligence from ſhore, that the janiſſaries and town's people, for a week, had been fighting together; I was very unwilling to interfere, wiſhing that they might have all leiſure to extirpate one another, if poſſible; and my Rais ſeemed moſt heartily to join me in my wiſhes

In the evening, the captain of the port came on board, and brought two janiſſaries with him, whom, with ſome difficulty, I ſuffered to enter the veſſel. Their firſt demand was gun-powder, which I poſitively refuſed. I then aſked them how many were killed in the eight days they had been engaged? They anſwered, with ſome indifference, not many, about a hundred every day, or a few leſs or more, chiefly Arabs. We heard afterwards, when we came on ſhore, one only had been wounded, and that a ſoldier, by a fall from his horſe. They inſiſted upon bringing the veſſel into the port; but I told them, on the contrary, that having no buſineſs at Yambo, and being by no means under the guns of their caſtle, I was at liberty to put to ſea without coming aſhore at all; therefore, if they did not leave us, as the wind was favourable, I would ſail, and, by force, carry them to Jidda. The janiſſaries began to talk, as their cuſtom is, in a very bluſtering and warlike tone; but I, who knew my intereſt at Jidda, and the force in my own hand; that my

veſſel

---

* Vide Irvine's letters.

vessel was afloat, and could be under weigh in an instant, never was less disposed to be bullied, than at that moment. They asked me a thousand questions, whether I was a Mamaluke, whether I was a Turk, or whether I was an Arab, and why I did not give them spirits and tobacco? To all which I answered, only, that they should know to-morrow who I was; then I ordered the Emir Bahar, the captain of the port, to carry them ashore at his peril, or I would take their arms from them, and confine them on board all night.

The Rais gave the captain of the port a private hint, to take care what they did, for they might lose their lives; and that private caution, understood in a different way perhaps than was meant, had effect upon the soldiers, to make them withdraw immediately. When they went away, I begged the Emir Bahar to make my compliments to his masters, Hassan and Hussein, Agas, to know what time I should wait upon them to-morrow; and desired him, in the mean time, to keep his soldiers ashore, as I was not disposed to be troubled with their insolence.

Soon after they went, we heard a great firing, and saw lights all over the town; and the Rais proposed to me to slip immediately, and set sail, from which measure I was not at all averse. But, as he said, we had a better anchoring place under the mosque of the Shekh, and, besides, that there we would be in a place of safety, by reason of the holiness of the saint, and that at our own choice might even put to sea in a moment, or stay till to-morrow, as we were in no sort of doubt of being able to repel, force by force, if attacked, we got under weigh for a few hundred yards, and dropt our anchor under the fhrine of one of the greateft faints in the world

At night the firing had abated, the lights diminifhed, and the captain of the port again came on board. He was furprifed at miffing us at our former anchoring place, and ftill more fo, when, on our hearing the noife of his oars, we hailed, and forbade him to advance any nearer, till he fhould tell us how many he had on board, or whether he had foldiers or not, otherwife we fhould fire upon them: to this he anfwered, that there were only himfelf, his boy, and three officers, fervants to the Aga. I replied, that three ftrangers were too many at that time of the night, but, fince they were come from the Aga, they might advance.

All our people were fitting together armed on the forepart of the veffel; I foon divined they intended us no harm, for they gave us the falute *Salam Alicum!* before they were within ten yards of us. I anfwered with great complacency; we handed them on board, and fet them down upon deck. The three officers were genteel young men, of a fickly appearance, dreffed in the fafhion of the country, in long burnoofes loofely hanging about them, ftriped with red and white; they wore a turban of red, green, and white, with ten thoufand taffels and fringes hanging down to the fmall of their backs. They had in their hand, each, a fhort javelin, the fhaft not above four feet and a half long, with an iron head about nine inches, and two or three iron hooks below the fhaft, which was bound round with brafs-wire, in feveral places, and fhod with iron at the farther end.

They

They afked me where I came from? I faid, from Conftantinople, laft from Cairo; but begged they would put no more queftions to me, as I was not at liberty to anfwer them. They faid they had orders from their mafters to bid me welcome, if I was the perfon that had been recommended to them by the Sherriffe, and was Ali Bey's phyfician at Cairo. I faid, if Metical Aga had advifed them of that, then I was the man. They replied he had, and were come to bid me welcome, and attend me on fhore to their mafters, whenever I pleafed. I begged them to carry my humble refpects to their mafters; and told them, though I did not doubt of their protection in any fhape, yet I could not think it confiftent with ordinary prudence, to rifk myfelf at ten o'clock at night, in a town fo full of diforder as Yambo appeared to have been for fome time, and where fo little regard was paid to difcipline or command, as to fight with one another. They faid that was true, and I might do as I pleafed; but the firing that I had heard did not proceed from fighting, but from their rejoicing upon making peace.

In fhort, we found, that, upon fome difcuffion, the garrifon and townfmen had been fighting for feveral days, in which diforders the greateft part of the ammunition in the town had been expended, but it-had fince been agreed on by the old men of both parties, that no body had been to blame on either fide, but the whole wrong was the work of *a Camel*. *A camel*, therefore, was feized, and brought without the town, and there a number on both fides having met, they upbraided the *camel* with every thing that had been either faid or done. The *camel* had killed men, *he* had threatened to fet the town on fire; the *camel* had threatened to burn the Aga's houfe, and the caftle; *he* had curfed the

Grand Signior, and the Sherriffe of Mecca, the fovereigns of the two parties; and, the only thing the poor animal was interested in, *he* had threatened to deftroy the wheat that was going to Mecca. After having fpent great part of the afternoon in upbraiding the *camel*, whofe meafure of iniquity, it feems, was near full, each man thruft him through with a lance, devoting him *Diis manibus & Diris*, by a kind of prayer, and with a thoufand curfes upon his head. After which, every man retired, fully fatisfied as to the wrongs he had received from the *camel*.

The reader will eafily obferve in this, fome traces of the *azazel, or fcape-goat of the Jews, which was turned out into the wildernefs, loaded with the fins of the people.

Next morning I went to the palace, as we call it, in which were fome very handfome apartments. There was a guard of janiffaries at the door, who, being warriors, lately come from the bloody battle with the *camel*, did not fail to fhew marks of infolence, which they wifhed to be miftaken for courage.

The two Agas were fitting on a high bench upon Perfian carpets; and about forty well-dreffed and well-looking men, (many of them old) fitting on carpets upon the floor, in a femi-circle round them. They behaved with great politenefs and attention, and afked no queftions but general ones; as, How the fea agreed with me? If there was plenty at Cairo?

till

---

* Levit. chap. xvi. ver. 5.

till I was going away, when the youngeſt of the Agas inquired, with a ſeeming degree of diffidence, Whether Mahomet Bey Abou Dahab, was ready to march? As I knew well what this queſtion meant, I anſwered, I know not if he is ready, he has made great preparations. The other Aga ſaid, I hope you will be a meſſenger of peace? I anſwered, I intreat you to aſk me no queſtions; I hope, by the grace of God, all will go well. Every perſon preſent applauded the ſpeech; agreed to reſpect my ſecret, as they ſuppoſed I had one, and they all were inclined to believe, that I was a man in the confidence of Ali Bey, and that his hoſtile deſigns againſt Mecca were laid aſide: this was juſt what I wiſhed them to ſuppoſe; for it ſecured me againſt ill-uſage all the time I choſe to ſtay there; and of this I had a proof in the inſtant, for a very good houſe was provided for me by the Aga, and a man of his ſent to ſhew me to it.

I WONDERED the Rais had not come home with me; who, in about half an hour after I had got into my houſe, came and told me, that, when the captain of the boat came on board the firſt time with the two ſoldiers, he had put a note, which they call *tiſkera*, into his hand, preſſing him into the Sherriffe's ſervice, to carry wheat to Jidda, and, with the wheat, a number of *poor pilgrims* that were going to Mecca at the Sherriffe's expence. Finding us, however, out of the harbour, and, ſuſpecting from our manners and carriage towards the janiſſaries, that we were people who knew what we had to truſt to, he had taken the two ſoldiers a-ſhore with him, who were by no means fond of their reception, or inclined to ſtay in ſuch company; and, indeed, our dreſſes and appearances in the boat were fully as likely to make ſtrangers believe we ſhould rob them, as theirs were to impress us with an apprehension that they would rob us. The Rais said also, that, after my audience, the Aga had called upon him, and taken away the *tiskera*, telling him he was free, and to obey nobody but me; and sent me one of his servants to sit at the door, with orders to admit nobody but whom I pleased, and that I might not be troubled with the people of Yambo.

Hitherto all was well; but it had been with me an observation, which had constantly held good, that too prosperous beginnings in these countries always ended in ill at the last. I was therefore resolved to use my prosperity with great temperance and caution, make myself as strong, and use my strength as little, as it was possible for me to do.

There was a man of considerable weight in Aleppo, named *Sidi Ali Taraboloussi, who was a great friend of Dr Russel, our physician, through whom I became acquainted with him. He was an intimate friend and acquaintance of the cadi of Medina, and had given me a letter to him, recommending me, in a very particular manner, to his protection and services. I inquired about this person, and was told he was in town, directing the distribution of the corn to be sent to his capital. Upon my inquiry, the news were carried to him as soon almost as his name was uttered; on which, being desirous of knowing what sort of man I was, about eight o'clock in the evening he sent me a message, and, immediately after, I received a visit from him.

I was

---

* Native of Tripoli: it is Turkish.

I was putting my telescopes and time-keeper in order, and had forbid admittance to any one; but this was so holy and so dignified a person, that all doors were open to him. He observed me working about the great telescope and quadrant in my shirt, for it was hot beyond conception upon the smallest exertion. Without making any apology for the intrusion at all, he broke out into exclamation, how lucky he was! and, without regarding me, he went from telescope to clock, from clock to quadrant, and from that to the thermometer, crying, *Ah tibe, ah tibe!* This is fine, this is fine! He scarcely looked upon me, or seemed to think I was worth his attention, but touched every thing so carefully, and handled so properly the brass cover of the alidade, which inclosed the horse-hair with the plummet, that he seemed to be a man more than ordinarily versed in the use of astronomical instruments. In short, not to repeat useless matter to the reader, I found he had studied at Constantinople, understood the principles of geometry very tolerably, was master of Euclid so far as it regarded plain trigonometry; the demonstrations of which he rattled off so rapidly, that it was impossible to follow, or to understand him. He knew nothing of spherics, and all his astronomy resolved itself at last into maxims of judicial astrology, first and second houses of the planets and ascendancies, very much in the style of common almanacks.

He desired that my door might be open to him at all times, especially when I made observations; he also knew perfectly the division of our clocks, and begged he might count time for me. All this was easily granted, and I had from him, what was most useful, a history of the situation of the government of the place, by which I learned, that

that the two young men (the governors) were flaves of the Sherriffe of Mecca; that it was impoffible for any one, the moft intimate with them, to tell which of the two was moft bafe or profligate; that they would have robbed us all of the laft farthing, if they had not been reftrained by fear; and that there was a foreigner, or a frank, very lately going to India, who had difappeared, but, as he believed, had been privately put to death in prifon, for he had never after been heard of.

THOUGH I cannot fay I relifhed this account, yet I put on the very beft face poffible, "Here, in a garrifon town, faid I, with very worthlefs foldiers, they might do what they pleafed with fix or feven ftrangers, but I do not fear them; I now tell them, and the people of Yambo, all and each of them, they had better be in their bed fick of the plague, than touch a hair of my dog, if I had one." "And fo, fays he they know, therefore reft and rejoice, and ftay as long with us as you can." "As fbort time as poffible, faid I, Sidi Mabomet; although I do not fear wicked people, I don't love them fo much as to ftay long with them."

HE then afked me a favour, that I would allow my Rais to carry a quantity of wheat for him to Jidda; which I wil lingly permitted, upon condition, that he would order but one man to go along with it; on which he declared folemnly, that none but one fhould go, and that I might *throw* him even into the *fea*, if he behaved improperly. However, afterwards he fent three; and one who deferved often to be *thrown* into the *fea*, as he had permitted. "Now friend, faid I, I have done every thing that you have defired, though favours fhould have begun with you upon

your

THE SOURCE OF THE NILE.   257

your own principle, as I am the ftranger. Now, what I have to afk you is this,—Do you know the Shekh of Beder Hunein? Know him! fays he, I am married to his fifter, a daughter of Harb; he is of the tribe of Harb." "Harb be it then (faid I) your trouble will be the lefs; then you are to fend a camel to your brother-in-law, who will procure me the largeft, and moft perfect plant poffible of the Balfam of Mecca. He is not to break the ftem, nor even the branches, but to pack it entire, with fruit and flower, if poffible, and wrap it in a mat." He looked cunning, fhrugged up his fhoulders, drew up his mouth, and putting his finger to his nofe, faid, "Enough, I know all about this, you fhall find what fort of a man I am, I am no fool, as you fhall fee."

I RECEIVED this the third day at dinner, but the flower (if there had been any) was rubbed off. The fruit was in feveral ftages, and in great perfection. The drawing, and defcription from this *plant, will, I hope, for ever obviate all difficulty about its hiftory. He fent me, likewife, a quart bottle of the pure balfam, as it had flowed that year from the tree, with which I have verified what the old botanifts in their writings have faid of it, in its feveral ftages. He told me alfo the circumftances I have related in my defcription of the balfam, as to the gathering and preparing of the feveral kinds of it, and a curious anecdote as to its origin. He faid the plant was no part of the creation of God in the fix days, but that, in the laft of three very bloody battles, which Mahomet fought with the noble Arabs of Harb, and his kinf-

---

* See the article Baleffan in the Appendix.

men the Beni Koreifh, then Pagans at Beder Hunein, that Mahomet prayed to God, and a grove of balfam-trees grew up from the blood of the flain upon the field of battle; and, that with the balfam that flowed from them he touched the wounds even of thofe that were dead, and all thofe pre-deftined to be good *Muffulmen* afterwards, immediately came to life. "I hope, faid I, friend, that the other things you told me of it, are fully as true as this, for they will other-wife laugh at me in England" "No, no, fays he, not half fo true, nor a quarter fo true, there is nothing in the world fo certain as this." But his looks, and his laughing very heartily, fhewed me plainly he knew better, as indeed moft of them do.

In the evening, before we departed, about nine o'clock, I had an unexpected vifit from the youngeft of the two Agas; who, after many pretended complaints of ficknefs, and injunctions of fecrecy, at laft *modeftly* requefted me to give him fome *flow poifon*, that might kill *his brother*, without fufpicion, and after fome time fhould elapfe. I told him, fuch propofals were not to be made to a man like me; that all the gold, and all the filver in the world, would not engage me to poifon the pooreft vagrant in the ftreet, fuppofing it never was to be fufpected, or known but to my own heart. All he faid, was, "Then your manners are not the *fame* as ours."—I anfwered, dryly, "*Mine*, I thank God, are not," and fo we parted.

Yambo, or at leaft the prefent town of that name, I found, by many obfervations of the fun and ftars, to be in latitude 24° 3′ 35″ north, and in long. 38° 16′ 30″ eaft from the meridian of Greenwich. The barometer, at its higheft, on the 23d

of

of April, was 27° 8′, and, the lowest on the 27th, was 26° 11′. The thermometer, on the 24th of April, at two o'clock in the afternoon, stood at 91°, and the lowest was 66° in the morning of the 26th of same month. Yambo is reputed very unwholesome, but there were no epidemical diseases when I was there.

The many delays of loading the wheat, the desire of *doubling* the quantity I had permitted, in which both the Rais and my friend the cadi conspired for their mutual interest, detained me at Yambo all the 27th of April, very much against my inclination. For I was not a little uneasy at thinking among what banditti I lived, whose daily wish was to rob and murder me, from which they were restrained by fear only; and this, a fit of drunkenness, or a piece of bad news, such as a report of Ali Bey's death, might remove in a moment. Indeed we were allowed to want nothing. A sheep, some bad beer, and some very good wheat-bread, were delivered to us every day from the Aga, which, with dates and honey, and a variety of presents from those that I attended as a physician, made us pass our time comfortably enough; we went frequently in the boats to fish at sea, and, as I had brought with me three fizgigs of different sizes, with the proper lines, I seldom returned without killing four or five dolphins. The sport with the line was likewise excellent. We caught a number of beautiful fish from the very house where we lodged, and some few good ones. We had vinegar in plenty at Yambo; onions, and several other greens, from Raddua; and, being all cooks, we lived well.

On the 28th of April, in the morning, I failed with a cargo of wheat that did not belong to me, and three paffengers, inftead of one, for whom only I had undertaken. The wind was fair, and I faw one advantage of allowing the Rais to load, was, that he was determined to carry fail to make amends for the delay. There was a tumbling, difagreeable fwell, and the wind feemed dying away. One of our paffengers was very fick. At his requeft, we anchored at Djar, a round fmall port, whofe entrance is at the north-eaft. It is about three fathoms deep throughout, unlefs juft upon the fouth fide, and perfectly fheltered from every wind. We faw here, for the firft time, feveral plants of rack tree, growing confiderably within the fea-mark, in fome places with two feet of water upon the trunk. I found the latitude of Djar to be 23° 36′ 9″ north. The mountains of Beder Hunein were S. S. W. of us.

The 29th, at five o'clock in the morning, we failed from Djar. At eight, we paffed a fmall cape called * Ras el Himma; and the wind turning ftill more frefh, we paffed a kind of harbour called Maibeed, where there is an anchoring place named El Horma. The fun was in the meridian when we paffed this; and I found, by obfervation, El Horma was in lat. 23° 0′ 30″ north. At ten we paffed a mountain on land called Soub; at two, the fmall port of Muftura, under a mountain whofe name is Hajoub; at half paft four we came to an anchor at a place called Harar. The wind had been contrary all the night, being fouth-eaft, and rather frefh;

---

* Cape Fever.

fresh; we thought, too, we perceived a current setting strongly to the westward.

On the 30th we sailed at eight in the morning, but the wind was unfavourable, and we made little way. We were surrounded with a great many sharks, some of which seemed to be large. Though I had no line but upon the small fizgigs for dolphins, I could not refrain from attempting one of the largest, for they were so bold, that some of them, we thought, intended to leap on board. I struck one of the most forward of them, just at the joining of the neck; but as we were not practised enough in laying our line, so as to run out without hitching, he leaped above two feet out of the water, then plunged down with prodigious violence, and our line taking hold of something standing in the way, the cord snapped asunder, and away went the shark. All the others disappeared in an instant; but the Rais said, as soon as they smelled the blood, they would not leave the wounded one, till they had torn him to pieces. I was truly sorry for the loss of my tackle, as the two others were really liker harpoons, and not so manageable. But the Rais, whom I had studied to keep in very good humour, and had befriended in every thing, was an old harpooner in the Indian Ocean, and he pulled out from his hold a compleat apparatus. He not only had a small harpoon like my first, but better constructed. He had, likewise, several hooks with long chains and lines, and a wheel with a long hair line to it, like a small windlass, to which he equally fixed the line of the harpoon, and those of the hooks. This was a compliment he saw I took very kindly, and did not doubt it would be rewarded in the proper time.

The wind freshening and turning fairer, at noon we brought to, within sight of Rabac, and at one o'clock anchored there. Rabac is a small port in lat. 22° 35′ 30″ north. The entry is E. N. E. and is about a quarter of a mile broad. The port extends itself to the east, and is about two miles long. The mountains are about three leagues to the north, and the town of Rabac about four miles north by east from the entrance to the harbour. We remained all day, the first of May, in the port, making a drawing of the harbour. The night of our anchoring there, the Emir Hadje of the pilgrims from Mecca encamped about three miles off. We heard his evening gun.

The passengers that had been sick, now insisted upon going to see the Hadje; but as I knew the consequence would be, that a number of fanatic wild people would be down upon us, I told him plainly, if he went from the boat, he should not again be received; and that we would haul out of the port, and anchor in the offing; this kept him with us. But all next day he was in very bad humour, repeating frequently, to himself, that he deserved all this for embarking with infidels.

The people came down to us from Rabac with water melons, and skins full of water. All ships may be supplied here plentifully from wells near the town; the water is not bad.

The country is level, and seemingly uncultivated, but has not so desert a look as about Yambo. I should suspect by its appearance, and the freshness of its water, that it rained

THE SOURCE OF THE NILE.

rained at times in the mountains here, for we were now confiderably within the tropic, which paffes very near Ras el Himma, whereas Rabac is half a degree to the fouthward.

On the 2d, at five o'clock in the morning, we failed from Rabac, with a very little wind, fcarcely making two knots an hour.

At half paft nine, Deneb bore eaft and by fouth from us. This place is known by a few palm-trees. The port is fmall, and very indifferent, at leaft for fix months of the year, becaufe it lies open to the fouth, and there is a prodigious fwell here.

At one o'clock we paffed an ifland called Hammel, about a mile off; at the fame time, another ifland, El Memifk, bore eaft of us, about three miles, where there is good anchorage.

At three and three quarters, we paffed an ifland called Gawad, a mile and a quarter fouth-eaft of us. The main bore likewife fouth-eaft, diftant fomething more than a league. We here changed our courfe from fouth to W. S. W. and at four o'clock came to an anchor at the fmall ifland of Lajack.

The 3d, we failed at half paft four in the morning, our courfe W. S. W. but it fell calm; after having made about a league, we found ourfelves off Ras Hateba, or the Woody Cape, which bore due eaft of us. After doubling the cape, the wind freshening, at four o'clock in the afternoon we anchored in the port of Jidda, close upon the key, where the officers of the custom-house immediately took possession of our baggage.

CHAP.

Arab Shekh;
Tribe Beni Koreish.

London Publish'd Dec.r 1st 1789. by G. Robinson & Co.

Heath Sc.

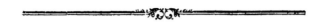

CHAP. XI.

Occurrences at Jidda—Visit of the Vizir—Alarm of the Factory—Great Civility of the English trading from India—Polygamy—Opinion of Dr Arbuthnot ill-founded—Contrary to Reason and Experience—Leave Jidda.

THE port of Jidda is a very extensive one, consisting of numberless shoals, small islands, and sunken rocks, with channels, however, between them, and deep water. You are very safe in Jidda harbour, whatever wind blows, as there are numberless shoals which prevent the water from ever being put into any general motion; and you may moor head and stern, with twenty anchors out if you please. But the danger of being lost, I conceive, lies in the going in and coming out of the harbour. Indeed the observation is here verified, the more *dangerous* the *port*, the *abler* the *pilots*, and no accidents ever happen.

There is a draught of the harbour of Jidda handed about among the English for many years, very inaccurately, and very ill laid down, from what authority I know not, often condemned, but never corrected; as also a pretended chart of the upper part of the Gulf, from Jidda to Mocha, full of soundings. As I was some months at Jidda, kindly entertained,

tained, and had abundance of time, Captain Thornhill, and some other of the gentlemen trading thither, wished me to make a survey of the harbour, and promised me the assistance of their officers, boats, and crews. I very willingly undertook it to oblige them. Finding afterwards, however, that one of their number, Captain Newland, had undertaken it, and that he would be hurt by my interfering, as he was in some manner advanced in the work, I gave up all further thoughts of the plan. He was a man of real ingenuity and capacity, as well as very humane, well behahaved, and one to whom I had been indebted for every sort of attention.

God forgive those who have taken upon them, very lately, to ingraft a number of new foundings upon that miserable bundle of errors, that Chart of the upper part of the Gulf from Jidda to Mocha, which has been tossed about the Red Sea these twenty years and upwards. One of these, since my return to Europe, has been sent to me new dressed like a bride, with all its original and mortal fins upon its head. I would beg leave to be understood, that there is not in the world a man more averse than I am to give offence even to a child. It is not in the spirit of criticism I speak this. In any other case, I would not have made any observations at all. But, where the lives and properties of so many are at stake yearly, it is a species of treason to conceal one's sentiments, if the publishing of them can any way contribute to safety, whatever offence it may give to unreasonable individuals

Of all the vessels in Jidda, two only had their log lines properly divided, and yet all were so fond of their supposed accuracy,

accuracy, as to aver they had kept their courfe within five leagues, between India and Babelmandeb. Yet they had made no eftimation of the currents without the * Babs, nor the different very ftrong ones foon after paffing Socotra; their half-minute glaffes upon a medium ran 57"; they had made no obfervation on the tides or currents in the Red Sea, either in the channel or in the inward paffage; yet there is delineated in this map a courfe of Captain Newland's, which he kept in the middle of the channel, full of fharp angles and fhort ftretches; you would think every yard was meafured and founded.

To the fpurious catalogue of foundings found in the old chart above mentioned, there is added a double proportion of new, from what authority is not known; fo that from Mocha, to lat. 17° you have as it were foundings every mile, or even lefs. No one can caft his eyes on the upper part of the map, but muft think the Red Sea one of the moft frequented places in the world. Yet I will aver, without fear of being contradicted, that it is a characteriftic of the Red Sea, fcarce to have foundings in any part of the channel, and often on both fides, whilft afhore foundings are hardly found a boat-length from the main. To this I will add, that there is fcarce one ifland upon which I ever was, where the boltfprit was not over the land, while there were no foundings by a line heaved over the ftern. I muft then proteft againft making thefe old moft erroneous maps a foundation for new ones, as they can be of no ufe, but muft be of detriment.

---

*.This is a common failor's phrafe for the Straits of Babelmandeb.

detriment. Many good feamen of knowledge and enterprife have been in that fea, within thefe few years. Let them fay, candidly, what were their inftruments, what their difficulties were, where they had doubts, where they fucceeded, and where they were difappointed? Were thefe acknowledged by one, they would be fpeedily taken up by others, and rectified by the help of mathematicians and good obfervers on fhore.

Mr Niebuhr has contributed much, but we fhould reform the map on both fides; though there is a great deal done, yet much remains ftill to do. I hope that my friend Mr Dalrymple, when he can afford time, will give us a foundation more proper to build upon, than that old rotten one; however changed in form, and fuppofed to have been improved, if he really has a number of obfervations by him that can be relied on, otherwife it is but continuing the delufion and the danger.

If fhips of war afterwards, that keep the channel, fhall come, manned with ftout and able feamen, and expert young officers, provided with lines, glaffes, good compaffes, and a number of boats, then we fhall know thefe foundings, at leaft in part. And then alfo we fhall know the truth of what I now advance, viz. that fhips like thofe employed hitherto in trading from India (manned and provided as the beft of them are) were incapable, amidft unknown tides and currents, and going before a monfoon, whether fouthern or northern, of knowing within three leagues where any one of them had ever dropt his founding line, unlefs he was clofe on board fome ifland, fhoal, remarkable point, or in a harbour.

Till that time, I would advife every man failing in the Red Sea, efpecially in the channel, where the pilots know no more than he, to truft to his own hands for fafety in the minute of danger, to heave the lead at leaft every hour, keep a good look-out, and fhorten fail in a frefh wind, or in the night-time, and to confider all maps of the channel of the Arabian Gulf, yet made, as matters of mere curiofity, and not fit to truft a man's life to. Any captain in the India fervice, who had run over from Jidda into the mouth of the river Frat, and the neighbouring port Kilfit, which might every year be done for L. 10 Sterling extra expences, would do more meritorious fervice to the navigation of that fea, than all the foundings that were ever yet made from Jibbel Zekir to the ifland of Sheduan

From Yambo to Jidda I had flept little, making my memoranda as full upon the fpot as poffible. I had, befides, an aguifh diforder, which very much troubled me, and in drefs and cleanlinefs was fo like a Galiongy (or Turkifh feaman) that the * Emir Bahar was aftonifhed at hearing my fervants fay I was an Englifhman, at the time they carried away all my baggage and inftruments to the cuftom-houfe. He fent his fervant, however, with me to the Bengal-houfe, who promifed me, in broken Englifh, all the way, a very magnificent reception from my countrymen. Upon his naming all the captains for my choice, I defired to be carried to a *Scotchman*, a *relation of my own*, who was then accidentally leaning over the rail of the ftair-cafe, leading up

to

---

* Captain of the port.

to his apartment. I saluted him by his name; he fell into a violent rage, calling me *villain, thief, cheat,* and *renegado rascal;* and declared, if I offered to proceed a step further, he would throw me over stairs. I went away without reply, his curses and abuse followed me long afterwards. The servant, my conductor, screwed his mouth, and shrugged up his shoulders. " Never fear, says he, I will carry you to the *best of them all.*" We went up an opposite stair-case, whilst I thought within myself, if those are their India manners, I shall keep my name and situation to myself while I am at Jidda. I stood in no need of them, as I had credit for 1000 sequins and more, if I should want it, upon Yousef Cabil, Vizir or Governor of Jidda.

I was conducted into a large room, where Captain Thornhill was sitting, in a white callico waistcoat, a very high-pointed white cotton night-cap, with a large tumbler of water before him, seemingly very deep in thought. The Emir Bahar's servant brought me forward by the hand, a little within the door; but I was not desirous of advancing much farther, for fear of the salutation of being thrown down stairs again. He looked very steadily, but not sternly, at me; and desired the servant to go away and shut the door. " Sir, says he, are you an Englishman?"—I bowed.— " You surely are sick, you should be in your bed, have you been long sick?"—I said, " long Sir," and bowed.—" Are you wanting a passage to India?"—I again bowed.—" Well, says he, you look to be a man in distress; if you have a secret, I shall respect it till you please to tell it me, but if you want a passage to India, apply to no one but Thornhill of the Bengal merchant. Perhaps you are afraid of somebody, if so, ask for Mr Greig, my lieutenant, he will carry you on board my ship
directly,

directly, where you will be safe."—"Sir, said I, I hope you will find me an honeft man, I have no enemy that I know, either in Jidda or elfewhere, nor do I owe any man any thing."—"I am fure, fays he, I am doing wrong, in keeping a poor man ftanding, who ought to be in his bed. Here! Philip! Philip!"—Philip appeared. "Boy," fays he, in Portuguefe, which, as I imagine, he fuppofed I did not underftand, "here is a poor Englifhman, that fhould be either in his bed or his grave; carry him to the cook, tell him to give him as much broth and mutton as he can eat; the *fellow* feems to have been ftarved, but I would rather have the feeding of ten to India, than the burying of one at Jidda."

PHILIP DE LA CRUZ was the fon of a Portuguefe lady, whom Captain Thornhill had married; a boy of great talents, and excellent difpofition, who carried me with great willingnefs to the cook. I made as aukward a bow as I could to Capt. Thornhill, and faid, "God will return this to your honour fome day." Philip carried me into a court-yard, where they ufed to expofe the famples of their India goods in large bales. It had a portico along the left-hand fide of it, which feemed defigned for a ftable. To this place I was introduced, and thither the cook brought me my dinner. Several of the Englifh from the veffels, lafcars, and others, came in to look at me; and I heard it, in general, agreed among them, that I was a very thief-like fellow, and certainly a Turk, and d——n them if they fhould like to fall into my hands.

I FELL faft afleep upon the mat, while Philip was ordering me another apartment. In the mean time, fome of my people had followed the baggage to the Cuftom-houfe, and fome of them ftaid on board the boat, to prevent the pilfering

pilfering of what was left. The keys had remained with me, and the Vizir had gone to sleep, as is usual, about midday. As soon as he awaked, being greedy of his prey, he fell immediately to my baggage, wondering that such a quantity of it, and that boxes in such a curious form, should belong to a mean man like me; he was therefore full of hopes, that a fine opportunity for pillage was now at hand. He asked for the keys of the trunks, my servant said, they were with me, but he would go instantly and bring them. That, however, was too long to stay; no delay could possibly be granted. Accustomed to pilfer, they did not force the locks, but, very artist like, took off the hinges at the back, and in that manner opened the lids, without opening the locks.

THE first thing that presented itself to the Vizir's sight, was the firman of the Grand Signior, magnificently written and titled, and the inscription powdered with gold dust, and wrapped in green taffeta. After this was a white sattin bag, addressed to the Khan of Tartary, with which Mr Peyssonel, French consul of Smyrna, had favoured me, and which I had not delivered, as the Khan was then prisoner at Rhodes. The next was a green and gold silk bag, with letters directed to the Sherriffe of Mecca; and then came a plain crimson-sattin bag, with letters addressed to Metical Aga, sword-bearer (or Selictar, as it is called) of the Sherriffe, or his great minister and favourite. He then found a letter from Ali Bey to himself, written with all the superiority of a Prince to a slave.

IN this letter the Bey told him plainly, that he heard the governments of Jidda, Mecca, and other States of the Sherriffe, were disorderly, and that merchants, coming about
their

their lawful bufinefs, were plundered, terrified, and detained. He therefore intimated to him, that if any fuch thing happened to me, he fhould not write or complain, but he would fend and punifh the affront at the very gates of Mecca. This was very unpleafant language to the Vizir, becaufe it was now publicly known, that Mahomet Bey Abou Dahab was preparing next year to march againft Mecca, for fome offence the Bey had taken at the Sherriffe. There was alfo another letter to him from Ibrahim Sikakeen, chief of the merchants at Cairo, ordering him to furnifh me with a thoufand fequins for my prefent ufe, and, if more were needed, to take my bill.

THESE contents of the trunk were fo unexpected, that Cabil the Vizir thought he had gone too far, and called my fervant in a violent hurry, upbraiding him, for not telling who I was. The fervant defended himfelf, by faying, that neither he, nor his people about him, would fo much as regard a word that he fpoke; and the cadi of Medina's principal fervant, who had come with the wheat, told the Vizir plainly to his face, that he had given him warning enough, if his pride would have fuffered him to hear it.

ALL was now wrong, my fervant was ordered to nail up the hinges, but he declared it would be the laft action of his life; that nobody opened baggage that way, but with intention of ftealing, when the keys could be got; and, as there were many rich things in the trunk, intended as prefents to the Sherriffe, and Metical Aga, which might have been taken out, by the hinges being forced off before he came, he wafhed his hands of the whole procedure, but knew his mafter would complain, and loudly too, and would be heard both at Cairo and Jidda. The Vizir took his refolution in a moment like a man. He nailed up the baggage, ordered his horfe to be brought, and attended by a number of naked blackguards (whom they call foldiers) he came down to the Bengal houfe, on which the whole factory took alarm.

ABOUT twenty-fix years before, the Englifh traders from India to Jidda, fourteen in number, were all murdered, fitting at dinner, by a mutiny of thefe wild people. The houfe has, ever fince, lain in ruins, having been pulled down and forbidden to be rebuilt.

GREAT inquiry was made after the Englifh nobleman, whom nobody had feen; but it was faid that one of his fervants was there in the Bengal houfe; I was fitting drinking coffee on the mat, when the Vizir's horfe came, and the whole court was filled. One of the clerks of the cuftom-houfe afked me where my mafter was? I faid, "In heaven." The Emir Bahar's fervant now brought forward the Vizir to me, who had not difmounted himfelf. He repeated the fame queftion, where my mafter was?—I told him, I did not know the purport of his queftion, that I was the perfon to whom the baggage belonged, which he had taken to the cuftom-houfe, and that it was in my favour the Grand Signior and Bey had written. He feemed very much furprifed, and afked me how I could appear in fuch a drefs? —"You cannot afk that ferioufly, faid I; I believe no prudent man would drefs better, confidering the voyage I have made. But, befides, you did not leave it in my power,

as

as every article, but what I have on me, has been thefe four hours at the cuftom-houfe, waiting your pleafure."

We then went all up to our kind landlord, Captain Thornhill, to whom I made my excufe, on acount of the ill ufage I had firft met with from my own relation. He laughed very heartily at the narrative, and from that time we lived in the greateft friendfhip and confidence. All was made up, even with Youfef Cabil; and all heads were employed to get the ftrongeft letters poffible to the Naybe of Mafuah, the king of Abyffinia, Michael Suhul the minifter, and the king of Sennaar.

Metical Aga, great friend and protector of the Englifh at Jidda, and in effect, we may fay, *fold to them*, for the great prefents and profits he received, was himfelf originally an Abyffinian flave, was the man of confidence, and directed the fale of the king's, and Michael's gold, ivory, civet, and fuch precious commodities, that are paid to them in kind; he furnifhed Michael, likewife, with returns in fire-arms; and this had enabled Michael to fubdue Abyffinia, murder the king his mafter, and feat another on his throne.

On the other hand, the Naybe of Mafuah, whofe ifland belonged to the Grand Signior, and was an appendage of the government of the Bafha of Jidda, had endeavoured to withdraw himfelf from his allegiance, and fet up for independency. He paid no tribute, nor could the Bafha, who had no troops, force him, as he was on the Abyffinian fide of the Red Sea. Metical Aga, however, and the Bafha, at laft agreed; the latter ceded to the former the ifland and territory of Mafuah, for a fixed fum annually;

and Metical Aga appointed Michael, governor of Tigré, receiver of his rents. The Naybe no sooner found that he was to account to Michael, than he was glad to pay his tribute, and give prefents to the bargain; for Tigré was the province from which he drew his fuftenance, and Michael could have over-run his whole territory in eight days, which once, as we fhall fee hereafter, belonged to Abyffinia. Metical's power being then univerfally acknowledged and known, the next thing was to get him to make ufe of it in my favour.

We knew of how little avail the ordinary futile recommendations of letters were. We were veteran travellers, and knew the ftyle of the Eaft too well, to be duped by letters of mere civility. There is no people on the earth more perfectly polite in their correfpondence with one another, than are thofe of the Eaft; but their civility means little more than the fame fort of expreffions do in Europe, to fhew you that the writer is a well-bred man. But this would by no means do in a journey fo long, fo dangerous, and fo ferious as mine.

We, therefore, fet about procuring effective letters, letters of bufinefs and engagement, between man and man; and we all endeavoured to make Metical Aga a very good man, but no great head-piece, comprehend this perfectly. My letters from Ali Bey opened the affair to him, and firft commanded his attention. A very handfome prefent of piftols, which I brought him, inclined him in my favour, becaufe, as I was bearer of letters from his fuperior, I might have declined beftowing any prefent upon him.

The English gentlemen joined their influence, powerful enough, to have accomplished a much greater end, as every one of thefe have feparate friends for their own affairs, and all of them were defirous to befriend me. Added to thefe was a friend of mine, whom I had known at Aleppo, Ali Zimzimiah, *i. e.* 'keeper of the holy well at Mecca,' a poft of great dignity and honour. This man was a mathematician, and an aftronomer, according to their degree of knowledge in that fcience.

ALL the letters were written in a ftyle fuch as I could have defired, but this did not fuffice in the mind of a very friendly and worthy man, who had taken an attachment to me fince my firft arrival. This was Captain Thomas Price, of the Lion of Bombay. He firft propofed to Metical Aga, to fend a man of his own with me, together with the letters, and I do firmly believe, under Providence, it was to this laft meafure I owed my life. With this Captain Thornhill heartily concurred, and an Abyffinian, called Mahomet Gibberti, was appointed to go with particular letters befides thofe I carried myfelf, and to be an eye-witnefs of my reception there.

THERE was fome time neceffary for this man to make ready, and a confiderable part of the Arabian Gulf ftill remained for me to explore. I prepared, therefore, to fet out from Jidda, after having made a confiderable ftay in it.

OF all the new things I yet had feen, what moft aftonifhed me was the manner in which trade was carried on at this place. Nine fhips were there from India; fome of them worth, I fuppofe, L. 200,000. One merchant, a Turk, living

at

at Mecca, thirty hours journey off, where no Christian dares go, whilst the whole Continent is open to the Turk for escape, offers to purchase the cargoes of four out of nine of these ships himself; another, of the same cast, comes and says, he will buy none, unless he has them all. The samples are shewn, and the cargoes of the whole nine ships are carried into the wildest part of Arabia, by men with whom one would not wish to trust himself alone in the field. This is not all, two India brokers come into the room to settle the price. One on the part of the India captain, the other on that of the buyer the Turk. They are neither Mahometans nor Christians, but have credit with both. They sit down on the carpet, and take an India shawl, which they carry on their shoulder, like a napkin, and spread it over their hands. They talk, in the mean time, indifferent conversation, of the arrival of ships from India, or of the news of the day, as if they were employed in no serious business whatever. After about twenty minutes spent in handling each others fingers below the shawl, the bargain is concluded, say for nine ships, without one word ever having been spoken on the subject, or pen or ink used in any shape whatever. There never was one instance of a dispute happening in *these sales*.

But this is not yet all, the money is to be paid. A private Moor, who has nothing to support him but his character, becomes responsible for the payment of these cargoes; his name was Ibrahim Saraf when I was there, *i. e.* Ibrahim the Broker. This man delivers a number of coarse hempen bags, full of what is supposed to be money. He marks the contents upon the bag, and puts his seal upon the string that ties the mouth of it. This is received for what is marked upon it, without any one ever having open-

ed

ed one of the bags, and, in India, it is current for the value marked upon it, as long as the bag lafts.

JIDDA is very unwholefome, as is, indeed, all the eaft coaft of the Red Sea. Immediately without the gate of that town, to the eaftward, is a defert plain filled with the huts of the Bedoweens, or country Arabs, built of long bundles of fpartum, or bent grafs, put together like fafcines. Thefe Bedoweens fupply Jidda with milk and butter. There is no ftirring out of town, even for a walk, unlefs for about half a mile, in the fouth fide by the fea, where there is a number of ftinking pools of ftagnant water, which contributes to make the town very unwholefome.

JIDDA, befides being in the moft unwholefome part of Arabia, is, at the fame time, in the moft barren and defert fituation. This, and many other inconveniencies, under which it labours, would, probably, have occafioned its being abandoned altogether, were it not for its vicinity to Mecca, and the great and fudden influx of wealth from the India trade, which, once a-year, arrives in this part, but does not continue, paffing on, as through a turnpike, to Mecca; whence it is difperfed all over the eaft. Very little advantage however accrues to Jidda. The cuftoms are all immediately fent to a needy fovereign, and a hungry fet of relations, dependents and minifters at Mecca. The gold is returned in bags and boxes, and paffes on as rapidly to the fhips as the goods do to the market, and leaves as little profit behind. In the mean time, provifions rife to a prodigious price, and this falls upon the townfmen, while all the profit of the traffic is in the hands of ftrangers; moft of whom, after the market is over, (which does not laft fix weeks)

weeks) retire to Yemen, and other neighbouring countries, which abound in every fort of provifion.

Upon this is founded the obfervation, that of all Mahometan countries none are fo monogam as thofe of Jidda, and no where are there fo many unmarried women, altho' this is the country of their prophet, and the permiffion of marrying four wives was allowed in this diftrict in the firft inftance, and afterwards communicated to all the tribes.

But Mahomet, in his permiffion of plurality of wives, feems conftantly to have been on his guard, againft fuffering that, which was intended for the welfare of his people, from operating in a different manner. He did not permit a man to marry two, three, or four wives, unlefs he could maintain them. He was interefted for the rights and rank of thefe women; and the man fo marrying was obliged to fhew before the Cadi, or fome equivalent officer, or judge, that it was in his power to fupport them, according to their birth. It was not fo with concubines, with women who were purchafed, or who were taken in war. Every man enjoyed thefe at his pleafure, and their peril, that is, whether he was able to maintain them or not.

From this great fcarcity of provifions, which is the refult of an extraordinary concourfe to a place almoft deftitute of the neceffaries of life, few inhabitants of Jidda can avail themfelves of the privilege granted him by Mahomet. He therefore cannot marry more than one wife, becaufe he cannot maintain more, and from this caufe arifes the want of people, and the large number of unmarried women.

When

WHEN in Arabia Felix, where every sort of provision is exceedingly cheap, where the fruits of the ground, the general food for man, are produced spontaneously, the supporting of a number of wives costs no more than so many slaves or servants; their food is the same, and a blue cotton shirt, a habit common to them all, is not more chargeable for the one than the other. The consequence is, that celibacy in women is prevented, and the number of people is increased in a fourfold ratio by polygamy, to what it is in those that are monogamous.

I KNOW there are authors fond of system, enemies to free inquiry, and blinded by prejudice, who contend that polygamy, without distinction of circumstances, is detrimental to the population of a country. The learned Dr Arbuthnot, in a paper addressed to the Royal Society*, has maintained this strange doctrine, in a still stranger manner. He lays it down, as his first position, that *in femine masculino* of our first parent Adam, there was impressed an original necessity of procreating, ever after, an equal number of males and females. The manner he proves this, has received great incense from the vulgar, as containing un unanswerable argument. He shews, by the casting of three dice, that the chances are almost infinite, that an equal number of males and females should *not* be born in any year; and he pretends to prove, that every year in twenty, as taken from the bills of mortality, the same number of males and females have constantly been produced, or at least a greater proportion of men than of women, to make up for the havock

---

* Philosoph. Transact. Vol. 27. p. 186.

vock occasioned by war, murder, drunkenness, and all species of violence to which women are not subject.

I NEED not say, that this, at least, sufficiently shews the weakness of the argument. For, if the *equal* proportion had been *in femine masculino* of our first parent, the consequence must have been, that male and female would have been invariably born, from the creation to the end of all things. And it is a supposition very unworthy of the wisdom of God, that, at the creation of man, he could make an allowance for any deviation that was to happen, from crimes, against the commission of which his positive precepts ran. Weak as this is, it is not the weakest part of this artificial argument, which, like the web of a spider too finely woven, whatever part you touch it on, the whole falls to pieces.

AFTER taking it for granted, that he has proved the equality of the two sexes in number, from the bills of mortality in London, he next supposes, as a consequence, that all the world is in the same predicament; that is, that an equal number of males and females is produced every where. Why Dr Arbuthnot, an eminent physician (which surely implies an informed naturalist) should imagine that this inference would hold, is what I am not able to account for. He should know, let us say, in the countries of the east, that fruits, flowers, trees, birds, fish, every blade of grass, is commonly different, and that man, in his appearance, diet, exercise, pleasure, government, and religion, is as widely different; why he should found the issue of an Asiatic, however, upon the bills of mortality in London, is to the full as absurd as to assert, that they do not wear either beard or whiskers in Syria, because that is not the case in London

I AM

I am well aware, that it may be urged by those who permit themselves to say every thing, because they are not at pains to consider any thing, that the course of my argument will lead to a defence of polygamy in general, the supposed doctrine of the Thelypthora *. Such reflections as these, unless introduced for merriment, are below my animadversion; all I shall say on that topic is, that they who find encouragement to polygamy in Mr Madan's book, the Thelypthora, have read it with a much more acute perception than perhaps I have done; and I shall be very much mistaken, if polygamy increases in England upon the principles laid down in the Thelypthora.

England, says Dr Arbuthnot, enjoys an equality of both sexes, and, if it is not so, the inequality is so imperceptible, that no inconvenience has yet followed. What we have now to inquire is, Whether other nations, or the majority of them, are in the same situation? For, if we are to decide by this, and if we should happen to find, that, in other countries, there are invariably born three women to one man, the conclusion, in regard to that country, must be, that three women to one man was the proportion of one sex to the other, impressed at the creation *in femine* of our first parent.

I confess I am not fond of meddling with the globe *before* the *deluge*. But as learned men seem inclined to think that Ararat and Euphrates are the mountain and river of antediluvian times, and that Mesopotamia, or Diarbekir, is the ancient situation of the terrestrial paradise, I cannot give

---

* A late publication of Dr Madan's, little understood, as it would seem.

Dr Arbuthnot's argument fairer play*, than to transport myself thither; and, in the same spot where the necessity was imposed of male and female being produced in equal numbers, inquire how that case stands now. The pretence that climates and times may have changed, the proportion cannot be admitted, since it has been taken for granted, that it exists in the bills of mortality in London, and governs them to this day; and, since it was founded on necessity, which must be eternal.

Now, from a diligent inquiry into the south, and scripture-part of Mesopotamia, Armenia, and Syria, from Mouful (or Nineveh) to Aleppo and Antioch, I find the proportion to be fully two women born to one man. There is indeed a fraction over, but not a considerable one. From Latikea, Laodicea ad mare, down the coast of Syria to Sidon, the number is very nearly three, or two and three-fourths to one man. Through the Holy Land, the country called *Horan*, in the Isthmus of Suez, and the parts of the Delta, unfrequented by strangers, it is something less than three. But, from Suez to the straits of Babelmandeb, which contains the three Arabias, the portion is fully four women to one man, which, I have reason to believe, holds as far as the Line, and 30° beyond it.

The Imam of Sana* was not an old man when I was in Arabia Felix in 1769; but he had 88 children then alive, of whom 14 only were sons.—The priest of the Nile had 70 and odd

---

* Sovereign of Arabia Felix, whose capital is *Sana*.

odd children; of whom, as I remember, above 50 were daughters.

It may be objected, that Dr Arbuthnot, in quoting the bills of mortality for twenty years, gave moſt unexceptionable grounds for his opinion, and that my ſingle aſſertion of what happens in a foreign country, without further foundation, cannot be admitted as equivalent teſtimony; and I am ready to admit this objection, as bills of mortality there are none in any of theſe countries. I ſhall therefore ſay in what manner I attained the knowledge which I have juſt mentioned. Whenever I went into a town, village, or inhabited place, dwelt long in a mountain, or travelled journies with any ſet of people, I always made it my buſineſs to inquire how many children they had, or their fathers, their next neighbours, or acquaintance. This not being a captious queſtion, or what any one would ſcruple to anſwer, there was no intereſt to deceive; and if it had been poſſible, that two or three had been ſo wrong-headed among the whole, it would have been of little conſequence.

I then aſked my landlord at Sidon, (ſuppoſe him a weaver,) how many children he has had? He tells me how many ſons, and how many daughters. The next I aſk is a ſmith, a tailor, a ſilk-gatherer, the Cadi of the place, a cowherd, a hunter, a fiſher, in ſhort every man that is not a ſtranger, from whom I can get proper information. I ſay, therefore, that a medium of both ſexes ariſing from three or four hundred families indiſcriminately taken, ſhall be the proportion in which one differs from the other; and this, I am confident, will give the reſult to be three women to one man in 50° out of the 90° under every meridian of the globe.

WITHOUT giving Mahomet all the credit for abilities that some have done, we may surely suppose him to know what happened in his own family, where he must have seen this great disproportion of four women born to one man; and from the obvious consequences, we are not to wonder that one of his first cares, when a legislator, was to rectify it, as it struck at the very root of his empire, power, and religion. With this view, he enacted, or rather revived, the law which gave liberty to every individual to marry four wives, each of whom was to be equal in rank and honour, without any preference but what the predilection of the husband gave her. By this he secured civil rights to each woman, and procured a means of doing away that reproach, of *dying without issue*, to which the minds of the whole sex have always been sensible, whatever their religion was, or from whatever part of the world they came.

MANY, who are not conversant with Arabian history, have imagined, that this permission of a plurality of wives was given in favour of men, and have taxed one of the most *political*, *necessary* measures, of that legislator, arising from motives merely civil, with a tendency to encourage lewdness, from which it was very far distant. But, if they had considered that the Mahometan law allows divorce without any *cause assigned*, and that, every day at the pleasure of the man; besides, that it permits him as many concubines as he can maintain, buy with money, take in war, or gain by the ordinary means of address and solicitations,—they will think

such

THE SOURCE OF THE NILE.   287

such a man was before sufficiently provided, and that there was not the least reason for allowing him to marry four wives at a time, when he was already at liberty to marry a new one every day.

Dr Arbuthnot lays it down as a self-evident position that four women will have more children by four men, than the same four women would have by one. This assertion may very well be disputed, but still it is not in point. For the question with regard to Arabia, and to a great part of the world besides, is, Whether or not four women and one man, married, or cohabiting at discretion, shall produce more children, than four women and one man who is debarred from cohabiting with any but one of the four, the others dying unmarried without the knowledge of man? or, in other words, Which shall have most children, one man and one woman, or one man and four women? This question I think needs no discussion.

Let us now consider, if there is any further reason why England should not be brought as an example, which Arabia, or the East in general, are to follow.

Women in England are commonly capable of child-bearing at fourteen, let the other term be forty-eight, when they bear no more; thirty-four years, therefore, an English woman bears children. At the age of fourteen or fifteen they are objects of our love; they are endeared by bearing us children after that time, and none I hope will pretend, that, at forty-eight and fifty, an English woman is not an agreeable companion. Perhaps the last years, to thinking minds, are fully more agreeable than the first. We grow old together,

ther, we have a near profpect of dying together; nothing can prefent a more agreeable picture of focial life, than monogamy in England.

The Arab, on the other hand, if fhe begins to bear children at eleven, feldom or never has a child after twenty. The time then of her child-bearing is nine years, and four women, *taken altogether*, have then the term of *thirty-fix*. So that the Englifh woman that bears children for thirty-four years, has only two years lefs than the term enjoyed by the four wives whom Mahomet has allowed; and if it be granted an Englifh wife may bear at fifty, the terms are equal.

But there are other grievous differences. An Arabian girl, at *eleven* years old, by her youth and beauty, is the object of man's defire; being an infant, however, in underftanding, fhe is not a rational companion for him. A man marries there, fay at *twenty*, and before he is thirty, his wife, improved as a companion, ceafes to be an object of his defires, and a mother of children; fo that all the beft, and moft vigorous of his days, are fpent with a woman he cannot love, and with her he would be deftined to live forty, or forty-five years, without comfort to himfelf by increafe of family, or utility to the public.

The reafons, then, againft polygamy, which fubfift in England, do not by any means fubfift in Arabia; and that being the cafe, it would be unworthy of the wifdom of God, and an unevennefs in his ways, which we fhall never fee, to fubject two nations, under fuch different circumftances, abfolutely to the fame obfervances.

I consider

THE SOURCE OF THE NILE.

I consider the prophecy concerning Ishmael, and his descendants the Arabs, as one of the most extraordinary that we meet with in the Old Testament. It was also one of the earliest made, and proceeded upon grounds of private reparation. Hagar had not sinned, though she had fled from Sarah with Ishmael her son into the wilderness. In that desert there were then no inhabitants, and though Ishmael's * succession was incompatible with God's promise to Abraham and his son Isaac, yet neither Hagar nor he having sinned, justice required a reparation for the heritage which he had lost. God gave him that very wilderness which before was the property of no man, in which Ishmael was to erect a kingdom under the most improbable circumstances possible to be imagined. His † hand was to be against every man, and every man's hand against him. By his sword he was to live, and pitch his tent in the *face* of his brethren.

Never has prophecy been so completely fulfilled. It subsisted from the earliest ages; it was verified before the time of Moses; in the time of David and Solomon; it subsisted in the time of Alexander and that of Augustus Cæsar; it subsisted in the time of Justinian,---all very distant, unconnected periods; and I appeal to the evidence of mankind, if, without apparent support or necessity, but what it has derived from God's promise only, it is not in full vigour at this very day. This prophecy alone, in the truth of which all sorts of

religions

---

* Gen. xv. 18.   † Gen. xvi. 12.

religions agree, is therefore of itself a sufficient proof, without other, of the Divine authority of the scripture.

MAHOMET prohibited all pork and wine; two articles which must have been, before, very little used in Arabia. Grapes, here, grow in the mountains of Yemen, but never arrive at maturity enough for wine. They bring them down for this purpose to Loheia, and there the heat of the climate turns the wine sour before they can clear it of its fæces so as to make it drinkable; and we know that, before the appearance of Mahomet, Arabia was never a wine country. As for swine, I never heard of them in the peninsula, of Arabia, (unless perhaps wild in the woods about Sana,) and it was from early times inhabited by Jews before the coming of Mahomet. The only people therefore that ate swine's flesh must have been Christians, and they were a sect of little account. Many of these, however, do not eat pork yet, but all of them were oppressed and despised every-where, and there was no inducement for any other people to imitate them.

MAHOMET then prohibiting only what was merely neutral, or indifferent to the Arabs, indulged them in that to which he knew they were prone.

AT the several conversations I had with the English merchants at Jidda, they complained grievously of the manner in which they were oppressed by the sherriffe of Mecca and his officers. The duties and fees were increased every voyage; their privileges all taken away, and a most destructive measure introduced of forcing them to give presents, which was only an inducement to oppress, that the gift might be the
greater

greater. I asked them if I should obtain from the Bey of Cairo permission for their ships to come down to Suez, whither there were merchants in India who would venture to undertake that voyage? Captain Thornhill promised, for his part, that the very season after such permission should arrive in India, he would dispatch his ship the Bengal Merchant, under command of his mate Captain Greig, to whose capacity and worth all his countrymen bore very ready testimony, and of which I myself had formed a very good opinion, from the several conversations we had together. This scheme was concerted between me and Captain Thornhill only; and tho' it must be confessed it had the appearance of an airy one, (since it was not to be attempted, till I had returned through Abyssinia and Nubia, against which there were many thousand chances,) it was executed, notwithstanding, in the very manner in which it had been planned, as will be after stated.

The kindness and attention of my countrymen did not leave me as long as I was on shore. They all did me the honour to attend me to the water edge. If others have experienced pride and presumption, from gentlemen of the East-Indies, I was most happily exempted from even the appearance of it at Jidda. Happy it would have been for me, if I had been more neglected.

All the quay of Jidda was lined with people to see the English salute, and along with my vessel there parted, at the same time, one bound to Masuah, which carried Mahomet Abd el cader, Governor of Dahalac, over to his government.

Dahalac* is a large island, depending upon Mafuah, but which has a feparate firman, or commiffion, renewed every two years. This man was a Moor, a fervant of the Naybe of Mafuah, and he had been at Jidda to procure his firman from Metical Aga, while Mahomet Gibberti was to come with me, and was to bring it to the Naybe. This Abd el cader no fooner was arrived at Mafuah, than, following the turn of his country for lying, he fpread a report, that a great man, or prince, whom he left at Jidda, was coming fpeedily to Mafuah; that he had brought great prefents to the Sherriffe and Metical Aga; that, in return, he had received a large fum in *gold* from the Sherriffe's Vizir, Youfef Cabil; befides as much as he pleafed from the Englifh, who had done nothing but feaft and regale him for the feveral months he had been at Jidda; and that, when he departed, as this great man was now going to vifit the Imam in Arabia Felix, all the Englifh fhips hoifted their colours, and fired their cannon from morning to night, for three days fucceffively, which was two days after he had failed, and therefore what he could not poffibly have feen. The confequence of all this was, the Naybe of Mafuah expected that a man with immenfe treafures was coming to put himfelf into *his hands*. I look therefore upon the danger I efcaped there as fuperior to all thofe put together, that I have ever been expofed to: of fuch material and bad confequence is the moft contemptible of all weapons, the tongue of a liar and a fool!

JIDDA

---

* The ifland of the Shepherds.

JIDDA is in lat. 28° 0' 1" north, and in long. 39° 16' 45" east of the meridian of Greenwich. Our weather there had few changes. The general wind was north-weft, or more northerly. This blowing along the direction of the Gulf brought a great deal of damp along with it; and this damp increafes as the feafon advances. Once in twelve or fourteen days, perhaps, we had a fouth wind, which was always dry. The higheft degree of the barometer at Jidda, on the 5th of June, wind north, was 26° 6', and the loweft on the 18th of fame month, wind north-weft, was 25° 7'. The higheft degree of the thermometer was 97° on the 12th of July, wind north, the loweft was 78° wind north.

CHAP.

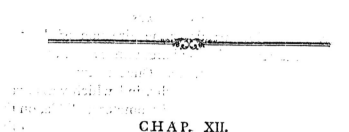

CHAP. XII.

Sails from Jidda—Konfodah—Ras Heli boundary of Arabia Felix— Arrives at Loheia—Proceeds to the Straits of the Indian Ocean—Arrives there—Returns by Azab to Loheia.

IT was on the 8th of July 1769 I sailed from the harbour of Jidda on board the same vessel as before, and I suffered the Rais to take a small loading for his own account, upon condition that he was to carry no passengers. The wind was fair, and we sailed through the English fleet at their anchors. As they had all honoured me with their regret at parting, and accompanied me to the shore, the Rais was surprised to see the respect paid to his little vessel as it passed under their huge sterns, every one hoisting his colours, and saluting it with eleven guns, except the ship belonging to my Scotch friend, who shewed his colours, indeed, but did not fire a gun, only standing upon deck, cried with the trumpet, " Captain ——— wishes Mr Bruce a good voyage." I stood upon deck, took my trumpet, and answered, " Mr Bruce wishes Captain ——— a speedy and perfect return of his understanding;" a wish, poor man, that has not yet been accomplished, and very much to my regret, it does not appear probable that ever it will. That night having passed

THE SOURCE OF THE NILE.

ed a cluster of shoals, called the Shoals of Safia, we anchored in a small bay, Merfa Gedan, about twelve leagues from the harbour of Jidda.

The 9th of July, we passed another small road called *Goofi*, and at a quarter past nine, Raghwan, east north-east two miles, and, at a quarter past ten, the small Port of Sodi, bearing east north-east, at the same distance. At one and three quarters we passed Markat, two miles distant north-east by east; and a rock called *Numan*, two miles distant to the south-west. After this the mountain of Somma, and, at a quarter past six, we anchored in a small unsafe harbour, called *Merfa Brahim*, of which we had seen a very rough and incorrect design in the hands of the gentlemen at Jidda. I have endeavoured, with that draught before me, to correct it so far that it may now be depended upon

The 10th, we sailed, at five o'clock in the morning, with little wind, our course south and by west; I suppose we were then going something less than two knots an hour. At half after seven we passed the island Abeled, and two other small mountains that bore about a league south-west and by west of us. The wind freshened as it approached midday, so that at one o'clock we went full three knots an hour, being obliged to change our course according to the lying of the islands. It came to be about south south-east in the end of the day.

At a quarter after one, we passed Ras el Afkar, meaning the Cape of the Soldiers, or of the Army. Here we saw some trees, and, at a considerable distance within the Main, mountains to the north-east of us. At two o'clock we passed in the

the middle channel, between five fandy iflands; all covered with kelp, three on the eaft or right hand, and two on the weft. They are called *Ginnan el Abiad*, or the White Gardens, I fuppofe from the green herb growing upon the white fand. At half after two, with the fame wind, we paffed an ifland bearing eaft from us, the Main about a league diftant. At three we paffed clofe to an ifland bearing fouthweft of us, about a mile off. It is of a moderate height, and is called *Jibbel Surreine*. At half paft four our courfe was fouth-eaft and by fouth; we paffed two iflands to the foutheaft of us, at two miles, and a fmaller, weft fouth-weft a quarter of a mile diftant. From this to the Main will be about five miles, or fomething more. At fifty minutes after four, came up to an ifland which reached to Konfodah. We faw to the weft, and weft fouth-weft of us, different fmall iflands, not more than half a mile diftant. We heaved the line, and had no foundings at thirty-two fathom, yet, if any where, I thought there we were to find fhoal water. At five o'clock, our courfe being fouth-eaft and by fouth, we paffed an ifland a quarter of a mile to the weft of us, and afterwards a number of others in a row; and, at half paft eight, we arrived at an anchoring-place, but which cannot be called a harbour, named *Merfa Hadou*.

THE 11th, we left Merfa Hadou at four o'clock in the morning. Being calm, we made little way; our courfe was fouth fouth-eaft, which changed to a little more eafterly. At fix, we tacked to ftand in for Konfodah harbour, which is very remarkable for a high mountain behind it, whofe top is terminated by a pyramid or cone of very regular proportion. There was no wind to carry us in; we hoifted out the boat which I had bought at Jidda for my
pleafure

pleasure and safety, intending it to be a present to my Rais at parting, as he very well knew. At a quarter past eight, we were towed to our anchorage in the harbour of Konfodah.

Konfodah means the town of the hedge-hog*. It is a small village, consisting of about two hundred miserable houses, built with green wood, and covered with mats, made of the doom, or palm-tree; lying on a bay, or rather a shallow bason, in a desert waste or plain. Behind the town are small hillocks of white sand. Nothing grows on shore excepting kelp, but it is exceedingly beautiful, and very luxuriant; farther in, there are gardens. Fish is in perfect plenty; butter and milk in great abundance; even the desert looks fresher than other deserts, which made me imagine that rain fell sometimes here, and this the Emir told me was the case.

Although I made a draught of the port, it is not worth the publishing. For though in all probability it was once deep, safe, and convenient, yet there is nothing now but a kind of road, under shelter of a point, or ridge of land, which rounds out into the sea, and ends in a Cape, called *Ras Mozeffa*. Behind the town there is another small Cape, upon which there are three guns mounted, but with what intention it was not possible to guess.

The Emir Ferhan, governor of the town, was an Abyssinian slave, who invited me on shore, and we dined together

---

* Or Porcupine.

on very excellent provifion, dreffed according to their cuftom. He faid the country near the fhore was defert, but a little within land, or where the roots and gravel had fixed the fand, the foil produced every thing, efpecially if they had any fhowers of rain. It was fo long fince I had heard mention of a fhower of rain, that I could not help laughing, and he feemed to think that he had faid fomething wrong, and begged fo politely to know what I laughed at, that I was obliged to confefs. " The reafon, faid I, Sir, is an abfurd one. What paffed in my mind at that time was, that I had travelled about two thoufand miles, and above twelve months, and had neither feen nor heard of a *fhower of rain,* till now, and though you will perceive by my converfation that I underftand your language well, for a ftranger, yet I declare to you, the moment you fpoke it, had you afked, what was the Arabic for a fhower of rain, I could not have told you. I declare to you, upon my word, it was that which I laughed at, and upon no other account whatever." " You are going, fays he, to countries where you will have rain and wind, fufficiently cold, and where the water in the mountains is harder than the dry land, and people ftand upon it *. We have only the remnant of their fhowers, and it is to that we owe our greateft happinefs."

I was very much pleafed with his converfation. He feemed to be near fifty years of age, was exceedingly well dreffed, had neither gun nor piftol about him, not even a knife,

---

* Yemen, or the high land of Arabia Felix, where water freezes,

knife, nor an Arab fervant armed, though they were all well dreffed; but he had in his court-yard about threefcore of the fineft horfes I had for a long time feen. We dined juft oppofite to them, in a fmall faloon ftrowed with India carpets; the walls were covered with white tiles, which I fuppofe he had got from India; yet his houfe, without, was a very common one, diftinguifhed only from the reft in the village by its fize.

He feemed to have a more rational knowledge of things, and fpoke more elegantly than any man I had converfed with in Arabia. He faid he had loft the only feven fons he had, in one month, by the fmall-pox: And when I attempted to go away, he wifhed I would ftay with him fome time, and faid, that I had better take up my lodgings in his houfe, than go on board the boat that night, where I was not perfectly in fafety. On my feeming furprifed at this, he told me, that laft year, a veffel from Mafcatte, on the Indian Ocean, had quarrelled with his people; that they had fought on the fhore, and feveral of the crew had been killed; that they had obftinately cruized in the neighbourhood, in hopes of reprifals, till, by the change of the monfoon, they had loft their paffage home, and fo were necef-farily confined to the Red Sea for fix months afterwards; he added, they had four guns, which they called patareroes, and that they would certainly cut us off, as they could not mifs to fall in with us. This was the very worft news that I had ever heard, as to what might happen at fea. Before this, we thought all ftrangers were our friends, and only feared the natives of the coaft for enemies; now, upon a bare defencelefs fhore, we found ourfelves likely to be a prey to both natives and ftrangers.

Our Rais, above all, was feized with a panic; his country was juft adjoining to Mafcatte upon the Indian Ocean, and they were generally at war. He faid he knew well who they were, that there was no country kept in better order than Mafcatte; but that thefe were a fet of pirates, belonging to the Bahareen; that their veffels were ftout, full of men, who carried incenfe to Jidda, and up as far as Madagafcar; that they feared no man, and loved no man, only were true to their employers for the time. He imagined (I fuppofe it was but imagination,) that he had feen a veffel in the morning, (a lug-fail veffel, as the pirate was defcribed to be,) and it was with difficulty we could prevail on the Rais not to fail back to Jidda. I took my leave of the Emir to return to my tent, to hold a confultation what was to be done.

Konfodah is in the lat. 19° 7' North. It is one of the moft unwholefome parts on the Red Sea, provifion is very dear and bad, and the water, (contrary to what the Emir had told me) execrable. Goats flefh is the only meat, and that very dear and lean. The anchorage, from the caftle, bears north-weft a quarter of a mile diftant, from ten to feven fathoms, in fand and mud.

On the 14th, our Rais, more afraid of dying by a fever than by the hands of the pirates, confented willingly to put to fea. The Emir's good dinners had not extended to the boat's crew, and they had been upon fhort commons. The Rais's fever had returned fince he left Jidda, and I gave him fome dofes of bark, after which he foon recovered. But he was always complaining of hunger, which the black flefh of an old goat, the Emir had given us, did not fatisfy.

We

We failed at fix o'clock in the morning, having firft, by way of precaution, thrown all our ballaft over-board, that we might run into fhoal water upon the appearance of the enemy. We kept a good look-out toward the horizon all around us, efpecially when we failed in the morning. I obferved we became all fearlefs, and bold, about noon; but towards night the panic again feized us, like children that are afraid of ghofts; though at that time we might have been fure that all ftranger veffels were at anchor.

We had little wind, and paffed between various rocks to the weftward, continuing our courfe S. S. E. nearly, fomewhat more eafterly, and about three miles diftant from the fhore. At four o'clock, noon, we paffed Jibbel Sabeia, a fandy ifland, larger than the others, but no higher. To this ifland the Arabs of Ras Heli fend their wives and children in time of war; none of the reft are inhabited. At five we paffed Ras Heli, which is the boundary between Yemen, or Arabia Felix, and the * Hejaz, or province of Mecca, the firft belonging to the Imam, or king of Sana, the other to the Sherriffe lately fpoken of.

I desired my Rais to anchor this night clofe under the Cape, as it was perfectly calm and clear, and, by taking a mean of five obfervations of the paffage of fo many ftars, the moft proper for the purpofe, over the meridian, I determined the latitude of Ras Heli, and confequently the boundary of the

---

* Arabia Deferta,

the two ſtates, Hejaz and Yemen, or Arabia Felix and Arabia Deſerta, to be 18° 36' north.

THE mountains reach here nearer to the ſea. We anchored a mile from the ſhore in 15 fathoms, the banks were ſand and coral; from this the coaſt is better inhabited. The principal Arabs to which the country belongs are Cotruſhi, Sebahi, Helali, Mauchlota, and Menjahi. Theſe are not Arabs by origin, but came from the oppoſite coaſt near Azab, and were *Shepherds*, who were ſtubborn enemies to Mahomet, but at laſt converted; they are black, and woolly-headed. The mountains and ſmall iſlands on the coaſt, farther inland to the eaſtward, are in poſſeſſion of the *Habib*. Theſe are white in colour, rebellious, or independent Arabs, who pay no ſort of obedience to the Imam, or the Sherriffe of Mecca, but occaſionally plunder the towns on the coaſt.

ALL the ſandy deſert at the foot of the mountains is called *Tehama*, which extends to Mocha. But in the maps it is marked as a ſeparate country from Arabia Felix, whereas it is but the low part, or ſea-coaſt of it, and is not a ſeparate juriſdiction. It is called *Tema* in ſcripture, and derives its name from *Taami* in Arabic, which ſignifies the ſea-coaſt. There is little water here, as it never rains; there is alſo no animal but the gazel or antelope, and but a few of them. There are few birds, and thoſe which may be found are generally mute.

THE 15th, we ſailed with little wind, coaſting along the ſhore, ſometimes at two miles diſtance, and often leſs. The mountains now ſeemed high. I founded ſeveral times, and found no ground at thirty fathoms, within a mile of the ſhore.

shore. We passed several ports or harbours; first Merſa Amec, where there is good anchorage in eleven fathom of water, a mile and a half from the shore; at eight o'clock, Nohoude, with an island of the same name; at ten, a harbour and village called Dahaban. As the sky was quite overcast, I could get no observation, though I watched very attentively. Dahaban is a large village, where there is both water and provision, but I did not see its harbour. It bore E. N. E. of us about three miles distant. At three quarters past eleven we came up to a high rock, called *Kotumbal*, and I lay to, for observation. It is of a dark-brown, approaching to red; is about two miles from the Arabian shore, and produces nothing. I found its latitude to be 17° 57' north. A small rock stands up at one end of the base of the mountain.

We came to an anchor in the port of Sibt, where I went ashore under pretence of seeking provisions, but in reality to see the country, and observe what sort of people the inhabitants were. The mountains from Kotumbal ran in an even chain along the coast, at no great distance, but of such a height, that as yet we had seen nothing like them. Sibt is too mean, and too small to be called a village, even in Arabia. It consists of about fifteen or twenty miserable huts, built of straw; around it there is a plantation of doomtrees, of the leaves of which they make mats and sails, which is the whole manufacture of the place.

Our Rais made many purchases here. The *Cotrushi*, the inhabitants of this village, seem to be as brutish a people as any in the world. They are perfectly lean, but muscular, and apparently strong; they wear all their own hair, which they divide upon the crown of their head. It is black and bushy, and, although sufficiently long, seems to partake of the woolly quality of the Negro. Their head is bound round with a cord or fillet of the doom leaf, like the ancient diadem. The women are generally ill-favoured, and go naked like the men. Those that are married have, for the most part, a rag about their middle, some of them not that. Girls of all ages go quite naked, but seem not to be conscious of any impropriety in their appearance. Their lips, eye-brows, and foreheads above the eye-brow, are all marked with stibium, or antimony, the common ornament of savages throughout the world. They seemed to be perfectly on an equality with the men, walked, sat, and smoked with them, contrary to the practice of all women among the Turks and Arabs.

WE found no provisions at Sibt, and the water very bad. We returned on board our vessel at sun-set, and anchored in eleven fathom, little less than a mile from the shore. About eight o'clock, two girls, not fifteen, swam off from the shore, and came on board. They wanted stibium for their eye-brows. As they had laboured so hard for it, I gave them a small quantity, which they tied in a rag about their neck. I had killed three sharks this day; one of them, very large, was lying on deck. I asked them if they were not afraid of that fish? They said, they knew it, but it would not hurt them, and desired us to eat it, for it was good, and made men strong. There appeared no symptoms of jealousy among them. The harbour of Sibt is of a semi-circular form, screened between N. N. E. and S. S. W. but to the south, and south west, it is exposed, and therefore is good only in summer.

THE SOURCE OF THE NILE.

THE 16th, at five in the morning, we failed from the port of Sibt, but, the wind being contrary, were obliged to steer to the W. S. W. and it was not till nine o'clock we could resume our true course, which was south-east. At half past four in the afternoon the main bore seven miles east, when we passed an island a quarter of a mile in length, called *Jibbel Foran*, the Mountain of Mice. It is of a rocky quality, with some trees on the south end, thence it rises infensibly, and ends in a precipice on the north. At six, we passed the island * Deregé, low and covered with grass, but round like a shield, which is the reason of its name. At half past six Ras Tarfa bore E. S. E. of us, distant about two miles; and at three quarters after six we passed several other islands, the largest of which is called *Saraffer*. It is covered with grass, has small trees upon it, and, probably, therefore water, but is uninhabited. At nine in the evening we anchored before Djezan.

DJEZAN is in lat. 16° 45' north, situated on a cape, which forms one side of a large bay. It is built, as are all the towns on the coast, with straw and mud. It was once a very considerable place for trade, but since coffee hath been so much in demand, of which they have none, that commerce is moved to Loheia and Hodeida. It is an usurpation from the territory of the Imam, by a Sherriffe of the family of Beni Hassan, called *Booarish*. The inhabitants are all Sherriffes, in other terms, troublesome, ignorant fanatics. Djezan is one of the towns most subject to fevers. The

---

* Der-gé, from that word in Hebrew.

Farenteit *, or worm, is very frequent here. They have great abundance of excellent fish, and fruit in plenty, which is brought from the mountains, whence also they are supplied with very good water,

The 17th, in the evening, we sailed from Djezan; in the night we passed several small villages called *Dueime*, which I found to be in lat. 16° 12′ 5″ north. In the morning, being three miles distant from the shore, we passed Cape Cofferah, which forms the north side of a large Gulf. The mountains here are at no great distance, but they are not high. The whole country seems perfectly bare and desert, without inhabitants. It is reported to be the most unwholesome part of Arabia Felix.

On the 18th, at seven in the morning, we first discovered the mountains, under which lies the town of Loheia. These mountains bore north north-east of us, when anchored in three-fathom water, about five miles from the shore. The bay is so shallow, and the tide being at ebb, we could get no nearer; the town bore east north-east of us. Loheia is built upon the south-west side of a peninsula, surrounded every where, but on the east, by the sea. In the middle of this neck there is a small mountain which serves for a fortress, and there are towers with cannon, which reach across on each side of the hill to the shore. Beyond this is a plain, where the Arabs intending to attack the town, generally, assemble. The ground upon which Loheia stands is black earth,

---

* It signifies Pharaoh's worm.

earth, and seems to have been formed by the retiring of the sea. At Loheia we had a very uneasy sensation, a kind of prickling came into our legs, which were bare, occasioned by the salt effluvia, or steams, from the earth, which all about the town, and further to the south, is strongly impregnated with that mineral.

Fish, and butcher meat, and indeed all sorts of provision, are plentiful and reasonable at Loheia, but the water is bad. It is found in the sand at the foot of the mountains, down the sides of which it has fallen in the time of the rain, and is brought to the town in skins upon camels. There is also plenty of fruit brought from the mountains by the Bedowé, who live in the skirts of the town, and supply it with milk, firewood, and fruit, chiefly grapes and bananas.

The government of the Imam is much more gentle than any Moorish government in Arabia or Africa; the people too are of gentler manners, the men, from early ages, being accustomed to trade. The women at Loheia are as solicitous to please as those of the most polished nations in Europe; and, though very retired, whether married or unmarried, they are not less careful of their dress and persons. At home they wear nothing but a long shift of fine cotton-cloth, suitable to their quality. They dye their feet and hands with *henna, not only for ornament, but as an astringent, to keep them dry from sweat: they wear their own hair, which is plaited, and falls in long tails behind.

---

* Liguftrum Ægyptiacum Latifolium.

The Arabians confider long and ftraight hair as beauti-ful. The Abyffinians prefer the fhort and curled. The Arabians perfume themfelves and their fhifts with a com-pofition of mufk, ambergreafe, incenfe, and benjoin, which they mix with the fharp horny nails that are at the extre-mity of the fifh furrumbac; but why this ingredient is added I know not, as the fmell of it, when burnt, does not at all differ from that of horn. They put all thefe ingredients into a kind of cenfer on charcoal, and ftand over the fmoke of it. The fmell is very agreeable; but, in Europe, it would be a very expenfive article of luxury.

The Arab women are not black, there are even fome ex-ceedingly fair. They are more corpulent than the men, but are not much efteemed.—The Abyffinian girls, who are bought for money, are greatly preferred; among other reafons, becaufe their time of bearing children is longer; few Arabian women have children after the age of twenty.

At Loheia we received a letter from Mahomet Gibberti, telling us, that it would yet be ten days before he could join us, and defiring us to be ready by that time. This hur-ried us extremely, for we were much afraid we fhould not have time to fee the remaining part of the Arabian Gulf, to where it joins with the Indian Ocean.

On the 27th, in the evening, we parted from Loheia, but were obliged to tow the boat out. About nine, we anchor-ed between an ifland called *Ormook*, and the land; about eleven we fet fail with a wind at north-eaft, and paffed a clufter of iflands on our left.

Arab of Loheia,
Tribe Beni Koreish.

London Publyhd Decr 1st 1789 by G Robinson & Co

THE SOURCE OF THE NILE.

The 28th, at five o'clock in the morning, we saw the small island of Rafah; at a quarter after six we passed between it and a large island called *Camaran*, where there is a Turkish garrison and town, and plenty of good water. At twelve we passed a low round island, which seemed to consist of white sand. The weather being cloudy, I could get no observation. At one o'clock we were off Cape Israel.

As the weather was fair, and the wind due north and steady, though little of it, my Rais said that we had better stretch over to Azab, than run along the coast in the direction we were now going, because, somewhere between Hodeida and Cape Nummel, there was foul ground, with which he should not like to engage in the night. Nothing could be more agreeable to me. For, though I knew the people of Azab were not to be trusted, yet there were two things I thought I might accomplish, by being on my guard. The one was, to learn what those ruins were that I had heard so much spoken of in Egypt and at Jidda, and which are supposed to have been works of the Queen of Sheba, whose country this was. The other was, to obtain the myrrh and frankincense-tree, which grow upon that coast only, but neither of which had as yet been described by any author.

At four o'clock we passed a dangerous shoal, which is the one I suppose our Rais was afraid of. If so, he could not have adopted a worse measure, than by stretching over from Cape Israel to Azab in the night; for, had the wind come westerly, as it soon after did, we should have probably been on the bank; as it was, we passed it something less than a mile, the wind was north, and we were going at a great rate. At sun-set we saw Jibbel Zekir, with three small islands, iflands, on the north fide of it. At twelve at night the wind failing, we found ourfelves about a league from the weft end of Jibbel Zekir, but it then began to blow frefh from the weft; fo that the Rais begged liberty to abandon the voyage to Azab, and to keep our firft intended one to Mocha. For my part, I had no defire at all to land at Mocha. Mr Niebuhr had already been there before us; and I was fure every ufeful obfervation had been made as to the country, for he had ftaid there a very confiderable time, and was ill ufed. We kept our courfe, however, upon Mocha town.

THE 29th, about two o'clock in the morning, we paffed fix iflands, called Jibbel el Ourèe; and having but indifferent wind, we anchored about nine off the point of the fhoal, which lies immediately eaft of the north fort of Mocha.

THE town of Mocha makes an agreeable appearance from the fea. Behind it there is a grove of palm-trees, that do not feem to have the beauty of thofe in Egypt, probably owing to their being expofed to the violent fouth-wefters that blow here, and make it very uneafy riding for veffels; there is, however, very feldom any damage done. The port is formed by two points of land, which make a femi-circle. Upon each of the points is a fmall fort; the town is in the middle, and if attacked by an enemy, thefe two forts are fo detached that they might be made of more ufe to annoy the town, than they could ever be to defend the harbour. The ground for anchorage is of the very beft kind, fand without coral, which laft chafes the cables all over the Red Sea.

ON the 30th, at feven o'clock in the morning, with a gentle but fteady wind at weft, we failed for the mouth of the
Indian

Indian Ocean. Our Rais became more lively and bolder as he approached his own coaſt, and offered to carry me for nothing, if I would go home with him to Sheher, but I had already enough upon my hand. It is, however, a voyage ſome man of knowledge and enterpriſe ſhould attempt, as the country and the manners of the people are very little known. But this far is certain, that there all the precious gums grow; all the drugs of the *galenical ſchool*, the frankincenſe, myrrh, benjoin, dragons-blood, and a multitude of others, the natural hiſtory of which no one has yet given us

The coaſt of Arabia, all along from Mocha to the Straits, is a bold coaſt, cloſe to which you may run without danger night or day. We continued our courſe within a mile of the ſhore, where in ſome places there appeared to be ſmall woods, in others a flat bare country, bounded with mountains at a conſiderable diſtance. Our wind freſhened as we advanced. About four in the afternoon we ſaw the mountain which forms one of the Capes of the Straits of Babelmandeb, in ſhape reſembling a gunner's quoin. About ſix o'clock, for what reaſon I did not know, our Rais inſiſted upon anchoring for the night behind a ſmall point. I thought, at firſt, it had been for pilots.

The 31ſt, at nine in the morning, we came to an anchor above Jibbel Raban, or Pilots Iſland, juſt under the Cape which, on the Arabian ſide, forms the north entrance of the Straits. We now ſaw a ſmall veſſel enter a round harbour, divided from us by the Cape. The Rais ſaid he had a deſign to have anchored there laſt night; but as it was troubleſome to get out in the morning by the weſterly wind, he intended to run over to Perim iſland to paſs the night,

and

and give us an opportunity to make what obfervations we pleafed in quiet.

We caught here a prodigious quantity of the fineft fifh that I had ever before feen, but the filly Rais greatly troubled our enjoyment, by telling us, that many of the fifh in that part were poifonous. Several of our people took the alarm, and abftained; the rule I made ufe of in choofing mine, was to take all thofe that were likeft the fifh of our own northern feas, nor had I ever any reafon to complain.

At noon, I made an obfervation of the fun, juft under the Cape of the Arabian fhore, with a Hadley's quadrant, and found it to be in lat. 12° 38' 30", but by many paffages of the ftars, obferved by my large aftronomical quadrant in the ifland of Perim, all dedu&tions made, I found the true latitude of the Cape fhould be rather 12° 39' 20" north.

Perim is a low ifland, its harbour good, fronting the Abyffinian fhore. It is a barren, bare rock, producing, on fome parts of it, plants of abfynthium, or rue, in others kelp, that did not feem to thrive; it was at this time perfectly fcorched by the heat of the fun, and had only a very faint appearance of having ever vegetated. The ifland itfelf is about five miles in length, perhaps more, and about two miles in breadth. It becomes narrower at both ends. Ever fince we anchored at the Cape, it had begun to blow ftrongly from the weft, which gave our Rais great apprehenfion, as, he faid, the wind fometimes continued in that point for fifteen days together. This alarmed me not a little, leaft, by miffing Mahomet Gibberti, we fhould lofe our voyage. We had rice and butter, honey and flour.

The

The fea afforded us plenty of fifh, and I had no doubt but hunger would get the better of our fears of being poifoned: with water we were likewife pretty well fupplied, but all this was rendered ufelefs by our being deprived of fire. In fhort, though we could have killed twenty turtles a-day, all we could get to make fire of, were the rotten dry roots of the rue that we pulled from the clefts of the rock, which, with much ado, ferved to make fire for boiling our coffee.

The 1ft of Auguft we ate drammock, made with cold water and raw flour, mixed with butter and honey, but we foon found this would not do, though I never was hungry, in my life, with fo much good provifion about me; for, befides the articles already fpoken of, we had two fkins of wine from Loheia, and a fmall jar of brandy, which I had kept exprefsly for a feaft, to drink the King's health on arriving in his dominions, the *Indian Ocean*. I therefore propofed, that, leaving the Rais on board, myfelf and two men fhould crofs over to the fouth fide, to try if we could get any wood in the kingdom of Adel. This, however, did not pleafe my companions. We were much nearer the Arabian fhore, and the Rais had obferved feveral people on land, who feemed to be fifhers.

If the Abyffinian fhore was bad by its being defert, the danger of the Arabian fide was, that we fhould fall into the hands of thieves. But the fear of wanting, even coffee, was fo prevalent, and the repetition of the drammock dofe fo difgufting, that we refolved to take a boat in the evening, with two men armed, and fpeak to the people we had feen. Here again the Rais's heart failed him. He faid the inhabitants on that coaft had fire-arms as well as we, and they could bring a million together, if they wanted them, in a moment; therefore we fhould forfake Perim ifland for the time, and, without hoifting in the boat, till we faw further, run with the veffel clofe to the Arabian fhore. There, it was conceived, armed as we were, with ammunition in plenty, we fhould be able to defend ourfelves, if thofe we had feen were pirates, of which I had not any fufpicion, as they had been eight hours in our fight,. without having made one movement nearer us; but I was, the only perfon on board that was of that opinion.

Upon attempting to get our veffel out, we found the wind ftrong againft us; fo that we were obliged, with great difficulty and danger, to tow her round the weft point, at the expence of many hard knocks, which fhe got by the way. During this operation, the wind had calmed confiderably; my quadrant, and every thing was on board; all our arms, new charged and primed, were laid, covered with a cloth, in the cabbin, when we found happily that 'the wind became due caft, and with the wind our refolution changed. We were but twenty leagues to Mocha, and not above twenty-fix from Azab, and we thought it better, rather to get on our return to Loheia, than to ftay and live upon drammock, or fight with the pirates for firewood. About fix o'clock, we were under weigh. The wind being perfectly fair, we carried as much fail as our veffel would bear, indeed, till her mafts nodded again. But before we begin the account of our return, it will be neceffary to fay fomething of thefe famous Straits, the communication between the Red Sea and Indian Ocean.

THE SOURCE OF THE NILE. 315

This entrance begins to shew itself, or take a shape between two capes; the one on the continent of Africa, the other on the peninsula of Arabia. That on the African side is a high land, or cape, formed by a chain of mountains, which run out in a point far into the sea. The Portuguese, or Venetians, the first Christian traders in those parts, have called it *Gardefui*, which has no signification in any language. But, in that of the country where it is situated, it is called *Gardefan*, and means the *Straits of Burial*, the reason of which will be seen afterwards. The opposite cape is Fartack, on the east coast of Arabia Felix, and the distance between them, in a line drawn across from one to another, not above fifty leagues. The breadth between these two lands diminishes gradually for about 150 leagues, till at last it ends in the Straits, whose breadth does not seem to me to be above six leagues.

After getting within the Straits, the channel is divided into two, by the island of Perim, otherwise called *Mehun*. The inmost and northern channel, or that towards the Arabian shore, is two leagues broad at most, and from twelve to seventeen fathom of water. The other entry is three leagues broad, with deep water, from twenty to thirty fathom. From this, the coast on both sides runs nearly in a north-west direction, widening as it advances, and the Indian Ocean grows straiter. The coast upon the left hand is part of the kingdom of Adel, and, on the right, that of Arabia Felix. The passage on the Arabian shore, though the narrowest and shallowest of the two, is that most frequently sailed through, and especially in the night; because, if you do not round the south-point of the island, as near as possible, in attempting to enter the broad one, but are going large with the

R r
wind

wind favourable, you fall in with a great number of low small iflands, where there is danger. At ten o'clock, with the wind fair, our courfe almoft north-eaft, we paffed three rocky iflands about a mile on our left.

On the 2d, at fun-rife, we faw land a-head, which we took to be the Main, but, upon nearer approach, and the day becoming clearer, we found two low iflands to the leeward; one of which we fetched with great difficulty. We found there the ftock of an old acacia-tree, and two or three bundles of wreck, or rotten fticks, which we gathered with great care; and all of us agreed, we would eat breakfaft, dinner and fupper hot, inftead of the cold repaft we had made upon the drammock in the Straits. We now made feveral large fires; one took the charge of the coffee, another boiled the rice; we killed four turtles, made ready a dolphin; got beer, wine, and brandy, and drank the King's health in earneft, which our regimen would not allow us to do in the Straits of Babelmandeb. While this good chear was preparing, I faw with my glafs, firft one man running along the coaft weftward, who did not ftop; about a quarter of an hour after, another upon a camel, walking at the ordinary pace, who difmounted juft oppofite to us, and, as I thought, kneeled down to fay his prayers upon the fand. We had launched our boat immediately upon feeing the trunk of the tree on the ifland; fo we were ready, and I ordered two of the men to row me on fhore, which they did.

It is a bay of but ordinary depth, with ftraggling trees, and fome flat ground along the coaft. Immediately behind is a row of mountains of a brownifh or black colour. The man remained motionlefs, fitting on the ground, till the

boat

boat was afhore, when I jumped out upon the fand, being armed with a fhort double-barrelled gun, a pair of piftols, and a crooked knife. As foon as the favage faw me afhore, he made the beft of his way to his camel, and got upon his back, but did not offer to go away.

I SAT down on the ground, after taking the white turban off my head, and waving it feveral times in token of peace, and feeing that he did not ftir, I advanced to him about a hundred yards. Still he ftood, and after again waving to him with my hands, as inviting him to approach, I made a fign as if I was returning to the fhore. Upon feeing this, he advanced feveral paces, and ftopt. I then laid my gun down upon the land, thinking that had frightened him, and walked up as near him as he would fuffer me; that is, till I faw he was preparing to go away. I then waved my turban, and cried, *Salam, Salam*. He ftaid till I was within ten yards of him. He was quite naked, was black, and had a fillet upon his head, either of a black or blue rag, and bracelets of white beads upon both his arms. He appeared as undetermined what to do. I fpoke as diftinctly to him as I could, *Salam Alicum*.—He anfwered fomething like Salam, but what it was I know not. I am, faid I, a ftranger from India, who came laft from Tajoura in the bay of Zeyla, in the kingdom of Adel. He nodded his head, and faid fomething in an unknown language, in which I heard the repetition of Tajoura and Adel. I told him I wanted water, and made a fign of drinking. He pointed up the coaft to the eaftward, and faid, *Raheeda*, then made a fign of drinking, and faid *Tybe*. I now found that he underftood me, and afked him where Azab was? he pointed to a mountain

juft

just before him, and said, Eh owah Azab Tybe, still with a representation of drinking.

I DEBATED with myself, whether I should not take this savage prisoner. He had three short javelins in his hand, and was mounted upon a camel. I was on foot, and above the ancles in sand, with only two pistols, which, whether they would terrify him to surrender or not, I did not know; I should, otherwise, have been obliged to have shot him, and this I did not intend. After having invited him as courteously as I could, to the boat, I walked towards it myself, and, in the way, took up my firelock, which was lying hid among the sand. I saw he did not follow me a step, but when I had taken the gun from the ground, he set off at a trot as fast as he could, to the westward, and we presently lost him among the trees.

I RETURNED to the boat, and then to dinner on the island, which we named Traitor's Island, from the suspicious behaviour of that only man we had seen near it. This excursion lost me the time of making my observation; all the use I made of it was to gather some sticks and camel's dung, which I heaped up, and made the men carry to the boat, to serve us for firing, if we should be detained. The wind was very fair, and we got under weigh by two o'clock.

ABOUT four we passed a rocky island with breakers on its south end, we left it about a mile to the windward of us. The Rais called it Crab-island. About five o'clock we came to an anchor close to a cape of no height, in a small bay, in three fathom of water, and leaving a small island just on our stern. We had not anchored here above ten minutes, before

before an old man and a boy came down to us. As they had no arms, I went afhore, and bought a fkin of water. The old man had a very thievifh appearance, was quite naked, and laughed or fmiled at every word he faid. He fpoke Arabic, but very badly; told me there was great plenty of every thing in the country whither he would carry me. He faid, moreover, that there was a king there, and a people that loved ftrangers.

THE murder of the boat's crew of the Elgin Eaft-Indiaman, in that very fpot where he was then fitting and praifing his countrymen, came prefently into my mind. I found my hand involuntarily take hold of my piftol, and I was, for the only time in my life, ftrongly tempted to commit murder. I thought I faw in the looks of that old vagrant, one of thofe who had butchered fo many Englifhmen in cold blood.

FROM his readinefs to come down, and being fo near the place, it was next to impoffible that he was not one of the party. A little reflection, however, faved his life; and I afked him if he could fell us a fheep, when he faid they were coming. Thefe words put me on my guard, as I did not know how many people might accompany them. I therefore defired him to bring me the water to the boat, which the boy accordingly did, and we paid him, in cohol, or ftibium, to his wifhes.

IMMEDIATELY upon this I ordered them to put the boat afloat, demanding, all the time, where were the fheep? A few minutes afterwards, four ftout young men came down, dragging after them two lean goats, which the old man

main-

maintained to me were sheep. Each man had three light javelins in his hand, and they began to wrangle exceedingly about the animals, whether they were sheep or goats, though they did not seem to underſtand one word of our language, but the words *sheep* and *goat* in Arabic. In five minutes after, their number increaſed to eleven, and I thought it was then full time for me to go on board, for every one of them ſeemed, by his diſcourſe and geſtures, to be violently agitated, but what they ſaid I could not comprehend. I drew to the ſhore, and then put myſelf on board as ſoon as poſſible. They ſeemed to keep at a certain diſtance, crying out *Belled, belled!* and pointing to the land, invited me to come aſhore; the old hypocrite alone ſeemed to have no fear, but followed me cloſe to the boat. I then reſolved to have a free diſcourſe with him. "There is no need, ſaid I to the old man, to ſend for thirteen men to bring two goats. We bought the water from people that had no lances, and we can do without the ſheep, though we could not want the water, therefore, every man that has a lance in his hand let him go away from me, or I will fire upon him."

They ſeemed to take no ſort of notice of this, and came rather nearer. "You old-grey headed traitor, ſaid I, do you think I don't know what you want, by inviting me on ſhore; let all thoſe about you with arms go home about their buſineſs, or I will in a minute blow them all off the face of the earth. He then jumped up, with rather more agility than his age ſeemed to promiſe, and went to where the others were ſitting in a cluſter, and after a little converſation the whole of them retired.

THE old fellow and the boy now came down without fear to the boat, when I gave them tobacco, some beads, and antimony, and did every thing to gain the father's confidence. But he still smiled and laughed, and I saw clearly he had taken his resolution. The whole burden of his song was, to persuade me to come on shore, and he mentioned every inducement, and all the kindness that he would shew me. " It is fit, you old rogue, said I, that, now your life is in my hands, you should know how much better men there are in the world than you. They were my *countrymen*, eleven or twelve of whom you murdered about three years ago, in the very place where you are now sitting, and though I could have killed the same number to-day, without any danger to myself, I have not only let them go away, but have bought and sold with you, and given you presents, when, according to your own law, I should have killed both you and your son. Now do not imagine, knowing what I know, that ever you shall decoy me ashore; but if you will bring me a branch of the myrrh tree, and of the incense tree to-morrow, I will give you two fonduclis for each of them." He said, he would do it that night. " The sooner the better, said I, for it is now becoming dark." Upon this he sent away his boy, who in less than a quarter of an hour came back with a branch in his hand.

I could not contain my joy, I ordered the boat to be drawn upon the shore, and went out to receive it; but, to my great disappointment, I found that it was a branch of Acacia, or Sunt, which we had every where met with in Egypt, Syria, and Arabia. I told him, this was of no use, repeating the word *Gerar*, *Saiël*, *Sunt*. He answered Eh owah *Saiël;* but being asked for the myrrh (mour), he said it was far up in the mountains, but would bring it to me if I would go to the town. Providence, however, had dealt more kindly with us in the moment than we expected. For, upon going afhore out of eagernefs to get the myrrh, I faw, not a quarter of a mile from us, fitting among the trees, at leaft thirty men, armed with javelins, who all got up the moment they faw me landed. I called to the boatmen to fet the boat afloat, which they immediately did, and I got quickly on board; near up to the middle in water; but as I went by the old man, I gave him fo violent a blow upon the face with the thorny branch in my hand, that it felled him to the ground. The boy fled, and we rowed off; but before we took leave of thefe traitors, we gave them a difcharge of three blunderbuffes loaded with piftol-fhot, in the direction where, in all probability, they were lying to fee the boat go off.

I DIRECTED the Rais to ftand out towards Crab-ifland, and there being a gentle breeze from the fhore, carrying an eafy fail, we ftood over upon Mocha town, to avoid fome rocks or iflands, which he faid were to the weftward. While lying at Crab-ifland, I obferved two ftars pafs the meridian, and by them I concluded the latitude of that ifland to be 13° 2′ 45″ North

THE wind continuing moderate, but more to the fouth ward, at three o'clock in the morning of the 3d, we paffed Jibbel el Ourèe, then Jibbel Zekir; and having a fteady gale, with fair and moderate weather, pafling to the weftward of the ifland Rafab, between that and fome other iflands to the north-eaft, where the wind turned contrary, we arrived at Loheia, the 6th, in the morning, being the
third

third day from the time we quitted Azab. We found every thing well on our arrival at Loheia; but no word of Mahomet Gibberti, and I began now to be uneasy. The rains in Abyssinia were to cease the 6th of next month, September, and then was the proper time for our journey to Gondar.

The only money in the country of the * Imam, is a small piece less than a sixpence, and by this the value of all the different denominations of foreign coin is ascertained. It has four names, Commesh, Loubia, Muchsota, and Harf, but the first two of these are most commonly used.

This money is very base adulterated silver, if indeed there is any in it. It has the appearance of pewter; on the one side is written *Olmass*, the name of the Imam; on the other, *Emir el Moumeneen*, Prince of the Faithful, or True Believers; a title, first taken by Omar after the death of Abou Beer; and since, borne by all the legitimate Caliphs. There are likewise Half-commeshes, and these are the smallest specie current in Yemen.

1 VENETIAN SEQUIN, - - - - 90	
1 FONDUCLI, - - - - - - - - 80	COMMESHES.
1 BARBARY SEQUIN, - - - - - 80	
1 PATAKA, *or* IMPERIAL DOLLAR, 40	

When the Indian merchants or vessels are here, the fonducli is raised three commeshes more, though all specie is

---

* Arabia Felix, or Yemen.

scarce in the Imam's country, notwithstanding the quantity continually brought hither for coffee, in silver patakas, that is, dollars, which is the coin in which purchases of any amount are paid. When they are to be changed into commeshes, the changer or broker gives you but 39 instead of 40, so he gains $2\frac{1}{2}$ *per cent.* for all money he changes, that is, by giving bad coin for good.

The long measure in Yemen is the peek of Stamboul, as they call it; but, upon measuring it with a standard of a Stamboul peek, upon a brass rod made on purpose, I found it $26\frac{5}{8}$ inches, which is neither the Stambouline peek, the Hendaizy peek, nor the el Belledy peek. The peek of Stamboul is $23\frac{3}{4}$ inches, so this of Loheia is a distinct peek, which may be called *Yemani.

The weights of Loheia are the rotolo, which are of two sorts, one of 140 drachms, and used in selling fine, the other 160 drachms, for ordinary and coarser goods. This last is divided into 16 ounces, each ounce into 10 drachms; 100 of these rotolos are a *kantar*, or *quintal.* The quintal of Yemen, carried to Cairo or Jidda, is 113 rotolo, because the rotolo of these places is 144 drachms. Their weights appear to be of Italian origin, and were probably brought hither when the Venetians carried on this trade. There is another weight, called *faranzala*, which I take to be the native one of the country. It is equal to 20 rotolo, of 160 drachms each.

The

---

* That is, the Peek of Arabia Felix, or Yemen.

THE SOURCE OF THE NILE. 325

The cuftoms, which at Mocha are three *per cent.* upon India goods, are five here, when brought directly from India; but all goods whatever, brought from Jidda by merchants, whether Turks or natives, pay feven *per cent.* at Loheia.

Loheia is in lat. 15° 40′ 52″ north, and in long. 42° 58′ 15″ eaft of the meridian of Greenwich.---The barometer, at its higheft on the 7th day of Auguft, was 26° 9′, and its loweft 26° 1′, on the 30th of July.---The thermometer, when at its higheft, was 99° on the 30th of the fame month, wind north-eaft; and its loweft was 81° on the 9th of Auguft, wind fouth by eaft.

On the 31ft of Auguft, at four o'clock in the morning, I faw a comet for the firft time. The head of it was fcarcely vifible in the telefcope, that is, its precife form, which was a pale indiftinct luminous body, whofe edges were not at all defined. Its tail extended full 20°. It feemed to be a very thin vapour, for through it I diftinguifhed feveral ftars of the fifth magnitude, which feemed to be increafed in fize. The end of its tail had loft all its fiery colour, and was very thin and white. I could diftinguifh no nucleus, nor any part that feemed redder or deeper than the reft; for all was a dim-ill-defined fpot. At $4^{hrs.}$ 1′ 24″, on the morning of the 31ft, it was diftant 20° 40′ from Rigel; its tail extended to three ftars in Eridanus.

The 1ft of September Mahomet Gibberti arrived, bringing with him the firman for the Naybe of Mafuah, and letters from Metical Aga to *Ras Michael. He alfo brought
a letter

---

* Governor of the Province of Tigré in Abyffinia.

a letter to me, and another to Achmet, the Naybe's nephew, and future succeffor, from Sidi Ali Zimzimia, that is, 'the keeper of Ifhmael's well at Mecca, called *Zimzim*.' In this letter, Sidi Ali defires me to put little truft in the Naybe, but to keep no fecret from Achmet his nephew, who would certainly be my friend.

CHAP.

CHAP. XIII.

Sails for Mafuah—Paffes a Volcano—Comes to Dahalac—Troubled with a Ghoft—Arrives at Mafuah.

ALL being prepared for our departure, we failed from Loheia on the 3d of September 1769, but the wind failing, we were obliged to warp the veffel out upon her anchors. The harbour of Loheia, which is by much the largeft in the Red Sea, is now fo fhallow, and choked up, that, unlefs by a narrow canal through which we enter and go out, there is no where three fathom of water, and in many places not half that depth. This is the cafe with all the harbours on the eaft-coaft of the Red Sea, while thofe on the weft are deep, without any banks or bars before them, which is probably owing, as I have already faid, to the violence of the north-weft winds, the only conftant ftrong winds to be met with in this Gulf. Thefe occafion ftrong currents to fet in upon the eaft-coaft, and heap up the fand and gravel which is blown in from Arabia.

ALL next day, the 4th, we were employed at warping out our veffel againft a contrary wind. The 5th, at three quarters paft five in the morning, we got under fail with little wind.

wind. At half paſt nine, Loheia bore eaſt north-eaſt about four leagues diſtant; and here we came in ſight of ſeveral ſmall, barren, and uninhabited iſlands. Booariſh bore ſouth-weſt two miles off; Zebid one mile and a half diſtant, eaſt and by north; Amar, the ſmalleſt of all, one mile ſouth; and Ormook, ſouth-eaſt by eaſt two miles.

THE Arabs of the mountain, who had attempted to ſurpriſe Loheia in the ſpring, now prepared for another attack againſt it, and had advanced within three days journey. This obliged the Emir to draw together all his troops from the neighbourhood; all the camels were employed to lay in an extraordinary ſtock of water.

OUR Rais, who was a ſtranger, and without connections in this place, found himſelf under great difficulties to provide water enough for the voyage, for we had but a ſcanty proviſion left, and though our boat was no more than ſixty feet long, we had about forty people on board of her. I had indeed hired the veſſel for myſelf, but gave the Rais leave to take ſome known people paſſengers on board, as it was very dangerous to make enemies in the place to which I was going, by fruſtrating any perſon of his voyage home, even though I paid for the boat, and ſtill as dangerous to take a perſon unknown, whoſe end in the voyage might be to defeat my deſigns. We were reſolved, therefore, to bear away for an iſland to the northward, where they ſaid the water was both good, and in plenty.

IN the courſe of this day, we paſſed ſeveral ſmall iſlands, and, in the evening, anchored in ſeven fathom and a half of water, near a ſhoal diſtant four leagues from Loheia. We there

there observed the bearings and distances of several islands, with which we were engaged; Foosht, W.b.N.¼ north, four leagues; Baccalan N.W.b.W. three leagues; Baida, a large high rock above the water, with white steep cliffs, and a great quantity of sea-fowl; Djund, and Mufracken, two large rocks off the west point off Baccalan, W.N.W.¼ west, eleven miles; they appear, at a distance, like a large heap of ruins: Umsegger, a very small island, nearly level with the water, W.N.W.¼ west four miles distant; Nachel, S.E.¼E. one league off; Ajerb S.E.b.E.½ south, two leagues; Surbat, an island S.E.b.E.¼ south, distant ten miles; it has a marabout or Shekh's tomb upon it: Dahu and Dee, two small islands, close together, N.W.¼ west, about eleven miles distant; Djua S.E.½ south; it is a small white island four leagues and a half off: Sahar, W.¼ north, nine miles off.

On the 6th, we got under sail at five o'clock in the morning. Our water had failed us as we foresaw, but in the evening we anchored at Foosht, in two fathoms water east of the town, and here staid the following day, our sailors being employed in filling our skins with water, for they make no use of casks in this sea.

Foosht is an island of irregular form. It is about five miles from south to north, and about nine in circumference. It abounds in good fish. We did not use our net, as our lines more than supplied us. There were many kinds, painted with the most beautiful colours in the world, but I always observed, the more beautiful they were, the worse for eating. There were indeed none good but those that resembled the fish of the north in their form, and plainness of their colours. Foosht is low and sandy on the south, and on the north is a black hill or cape of no confiderable height, that may be feen at four leagues off. It has two watering-places; one on the eaft of the ifland, where we now were, the other on the weft. The water there is bitter, but it had been troubled by a number of little barks, that had been taking in water juft before us. The manner of filling their goat fkins being a very flovenly one, they take up much of the mud along with it, but we found the water excellent, after it had fettled two or three days; when it came on board, it was as black as ink. It was incomparably the beft water we had drank fince that of the Nile.

This ifland is covered with a kind of bent grafs, which want of rain, and the conftant feeding of the few goats that are kept here, prevent from growing to any height. The end of the ifland, near the north cape, founds very hollow, underneath, like Solfaterra, near Naples; and as quantities of pumice ftones are found here, there is great appearance that the black hill was once a volcano. Several large fhells from the fifh called Biffer, fome of them twenty inches long, are feen turned upon their faces, on the furface of large ftones, of ten or twelve ton weight. Thefe fhells are funk into the ftones, as if they were into pafte, and the ftone raifed round about, fo as to conceal the edge of the fhell; a proof that this ftone has, fome time lately, been foft or liquified. For, had it been long ago, the weather and fun would have worn the furface of the fhell, but it feems perfectly entire, and is fet in that hard brown rock, as the ftone of a ring is in a golden chafing.

The inhabitants of Foofht are poor fifhermen, of the fame degree of blacknefs as thofe between Heli and Djezan; like them

THE SOURCE OF THE NILE. 331

them too, they were naked, or had only a rag about their waift. Their faces are neither ftained nor painted. They catch a quantity of fifh called Seajan, which they carry to Loheia, and exchange for Dora and Indian corn, for they have no bread, but what is procured this way. They alfo have a flat fifh, with a long tail to it, whofe fkin is a fpecies of fhagreen, with which the handles of knives and fwords are made. Pearls too are found here, but neither large nor of a good water, on the other hand, they are not dear; they are the produce of various fpecies of fhells, all Bivalves *

THE town confifts of about thirty huts, built with faggots of bent grafs or fpartum, and thefe are fupported within with a few fticks, and thatched with the grafs, of which they are built. The inhabitants feemed to be much terrified at feeing us come a-fhore all armed; this was not done out of fear of them, but, as we intended to ftay on fhore all night, we wifhed to be in a fituation to defend ourfelves againft boats of ftrollers from the main. The faint, or Marabout, upon feeing me pafs near him, fell flat upon his face, where he lay for a quarter of an hour; nor would he get up till the guns, which I was told had occafioned his fears, were ordered by me to be immediately fent on board.

ON the 7th, by an obfervation of the meridian altitude of the fun, I found the latitude of Foofht to be 15° 59' 43" north. There are here many beautiful fhell-fifh; the concha veneris, of feveral fizes and colours, as alfo fea urchins,

---

* See the article Pearl in the Appendix.

or fea-eggs. I found, particularly, one of the pentaphylloid kind, of a very particular form. Spunges of the common fort are likewife found all along this coaft. The bearings and diftances of the principal iflands from Foofht are:

 Baccalan, and the two rocks Djund } 4 miles.
  and Mufracken, E. N. E.
 Baida rock, E. by N. 4 miles.
 Sahar, - - S. E. 3 do.
 Ardaina, - W.N.W. 8 do.
 Aideen, - - N.½E. 9 do.

BACCALAN is an ifland, low, long, and as broad as Foofht, inhabited by fifhermen; without water in fummer, which is then brought from Foofht, but in winter they preferve the rain-water in cifterns. Thefe were built in ancient times, when this was a place of importance for the fifhing of pearls, and they are in perfect repair to this day; neither the cement of the work, nor the ftucco within, having at all fuffered. Very violent fhowers fall here from the end of October to the beginning of March, but at certain intervals

ALL the iflands on this eaft-fide of the channel belong to the Sherriffe Djezan Booarifh, but none are inhabited except Baccalan and Foofht. This laft ifland is the moft convenient watering-place for fhips, bound up the channel from Jibbel Teir, from which it bears N. E. by E. ¾ E. by the compafs, nineteen leagues diftant. It fhould be remembered, however, that the weftern watering-place is moft eligible, becaufe, in that cafe, navigators need not engage themfelves among the iflands to the eaftward, where they will have uneven foundings two leagues from the land; but, though they

THE SOURCE OF THE NILE. 333

they ſhould fall to the eaſtward of this iſland, they will have good anchorage, from nine to eighteen fathoms water; the bottom being good ſand, between the town and the white rock Baida.

Having ſupplied our great and material want of water, we all repaired on board in the evening of the 7th; we then found ourſelves unprovided with another neceſſary, namely fire; and my people began to remember how cold our ſtomachs were from the drammock at Babelmandeb. Firewood is a very ſcarce article in the Red Sea. It is, nevertheleſs, to be found in ſmall quantities, and in ſuch only it is uſed. Zimmer, an iſland to the northward, was known to afford ſome; but, from the time I had landed at Fooſht, on the 6th, a trouble of a very particular kind had fallen upon our veſſel, of which I had no account till I had returned on board.

An Abyſſinian, who had died on board, and who had been buried upon our coming out from Loheia bay, had been ſeen upon the boltſprit for two nights, and had terrified the ſailors very much; even the Rais had been not a little alarmed; and, though he could not directly ſay that he had ſeen him, yet, after I was in bed on the 7th, he complained ſeriouſly to me of the bad conſequences it would produce if a gale of wind was to riſe, and the ghoſt was to keep his place there, and deſired me to come forward and ſpeak to him. "My good Rais," ſaid I, " I am exceedingly tired, and my head achs much with the ſun, which hath been violent to-day. You know the Abyſſinian paid for his paſſage, and, if he does not overload the ſhip, (and I apprehend he ſhould be lighter than when we took him on board)

I do

"I do not think, that in juftice or equity, either you or I can hinder the ghoft from continuing his voyage to Abyffinia, as we cannot judge what ferious bufinefs he may have there." The Rais began to blefs himfelf that he did not know any thing of his affairs.—" Then, faid I," " if you do not find he makes the veffel too heavy before, do not moleft him; becaufe, certainly if he was to come into any other part of the fhip, or if he was to infift to fit in the middle of you (in the difpofition that you all are) he would be a greater inconvenience to you than in his prefent poft." The Rais began again to blefs himfelf, repeating a verfe of the *Koran;* " bifmilla fheitan rejem," in the name of God keep the devil far from me. "Now, Rais," faid I, "if he does us no harm, you will let him ride upon the boltfprit till he is tired, or till he comes to Mafuah, for I fwear to you, unlefs he hurts or troubles us, I do not think I have any obligation to get out of my bed to moleft him, only fee that he carries nothing off with him.

THE Rais now feemed to be exceedingly offended, and faid, for his part he did not care for his life more than any other man on board; if it was not from fear of a gale of wind, he might ride on the boltfprit and be d———n'd; but that he had always heard learned people could fpeak to ghofts. Will you be fo good, Rais, faid I, to ftep forward, and tell him, that I am going to drink coffee, and fhould be glad if he would walk into the cabbin, and fay any thing he has to communicate to me, if he is a Chriftian, and if not, to Mahomet Gibberti. The Rais went out, but, as my fervant told me, he would neither go himfelf, nor could get any perfon to go to the ghoft for him. He came back, however, to drink coffee with me. I was very ill, and ap-

prehenfive

THE SOURCE OF THE NILE: 335

prehenfive of what the French call a *Coup de foleil*. " Go, faid I to the Rais, to Mahomet Gibberti, who was lying juft before us, tell him that I am a Chriftian, and have no jurifdiction over ghofts in thefe feas."

A MOOR called *Yafine*, well known to me afterwards, now came forward, and told me, that Mahomet Gibberti had been very bad ever fince we failed, with fea-ficknefs, and begged that I would not laugh at the fpirit, or fpeak fo familiarly of him, becaufe it might very poffibly be the devil, who often appeared in thefe parts. The Moor alfo defired I would fend Gibberti fome coffee, and order my fervant to boil him fome rice with frefh water from Foofht; for hitherto our fifh and our rice had been boiled in fea water, which I conftantly preferred. This bad news of my friend Mahomet banifhed all merriment, I gave therefore the neceffary orders to my fervant to wait upon him, and at the fame time recommended to Yafine to go forward with the Koran in his hand, and read all night, or till we fhould get to Zimmer, and then, or in the morning, bring me an account of what he had feen.

THE 8th, early in the morning, we failed from Foofht; but the wind being contrary, we did not arrive at our deftination till near mid-day, when we anchored in an open road about half a mile from the ifland, for there is no harbour in Baccalan, Foofht, nor Zimmer. I then took my quadrant, and went with the boat afhore, to gather wood. Zimmer is a much fmaller ifland than Foofht, without inhabitants, and without water; though, by the cifterns which ftill remain, and are fixty yards fquare, hewed out of the folid rock, we may imagine this was once a place of confequence;

quence: rain in abundance, at certain feafons, ftill falls there. It is covered with young plants of rack tree, whofe property it is, as I have already faid, to vegetate in falt water. The old trees had been cut down, but there was a confiderable number of Saiel, or Acacia trees, and of thefe we were in want.

ALTHOUGH Zimmer is faid to be without water, yet there are antelopes upon it, as alfo hyænas in number, and it is therefore probable that there is water in fome fubterraneous caves or clefts of the rocks, unknown to the Arabs or fifhermen, without which thefe animals could not fubfift. It is probable the antelopes were brought over from Arabia for the Sherriffe's pleafure, or thofe of his friends, if they did not fwim from the main, and an enemy afterwards brought the hyæna to difappoint that amufement.. Be that as it will, though I did not myfelf fee the animals, yet I obferved the dung of each of them upon the fand, and in the cifterns; fo the fact does not reft wholly upon the veracity of the boatman. We found at Zimmer plenty of the large fhell fifh called Biffer and Surrumbac, but no other. I found Zimmer, by an obfervation of the fun at noon, to be in lat. 16° 7′ North, and from it we obferved the following bearings and diftances,

Sahaanah,	dift.	9 miles,	- - S. by W.
Foofht, -	do.	8 do.	N. W. by N. $\frac{1}{4}$ W.
Aideen, -	do.	7 do.	E.
Ardaina, -	do.	2 do.	- E. by S.
Rabha.	do.	6 do.	N. W. $\frac{1}{4}$ N.
Doohaarab	do,	21 do,	W. N. W. $\frac{1}{4}$ W.

WE

THE SOURCE OF THE NILE.

We failed in the night from Zimmer. When we came nearer the channel, the iflands were fewer, and we had never lefs than twenty-five fathom water. The wind was conftantly to the north and weft, and, during all the heat of the day, N. N. W. At the fame time we had vifibly a ftrong current to the northward.

The 9th, at fix o'clock in the morning, the ifland Rapha bore N. E. by eaft, diftant about two leagues, and in the fame direction we faw the tops of very high mountains in Arabia Felix, which we imagined to be thofe above Djezan; and though thefe could not be lefs than twenty-fix leagues diftance, yet I diftinguifhed their tops plainly, fome minutes before fun-rife. At noon I obferved our latitude to be 16° 10′ 3″ north, fo we had made very little way this day, it being for the moft part calm. Rapha then bore E.¾ north, diftant thirteen miles, and Doohaarab N. N. W. five miles off. We continued under fail all the evening, but made little way, and ftill lefs during the night.

On the 10th, at feven in the morning, I firft faw Jibbel Teir, till then it had been covered with a mift. I ordered the pilot to bear down directly upon it. All this forenoon our veffel had been furrounded with a prodigious number of fharks. They were of the hammer-headed kind, and two large ones feemed to vie with each other which fhould come neareft our veffel. The Rais had fitted a large, harpoon with a long line for the large fifh in the channel, and I went to the boltfprit to wait for one of the fharks, after having begged the Rais, firft to examine if all was tight there, and if the ghoft had done it no harm by fitting fo many nights upon it. He fhook his head, laughing, and

Vol. I. U u faid,

said, " The sharks seek something more substantial than ghosts." "If I am not mistaken, Rais, said I, this ghost seeks something more substantial too, and you shall see the end of it."

I STRUCK the largest shark about a foot from the head, with such force, that the whole iron was buried in his body. He shuddered, as a person does when cold, and shook the shaft of the harpoon out of the socket, the weapon being made so on purpose; the shaft fell across, kept fixt to the line, and served as a float to bring him up when he dived, and impeded him when he swam. No salmon fisher ever saw finer sport with a fish and a rod. He had thirty fathom of line out, and we had thirty fathom more ready to give him. He never dived, but sailed round the vessel like a ship, always keeping part of his back above water. The Rais, who directed us, begged we would not pull him, but give him as much more line as he wanted; and indeed we saw it was the weight of the line that galled him, for he went round the vessel without seeking to go farther from us. At last he came nearer, upon our gathering up the line, and upon gently pulling it after, we brought him alongside, till we fastened a strong boat-hook in his throat: a man swung upon a cord was now let down to cut his tail, while hanging on the ship's side, but he was, if not absolutely dead, without the power of doing harm. He was eleven feet seven inches from his snout to his tail, and nearly four feet round in the thickest part of him. He had in him a dolphin very lately swallowed, and about half a yard of blue cloth. He was the largest, the Rais said, he had ever seen, either in the Red Sea or the Indian Ocean.

THE SOURCE OF THE NILE.

About twenty minutes before twelve o'clock we were about four leagues distant from the island, as near as I could judge upon a parallel. Having there taken my observation, and all deductions made, I concluded the latitude of the north end of Jibbel Teir to be 15° 38' north; thirty-two leagues west longitude from Loheia, fifty-three east longitude from Masuah, and forty-six leagues east of the meridian of Jidda. Jibbel Teir, or the Mountain of the Bird, is called by others, Jibbel Douhan, or the Mountain of Smoke. I imagine that the same was the origin of our name of * *Gibraltar*, rather than from *Tarik*, who first landed in Spain; and one of my reasons is, that so conspicuous a mountain, near, and immediately in the face of the moors of Barbary, must have been known by some name, long before Tarik with his Arabs made his descent into Spain.

The reason of its being called Jibbel Douhan, the Mountain of Smoke, is, that though, in the middle of the sea, it is a volcano, which throws out fire, and though nearly extinguished, smokes to this day. It probably has been the occasion of the creation of great part of the neighbouring islands. Did it burn now, it would be of great use to shipping in the night, but in the earliest history of the trade of that sea, no mention is made of it, as in a state of conflagration. It was called *Orneón* in Ptolemy, the Bird-Island, the same as Jibbel Teir. It is likewise called Sheban, from the white spot at the top of it, which seems to be sulphur, and a part seems to have fallen in, and to have

---

* Jibbel Teir, the Mountain of the Bird; corruptly, *Gibraltar*.

have enlarged the crater on this fide. The ifland is four miles from fouth to north, has a peek in form of a pyramid in the middle of it, and is about a quarter of a mile high. It defcends, equally, on both fides, to the fea; has four openings at the top, which vent fmoke, and fometimes, in ftrong foutherly winds it is faid to throw out fire. There was no fuch appearance when we paffed it. The ifland is perfectly defert, being covered with fulphur and pumice ftones.

SOME journals that I have feen are full of indraughts, whirlpools, and unfathomable depths, all around this ifland. I muft however take the liberty of faying to thefe gentlemen, who are otherwife fo very fond of foundings as to diftribute them all over the channel, that they have been unfortunate in placing their unfathomable depths here, and even foundings. It is probable thefe are occafioned by the convulfions in the earth made by this volcano; but the only indraught we faw was a ftrong current fetting northward, and there are foundings as far as three leagues eaft of it, in 33 fathom water, with a fandy bottom. Between this and the ifland Rafab you have foundings from 20 to 35 fathom, with fand and rocks; and on the north-eaft fide you have good anchoring, from a league's diftance, till within a cable's length of the fhore, and there is anchorage five leagues S. W. by. W. in twenty-five fathoms, and I believe alfo, in the line from Loheia to Dahalac, the effects of the convulfions of this vulcano. Such, at leaft, is the information I procured at Mafuah from the pilots ufed to this navigation in fearch of fulphur; fuch was the information alfo of my Rais, who went twice loaded with that commodity to his own country at Mafcatte; no other people go there. Both Abyffinians and Arabians believe that this is

the

the entry or paſſage by which the devil comes up to this world.

Six leagues E. by S. of this iſland there is a dangerous ſhoal with great overfalls, on which a French ſhip ſtruck in the year 1751, and was ſaved with very great difficulty. Jibbel Teir is the point from which all our ſhips, going to Jidda, take their departure, after ſailing from Mocha, and paſſing the iſlands to the ſouthward.

We left Jibbel Teir on the 11th with little wind at weſt, but towards mid-day it freſhened as uſual, and turned northward to N.N. eaſt. We were now in mid-channel, ſo that we ſtood on ſtraight for Dahalac till half paſt four, when a boy, who went aloft, ſaw four iſlands in a direction N. W. by W. $\frac{1}{4}$ weſt. We were ſtanding on with a freſh breeze, and all our ſails full, when I ſaw, a little before ſun-ſet, a white-fringed wave of the well-known figure of a breaker. I cried to the Rais for God's ſake to ſhorten ſail, for I ſaw a breaker a-head, ſtraight in our way. He ſaid there was no ſuch thing; that I had miſtaken it, for it was a ſea-gull. About ſeven in the evening we ſtruck upon a reef of coral rocks. Arabs are cowards in all ſudden dangers, which they conſider as particular directions or mandates of providence, and therefore not to be avoided. Few uncultivated minds indeed have any calmneſs, or immediate reſource in themſelves when in unexpected danger. The Arab ſailors were immediately for taking the boat, and ſailing to the iſlands the boy had ſeen. The Abyſſinians were for cutting up the planks and wood of the inſide of the veſſel, and making her a raft.

A VIOLENT

A VIOLENT difpute enfued, and after that a battle, when night overtook us, ftill faft upon the rock. The Rais and Yafine, however, calmed the riot, when I begged the paffengers would hear me. I told them, "You all know, or fhould know, that the boat is mine, as I bought it with my money, for the fafety and accommodation of myfelf and fervants; you know, likewife, that I and my men are all well armed, while you are naked; therefore do not imagine that we will fuffer any of you to enter that boat, and fave your lives at the expence of ours. On this veffel of the Rais is your dependence, in it you are to be faved or to perifh; therefore all hands to work, and get the veffel off, while it is calm; if fhe had been materially damaged, fhe had been funk before now." They all feemed on this to take courage, and faid, they hoped I would not leave them. I told them, if they would be men, I would not leave them while there was a bit of the veffel together.

THE boat was immediately launched, and one of my fervants, the Rais, and two failors, were put on board. They were foon upon the bank, where the two failors got out, who cut their feet at firft upon the white coral, but afterwards got firmer footing. They attempted to pufh the fhip backwards, but fhe would not move. Poles and handfpikes were tried in order to ftir her, but thefe were not long enough. In a word, there was no appearance of getting her off before morning, when we knew the wind would rife, and it was to be feared fhe would then be dafhed to pieces. Mahomet Gibberti, and Yafine, had been reading the Koran aloud ever fince the veffel ftruck. I faid to them in paffing, "Sirs, would it not be as wife for you to leave your books till you get a-fhore, and lend a hand to the people?"

people?" Mahomet anfwered, " that he was fo weak and fick, that he could not ftand." But Yafine did not flight the rebuke, he ftripped himfelf naked, went forward on the veffel, and then threw himfelf into the fea. He, firft, very judicioufly, felt what room there was for ftauding, and found the bank was of confiderable breadth, and that we were ftuck upon the point of it; that it rounded, flanting away afterwards, and feemed very deep at the fides, fo the people, ftanding on the right of it, could not reach the vef- fel to pufh it, only thofe upon the point. The Rais and Yafine now cried for poles and handfpikes, which were given them; two more men let themfelves down by the fide, and ftood upon the bank. I then defired the Rais to get out a line, come a-ftern with the boat, and draw her in the fame direction that they pufhed.

As foon as the boat could be towed a-ftern, a great cry was fet up, that fhe began to move. A little after, a gentle wind juft made itfelf felt from the caft, and the cry from the Rais was, Hoift the fore-fail and put it a-back. This being immediately done, and a gentle breeze filling the fore-fail at the time, they all pufhed, and the veffel flid gently off, free from the fhoal. I cannot fay I partook of the joy fo fuddenly as the others did. I had always fome fears a plank might have been ftarted; but we faw the advantage of a veffel being fewed, rather than nailed together, as fhe not only was unhurt, but made very little water. The people were all exceedingly tired, and nobody thought they could enough praife the courage and readinefs of Yafine. From that day he grew into confideration with me, which increa- fed ever after, till my departure from Abyffinia.

THE

The latitude of our place, at noon, had been 15° 32′ 12″. I rectified my quadrant, and hung it up. Seeing the clear of the *Lyre* not far from the meridian, I was willing to be certain of that dangerous place we had fallen upon. By two observations of *Lucida Lyræ*, and *Lucida Aquilæ*, and by a mean of both, I found the bank to be in lat. 15° 28′ 15″ north.

There was a circumstance, during the hurry of this transaction, that gave us all reason to be surprised. The ghost was supposed to be again seen on the boltsprit, as if pushing the vessel ashore; and as this was breaking covenant with me, as a passenger, I thought it was time some notice should be taken of him, since the Rais had referred it entirely to me. I inquired who the persons were that had seen him. Two moors of Hamazen were the first that perceived him, and afterwards a great part of the crew had been brought to believe the reality of this vision. I called them forward to examine them before the Rais, and Mahomet Gibberti, and they declared that, during the night, they had seen him go and come several times; once, he was pushing against the boltsprit, another time he was pulling upon the rope, as if he had an anchor ashore; after this he had a very long pole, or stick, in his hand, but it seemed heavy and stiff, as if it had been made of iron, and when the vessel began to move, he turned into a small blue flame, ran along the gunnel on the larboard side of the ship, and, upon the vessel going off, he disappeared. " Now, said I, " it is plain by this change of shape, that he has left us for ever, let us therefore see whether he has done us any harm or not. Hath any of you any baggage stowed forwards ?" The strangers answered, " Yes, it is all there." Then

said

said I, go forward, and see if every man has got his own. They all did this without loss of time, when a great noise and confusion ensued; every one was plundered of something, stibium, nails, brass wire, incense and beads; in short, all the precious part of their little stores was stolen.

All the passengers were now in the utmost despair, and began to charge the sailors. "I appeal to you, Yasine and Mahomet Gibberti, said I, whether these two moors who saw him oftenest, and were most intimate with him, have not a chance of knowing where the things are hid; for in my country, where ghosts are very frequent, they are always assisted in the thefts they are guilty of, by those that see and converse with them. I suppose therefore it is the same with Mahometan ghosts." "The very same, said Mahomet Gibberti and Yasine, as far as ever we heard." "Then go, Yasine, with the Rais, and examine that part of the ship where the moors slept, while I keep them here; and take two sailors with you, that know the secret places." Before the search began, however, one of them told Yasine where every thing was, and accordingly all was found and restored. I would not have the reader imagine, that I here mean to value myself, either upon any supernatural knowledge, or extreme sagacity, in supposing that it was a piece of roguery from the beginning, of which I never doubted. But while Yasine and the sailors were busy pushing off the vessel, and I a-stern at an observation, Mahomet Gibberti's servant, sitting by his master, saw one of the moors go to the repository of the baggage, and, after staying a little, come out with a box and package in his hand. This he told his master, who informed me, and the ghost finding his associates discovered, never was seen any more.

THE 12th, in the morning, we found that this shoal was a sand bank, with a ridge of coral rocks upon it, which stretches hither from Selma, and ends a little farther to the northward in deep water. At sun-rise the islands bore as follow :—

Wowcan,	distant	5	miles	S. S. E. ¼ E.
Selma	do.	3	do.	S.
Megaida	do.	4	do.	S. W. ½ S.
Zober	do.	4	do.	W. by S. ¼ S.
Raeka	do.	5	do.	N. N. W.
Furſh	do.	4	do.	N. W. by N. ¼ N.

THESE islands lie in a semi-circle round this shoal. There were no breakers upon it, the sea being so perfectly calm. I suppose if there had been wind, it would have broken upon it, as I certainly saw it do before we struck; between Megaida and Zober is a small sharp rock above the surface of the sea.

WE got under sail at six in the morning, but the wind was very fast decaying, and soon after fell dead-calm. Towards eleven, as usual, it freshened, and almost at due north. At noon I found our lat. to be 15° 29′ 33″ north, from which we had the following bearings :—

Selma,	distant	5	miles,	S. E. ½ S.
Megaida,	do.	4	do.	S. S. E.
Zober,	do.	2	do.	S.
Dubia,	do.	5	do.	W. by S. ¼ S.
Racka,	do.	1	do.	N. W.
Beyoume,	do.	5	do.	N. W. by N.

Cigala,

THE SOURCE OF THE NILE.

Cigala,	diſtant	6 miles,	N.
Furſh,	do.	3 do.	N.E.byN.¼N.

---and the rocks upon which we ſtruck, E. by S.½S. ſomething leſs than five miles off.

At four o'clock in the afternoon we ſaw land, which our pilot told us was the ſouth end of Dahalac. It bore weſt by ſouth, and was diſtant about nine leagues. As our courſe was then weſt by north, I found that we were going whither I had no intention to land, as my agreement was to touch at Dahalac el Kibeer, which is the principal port, and on the ſouth end of the iſland, where the India ſhips formerly uſed to reſort, as there is deep water, and plenty of ſea-room between that and the main. But the freight of four ſacks of dora, which did not amount to ten ſhillings, was ſufficient to make the Rais break his word, and run a riſk of cancelling all the meritorious ſervices he had ſo long performed for me. So certain is it, that none of theſe people can ever do what is right, where the ſmalleſt trifle is thrown into the ſcale to bias them from their duty.

At ſix in the evening we anchored near a ſmall iſland called *Racka Garbia*, or Weſt Racka, in four fathom of ſtonyground. By a meridian altitude of *Lucida Aquilæ*, I concluded the lat. to be 15° 31′ 30″ north, and our bearings as follow:—

Dallacken,	diſtant	3 miles,	N.E.¾E.
Dalgrouſht,	do.	5 do.	S.E.byE.½S.
Delleſheb,	do.	6 do.	E.N.E.¾E.
Dubia,	do.	11 do.	E.byS.½S.
Racka Garbia,	do.	2 do.	S.W.byW.¼S.

On the 13th, a little after fun-rife, we continued our courfe weft, and a very little foutherly, with little wind. At eight o'clock we paffed Dalgroufht, north by eaft about a league diftance, and a new ifland, Germ Malco, weft by north. At noon, I obferved our latitude to be 15° 33′ 13″ north; and our bearings as follow:—

Dallacken,	diftant	6 miles;	E. by S.
Racka,	do.	6 do.	S. E. by S.
Germ Malco,	do.	6. do.	S. S. W.
Dalgroufht,	do.	4 do.	E. N. E.
Dennifarek,	do.	7 do.	N. N. W.
Seide el Arabi,	do.	4 do.	W. by S.
Dahal Coufs,	do.	9 do.	N. W. by N.

The fouth cape of the ifland of Dahalac is called *Ras Shouke*, which, in Arabic, means the Cape of Thorns, becaufe upon it are a quantity of funt, or acacia, the thorny-tree which bears the gum-arabic. We continued our courfe along the eaft fide of Dahalac, and, at four o'clock in the afternoon, faw Irwée, which is faid to anfwer to the centre of the ifland. It bore then fouth-weft of us four miles. We alfo faw two fmall iflands, Tarza and Siah el Sezan; the firft, north by weft three miles; the fecond, north-eaft by eaft, but fomething farther. After having again violently ftruck on the coral rocks in the entry, at fun-fet we anchored in the harbour of Dobelew.

This harbour is in form circular, and fufficiently defended from all winds, but its entrance is too narrow, and within, it is full of rocks. The bottom of the whole port is covered with large ramifications of white coral, with huge black

THE SOURCE OF THE NILE. 349

black stones; and I could no where observe there were above three fathom water, when it was full sea. The pilot indeed said there were seven, or twelve at the mouth; but so violent a tide rushed in through the entrance, that no vessel could escape being driven upon the rocks, therefore I made no draught of it.

DOBELEW is a village three miles south-west of the harbour. It consists of about eighty houses, built of stone drawn from the sea; these calcine like shells, and make good enough morter, as well as materials for building before burning. All the houses are covered with bent-grafs, like those of Arabia. The 17th, I got my large quadrant a-shore, and observed the sun in the meridian in that village, and determined the lat. of its south-west extremity, to be 15° 42′ 22″ north.

IRWEE is a village still smaller than Dobelew, about four miles distant. From this observation, compared with our account, we computed the southern cape of Dahalac, called *Ras Shouke*, to be in lat. 15° 27′ 30″; and Ras Antalou, or the north cape, to be in lat. 15° 54′ 30″ north.

THE whole length of the island, whose direction is from north-west to south-east, is thirty-seven miles, and its greatest breadth eighteen, which did within a very little agree with the account the inhabitants gave us, who made its length indeed something more.

DAHALAC is by far the largest island in the Red Sea, as none, that we had hitherto seen, exceeded five miles in length. It is low and even, the soil fixed gravel and white sand,

sand, mixed with shells and other marine productions. It is destitute of all sorts of herbage, at least in summer, unless a small quantity of bent grass, just sufficient to feed the few antelopes and goats that are on the island. There is a very beautiful species of this last animal found here, small, short-haired, with thin black sharp horns, having rings upon them, and they are very swift of foot.

This island is, in many places, covered with large plantations of Acacia trees, which grow to no height, seldom above eight feet, but spread wide, and turn flat at top, probably by the influence of the wind from the sea. Though in the neighbourhood of Abyssinia, Dahalac does not partake of its seasons: no rain falls here, from the end of March to the beginning of October; but, in the intermediate months, especially December, January, and February, there are violent showers for twelve hours at a time, which deluge the island, and fill the cisterns so as to serve all next summer; for there are no hills nor mountains in Dahalac, and consequently no springs. These cisterns alone preserve the water, and of them there yet remain three hundred and seventy, all hewn out of the solid rock. They say these were the works of the Persians; it is more probable they were those of the first Ptolemies. But whoever were the constructors of these magnificent reservoirs, they were a very different people from those that now possess them, who have not industry enough to keep one of the three hundred and seventy clear for the use of man. All of them are open to every sort of animal, and half full of the filth they leave there, after drinking and washing in them. The water of Dobelew, and Irwée, tasted strong of musk, from the dung of the goats and antelopes, and the smell before you

you drink it is more naufeous than the tafte; yet one of thefe cifterns, cleaned and fhut up with a door, might afford them wholefome fweet water all the year over.

AFTER the rains fall, a prodigious quantity of grafs immediately fprings up; and the goats give the inhabitants milk, which in winter is the principal part of their fubfiftence, for they neither plow nor fow. All their employment is to work the veffels which trade to the different parts of the coaft. One half of the inhabitants is conftantly on the Arabian fide, and by their labour is enabled to furnifh with * dora, and other provifions, the other half who ftay at home; and when their time is expired, they are relieved by the other half, and fupplied with neceffaries in their turn. But the fuftenance of the poorer fort is entirely fhell and other fifh. Their wives and daughters are very bold, and expert fifher-women. Several of them, entirely naked, fwam off to our veffel before we came to an anchor, begging handfuls of wheat, rice, or dora. They are very importunate and fturdy beggars, and not eafily put off with denials. Thefe miferable people, who live in the villages not frequented by barks from Arabia, are fometimes a whole year without tafting bread. Yet fuch is the attachment to the place of their nativity, they prefer living in this bare, barren, parched fpot, almoft in want of neceffaries of every kind, especially of thefe effential ones, bread and water, to thofe pleafant and plentiful countries on both fides of them. This preference we muft not call ftrange, for it is univerfal: A ftrong attachment to our native country,

---

* Millet, or Indian corn.

country, whatever is its condition, has been impreſſed by Providence, for wiſe ends, in the breaſts of all nations; from Lapland to the Line, you find it written preciſely in the ſame character.

There are twelve villages, or towns, in Dahalac, little different in ſize from Dobelew; each has a plantation of doom-trees round it, which furniſh the only manufacture in the iſland. The leaves of this tree, when dried, are of a gloſſy white, which might very eaſily be miſtaken for ſattin; of theſe they make baſkets of ſurpriſing beauty and neatneſs, ſtaining part of the leaves with red or black, and working them into figures very artificially. I have known ſome of theſe, reſembling ſtraw-baſkets, continue full of water for twenty-four hours, without one drop coming through. They ſell theſe at Loheia and Jidda, the largeſt of them for four commeſh, or ſixpence. This is the employment, or rather amuſement of the men who ſtay at home; for they work but very moderately at it, and all of them indeed take ſpecial care, not to prejudice their health by any kind of fatigue from induſtry.

People of the better ſort, ſuch as the Shekh and his relations, men privileged to be idle, and never expoſed to the ſun, are of a brown complexion, not darker than the inhabitants of Loheia. But the common ſort employed in fiſhing, and thoſe who go conſtantly to ſea, are not indeed black, but red, and little darker than the colour of new mohogany. There are, beſides, blacks among them, who come from Arkeeko and the Main, but even theſe, upon marrying, grow leſs black in a generation.

THE

THE SOURCE OF THE NILE.

The inhabitants of Dahalac feemed to be a fimple, fearful, and inoffenfive people. It is the only part of Africa, or Arabia, (call it which you pleafe) where you fee no one carry arms of any kind; neither gun, knife, nor fword, is to be feen in the hands of any one. Whereas, at Loheia, and on all the coaft of Arabia, and more particularly at Yambo, every perfon goes armed; even the porters, naked, and groaning under the weight of their burden, and heat of the day, have yet a leather belt, in which they carry a crooked knife, fo monftroufly long, that it needs a particular motion and addrefs in walking, not to lame the bearer. This was not always the cafe at Dahalac; feveral of the Portuguefe, on their firft arrival here, were murdered, and the ifland often treated ill, in revenge, by the armaments of that nation. The men feem healthy. They told me they had no difeafes among them, unlefs fometimes in Spring, when the boats of Yemen and Jidda bring the fmall-pox among them, and very few efcape with life that are infected. I could not obferve a man among them that feemed to be fixty years old, from which I infer, they are not long livers, though the air fhould be healthy, as being near the channel, and as they have the north wind all fummer, which moderates the heat.

Or all the iflands we had paffed on this fide the channel, Dahalac alone is inhabited. It depends, as do all the reft, upon Mafuah, and is conferred by a firman from the Grand Signior, on the Bafha of Jidda; and, from him, on Metical Aga, then on the Naybe and his fervants. The prefent governor's name was Hagi Mahomet Abd el cader, of whom I have before fpoken, as having failed from Jidda to Mafuah before me, where he did me all the dif-fervice in his power, and nearly procured my aſſaſſination. The revenue of this governor confiſts in a goat brought to him monthly by each of the twelve villages. Every veſſel, that puts in there for Maſuah, pays him alſo a pound of coffee, and every one from Arabia, a dollar or pataka. No ſort of ſmall money is current at Dahalac, excepting Venetian glaſs-beads, old and new, of all ſizes and colours, broken and whole.

ALTHOUGH this is the miſerable ſtate of Dahalac at preſent, matters were widely different in former times. The pearl fiſhery flouriſhed greatly here, under the Ptolemies; and even long after, in the time of the Caliphs, it produced a great revenue, and, till the ſovereigns of Cairo, of the preſent miſerable race of ſlaves, began to withdraw themſelves from their dependency on the port (for even after the reign of Selim, and the conqueſts of Arabia, under Sinan Baſha, the Turkiſh gallies were ſtill kept up at Suez, whilſt Maſuah and Suakem had Baſhas) Dahalac was the principal iſland that furniſhed the pearl fiſhers, or divers. It was, indeed, the chief port for the fiſhery on the ſouthern part of the Red Sea, as Suakem was on the north; and the Baſha of Maſuah paſſed part of every ſummer here, to avoid the heat at his place of reſidence on the Continent.

THE fiſhery extended from Dahalac and its iſlands nearly to lat. 20°. The inhabited iſlands furniſhed each a bark, and ſo many divers, and they were paid in wheat, flour, &c. ſuch a portion to each bark, for their uſe, and ſo much to leave with their family, for their ſubſiſtence; ſo that a few months employment furniſhed them with every thing neceſſary for the reſt of the year. The fiſhery was rented, in latter times, to the Baſha of Suakem, but there was a place between

between Suakem, and the suppofed river Frat, in lat. 21° 28' north, called *Gungunnah*, which was referved to the Grand Signior in particular, and a fpecial officer was appointed to receive the pearls on the fpot, and fend them to Conftantinople. The pearls found there were of the largeft fize, and inferior to none in water, or roundnefs. Tradition fays, that this was, exclufively, the property of the Pharaohs, by which is meant, in Arabian manufcrip's, the old kings of Egypt before Mahomet.

In the fame extent, between Dahalac and Suakem, was another very valuable fifhery, that of * tortoifes, from which the fineft fhells of that kind were produced, and a great trade was carried on with the Eaft Indies, (China efpecially) at little expence, and with very confiderable profits. The animal itfelf (the turtle) was in great plenty, between lat. 18° and 20°, in the neighbourhood of thofe low fandy iflands, laid down in my chart.

The India trade flourifhed exceedingly at Suakem and Mafuah, as it had done in the profperous time of the Caliphs. The Banians, (then the only traders from the Eaft Indies) being prohibited by the Mahometans to enter the Holy Land of the Hejaz, carried all their veffels to Konfodah in Yemen, and from thefe two ports had, in return, at the firft hand, pearls, tortoife-fhell, which fold for its weight of gold, in China; Tibbar, or pure gold of Sennaar, (that from Abyffinia being lefs fo) elephant's teeth, rhinoceros horns

---

* See the article Tortoife in the Appendix.

horns for turning, plenty of gum Arabic, caffia, myrrh, frankincenfe, and many other precious articles; thefe were all bartered, at Mafuah and Suakem, for India goods. But nothing which violence and injuftice can ruin, ever can, fubfift under Turkifh government. The Bafhas paying dearly for their confirmation at Conftantinople, and uncertain if they fhould hold this office long enough to make reimburfements for the money they had already advanced, had not patience to ftay till the courfe of trade gradually indemnified them, but proceeding from extortion to extortion, they at laft became downright robbers, feizing the cargo of the fhips wherever they could find them, and exercifing the moft fhocking cruelties on the perfon they belonged to, flaying the factors alive, and impaling thofe that remained in their hands, to obtain, by terror, remittances from India. The trade was thus abandoned, and the revenue ceafed. There were no bidders at Conftantinople for the farm, nobody had trade in their heads when their lives were every hour in danger. Dahalac became therefore dependent on the Bafha of Jidda, and he appointed an * Aga, who paid him a moderate fum, and appropriated to himfelf the provifions and falary allowed for the pearl fifhery, or the greateft part of them.

The Aga at Suakem endeavoured, in vain, to make the Arabs and people near him work without falary, fo they abandoned an employment which produced nothing but punifhment; and, in time, they grew ignorant of the fifhery
in

---

* A Subaltern Governor.

in which they once were so well skilled and had been educated. This great nursery of seamen therefore was lost, and the gallies, being no longer properly manned, were either given up to rot, or turned into merchant-ships for carrying the coffee between Yemen and Suez, these vessels were unarmed, and indeed incapable of armament, and unserviceable by their construction; besides, they were ill-manned, and so carelessly and ignorantly navigated, that there was not a year, that one or more did not founder, not from stress of weather, (for they were sailing in a pond) or from any thing, but ignorance, or inattention.

Trade took again its ancient course towards Jidda. The Sherriffe of Mecca, and all the Arabs, were interested to get it back to Arabia, and with it the government of their own countries. That the pearl fishing might, moreover, no longer be an allurement for the Turkish power to maintain itself here, and oppress them, they discouraged the practice of diving, till it grew into desuetude; this brought insensibly all the people of the islands to the continent, where they were employed in coasting vessels, which continues their only occupation to this day. This policy succeeded; the princes of Arabia became again free from the Turkish power, now but a shadow, and Dahalac, Masuah, and Suakem, returned to their ancient masters, to which they are subject at this instant, governed indeed by Shekhs of their own country, and preserving only the name of Turkish government, each being under the command of a robber and assassin.

The immense treasures in the bottom of the Red Sea have thus been abandoned for near two hundred years, though

though they never were richer in all probability than at prefent. No nation can now turn them to any profit, but the Englifh Eaft India Company, more intent on multiplying the number of their enemies, and weakening themfelves by fpreading their inconfiderable force over new conquefts, than creating additional profit by engaging in new articles of commerce. A fettlement upon the river Frat, which never yet has belonged to any one but wandering Arabs, would open them a market both for coarfe and fine goods from the fouthern frontiers of Morocco, to Congo and Angola, and fet the commerce of pearls and tortoife fhell on foot again. All this fection of the Gulf from Suez, as I am told, is in their charter, and twenty fhips might be employed on the Red Sea, without any violation of territorial claims. The myrrh, the frànkincenfe, fome cinnamon, and variety of drugs, are all in the poffeffion of the weak king of Adel, an ufurper, tyrant, and Pagan, without protection, and willing to trade with any fuperior power, that only would fecure him a miferable livelihood.

If this does not take place, I am perfuaded the time is not far off, when thefe countries fhall, in fome fhape or other, be fubjects of a new mafter. Were another Peter, another Elizabeth, or, better than either, another Catharine to fucceed the prefent, in an empire already extended to China;—were fuch a fovereign, unfettered by European politics, to profecute that eafy tafk of pufhing thofe mountebanks of fovereigns and ftatefmen, thefe ftage-players of government, the Turks, into Afia, the inhabitants of the whole country, who in their hearts look upon her already as their fovereign, becaufe fhe is the head of their religion, would, I am perfuaded, fubmit without a blow that inftant ſtant the Turks were removed on the other ſide of the Hellefpont.

There are neither horſes, dogs, ſheep, cows, nor any ſort of quadruped, but goats, aſſes, a few half-ſtarved camels and antelopes at Dahalac, which laſt are very numerous. The inhabitants have no knowledge of fire-arms, and there are no dogs, nor beaſts of prey in the iſland to kill them; they catch indeed ſome few of them in traps.

On our arrival at Dahalac, on the 14th, we ſaw ſwallows there, and, on the 16th, they were all gone. On our landing at Maſuah, on the 19th, we ſaw a few; the 21ſt and 22d they were in great flocks; on the 2d of October they were all gone. It was the blue long-tailed ſwallow, with the flat head; but there was, likewiſe, the Engliſh martin, black, and darkiſh grey in the body, with a white breaſt.

The language at Dahalac is that of the *Shepherds*; Arabic too is ſpoken by moſt of them. From this iſland we ſee the high mountains of *Habeſh*, running in an even ridge like a wall, parallel to the coaſt, and down to Suakem.

Before I leave Dahalac, I muſt obſerve, that, in a wretched chart, in the hands of ſome of the Engliſh gentlemen at Jidda, there were foundings marked all along the eaſt-coaſt of Dahalac, from thirteen to thirty fathoms, within two leagues of the ſhore. Now, the iſlands I have mentioned occupy a much larger ſpace than that; yet none of them are ſet down in the chart; and, where the foundings are marked thirty, forty, and even ninety fathom, all is full of ſhoals under water, with iſlands and ſunken coral rocks, some of them near the surface, though the breakers do not appear upon them, partly owing to the waves being steadied by the violence of the current, and somewhat kept off by the island. This dangerous error is, probably, owing to the draughts being composed from different journals, where the pilot has had different ways of measuring his distance; some using forty-two feet to a thirty-second glass, and some twenty-eight, both of them being considered as one competent division of a degree; the distances are all too short, and the soundings, and every thing else, consequently out of their places.

Whoever has to navigate in the Abyssinian side of the channel, will do well to pass the island Dahalac on the east side, or, at least, not approach the outmost island, Wowcan, nearer than ten leagues; but, keeping about twelve leagues meridian distance west of Jibbel Teir, or near mid-channel between that and the island, they will then be out of danger; being between lat. 15° 20′ and 15° 40′, which last is the latitude, as I observed, of Saiel Noora, and which is the northern island, we saw, three leagues off Ras Antalou, the northmost cape of Dahalac.

Both at our entering into the port of Dobelew on the 14th, and our going out of it on the 17th, we found a tide running like a sluice, which we apprehended, in spite of our sails being full, would force us out of our course upon the rocks. I imagine it was then at its greatest strength, it now being near the equinoctial full moon. The channel between Terra Firma and the island being very narrow, and the influence of the sun and moon then nearly in the equator,

had

THE SOURCE OF THE NILE.

had occafioned this unufual violence of the tide, by forcing a large column of water through fo narrow a fpace.

On the 17th, after we had examined our veffel, and found fhe had received no damage, and provided water (bad as it was) for the remainder of our voyage, we failed from Dobelew, but, the wind being contrary, we were obliged to come to an anchor, at three quarters paft four o'clock, in ten fathom water, about three leagues from that port, which was to the fouth-weft of us; the bearings and diftances are as follow:—

Derghiman Kibeer,	diftant 10 miles,		W.S.W.
Deleda, -	do. 7 do.		W. by N.
Saiel Sezan, -	do. 4 do.	- -	S. E.
Zeteban, -	do. 5 do.	- -	N. E.
Dahalac, -	do. 12 do.	-	S.S.W.
Dahalhalem, -	do. 12 do.		N.W. by N.

On the 18th, we failed, ftanding off and on, with a contrary wind at north-weft; and a ftrong current in the fame direction. At half paft four in the morning we were forced to come to an anchor. There is here a very fhallow and narrow paffage, which I founded myfelf in the boat, barely one and a half fathom, or nine feet of water, and we were obliged to wait the filling of the tide. This is called the *Bogaz*, which fignifies, as I have before obferved, the narrow and fhallow paffage. It is between the ifland Dahalac and the fouth point of the ifland of Noora, about forty fathom broad, and, on each fide, full of dangerous rocks. The iflands then bore,

Derghiman Seguier,	diftant	3 miles,	- - S. W.
Derghiman Kibeer,	- do.	5 do.	- - S.
Dahalhalem,	- - - do.	4 do.	- - E. N. E.
Noora,	- - - - do.	2 do.	- - N. E b. N.

THE tide now entered with an unufual force, and ran more like the Nile, or a torrent, or ftream conducted to turn a mill, than the fea, or the effects of a tide. At half paft one o'clock, there was water enough to pafs, and we foon were hurried through it by the violence of the current; driving us in a manner truly tremendous.

AT half after three, we paffed between Ras Antalou, the North Cape of Dahalac, and the fmall ifland Dahalottom, which has fome trees upon it. On this ifland is the tomb of Shekh * Abou Gafar, mentioned by Poncet, in his voyage, who miftakes the name of the faint for that of the ifland. The ftrait between the Cape and the ifland is a mile and a half broad. At four in the afternoon, we anchored near a a fmall ifland called *Surat*. All between this and Dahalac; there is no water exceeding feven fathom, till you are near Dahalac Kibeer, whofe port has water for large veffels, but is open to every point, from fouth-weft to north-weft, and has a great fwell.

ALL fhips coming to the weftward of Dahalac had better keep within the ifland Drugerut, between that and the main, where there is plenty of water, and room enough to work.

---

* Poncet's Voyage, tranflated into Englifh, printed for W. Lewis in 1709, in 12mo, page 121.

THE SOURCE OF THE NILE. 363

work, tho', even here, there are iflands a-head; and clear weather, as well as a good look-out, will always be neceffary.

On the 19th of September, at three quarters paft fix in the morning, we failed from our anchorage near Surat. At a quarter paft nine, Dargeli, an ifland with trees upon it, bore N. W. by W. two miles and a half diftant; and Drugerut three leagues and a half north and by eaft, when it fell calm.

At eleven o'clock, we paffed the ifland of Dergaiham, bearing N. by Eaft, three miles diftant, and at five in the afternoon we came to an anchor in the harbour of Mafuah, having been * feventeen days on our paffage, including the day we firft went on board, though this voyage, with a favourable wind, is generally made in three days; it often has, indeed, been failed in lefs.

The reader will obferve, that many of the iflands begin with Dahal, and fome with Del, which laft is only an abbreviation of the former, and both of them fignify *ifland*, in the language of Beja, otherwife called *Geez*, or the language of the fhepherds. Maffowa, too, though generally fpelled in the manner I have here expreffed it, fhould properly be written *Mafuah*, which is the harbour or water of the *Shepherds*. Of this nation, fo often mentioned already in this work, as well as the many other people lefs powerful and numerous than they that inhabit the countries between the tropics, or frontiers of Egypt and the Line, it will

---

* This muft not be attributed wholly to the weather. We fpent much time in furveying the iflands, and in obfervation.

be necessary now to speak in some detail, although the connection they all have with the trade of the Red Sea, and with each other, will oblige me to go back to very early times, to the invention of letters, and all the useful arts, which had their beginning here, were carefully nourished, and came probably to as great a perfection as they did ever since arrive at any other period.

TRAVELS

TO DISCOVER

THE SOURCE OF THE NILE.

BOOK II.

ACCOUNT OF THE FIRST AGES OF THE INDIAN AND AFRICAN TRADE—THE FIRST PEOPLING OF ABYSSINIA AND ATBARA—SOME CONJECTURES CONCERNING THE ORIGIN OF LANGUAGE THERE.

CHAP. I.

Of the India trade in its earliest ages—Settlement of Ethiopia—Troglodytes---Building of the first Cities.

THE farther back we go into the history of Eastern nations, the more reason we have to be surprised at the accounts of their immense riches and magnificence. One who reads the history of Egypt is like a traveller walking through its ancient, ruined, and deserted towns, where all are palaces and temples, without any trace of private or ordinary habitation. So in the earliest, though now mutilated

ted, accounts which we have of them, all is power, splendour, and riches, attended by the luxury which was the neceffary confequence, without any clue or thread left us by which we can remount, or be conducted, to the fource or fountain whence this variety of wealth had flowed; without ever being able to arrive at a period, when thefe people were poor and mean, or even in a ftate of mediocrity, or upon a footing with European nations.

The facred fcriptures, the moft ancient, as well as the moft credible of all hiftories, reprefent Paleftine, of which they particularly treat, in the earlieft ages, as not only full of polifhed, powerful, and orderly ftates, but abounding alfo in filver and gold *, in a greater proportion than is to be found this day in any ftate in Europe, though immenfely rich dominions in a new world have been added to the poffeffion of that territory, which furnifhed the greateft quantity of gold and filver to the old. Paleftine, however, is a poor country, left to its own refources and produce merely. It muft have been always a poor country, without fome extraordinary connection with foreign nations. It never contained either mines of gold or filver, and though, at moft periods of its hiftory, it appears to have been but thinly inhabited, it never of itfelf produced wherewithal to fupport and maintain the few that dwelt in it.

Mr de Montesquieu †, fpeaking of the wealth of Semiramis, imagines that the great riches of the Affyrian empire

---

* Exod. xxxviii 39. † Lib. 21. cap. 6.

empire in her reign, arofe from this queen's having plundered fome more ancient and richer nation, as they, in
their turn, fell afterwards a prey to a poorer, but more
warlike enemy. But however true this fact may be with
regard to Semiramis, it does not folve the general difficulty,
as ftill the fame queftion recurs, concerning the wealth of
that prior nation, which the Affyrians plundered, and
from which they received their treafure. I believe the example is rare, that a large kingdom has been enriched by
war. Alexander conquered all Afia, part of Africa, and a
confiderable portion of Europe; he plundered Semiramis's
kingdom, and all thofe that were tributary to her; he went
farther into the Indies than ever fhe did, though her territories bordered upon the river Indus itfelf; yet neither Ma-
cedon, nor any of the neighbouring provinces of Greece,
could ever compare with the fmall diftricts of Tyre and Sidon for riches.

WAR difperfes wealth in the very inftant it acquires it;
but commerce, well regulated, conftantly and honeftly fupported, carried on with œconomy and punctuality, is the
only thing that ever did enrich extenfive kingdoms; and
one hundred hands employed at the loom will bring to a
country more riches and abundance, than ten thoufand
bearing fpears and fhields. We need not go far to produce an example that will confirm this. The fubjects
and neighbours of Semiramis had brought fpices by land
into Affyria. The Ifhmaelites and Midianites, the merchants and carriers of gold from Ethiopia, and more immediately from Paleftine, met in her dominions; and there
was, for a time, the mart of the Eaft India trade. But, by
an abfurd expedition with an army into India, in hopes to
enrich

enrich herself all at once, she effectually ruined that commerce, and her kingdom fell immediately afterwards.

Whoever reads the history of the most ancient nations, will find the origin of wealth and power to have risen in the east; then to have gradually advanced westward, spreading itself at the same time north and south. They will find the riches and population of those nations decay in proportion as this trade forsakes them; which cannot but suggest to a good understanding, this truth constantly to be found in the disposition of all things in this universe, that God makes use of the smallest means and causes to operate the greatest and most powerful effects. In his hand a pepper-corn is the foundation of the power, glory, and riches of India; he makes an acorn, and by it communicates power and riches to nations divided from India by thousands of leagues of sea.

Let us pursue our consideration of Egypt. Sesostris, before the time we have been just speaking of, passed with a fleet of large ships from the Arabian Gulf into the Indian Ocean; he conquered part of India, and opened to Egypt the commerce of that country by sea. I enter not into the credibility of the number of his fleet, as there is scarce any thing credible left us about the shipping and navigation of the ancients, or, at least, that is not full of difficulties and contradictions; my business is with the expedition, not with the number of the ships. It would appear he revived, rather than first discovered, this way of carrying on the trade to the East Indies, which, though it was at times intermitted, (perhaps forgot by the Princes who were contending for the sovereignty of the continent of Asia), was, nevertheless,

THE SOURCE OF THE NILE.

lefs, perpetually kept up by the trading nations themfelves, from the ports of India and Africa, and on the Red Sea from Edom.

THE pilots from thefe ports alone, of all the world, had a fecret confined to their own knowledge, upon which the fuccefs of thefe voyages depended. This was the phænomena of the trade-winds* and monfoons, which the pilots of Sefoftris knew; and which thofe of Nearchus feem to have taught him only in part, in his voyage afterwards, and of which we are to fpeak in the fequel. Hiftory fays further of Sefoftris, that the Egyptians confidered him as their greateft benefactor, for having laid open to them the trade both of India and Arabia, for having overturned the dominion of the *Shepherd* kings; and, laftly, for having reftored to the Egyptian individuals each their own lands, which had been wrefted from them by the violent hands of the Ethiopian *Shepherds*, during the firft ufurpation of thefe princes.

IN memory of his having happily accomplifhed thefe events, Sefoftris is faid to have built a fhip of cedar of a hundred and twenty yards in length, the outfide of which he covered with plates of gold, and the infide with plates of filver, and this he dedicated in the temple of Ifis. I will not enter into the defence of the probability of his reafons for having built a fhip of this fize, and for fuch a purpofe, as one of ten yards would have fufficiently anfwered. The

---

* Thefe are far from being fynonymous terms, as we fhall fee afterwards.

use it was made for, was apparently to serve for a hieroglyphic, of what he had accomplished, viz. that he had laid open the gold and silver trade from the mines in Ethiopia, and had navigated the ocean in ships made of wood, which were the only ones, he thereby insinuated, that could be employed in that trade. The Egyptian ships, at that time, were all made of the reed papyrus*, covered with skins or leather, a construction which no people could venture to present to the ocean.

There is much to be learned from a proper understanding of these last benefits conferred by Sesostris upon his Egyptian subjects. When we understand these, which is very easy to any that have travelled in the countries we are speaking of, (for nations and causes have changed very little in these countries to this day), it will not be difficult to find a solution of this problem, What was the commerce that, progressively, laid the foundation of all that immense grandeur of the east; what polished them, and cloathed them with silk, scarlet, and gold; and what carried the arts and sciences among them, to a pitch, perhaps, never yet surpassed, and this some thousands of years before the nations in Europe had any other habitation than their native woods, or cloathing than the skins of beasts, wild and domestic, or government, but that first, innate one, which nature had given to the strongest?

Let us inquire what was the connection Sesostris brought about between Egypt and India; what was that commerce

---

* See the article papyrus in the Appendix.

of Ethiopia and Arabia, by which he enriched Egypt, and what was their connection with the peninsula of India; who were those kings who bore so opposite an office, as to be at the same time *Shepherds*; and who were those *Shepherds*, near, and powerful enough to wrest the property of their lands from four million of inhabitants.

To explain this, it will be necessary to enter into some detail, without which no person dipping into the ancient or modern history of this part of Africa, can have any precise idea of it, nor of the different nations inhabiting the peninsula, the source of whose wealth consisted entirely in the early, but well-established commerce between Africa and India. What will make this subject of more easy explanation is, that the ancient employment and occupations of these people in the first ages, were still the same that subsist at this day. The people have altered a little by colonies of strangers being introduced among them, but their manners and employments are the same as they originally were. What does not relate to the ancient history of these people, I shall only mention in the course of my travels when passing through, or sojourning amongst them.

Providence had created the inhabitants of the peninsula of India under many disadvantages in point of climate. The high and wholesome part of the country was covered with barren and rugged mountains; and, at different times of the year, violent rains fell in large currents down the sides of these, which overflowed all the fertile land below; and these rains were no sooner over, than they were succeeded by a scorching sun, the effect of which upon the human body, was to render it feeble, enervated, and incapable of the efforts neceffary for agriculture. In this flat country, large rivers, that fcarce had declivity enough to run, crept flowly along, through meadows of fat black earth, ftagnating in many places as they went, rolling an abundance of decayed vegetables, and filling the whole air with exhalations of the moft corrupt and putrid kind. Even rice, the general food of man, the fafeft and moft friendly to the inhabitants of that country, could not grow but by laying under water the places where it was fown, and thereby rendering them, for feveral months, abfolutely improper for man's dwelling. Providence had done this, but, never failing in its wifdom, had made to the natives a great deal more than a fufficient amends.

THEIR bodies were unfit for the fatigues of agriculture, nor was the land proper for common cultivation. But this country produced fpices of great variety, efpecially a fmall berry called Pepper, fuppofed, of all others, and with reafon, to be the greateft friend to the health of man. This grew fpontaneoufly, and was gathered without toil. It was, at once, a perfect remedy for the inclemencies and difeafes of the country, as well as the fource of its riches, from the demand of foreigners. This fpecies of fpice is no where known but in India, though equally ufeful in every putrid region, where, unhappily, thefe difeafes reign. Providence has not, as in India, placed remedies fo near them, thus wifely providing for the welfare of mankind in general, by the dependency it has forced one man to have upon another. In India, and fimilar climates, this fpice is not ufed in fmall quantities, but in fuch, as to be nearly equal to that of bread.

THE SOURCE OF THE NILE. 373

In cloathing, Providence had not been lefs kind to India. The filk worm, with little fatigue and trouble to man, almoft without his interference, provided for him a ftuff, at once the fofteft, the moft light and brilliant, and confequently the beft adapted to warm countries; and cotton, a vegetable production, growing every where in great abundance, without care, which may be confidered as almoft equal to filk, in many of its qualities, and fuperior to it in fome, afforded a variety ftill cheaper for more general ufe. Every tree without culture produced them fruit of the moft excellent kind; every tree afforded them fhade, under which, with a very light and portable *loom* of cane, they could pafs their lives delightfully in a calm and rational enjoyment, by the gentle exercife of weaving, at once providing for the health of their bodies, the neceffities of their families, and the riches of their country.

But however plentifully their fpices grew, in whatever quantity the Indians confumed them, and however generally they wore their own manufactures, the fuperabundance of both was fuch, as naturally led them to look out for articles againft which they might barter their fuperfluities. This became neceffary to fupply the wants of thofe things that had been with-held from them, for wife ends, or which, from wantonnefs, luxury, or flender neceffity, they had created in their own imaginations.

Far to the weftward of them, but part of the fame continent, connected by a long defert, and dangerous coaft, was the peninfula of Arabia, which produced no fpices, tho' the neceffities of its climate fubjected its inhabitants to the fame difeafes as thofe in India. In fact, the country and
climate

climate were exactly similar, and, consequently, the plentiful use of these warm productions was as necessary there, as in India, the country where they grew.

It is true, Arabia was not abandoned wholly to the inclemency of its climate, as it produced myrrh and frankincense, which, when used as perfumes or fumigations, were powerful antiseptics of their kind, but administered rather as preventatives, than to remove the disorder when it once prevailed. These were kept up at a price, of which, at this day, we have no conception, but which never diminished from any circumstance, under which the country where they grew, laboured.

The silk and cotton of India were white and colourless, liable to soil, and without any variety; but Arabia produced gum and dyes of various colours, which were highly agreeable to the taste of the Asiatics. We find the sacred scriptures speak of the party-coloured garment as the mark of the greatest honour *. Solomon, in his proverbs, too, says, that he decked his bed with coverings of tapestry of Egypt †. But Egypt had neither silk nor cotton manufactory, no, nor even wool. Solomon's coverings, though he had them from Egypt, were therefore an article of barter with India.

Balm, or Balsam ‡, was a commodity produced in Arabia, sold at a very high price, which it kept up till within these few

---

* Gen. xxxvii. 3 and 2 Sam. xiii. 18. † Prov. vii. 16.
‡ Vide Appendix, where this tree is described.

few centuries in the eaft; when the Venetians carried on the India trade by Alexandria, this Balfam then fold for its weight in gold; it grows in the fame place, and, I believe, nearly in the fame quantity as ever, but, for very obvious reafons*, it is now of little value.

The bafis of trade, or a connection between thefe two countries, was laid, then, from the beginning, by the hand of Providence. The wants and neceffities of the one found a fupply, or balance from the other. Heaven had placed them not far diftant, could the paffage be made by fea; but violent, fteady, and unconquerable winds prefented themfelves to make that paffage of the ocean impoffible, and we are not to doubt, but, for a very confiderable time, this was the reafon why the commerce of India was diffufed through the continent, by land only, and from this arofe the riches of Semiramis.

But, however precious the merchandife of Arabia was, it was neither in quantity, nor quality, capable of balancing the imports from India. Perhaps they might have paid for as much as was ufed in the peninfula of Arabia itfelf, but, beyond this there was a vaft continent called Africa, capable of confuming many hundred fold more than Arabia; which lying under the fame parallel with India, part of it ftill farther fouth, the difeafes of the climate, and the wants of its numerous inhabitants, were, in many parts of it, the fame as thofe of Arabia and India; befides which there was the

---

* The quantity of fimilar drugs brought from the New World.

the Red Sea, and divers communications to the northward.

Neither their luxuries nor neceffaries were the fame as thofe of Europe. And indeed Europe, at this time, was probably inhabited by fhepherds, hunters, and fifhers, who had no luxury at all, or fuch as could not be fupplied from India; they lived in woods and marfhes, with the animals which made their fport, food, and cloathing.

The inhabitants of Africa then, this vaft Continent, were to be fupplied with the neceffaries, as well as the luxuries of life, but they had neither the articles Arabia wanted, nor thofe required in India, at leaft, for a time they thought fo; and fo long they were not a trading people.

It is a tradition among the Abyffinians, which they fay they have had from time immemorial, and which is equally received among the Jews and Chriftians, that almoft immediately after the flood, Cufh, grandfon of Noah, with his family, paffing through Atbara from the low country of Egypt, then without inhabitants, came to the ridge of mountains which ftill feparates the flat country of Atbara from the more mountainous high-land of Abyffinia.

By cafting his eye upon the map, the reader will fee a chain of mountains, beginning at the Ifthmus of Suez, that runs all along like a wall, about forty miles from the Red Sea, till it divides in lat. 13°, into two branches. The one goes along the northern frontiers of Abyffinia, croffes the Nile, and then proceeds weftward, through Africa towards the Atlantic Ocean. The other branch goes fouthward, and then

THE SOURCE OF THE NILE. 377

then eaft, taking the form of the Arabian Gulf; after which, it continues fouthward all along the Indian Ocean, in the fame manner as it did in the beginning all along, the Red Sea, that is parallel to the coaft.

THEIR tradition fays, that, terrified with the late dreadful event the flood, ftill recent in their minds, and apprehenfive of being again involved in a fimilar calamity, they chofe for their habitation caves in the fides of thefe mountains, rather than truft themfelves again on the plain. It is more than probable, that, foon after their arrival, meeting here with the tropical rains, which, for duration, ftill exceed the days that occafioned the flood, and obferving, that going through Atbara, that part of Nubia between the Nile and Aftaboras, afterwards called Meroë, from a dry climate at firft, they had after fallen in with rains, and as thofe rains increafed in proportion to their advancing fouthward, they chofe to ftop at the firft mountains, where the country was fertile and pleafant, rather than proceed farther at the rifk of involving themfelves, perhaps in a land of floods, that might prove as fatal to their pofterity as that of Noah had been to their anceftors.

THIS is a conjecture from probability, only mentioned for illuftration, for the motives that guided them cannot certainly be known; but it is an undoubted fact, that here the Cufhites, with unparalleled induftry, and with inftruments utterly unknown to us, formed for themfelves commodious, yet wonderful habitations in the heart of mountains of granite and marble, which remain entire in great numbers to this day, and promife to do fo till the confummation of all things. This original kind of dwellings foon extended

tended themselves through the neighbouring mountains. As the Cushites grew populous, they occupied those that were next them, spreading the industry and arts which they cultivated, as well to the eastern as to the western ocean, but, content with their first choice, they never descended from their caves, nor chose to reside at a distance on the plain.

It is very singular that St Jerome does not know where to look for this family, or descendents of Cush; though they are as plainly pointed out, and as often alluded to by scripture, as any nation in the Old Testament. They are described, moreover, by the particular circumstances of their country, which have never varied, to be in the very place where I now fix them, and where, ever since, they have remained, and still do to this present hour, in the same mont ains, and the same houses of stone they formed for themselves in the beginning. And yet Bochart *, professedly treating this subject, as it were industriously, involves it in more than Egyptian darkness. I rather refer the reader to his work, to judge for himself, than, quoting it by extracts, communicate the confusion of his ideas to my narrative.

The Abyssinian tradition further says, they built the city of Axum some time early in the days of Abraham. Soon after this, they pushed their colony down to Atbara, where we know from Herodotus *, they early and successfully pursued their studies, from which, Josephus says‡, they were called Meroëtes, or inhabitants of the island of Meroë.

The

---

* Boch. lib. 4. cap. 3. † Herod. lib. 2. cap. 29. ‡ Joseph. antiquit. Jud.

THE SOURCE OF THE NILE.

The prodigious fragments of coloffal ftatues of the dog-ftar, ftill to be feen at Axum, fufficiently fhew what a material object of their attention they confidered him to be; and Seir, which in the language of the Troglodytes, and in that of the low country of Meroë, exactly correfponding to it, fignifies a *dog*, inftructs us in the reafon why this province was called *Sirè*, and the large river which bounds it, *Siris*.

I APPREHEND the reafon why, without forfaking their ancient domiciles in the mountains, they chofe this fituation for another city, Meroë, was owing to an imperfection they had difcovered (both in Sirè and in their caves below it) to refult from their climate. They were within the tropical rains; and, confequently, were impeded and interrupted in the neceffary obfervations of the heavenly bodies, and the progrefs of aftronomy which they fo warmly cultivated. They muft have feen, likewife, a neceffity of building Meroë farther from them than perhaps they wifhed, for the fame reafon they built Axum in the high country of Abyffinia in order to avoid the fly (a phænomenon of which I fhall afterwards fpeak) which purfued them everywhere within the limits of the rains, and which muft have given an abfolute law in thofe firft times to the regulations of the Cufhite fettlements. They therefore went the length of lat. 16°, where I faw the ruins fuppofed to be thofe of Meroë*, and caves in the mountains immediately above that fituation, which I cannot doubt were the temporary habitation of the builders of that firft feminary of learning.

---

* At Gerri in my return through the defert.

It is probable that, immediately upon their fuccefs at Meroë, they loft no time in ftretching on to Thebes. We know that it was a colony of Ethiopians, and probably from Meroë, but whether directly, or not, we are not certain. A very fhort time might have paffed between the two eftablifhments, for we find above Thebes, as there are above Meroë, a vaft number of caves, which the colony made provifionally, upon its firft arrival, and which are very near the top of the mountain, all inhabited to this day.

Hence we may infer, that their ancient apprehenfions of a deluge had not left them whilft, they faw the whole land of Egypt could be overflowed every year without rain falling upon it; that they did not abfolutely, as yet, truft to the ftability of towns like thofe of Sirè and Meroë, placed upon columns or ftones, one laid upon the other, or otherwife, that they found their excavations in the mountains were finifhed with lefs trouble, and more comfortable when complete, than the houfes that were built. It was not long before they affumed a greater degree of courage.

CHAP.

CHAP. II.

Saba and the South of Africa peopled—Shepherds, their particular Employment and Circumstances—Abyssinia occupied by seven stranger Nations—Specimens of their several Languages—Conjectures concerning them.

WHILE these improvements were going on so prosperously in the central and northern territory of the descendents of Cush, their brethren to the south were not idle, they had extended themselves along the mountains that run parallel to the Arabian Gulf; which was in all times called Saba, or Azabo, both which signify *South*, not because Saba was south of Jerusalem, but because it was on the south coast of the Arabian Gulf, and, from Arabia and Egypt, was the first land to the southward which bounded the African Continent, then richer, more important, and better known, than the rest of the world. By that acquisition, they enjoyed all the perfumes and aromatics in the east, myrrh, and frankincense, and caffia; all which grow spontaneously in that stripe of ground, from the Bay of Bilur west of Azab, to Cape Gardefan, and then southward up in the Indian Ocean, to near the coast of Melinda, where there is cinnamon, but of an inferior kind.

ARABIA probably had not then fet itfelf up as a rival to this fide of the Red Sea, nor had it introduced from Abyffinia the myrrh and frankincenfe, as it did afterwards, for there is no doubt that the principal mart, and growth of thefe gums, were always near Saba. Upon the confumption increafing, they, however, were tranfplanted thence into Arabia, where the myrrh has not fucceeded.

THE Troglodyte extended himfelf ftill farther fouth. As an aftronomer, he was to difengage himfelf from the tropical rains and cloudy fkies that hindered his correfpondent obfervations with his countrymen at Meroë and Thebes. As he advanced within the fouthern tropic, he, however, ftill found rains, and made his houfes fuch as the fears of a deluge had inftructed him to do. He found there folid and high mountains, in a fine climate; but, luckier than his countrymen to the northward, he found gold and filver in large quantities, which determined his occupation, and made the riches and confequence of his country. In thefe mountains, called *the Mountains of Sofala*, large quantities of both metals were difcovered in their pure unmixed ftate, lying in globules without alloy, or any neceffity of preparation or feparation.

THE balance of trade, fo long againft the Arabian and African continents, turned now in their favour from the immenfe influx of thefe precious metals, found in the mountains of Sofala, juft on the verge of the fouthern tropical rains.

GOLD and filver had been fixed upon in India as proper returns for their manufactures and produce. It is impoffible

ble to say whether it was from their hardness or beauty, or what other reason governed the mind of man in making this standard of barter. The history of the particular transactions of those times is lost, if, indeed, there ever was such history, and, therefore, all further inquiries are in vain. The choice, it seems, was a proper one, since it has continued unaltered so many ages in India, and has been universally adopted by all nations pretty much in the proportion or value as in India, into which continent gold and silver, from this very early period, began to flow, have continued so to do to this day, and in all probability will do to the end of time. What has become of that immense quantity of bullion, how it is consumed, or where it is deposited, and which way, if ever it returns, are doubts which I never yet found a person that could satisfactorily solve.

The Cushite then inhabited the mountains, whilst the northern colonies advanced from Meroë to Thebes, busy and intent upon the improvement of architecture, and building of towns, which they began to substitute for their caves; they thus became traders, farmers, artificers of all kinds, and even practical astronomers, from having a meridian night and day free from clouds, for such was that of the Thebaid. As this was impossible to their brethren, and six months continual rain confined them to these caves, we cannot doubt but that their sedentary life made them useful in reducing the many observations daily made by those of their countrymen who lived under a purer sky. Letters too, at least one sort of them, and arithmetical characters, we are told, were invented by this middle part of the Cushites, while trade and astronomy, the natural history of the winds and seasons, were what necessarily employed the part of the colony established at Sofala most to the southward.

THE very nature of the Cushites commerce, the collecting of gold, the gathering and preparing his spices, necessarily fixed him perpetually at home; but his profit lay in the dispersing of these spices through the continent, other wise his mines, and the trade produced by the possession of them, were to him of little avail.

A CARRIER was absolutely necessary to the Cushite, and Providence had provided him one in a nation which were his neighbours. These were in most respects different, as they had long hair, European features, very dusky and dark complexion, but nothing like the black-moor or negro; they lived in plains, having moveable huts or habitations, attended their numerous cattle, and wandered from the necessities and particular circumstances of their country. These people were in the Hebrew called *Phut*, and, in all other languages, *Shepherds;* they are so still, for they still exist; they subsist by the same occupation, never had another, and therefore cannot be mistaken; they are called Balous, Bagla, Belowee, Berberi, Barabra, Zilla and Habab*, which all signify but one thing, namely that of *Shepherd.* From their place of habitation, the territory has been called *Barbaria* by the Greeks and Romans, from Berber, in the original signifying *shepherd.* The authors that speak of the Shepherds seem to know little of those of the *Thebaid*, and still less

---

* It is very probable, some of these words signified different degrees among them, as we shall see in the sequel.

THE SOURCE OF THE NILE.

less of those of *Ethiopia*, whilst they fall immediately upon the shepherds of the Delta, that they may get the sooner rid of them, and thrust them into Assyria, Palestine, and Arabia. They never say what their origin was; how they came to be so powerful; what was their occupation; or, properly, the land they inhabited; or what is become of them now, though they seem inclined to think the race extinct.

The whole employment of the shepherds had been the dispersing of the Arabian and African goods all over the continent; they had, by that employment, risen to be a great people: as that trade increased, their quantity of cattle increased also, and consequently their numbers, and the extent of their territory.

Upon looking at the map, the reader will see a chain of mountains which I have described, and which run in a high ridge nearly straight north, along the Indian Ocean, in a direction parallel to the coast, where they end at Cape Gardefan. They then take the direction of the coast, and run west from Cape Gardefan to the Straits of Babelmandeb, inclosing the frankincense and myrrh country, which extends considerably to the west of Azab. From Babelmandeb they run northward, parallel to the Red Sea, till they end in the sandy plain at the Isthmus of Suez, a name probably derived from Suah, *Shepherds.*

Although this stripe of land along the Indian Ocean, and afterwards along the Red Sea, was necessary to the shepherds, because they carried their merchandise to the ports there, and thence to Thebes and Memphis upon the Nile, yet the principal seat of their residence and power was that flat part of Africa between the northern tropic and the mountains of Abyssinia. This is divided into various districts; it reaches from Masuah along the sea-coast to Suakem, then turns westward, and continues in that direction, having the Nile on the south, the tropic on the north, to the deserts of Selima, and the confines of Libya on the west. This large extent of country is called *Beja*. The next is that district * in form of a shield, as Meroë is said to have been; this name was given it by Cambyses. It is between the Nile and Astaboras, and is now called Atbara. Between the river Mareb, the ancient Astusaspes on the east, and Atbara on the west, is the small plain territory of Derkin, another district of the shepherds. All that range of mountains running east and west, inclosing Derkin and Atbara on the south, and which begins the mountainous country of Abyssinia, is inhabited by the negro woolly-headed Cushite, or Shangalla, living as formerly in caves, who, from having been the most cultivated and instructed people in the world, have, by a strange reverse of fortune, relapsed into brutal ignorance, and are hunted by their neighbours like wild beasts in those forests, where they used to reign in the utmost luxury, liberty, and splendour. But the noblest, and most warlike of all the shepherds, were those that inhabited the mountains of the Habab, a considerable ridge reaching from the neighbourhood of Masuah to Suakem, and who still dwell there

In the ancient language of this country, *So*, or *Suah*, signified shepherd, or shepherds; though we do not know any particular rank or degrees among them, yet we may suppose these called simply *shepherds* were the common sort that attended the

---
D od. S.c. lib. 1. cap.

the flocks. Another denomination, part of them bore, was *Hycſos*, founded by us Agſos, which ſignifies *armed ſhepherds*, or ſuch as wore harneſs, which may be ſuppoſed the ſoldiers, or armed force of that nation. The third we ſee mentioned is Ag-ag, which is thought to be the nobles or chiefs of thoſe armed ſhepherds, whence came their title *King of Kings* *. The plural of this is Agagi, or, as it is written in the Ethiopic, Agaazi.

This term has very much puzzled both Scaliger and Ludolf; for, finding in the Abyſſinian books that they are called Agaazi, they torment themſelves about finding the etymology of that word. They imagine them to be Arabs from near the Red Sea, and Mr Ludolf† thinks the term ſignifies *baniſhed men*. Scaliger, too, has various gueſſes about them nearly to the ſame import. All this, however, is without foundation; the people aſſert themſelves at this day to be Agaazi, that is, a race of Shepherds inhabiting the mountains of the Habab, and have by degrees extended themſelves through the whole province of Tigré, whoſe capital is called Axum, from Ag and Suah, the metropolis, or principal city of the ſhepherds that wore arms.

Nothing was more oppoſite than the manners and life of the Cuſhite, and his carrier the ſhepherd. The firſt, though he had forſaken his caves, and now lived in cities which he had built, was neceſſarily confined at home by his commerce, amaſſing gold, arranging the invoices of his ſpices,

---

* This was the name of the king of Amalek; he was an Arab ſhepherd, ſlain by Samuel, 1 Sam. xv. 33.

† Ludolf lib. 1 cap. 4.

spices, hunting in the season to provide himself with ivory, and food throughout the winter. His mountains, and the cities he built afterwards, were situated upon a loomy, black earth, so that as soon as the tropical rains began to fall, a wonderful phænomenon deprived him of his cattle. Large swarms of flies appeared wherever that loomy earth was, which made him absolutely dependent in this respect upon the shepherd, but this affected the shepherd also

This insect is called *Zimb;* it has not been described by any naturalist. It is in size very little larger than a bee, of a thicker proportion, and his wings, which are broader than those of a bee, placed separate like those of a fly; they are of pure gauze, without colour or spot upon them; the head is large, the upper jaw or lip is sharp, and has at the end of it a strong-pointed hair of about a quarter of an inch long; the lower jaw has two of these pointed hairs, and this pencil of hairs, when joined together, makes a resistence to the finger nearly equal to that of a strong hog's bristle. Its legs are serrated in the inside, and the whole covered with brown hair or down. As soon as this plague appears, and their buzzing is heard, all the cattle forsake their food, and run wildly about the plain, till they die, worn out with fatigue, fright, and hunger. No remedy remains, but to leave the black earth, and hasten down to the sands of Atbara, and there they remain while the rains last, this cruel enemy never daring to pursue them farther.

What enables the shepherd to perform the long and toilsome journies across Africa is the camel, emphatically called by the Arabs, the *ship of the desert.* He seems to have been created for this very trade, endued with parts and qualities

qualities adapted to the office he is employed to difcharge. The drieft thiftle, and the bareft thorn, is all the food this ufeful quadruped requires, and even thefe, to fave time, he eats while advancing on his journey, without flopping, or occafioning a moment of delay. As it is his lot to crofs immenfe deferts, where no water is found, and countries not even moiftened by the dew of heaven, he is endued with the power at one watering-place to lay in a· ftore, with which he fupplies himfelf for thirty days to come. To contain this enormous quantity of fluid, Nature has formed large cifterns within him, from which, once filled, he draws at pleafure the quantity he wants, and pours it into his ftomach with the fame effect as if he then drew it from a fpring, and with this lle travels, patiently and vigoroufly, all day long, carrying a prodigious load upon him, through countries infected with poifonous winds, and glowing with parching and never-cooling fands. Though his fize is immenfe, as is his ftrength, and his body covered with a thick fkin, defended with ftrong hair, yet ftill he is not capable to fuftain the violent punctures the fly makes with his pointed probofcis. He muft lofe no time in removing to the fands of Atbara; for, when once attacked by this fly, his body, head, and legs break out into large boffes, which fwell, break, and putrify, to the certain deftruction of the creature.

EVEN the elephant and rhinoceros, who, by reafon of their enormous bulk, and the vaft quantity of food and water they daily need, cannot fhift to defert and dry places as the feafon may require, are obliged to roll themfelves in mud and mire, which, when dry, coats them over like armour, and enables them to ftand their ground againft this winged affaffin; yet I have found fome of thefe tubercules upon

upon almoft every elephant and rhinoceros that I have feen, and attribute them to this caufe.

ALL the inhabitants of the fea-coaft of Melinda, down to Cape Gardefan, to Saba, and the fouth coaft of the Red Sea, are obliged to put themfelves in motion, and remove to the next fand in the beginning of the rainy feafon, to prevent all their ftock of cattle from being deftroyed. This is not a partial emigration; the inhabitants of all the countries from the mountains of Abyffinia northward, to the confluence of the Nile and Aftaboras, are once a-year obliged to change their abode, and feek protection in the fands of Beja; nor is there any alternative, or means of avoiding this, though a hoftile band was in their way, capable of fpoiling them of half their fubftance; and this is now actually the cafe, as we fhall fee when we come to fpeak of Sennaar.

OF all thofe that have written upon thefe countries, the prophet Ifaiah alone has given an account of this animal, and the manner of its operation. Ifa. vii. ch. 18. and 19. ver. " And it fhall come to pafs, in that day, that the Lord fhall " *hifs* for the fly that is in the uttermoft part of the rivers of " Egypt,"---" And they fhall come, and fhall reft all of them " in the defolate vallies*, and in the holes of the rocks, and " upon all thorns, and upon all bufhes."

THE mountains that I have already fpoken of, as running through the country of the Shepherds, divide the feafons

by

---

* That is, they fhall cut off from the cattle their ufual retreat to the defert, by taking poffeffion of thofe places, and meeting them there where ordinarily they never come, and which therefore is the refuge of the cattle.

THE SOURCE OF THE NILE. 391

by a line drawn along their fummit, fo exactly, that, while the eaftern fide, towards the Red Sea, is deluged with rain for the fix months that conftitute our *winter* in Europe, the weftern fide towards Atbara enjoys a perpetual fun, and active vegetation. Again, the fix months, when it is our *fummer* in Europe, Atbara, or the weftern fide of thefe mountains, is conftantly covered with clouds and rain, while, for the fame time, the fhepherd on the eaftern fide, towards the Red Sea, feeds his flocks in the moft exuberant foliage and luxuriant verdure, enjoying the fair weather, free from the fly or any other moleftation. Thefe great advantages have very naturally occafioned thefe countries of Atbara and Beja to be the principal refidence of the fhepherd and his cattle, and have entailed upon him the neceffity of a perpetual change of places. Yet fo little is this inconvenience, fo fhort the peregrination, that, from the rain on the weft fide, a man, in the fpace of four hours, will change to the oppofite feafon, and find himfelf in fun-fhine to the eaftward.

When Carthage was built, the carriage of this commercial city fell into the hands of Lehabim, or Lubim, the Libyan peafants, and became a great acceffion to the trade, power, and number of the fhepherds. In countries to which there was no accefs by fhipping, the end of navigation was nearly anfwered by the immenfe increafe of camels; and this trade, we find, was carried on in the very earlieft ages on the Arabian fide, by the Ifhmaelite merchants trading to Paleftine and Syria, from the fouth end of the peninfula, with camels. This we learn particularly from Genefis, they brought myrrh and fpices, or pepper, and fold them for filver;

silver; they had also balm, or balsam, but this it seems, in those days, they brought from Gilead.

We are sorry, in reading this curious anecdote preserved to us in scripture, to find, in those early ages of the India trade, that another species of commerce was closely connected with it, which modern philanthropy has branded as the disgrace of human nature. It is plain, from the passage, the commerce of selling men was then universally established. Joseph* is bought as readily, and sold as currently immediately after, as any ox or camel could be at this day. Three nations, Javan, Tubal, and Meshech†, are mentioned as having their principal trade at Tyre in the selling of men; and, as late as St John's time‡, this is mentioned as a principal part of the trade of Babylon; notwithstanding which, no prohibition from God, or censure from the prophets, have ever stigmatized it either as irreligious or immoral; on the contrary, it is always spoken of as favourably as any species of commerce whatever. For this, and many other reasons which I could mention, I cannot think, that purchasing slaves is, in itself, either cruel or unnatural. To purchase any living creature to abuse it afterwards, is certainly both base and criminal; and the crime becomes still of a deeper dye, when our fellow-creatures come to be the sufferers. But, although this is an abuse which accidentally follow the trade, it is no necessary part of the trade itself; and, it is against this abuse the wisdom of the legislature should be directed, not against the trade itself.

On

---

* Gen. chap. xxxvii. ver. 25. 28.   † Ezek. chap. xvii. ver. 13.
‡ Rev. chap. xviii. ver. 13.

THE SOURCE OF THE NILE.

On the eaftern fide of the peninfula of Africa, many thoufand flaves are fold to Afia, perfectly in the fame manner as thofe on the weft fide are fent to the Weft Indies; but no one, that ever I heard, has as yet opened his mouth againft the fale of Africans to the Eaft Indies; and yet there is an aggravation in this laft fale of flaves that fhould touch us much more than the other, where no fuch additional grievance can be pretended. The flaves fold into Afia are moft of them Chriftians; they are fold to Mahometans, and, with their liberty, they are certainly deprived of their religion likewife. But the treatment of the Afiatics being much more humane than what the Africans, fold to the Weft Indies, meet with, no clamour has yet been raifed againft this commerce in Afia, becaufe its only bad confequence is apoftacy; a proof to me that religion has no part in the prefent difpute, or, as I have faid, it is the abufe that accidentally follows the purchafing of flaves, not the trade itfelf, that fhould be confidered as the grievance.

It is plain from all hiftory, that two abominable practices, the one the eating of men, the other of facrificing them to the devil, prevailed all over Africa. The India trade, as we have feen in very early ages, firft eftablifhed the buying and felling of flaves; fince that time, the eating of men, or facrificing them, has fo greatly decreafed on the eaftern fide of the peninfula, that now we fcarcely hear of an inftance of either of thefe that can be properly vouched. On the weftern part, towards the Atlantic Ocean, where the fale of flaves began a confiderable time later, after the difcovery of America and the Weft Indies, both of thefe horrid practices are, as it were, general, though, I am told, lefs fo to the northward fince that event.

There is still alive a man of the name of Matthews, who was present at one of those bloody banquets on the west of Africa, to the northward of Senega. It is probable the continuation of the slave-trade would have abolished these, in time, on the west side also. Many other reasons could be alledged, did my plan permit it. But I shall content myself at present, with saying, that I very much fear that a relaxation and effeminacy of manners, rather than genuine tenderness of heart, has been the cause of this violent paroxysm of philanthropy, and of some other measures adopted of late to the discouragement of discipline, which I do not doubt will soon be felt to contribute their mite to the decay both of trade and navigation that will necessarily follow.

The Ethiopian shepherds at first carried on the trade on their own side of the Red Sea; they carried their India commodities to Thebes, likewise to the different black nations to the south-west; in return, they brought back gold, probably at a cheaper rate, because certainly by a shorter carriage than by that from Ophir.

Thebes became exceedingly rich and proud, though, by the most extensive area that ever was assigned to it, it never could be either large or populous. Thebes is not mentioned in scripture by that name; it was destroyed before the days of Moses by Salatis prince of the Agaazi, or Ethiopian shepherds; at this day it has assumed a name very like the ancient one. The first signification of its name, Medinet Tabu, I thought was the Town of our Father. This, history says, was given it by Sesostris in honour of his father; in the ancient language, its name was *Ammon No*. The next that presented itself was Theba, which was the Hebrew name

name for the Ark when Noah was ordered to build it—
Thou shalt " make thee an Ark (Theba) of gopher-wood*."

The figure of the temples in Thebes do not seem to be far removed from the idea given us of the Ark. The third conjecture is, that being the first city built and supported on pillars, and, on different and separate pieces of stone, it got its name from the architects first expression of approbation or surprise, Tabu, that it stood insulated and alone, and this seems to me to be the most conformable both to the Hebrew and Ethiopic.

The shepherds, for the most part, friends and allies of the Egyptians, or Cushite, at times were enemies to them. We need not, at this time of day, seek the cause; there are many very apparent, from opposite manners, and, above all, the difference in the dietetique regimen. The Egyptians worshipped the cow, the Shepherds killed and ate her. The Shepherds were Sabeans, worshipping the host of heaven—the sun, moon, and stars. Immediately upon the building of Thebes and the perfection of sculpture, idolatry and the grossest materialism greatly corrupted the more pure and speculative religion of the Sabeans. Soon after the building of Thebes, we see that Rachel, Abraham's wife, had idols †; we need seek no other probable cause of the devastation that followed, than difference of religion.

Thebes was destroyed by Salatis, who overturned the first Dynasty of Cushite, or Egyptian kings, begun by Menes, in what is called the second age of the world, and founded

---

* Gen. vi. 14. † Gen. xxxv. 4.

founded the first Dynasty of the Shepherds, who behaved very cruelly, and wrested the lands from their first owners; and it was this Dynasty that Sesostris destroyed, after calling Thebes by his father's name, Ammon No, making those decorations that we have seen of the harp in the sepulchres on the west, and building Diospolis on the opposite side of the river. The second conquest of Egypt by the Shepherds was that under Sabaeo, by whom it has been imagined Thebes was destroyed, in the reign of Hezekiah king of Judah, who is said to have made peace with So * king of Egypt, as the translator has called him, mistaking So for the name of the king, whereas it only denoted his quality of shepherd.

From this it is plain, all that the scripture mentions about Ammon No, applies to Diospolis on the other side of the river. Ammon No and Diospolis, though they were on different sides of the river, were considered as one city, thro' which the Nile flowed, dividing it into two parts. This is plain from profane history, as well as from the prophet Nahum †, who describes it very exactly, if in place of the word *sea* was substituted *river*, as it ought to be

There was a third invasion of the Shepherds after the building of Memphis, where a ‡ king of Egypt § is said to have inclosed two hundred and forty thousand of them in a city called *Abaris;* they surrendered upon capitulation, and were banished the country into the land of Canaan. That two hundred and forty thousand men should be inclosed

---

* 2 Kings, xvii. 4.   † Nahum, chap. iii. 8.   ‡ Misphragmuthosis.   § Manethon, Apud. Josephum Apion. lib. 1. p. 460.

inclofed in one city, fo as to bear a fiege, feems to me extremely improbable; but be it fo, all that it can mean is, that Memphis, built in Lower Egypt near the Delta, had war with the Shepherds of the Ifthmus of Suez, or the diftricts near them, as thofe of Thebes had before with the Shepherds of the Thebaid. But, however much has been written upon the fubject, the total expulfion of the Shepherds at any one time by any King of Egypt, or at any one place, muft be fabulous, as they have remained in their ancient feats, and do remain to this day; perhaps in not fo great a number as when the India trade was carried on by the Arabian Gulf, yet ftill in greater numbers than any other nation of the Continent.

THE mountains which the Agaazi inhabit, are called *Habab*, from which it comes, that they themfelves have got that name. Habab, in their language, and in Arabic likewife, fignifies a *ferpent*, and this I fuppofe explains that hiftorical fable in the book of Axum, which fays, a ferpent conquered the province of Tigré, and reigned there.

IT may be afked, Is there no other people that inhabit Abyffinia, but thefe two nations, the Cufhites and the Shepherds? Are there no other nations, whiter or fairer than them, living to the fouthward of the Agaazi? Whence did thefe come? At what time, and by what name are they called? To this I anfwer, That there are various nations which agree with this defcription, who have each a particular name, and who are all known by that of *Habefh*, in Latin *Convenæ*, fignifying a number of diftinct people meeting accidentally in one place. The word has been greatly mifunderftood, and mifapplied, both by Scaliger and Ludolf, and

a numa number of others; but nothing is more confonant to the hiftory of the country than the tranflation I have given it, nor will the word itfelf bear any other.

The Chronicle of Axum, the moft ancient repofitory of the antiquities of that country, a book efteemed, I fhall not fay how properly, as the firft in authority after the holy fcriptures, fays, that between the creation of the world and the birth of our Saviour there were 5500 years *; that Abyffinia had never been inhabited till 1808 years before Chrift *; and 200 years after that, which was in the 1600, it was laid wafte by a flood, the face of the country much changed and deformed, fo that it was denominated at that time Ourè Midre, or, *the country laid wafte*, or, as it is called in fcripture itfelf, a land which the waters or floods had fpoiled †; that about the 1400 year before Chrift it was taken poffeffion of by a variety of people fpeaking different languages, who, as they were in friendfhip with the Agaazi, or Shepherds, poffeffing the high country of Tigrè, came and fat down befide them in a peaceable manner, each occupying the lands that were before him. This fettlement is what the Chronicle of Axum calls *Angaba*, the entry and eftablifhment of thefe nations, which finifhed the peopling of Abyffinia

Tradition further fays, that they came from Paleftine. All this feems to me to wear the face of truth. Some time after the year 1500, we know there happened a flood which
occafioned

---

* Eight years lefs than the Greeks and other followers of the Septuagint.
† Ifaiah, chap. xviii. ver. 2.

THE SOURCE OF THE NILE.

occasioned great devastation. Pausanius says, that this flood happened in Ethiopia in the reign of Cecrops; and, about the 1490 before Christ, the Israelites entered the land of promise, under Caleb and Joshua. We are not to wonder at the great impression that invasion made upon the minds of the inhabitants of Palestine. We see by the history of the harlot, that the different nations had been long informed by prophecies, current and credited among themselves, that they were to be extirpated before the face of the Israelites, who for some time had been hovering about their frontiers. But now when Joshua had passed the Jordan, after having miraculously dried up the river* before his army had invaded Canaan, and had taken and destroyed Jericho, a panic seized the whole people of Syria and Palestine.

THESE petty states, many in number, and who had all different languages, seeing a conqueror with an immense army already in possession of part of their country, and who did not conduct himself according to the laws of other conquerors, but put the vanquished under saws and harrows of iron, and destroyed the men, women, and children, and sometimes even the cattle, by the sword, no longer could think of waiting the arrival of such an enemy, but fought for safety by speedy flight or emigration. The Shepherds in Abyssinia and Atbara were the most natural refuge these fugitives could seek; commerce must have long made them acquainted with each others manners, and they must

---

* Joshua, iii. 16.

must have been already entitled to the rights of hospitality by having often passed through each other's country.

Procopius* mentions that two pillars were standing in his time on the coast of Mauritania, opposite to Gibraltar, upon which were inscriptions in the Phœnician tongue: " We are " Canaanites, flying from the face of Joshua, the son of Nun, " the *robber :*" A character they naturally gave him from the ferocity and violence of his manners. Now, if what these inscriptions contain is true, it is much more credible, that the different nations, emigrating at that time, should seek their safety near hand among their friends, rather than go to an immense distance to Mauritania, to risk a precarious reception among strangers, and perhaps that country not yet inhabited.

Upon viewing the several countries in which these nations have their settlements, it seems evident they were made by mutual consent, and in peace; they are not separated from each other by chains of mountains, or large and rapid rivers, but generally by small brooks, dry the greatest part of the year; by hillocks, or small mounds of earth, or imaginary lines traced to the top of some mountain at a distance; these boundaries have never been disputed or altered, but remain upon the old tradition to this day. These have all different languages, as we see from scripture all the petty states of Palestine had, but they have no letters, or written character, but the Geez, the character of

---

* Procop. de bello vind. lib 2. cap. 10.

* A Moorish author, Ibn el Raquique, says, this inscription was on a stone on a mountain at Carthage. Marmol. lib. 1. cap. 25.

Geez

መሐልየ፡ መሐልይ፡ ዝውእቲ፡ ዘሰሎሞን፡ ይሰሰምኒ፡ በእስመ፡ አፉሁ፡ አዳም፡ አጥበትኪ፡ እምወይን፡፡ ወመዓዛ፡ ሠፈረትኪ፡ እምኩሎ፡ አፋው፡፡፨ ዕፋረትሰ፡ ዘተወቅጠ፡ ስምከ፡ ወበ ለንተዝ፡ ደናግል፡ አፍቀራከ፡፡ ወሰ ሐበከ፡ ድኅሬከ፡ በመዓዛ፡ ዕፋረትከ፡ ንረውፅ፡፡ አብአኒ፡ ንጉሥ፡ ወስተ፡ ጽራሑ፡፡ ንትፈሣሕ፡ ወንትሐሠይ፡ ብከ፡ ናፈቅር፡ አጥበቲኪ፡ አምወይ እን፡፡ ወርቱዕ፡ ሰፉቅራትኪ፡ ጸሎሙ፡ እኒ፡ ወሠናይት፡ አመለወደ፡ ሲየሩ ሰሌም፡፡ ከመ፡ መጽለተ፡ ቄደር፡ ወ ሐየምታቱ፡ ሰሎሞን፡፡ ሲትርአያኒ፡ እስመ፡ አኒ፡ ሔሳም፡፡ እስመ፡ ሲርእያ ኒ፡ ጸሐይ፡፡ ደቂቀ፡ እምየ፡ ተበአሱ በለንቲአየ፡፡ አንበረኒ፡ ዓቃቢተ፡ ዓ ፀደ፡ ወይንዓፀደ፡ ወይን፡ ዘዚአያ፡ ሲአቀብኩ፡፡ ንገረኒ፡ ዘአፋቀረት፡ ነፍሰየ፡ አየቴ፡ ትሬሲ፡ ወአየቴ፡ ትሰክብ፡ ጊዜ፡ ቀትር፡ ከመ፡ ሲየኩ ኒ፡ ለእዘ፡ ለንገጌ፡ ውስተምርሰ የ፡ ክልአንከ፡፡ ሰመ፡ ሲያመርኪ፡ ርሰስኪ፡ ሠናይተ፡ ለዋለንሰተ፡ ባ ሲ፡ ለንቴ፡ ውስተ፡ ሰኩናሆሙ፡ ሰ መሬቴ፡፡ ወሬዲ፡ መሐኪፃ፡ አሣ ሴኪ፡፡ ውስተ፡ ስዕፃደቲሆሙ፡ ለ ኖሎት፡፡ ለፈረስየ፡ ወለሰገለተ፡ ፈራዖን፡፡ አስተጋሰልኩኪ፡ እንተ ንበየ..

Amhara

ይህ፡ ከመሰገን፡ ያሚበልጽ፡ ጥሰገን፡ የሰሎሞን፡ ነው፡፡ ባፉ፡ አሳላም፡ ይ አማናል፡፡ ከወይን፡ ይልቅ፡ ጡቶች፡ ኩ፡ ይሰ፡ ይላሉ፡ የስቴሳዎ፡ ሰታ ክስቴ፡ ሁስ፡ ይላሳል፡፡ በሸሜ፡ የተ ቀለቀለ፡ እምህ፡ እነይ፡ ለቴ፡ ያክወ ድይናል፡፡ አለዜህ፡ ቆናይት፡ ወደዳ ህ፡፡ ሁዋለከ፡ ተከተሌህ፡ በሸቴ ሀ፡ ከታ፡ ሰንቂደሰን፡፡ ነጉሠ፡ ከጮ ጉላዉ፡ ስገሰን፡፡ በኔች፡ ደስ፡ ይሰና ለ፡፡ ጠቶሰን፡ ኩወይን፡ ይልቅ፡ ከነ ወደክን፡፡ አነቶን፡ መወደድ፡ ቅን፡ ነገሪ፡ ነዉ፡፡ ከየረሳሴዎ፡ ቆነጅተ፡ ይልቅ፡ ጠቁረሰሁ፡፡ ከንደ፡ ዘባን፡ ሳጅ፡ ከነደ፡ ሰሉዋን፡ ድንኳን፡ ከጥ ሬ፡ ነበረ፡፡ ጠቁራሰሁና፡ ለቅደኛ ፀሐይ፡ ከሰዮጻዎኗ፡፡ የናቴ፡ ሌጆች፡ ሰሌኔ፡ ተጸሉ፡፡ ሠይን፡ ጠብቂ፡ ብሉ፡ እኖረኛ፡፡ የኔ፡ ወይን፡ አሌጠበቅሁ ም፡፡ ሌቡኖይ፡ የወደዳችሆይ፡ ንገረኝ፡ ወደተ፡ ተሰምራለህ፡፡ ወደተ፡ ተተ ኛለህ፡፡ በቀትር፡ ጊዜ፡፡ ስቅበዘበዝ እንደሌገኝ፡፡ ከባለንጀሮችህ፡ መነ ጎች፡፡ ራሷኒ፡ ከሰወቅሺ፡፡ ከሴ ቶች፡ የመታምሪ፡፡ የመነጎችን፡ ሰኮና፡ ቀተለሸ፡ ዉጪ፡፡ የፋሴ ትሸኒ፡ ጥቦተ፡ ጠብቂ፡፡ በረኞች፡ ቦታ፡ ያሱን፡፡ ፈረሴኛ፡ የፈሪን፡ ሬ ረስ፡፡ ሰሪገሰየን፡ የፈሪን፡ ሰረ ገስ፡፡

Falasha

የሰሎሟን፡ ባዝሊኪ፡ ባዝ፡ ሾራው፡
ባዝ፡ ነሞኬዝ፡ ይማሆኩ፡፡ ሾራ፡ ኪነ
ጕጉ፡ ወይነ፡ ወሸው፡ ኪኒራሰ፡ ነራ፡
ናሊኪ፡ ጌራ፡ ሾራ፡ ኪሺዌሊዝ፡ ኚራ፡
ተደባለቃ፡፡ አነዚ፡ ይቁነ፡ ይከልኛ፡
አነገጌሳ፡ ወተረኜዉ፡፡ ኪኒሪዝ፡ ኚራ፡
ጊሳኛ፡፡ አሾነ፡ ነነገሊ፡ ፋገው፡፡ወይነ፡
ሊዉሾዉ፡ ኪነጕጉሰ፡ ይከሴነዉ፡፡
ኪይከሴነ፡ሌታ፡፡ አነ፡ሿምነቲ፡ቀነኮ፡፡
አየሩሰሌም፡ ሾክነሊ፡ አነ፡ ኪዘኮ፡፡
ዘስነ፡ ጉጀ፡ ኪና፡፡ ሶሎዎኜዉ፡ ዶነ
ኧነ፡ ከና፡፡ ሰሞነቱ፡ አነኩ፡ ሐሴታ፡፡

ኧራ፡ሐሴከይ፡፡ ይገኛ፡ ሑራ፡ይገሪ፡ከራ
ኘሑረዉ፡፡ ወይነ፡ ሰብረሰ፡ ጌልታ፡፡
ከበኛ፡፡ ይከሞሰ፡ ወይነ፡ ሰብረሰ፡
ጌለትገሩ፡፡ ይት፡ ይከለይቲ፡ ዶዊ፡፡
አጉተ፡ ሰካብአያ፡፡ አጉተ፡ ጋነጅገነ፡
ሐሰሐሰ፡ ጉዘዝ፡፡ ሰገገና፡ ወነተ፡ተረ
ነጉ፡ ኪሞገዋ፡ ሊነያ፡፡ ኩያጊሰ፡ አህ
ከረ፡፡ ይዊነሊኪ፡ አነት፡ ሾራ፡፡ አነ
ተፉ፡፡ ናልኩሰ፡ ሰኮብሰዎሊ፡፡ ፋ
ነቲሪ፡ ተበተሰ፡ ጌለቲ፡፡ ሴተነ
ሰ፡ ናሲየዋ፡ ደፉረዘዝ፡ ፈረያነ፡
ሽረጋሰነ

Damot Agow

ማዜነ፡ ህዮ፡ ማዜነ፡ የሰሎጦን፡ ለኝ፡፡
ሞጀ፡ ለማቀ፡ ከወይን፡ ኔኩ፡ ኤቁሿ፡ ለ
ሞጥኸ፡፡ ሀርሸ፡ ሀሬ፡ ከሀር፡ ጆቅ፡ ለ
ሞተኑ፡፡ ይሹኝ፡ ሐብሬ፡ ክሹኝ፡
ሀሬካኝ፡ ለቀነሰኮ፡ ኛማተን፡ ሞቁ፡
ለቅኑ፡፡ ክጌሬ፡ ቲክኑ፡፡ ኮሀሬ፡ ሀሬ፡
ፉረነኩን፡፡ ነጉሡ፡ ፀወለ፡ ድቀ፡፡
ክጀቃ፡ ለሞተጠኩን፡ ለቁጠነ፡ ከወ
ይን፡ ህየኩ፡ ለቀነኩነ፡፡ ክተ፡ ቀናኩነ፡
ጮቄቁ፡ ገብ፡ ለኝ፡ ከየረሰሊም
ሞቁ፡ ህየኩ፡ ኛጮሬነ፡፡ ሞቃ፡
ጉጀኛ፡ ሰሎዋን፡ ደኮኝ፡፡ ገሬ

ሞ፡ ጽቡነ፡፡ ነጭሬኩነ፡ ለለታ፡
ኮሬ፡ ለልይ፡፡ ይጀሰ፡ ሁሬ፡ ይማጥኛ፡
ቃሬኸ፡፡ ወደን፡ ሞቃ፡ ይሬ፡ ሰቁሬ፡፡
የወ፡ ወይን፡ ልሚትቀሬ፡፡ ለዘን፡
ለክንደይን፡ ድቁ፡፡ ለወሬ፡ ፈተሬን፡
ለወሬ፡ ግዝሬን፡ ሰት፡ ጊዝ፡፡ ለሸ
ኸለ፡ ሐወክሰኮ፡ ኮፃሞጥ፡ ሜነጋ፡፡
ከወሬ፡ ኦረቅየሬ፡፡ ለቁን፡ ጊሬም
ሬ፡፡ የሞነሳችሸን፡ ሰወን፡ ቲክ፡
ደፉ፡፡ ፈጮሬ፡ ተቦተ፡ ሱሚጮ፡
ሞቃ፡ ቡታ፡ እኮ፡፡ ደፉረዛ፡ የፈሬዎን፡
ፉረዛ፡፡ ለሞደሬቃ፡ የፈሬዎን፡ ለጥደሬቀ፡

Tcheratz Agow

ለነ፡ ዋሰጋ፡ ጸዘጊ፡ ኝለዉ፡ ዋሰጋሉ፡ የሰሎዎነ፡ ኜ፡፡ ኽዋቢ፡ ኩሰኛዉ፡ ኩሰኚ፡፡ ከዋይነ፡ ኽሰ፡ ለነ፡ ደሳነ፡ ኩኒረኒ፡ ኜረ፡ ከኒረዉ፡ ዉሰ፡ ከሸኩ፡፡ ይዉሰኛሰ፡ አለቀጽትዊ፡፡ ኩ ሸዎሰ፡ ኜረታ፡ ለኸከነሰ፡፡ ለነክተ፡ ጸነ ከከ፡ ለከከኩ፡፡ ለነገረዎ፡ ታነኩኑ፡፡ ሃረደ፡ ሳረ፡ ከነ፡፡ ነጉሠኒ፡ ቻፑሊደ፡ ኜሽከ፡፡ ከደ ደሰዎ፡፡ ለነጦ፡ ከዎ ይነ፡ ደለነካነ፡፡ ኩዎ፡ ለነከነኛ፡ ገገረ፡ ደቢ፡ ኜ፡፡ ከየረሳዎ፡ ለነካ፡ ኽሰ ዛርከታ፡፡ ዚለኒት፡ ጉጅ፡ ሰሎዎነታ፡ ደነጵንታ፡ ለመረ፡ ሸኾነ፡ ዛርከታ፡ ካ

ነቲደነ፡፡ ነዊ፡ ከነቲየ፡፡ ይቹ፡ ይረ፡ ይባነ፡ ጆፋኛነ፡፡ ዎይነ፡ ዓነደነኩ፡ ነካግ፡ ለነኩረኒ፡፡ የዉሰ፡ ዎይነ፡ ዓነተየ፡፡ ይሸዎ፡ ለነካነተዎሰ፡ ዶ ኩ፡፡ ዉሸዎ፡ ዛነገረቲ፡፡ ዉሸዎ፡ ሁረ፡ ገርግ፡ ሸሸ፡፡ ለገበተረ፡ ለገለታ፡ ቲተ፡ ይሰብኪ፡ ዋረተሌ፡፡ ኛረይ፡ ተ ከሰ፡፡ ኹከነ፡ ለመርት፡፡ ዋረቲ ሳጉ፡ ተከነተታረ፡፡ ፋገይቲ፡ ሳ ዉነኩ፡ ምነቲ፡፡ ለበለዎ፡ ሰፈረይ፡ ዝኩነከሰ፡፡ ፈረሰይ፡ የፈረየነ፡ ፈ ረሳሰ፡ ሰረገሊያ፡ የፈረየነ፡ ሰረገሊ ያ፡፡

Gafat

ይህ፡ የሰሎሞን፡ ለጀዋት፡ ለጀ፤ ለጂ፡ በለዋት፡ ለጂ፡ ለፃፃዎ፡ አፃፃም ኛ፡፡ ዋይት፡ ለትለቁ፡ ጥበጂ፡ አዝንጄ፡ ጉና፡፡ አንፋጄሰ፡ አነፉ፡ አለም፡ ይጋጅ፡፡ ሐሙየትጄ፡ ደበሉ፡ ሕጦዉትህ፡ ለነደ፡ ገና፡ ለሸጥኬ፡፡ የዉታቶ፡ ዘያትጅ፡ ወደሃ፡፡ ማልፋኒ ሔነ፡ ቀጠለም፡፡ በነፈጂ፡ ለነረው፡ ለንታሁር፡፡ ንጉሡ ለትጌባኝ፡ በጪ ጉሳሸ፡፡ በይት፡ ደሰ፡ ደብል፡፡ ጥቡጂ፡ ዋይኑ፡ ይጋጂ፡ ለነወደ፡፡ ይት፡ ወዮደ፡ ጉና፡ ጸወተ፡ ደቀኒ፡፡ ክየረሳለም፡ መዛ የች፡ ጁተለቁ፡ ለገለጅሁ፡፡ ለነደ፡ ለ በለዋ፡ ደካመጂ፡ ለነደ፡ ሰሎዋን፡

መደነኋነ፡=፡ ጉና፡ ጋጅሁኀ፡ ደጀ፡፡ ለጉጸኯሞ፡ ለትጅኜ፡፡ ጠበሩት፡ ለ ላጅቸም፡፡ ለሙየት፡ ቡሹች፡ ያነት፡ ይብሉ፡ ይትጸጌም፡፡ ዋይኘሽ፡ ለቃቡ፡ ብል፡ ለትወን፡፡ ያነትነ፡ ወደነ፡ ለለ ቀብሁም፡፡ ልፀጄ፡ ያቃለነ፡ ይወደ፡፡ ይፉነ፡ ተዘነገር፡ ይፈነትትገደል፡ ቀንሽ ኩየ፡፡ ይትቷወደ፡ ማልሆነ፡ ማለቸ ጄ፡ ጠነገ፡፡ ድማሐሸ፡ ያትሸለ፡ ለ ነትቸ፡ ጉና፡ ቲሸለ፡፡ የጉናቸን፡ መ ሰጒሏ፡ ቀጉደ፡ ነደደ፡፡ የናየሎችሸን፡ ጥበት፡ ለቅበ፡ በቦ፡ ላመሽ፡ ቦቲ፡ ለቀ ቢ፡፡ ፈራያሸን፡ የፈራየነ፡ ፈርደሽ፡ ባልሽን፡ የፈራየነ፡ ባልሽ

Galla

ኩኖ፡ ገላተ፡ አረጀሬ፡ ገለተ፡ የሱሎሞን፡ ደነኳነ፡ ሚደገ፡ ቴሬ፡፡ ደታይ
ኔ፡ ይሰ፡፡ አፈኒ፡ ይላቲ፡ አኔድ፡ አነጦ ጅሬ፡ አናነሳ፡፡ ሊይ፡ አናነላሴ፡ ጎደ
ቲ፡፡ ወይኒ፡ አረጀሬ፡ ሐርሚኬ፡ ገሙ ኮ፡ ኔጀሴ፡ አንአፉጀያኒ፡ ወሉለኒ፡፡ ወ
ቱ፡፡ ዉራጎኬ፡ ዉርጋ፡ ዉርጋ፡ ዶደ፡ ይን፡ ደገይ፡ አአጀረስቸሰኒ፡፡ ወይንኩ፡
አረጀሬ፡፡ መቃኮቲ፡ ደበሴ፡ መቃኬ፡ ሂነገኒ፡፡ ቀልቢኮ፡ ከንጀለቲ፡ አናቲሃ
አከ፡ ወርጋወ፡ አነጀላችላ፡፡ ከናሬ ሚ፡ ሌሳ፡ አደሙፈቲ፡፡ ሌሰ፡ ቲጭ
ደበሩ፡ ሲጀለቲኒ፡፡ ደበኬ፡ ሲደከለይ ፉቲ፡ ሳፈወቲ፡ ጌና፡ ዋራሴ፡ ከሲኒ
ሙ፡ ወርጋኬቲ፡ ወረጋ፡ አደሞና፡፡ ሞ ተሃ፡፡ ኔሪያኬ፡ ኔደ፡፡ ኮተንኬ፡
ቲ፡ ደንቃ፡ አናሴንሲሴ፡፡ ሲቲ፡ ገሙ ቤኩባቴ፡ ነዶሲዋን፡ ከምበሬደ፡፡ ነደነ
ድና፡፡ ሐረሚኬ፡ ከወይን፡ አረጀሬ፡ በኬ፡ ኮቴ፡ ደካዴነቴ፡ በኑ፡፡ ሪየተኬ፡
ጀለና፡፡ ሲሂ፡ ጀለሳ፡ ቀጀለ፡ ደቢ ጥበት፡ ሌጊ፡፡ ኦገደዋን፡ ሲረጊ፡ ከ
ይሰ፡ ከየረሳሌም፡ ደበሬ፡ ይሬ፡ ደተ ንጀረን፡፡ ፈረደኮ፡ የፈሪየን፡ ፈሪየ፡ ሰረ
ያጀሬ፡፡ አከ፡ ቲክሲቱ፡ ቲዖ፡ ከሰሎ ገለየን፡ የፈረየን፡ ሰረገለ፡፡

THE SOURCE OF THE NILE. 401

of the Cushite shepherd by whom they were first invented and used, as we shall see hereafter. I may add in further proof of their origin, that the curse * of Canaan seems to have followed them, they have obtained no principality, but served the kings of the Agaazi or Shepherds, have been hewers of wood and drawers of water, and so they still continue.

The first and most considerable of these nations settled in a province called *Amhara*; it was, at first coming, as little known as the others; but, upon a revolution in the country, the king fled to that province, and there the court staid many years, so that the Geez, or language of the Shepherds, was dropt, and retained only in writing, and as a dead language; the sacred scriptures being in that language only, saved the Geez from going totally into disuse. The second were the Agows of Damot, one of the southern provinces of Abyssinia, where they are settled immediately upon the sources of the Nile. The third are the Agows of Lasta, or Tcheratz Agow, from Tchera, their principal habitation; theirs too is a separate language; they are Troglodytes that live in caverns, and seem to pay nearly the same worship to the Siris, or Tacazzè, that those of Damot pay to the Nile.

I take the old names of these two last-mentioned nations, to be sunk in the circumstances of this their new settlement, and to be a compound of two words Ag-oha, the Shepherds of the River, and I also imagine, that the idolatry

Vol. I. 3 E they

---

* Gen. ix. 25, 26, and 27. verses.

they introduced in the worſhip of the Nile, is a further proof that they came from Canaan, where they imbibed materialiſm in place of the pure Sabean worſhip of the Shepherds, then the only religion of this part of Africa.

THE fourth is a nation bordering upon the ſouthern banks of the Nile near Damot. It calls itſelf Gafat, which ſignifies oppreſſed by violence, torn, expelled, or chaced away by force. If we were to follow the idea ariſing merely from this name, we might be led to imagine, that theſe were part of the tribes torn from Solomon's ſon and ſucceſſor, Rehoboam. This, however, we cannot do confiſtent with the faith to be kept by a hiſtorian with his reader. The evidence of the people themſelves, and the tradition of the country, deny they ever were Jews, or ever concerned with that colony, brought with Menilek and the queen of Saba, which eſtabliſhed the Jewiſh hierarchy. They declare, that they are now Pagans, and ever were ſo; that they are partakers with their neighbours the Agows in the worſhip of the river Nile, the extent or particulars of which I cannot pretend to explain.—The fifth is a tribe, which, if we were to pay any attention to ſimilarity of names, we ſhould be apt to imagine we had found here in Africa a part of that great Gauliſh nation ſo widely extended in Europe and Aſia. A compariſon of their languages, with what we know exiſts of the former, cannot but be very curious.— Theſe are the Galla, the moſt confiderable of theſe nations, ſpecimens of whoſe language I have cited. This word, in their own language, ſignifies *Shepherd**; they ſay that formerly

---

* Theſe people likewiſe call themſelves Agaazi, or Agagi, they have over-run the kingdom of Congo ſouth of the Line, and on the Atlantic Ocean, as the Galla have done that part of the kingdom of Adel and Abyſſinia, on the Eaſtern, or Indian Ocean. Purch. lib. ii. chap. 4. Sect. 8.

THE SOURCE OF THE NILE. 403

merly they lived on the borders of the southern rains, within the southern tropic; and that, like these in Atbara, they were carriers between the Indian and Atlantic Oceans, and supplied the interior part of the peninsula with Indian commodities.

The history of this trade is unknown; it must have been little less ancient, and nearly as extensive, as the trade to Egypt and Arabia. It probably suffered diminution, when the mines of Sofala were given up, soon after the discovery of the new world. The Portuguese found it still flourishing, when they made their first conquests upon that coast; and they carry it on still in an obscure manner, but in the same tract to their settlements near Cape Negro on the western ocean. From these settlements would be the proper place to begin to explore the interior parts of the peninsula, on both sides of the southern tropic, as protection and assistance could probably be got through the whole course of it, and very little skill in language would be necessary.

When no employment was found for this multitude of men and cattle, they left their homes, and proceeding northward, they found themselves involved near the Line, in rainy, cold, and cloudy weather, where they scarcely ever saw the sun. Impatient of such a climate, they advanced still farther, till about the year 1537, they appeared in great numbers in the province of Bali, abandoning the care of camels for the breeding of horses. At present they are all cavalry. I avoid to say more of them in this place, as I shall be obliged to make frequent mention of them in the course of my narrative.

The Falasha, too, are a people of Abyssinia, having a particular language of their own; a specimen of which I have also published, as the history of the people seems to be curious. I do not, however, mean to say of them, more than of the Galla, that this was any part of those nations who fled from Palestine on the *invasion* of Joshua. For they are now, and ever were, Jews, and have traditions of their own as to their origin, and what reduced them to the present state of separation, as we shall see hereafter, when I come to speak of the translation of the holy scripture.

In order to gratify such as are curious in the study and history of language, I, with great pains and difficulty, got the whole book of the Canticles translated into each of these languages, by priests esteemed the most versant in the language of each nation. As this barbarous polyglot is of too large a size to print, I have contented myself with copying six verses of the first chapter in each language; but the whole book is at the service of any person of learning that will bestow his time in studying it, and, for this purpose, I left it in the British Museum, under the direction of Sir Joseph Banks, and the Bishop of Carlisle.

These *Convenæ*, as we have observed, were called *Habesh*, a number of distinct nations meeting in one place. Scripture has given them a name, which, though it has been ill translated, is precisely *Convenæ*, both in the Ethiopic and Hebrew. Our English translation calls them the *mingled people* *, whereas it should be the *separate nations*, who, though met and settled together, did not mingle, which is strictly *Convenæ*.

The

Jerem. chap. xliii. ver. 23.—id. xxv. 24.—Ezek. chap. xxx. ver. 5.

THE SOURCE OF THE NILE.

The inhabitants then who poffeffed Abyffinia, from its fouthern boundary to the tropic of Cancer, or frontiers of Egypt, were the Cufhites, or polifhed people, living in towns, firft Troglodytes, having their habitations in caves. The next were the Shepherds; after thefe were the nations who, as we apprehend, came from Paleftine—Amhara, Agow of Damot, Agow of Tchera, and Gafat.

INTERPRETERS, much lefs acquainted with the hiftorical circumftances of thefe countries than the prophets, have, either from ignorance or inattention, occafioned an obfcurity which otherwife did not arife from the text. All thefe people are alluded to in fcripture by defcriptions that cannot be miftaken. If they have occafioned doubts or difficulties, they are all to be laid at the door of the tranflators; chiefly the Septuagint. When Mofes returned with his wife Zipporah, daughter of the fovereign of the Shepherds of Midian, carriers of the India trade from Saba into Paleftine, and eftablifhed near their principal mart Edom, in Idumea or Arabia, Aaron, and Miriam his fifter, quarrelled with Mofes, becaufe he had married one who was, as the tranflator fays, an Ethiopian*. There is no fenfe in this caufe; Mofes was a fugitive when he married Zipporah; fhe was a noble-woman, daughter of the prieft of Midian, head of a people. She likewife, as it would feem, was a Jewefs †, and more attentive, at that time, to the prefervation of the precepts of the law, than Mofes was himfelf; no exception, then, could lie againft Zipporah, as fhe was furely, in every view, Mofes's fuperior. But if the tranflator had rendered

it,

---

* Numb. chap. xii. ver. 1. † Exod. chap. iv. ver. 25.

it, that Aaron and Miriam had quarrelled with Mofes, becaufe he had married a *negro*, or *black-moor*, the reproach was evident; whatever intrinfic merit Zipporah might have been found to have poffeffed afterwards, fhe muft have appeared before the people, at firft fight, as a *ftrange* woman, or Gentile, whom it was prohibited tomarry. Befides, the innate deformity of the complexion, negroes were, at all times, rather coveted for companions of men of luxury or pleafure, than fought after for wives of fober legiflators, and governors of a people.

The next inftance I fhall give is, Zerah of Gerar*, who came out to fight Afa king of Ifrael with an army of a million of men, and three hundred chariots, whilft both the quarrel and the decifion are reprefented as immediate.

Gerar was a fmall diftrict, producing only the Acacia or gum-arabic trees, from which it had its name; it had no water but what came from a few wells, part of which had been dug by Abraham †, after much ftrife with the people of the country, who fought to deprive him of them, as of a treafure.

Abraham and his brother Lot returning from Egypt, though poor fhepherds, could not fubfift there for want of food, and water, and they feparated accordingly, by confent‡.
Now

---

* 2 Chron. chap. xiv. ver. 9. † Gen chap. 21. ver. 30.
‡ Gen. chap. 13. ver. 6. and 9.

Now it muſt be confeſſed, as it is not pretended there was any miracle here, that there is not a more unlikely tale in all Herodotus, than this muſt be allowed to be upon the footing of the tranſlation. The tranſlator calls Zerah an Ethiopian, which ſhould either mean he dwelt in Arabia, as he really did, and this gave him no advantage, or elſe that he was a ſtranger, who originally came from the country above Egypt; and, either way, it would have been impoſſible, during his whole life-time, to have collected a million of men, one of the greateſt armies that ever ſtood upon the face of the earth, nor could he have fed them though they had ate the whole trees that grew in his country, nor could he have given every hundredth man one drink of water in a day from all the wells he had in his country.

Here, then, is an obvious triumph for infidelity, becauſe, as I have ſaid, no ſupernatural means are pretended. But had it been tranſlated, that Zerah was a *black-moor*, a *Cuſhite-negro*, and prince of the Cuſhites, that were carriers in the Iſthmus, an Ethiopian ſhepherd, then the wonder ceaſed. Twenty camels, employed to carry couriers upon them, might have procured that number of men to meet in a ſhort ſpace of time, and, as Zerah was the aggreſſor, he had time to chooſe when he ſhould attack his enemy; every one of theſe ſhepherds carrying with them their proviſion of flour and water, as is their invariable cuſtom, might have fought with Aſa at Gerar, without eating a loaf of Zerah's bread, or drinking a pint of his water.

The next paſſage I ſhall mention is the following: "The "labour of Egypt, and merchandiſe of Ethiopia, and of the "Sabeans,

"Sabeans, men of stature, shall come over unto thee, and "they shall be thine*." Here the several nations are distinctly and separately mentioned in their places, but the whole meaning of the passage would have been lost, had not the situation of these nations been perfectly known; or, had not the Sabeans been mentioned separately, for both the Sabeans and the Cushite were certainly Ethiopians. Now, the meaning of the verse is, that the fruit of the agriculture of Egypt, which is wheat, the commodities of the negro, gold, silver, ivory, and perfumes, would be brought by the Sabean shepherds, their carriers, a nation of great power, which should join themselves with you.

AGAIN, Ezekiel says,† "And they shall know that I am "the Lord, when I have set a fire in Egypt, and when all "her helpers shall be destroyed."—" In that day shall mes- "sengers go forth from me in ships, to make the careless " Ethiopians afraid." Now, Nebuchadnezzar was to destroy Egypt‡, from the frontiers of Palestine, to the mountains above Atbara, where the Cushite dwelt. Between this and Egypt is a great desert; the country beyond it, and on both sides, was possessed by half a million of men. The Cushite, or negro merchant, was secure under these circumstances from any insult by land, but they were open to the sea, and had no defender, and messengers, therefore, in ships or a fleet had easy access to them, to alarm and keep them at home, that they did not fall into danger by marching into Egypt against Nebuchadnezzar, or interrupting the service upon which God had sent him. But this does not appear from transla-

---

* Isa. chap. xlv. ver. 14.   † Ezek. chap. xxx. ver. 8. and 9.   ‡ Ezek. chap. xxix. ver. 10.

THE SOURCE OF THE NILE.

ting Cush, *Ethiopian;* the neareft Ethiopian to Nebuchadnezzar, the moft powerful and capable of oppofing him, were the Ethiopian fhepherds of the Thebaid, and thefe were not acceffible to fhips; and the fhepherds, fo pofted near to the fcene of deftruction to be committed by Nebuchadnezzar, were enemies to the Cufhites living in towns, and they had repeatedly themfelves deftroyed them, and therefore had no temptation to be other than fpectators.

In feveral other places, the fame prophet fpeaks of Cufh as the commercial nation, fympathifing with their countrymen dwelling in the towns in Egypt, independent of the fhepherds, who were really their enemies, both in civil and religious matters. "And the fword fhall come upon Egypt, "and great pain fhall be in Ethiopia, when the flain fhall "fall in Egypt*." Now Ethiopia, as I have before faid, that is, the low country of the fhepherds, neareft Egypt, had no common caufe with the Cufhites that lived in towns there; it was their countrymen, the Cufhites in Ethiopia, who mourned for thofe that fell in Egypt, who were merchants, traders, and dwelt in cities like themfelves.

I shall mention but one inftance more: "Can the Ethi-"opian change his fkin, or the leopard his fpots?†" Here Cufh is rendered Ethiopian, and many Ethiopians being white, it does not appear why they fhould be fixed upon, or chofen for the queftion more than other people. But had Cufh been tranflated Negro, or Black-moor, the queftion would

Vol. I. 3 F

---

* Ezek. chap. xxx. ver. 4. † Jerem. chap. xiii. ver. 23.

would have been very easily understood, Can the negro change his skin, or the leopard his spots?

JEREMIAH * speaks of the chiefs of the mingled people that dwell in the deserts. And Ezekiel† also mentions them independent of all the others, whether Shepherds, or Cushites, or Libyans their neighbours, by the name of the Mingled People. Isaiah ‡ calls them " a nation scattered " and peeled; a people terrible from their beginning hitherto; " a nation meted out and trodden down, whose land the ri- " vers have spoiled:" which is a sufficient description of them, as having been expelled their own country, and settled in one that had suffered greatly by a deluge a short time before.

---

* Jerem. chap. xxv. ver. 24.　　† Ezek. chap. xxx. ver. 5.　　‡ Isa. chap. xviii. ver. 2.

CHAP.

THE SOURCE OF THE NILE. 411

CHAP. III.

Origin of Characters or Letters—Ethiopic the first Language—How and why the Hebrew Letter was formed.

THE reader will observe what I have already said concerning the language of Habesh, or the Mingled Nations, that they have not characters of their own; but when written, which is very seldom, it must be by using the Geez alphabet. Kircher, however, says, there are two characters to be found in Abyssinia; one he calls the Sacred Old Syrian, the other the Vulgar, or Common Geez character, of which we are now speaking. But this is certainly a mistake; there never was, that I know, but two original characters which obtained in Egypt. The first was the Geez, the second the Saitic, and both these were the oldest characters in the world, and both derived from hieroglyphies.

ALTHOUGH it is impossible to avoid saying something here of the origin of languages, the reader must not expect that I should go very deep into the fashionable opinions concerning them, or believe that all the old deities of the

Pagan nations were the patriarchs of the Old Teftament. With all refpect to Sanchoniatho and his followers, I can no more believe that Ofiris, the firft king of Egypt, was a real perfonage, and that Tot was his fecretary, than I can believe Saturn to be the patriarch Abraham, and Rachel and Leah, Venus and Minerva. I will not fatigue the reader with a detail of ufelefs reafons; if Ofiris is a real perfonage, if he was king of Egypt, and Tot his fecretary, they furely travelled to very good purpofe; as all the people of Europe and Afia feem to be agreed, that in perfon they firft communicated letters and the art of writing to them, but at very different, and very diftant periods.

THEBES was built by a colony of Ethiopians from Sirè, the city of Seir, or the Dog Star. Diodorus Siculus fays, that the Greeks, by putting O before Siris, had made the word unintelligible to the Egyptians: Siris, then, was Ofiris; but he was not the Sun, no more than he was Abraham, nor was he a real perfonage. He was Syrius, or the dog-ftar, defigned under the figure of a dog, becaufe of the warning he gave to Atbara, where the firft obfervations were made at his heliacal rifing, or his difengaging himfelf from the rays of the fun, fo as to be vifible to the naked eye. He was the Latrator Anubis, and his firft appearance was figuratively compared to the barking of a dog, by the warning it gave to prepare for the approaching inundation. I believe, therefore, this was the firft hieroglyphic; and that Ifis, Ofiris, and Tot, were all after inventions relating to it; and, in faying this, I am fo far warranted, becaufe there is not in Axum (once a large city) any other hieroglyphic but of the dog-ftar, as far as I can judge from the huge fragments of figures of this animal, remains of which, in different

THE SOURCE OF THE NILE. 413

rent poftures, are ftill diftinctly to be feen upon the pedeftals everywhere among the ruins.

It is not to be doubted, that hieroglyphics then, but not aftronomy, were invented at Thebes, where the theory of the dog-ftar was particularly inveftigated, becaufe connected with their rural year. Ptolemy* has preferved us an obfervation of an helaical rifing of Sirius on the 4th day after the fummer folftice, which anfwers to the 2250 year before Chrift; and there are great reafons to believe the Thebans were good practical aftronomers long before that period†; early, as it may be thought, this gives to Thebes a much greater antiquity than does the chronicle of Axum juft cited.

As fuch obfervations were to be of fervice for ever, they became more valuable and ufeful in proportion to their priority. The moft ancient of them would be of ufe to the aftronomers of this day, for Sir Ifaac Newton appeals to thefe of Chiron the Centaur. Equations may indeed be difcovered in a number of centuries, which, by reafon of the fmallnefs of their quantities, may very probably have efcaped the moft attentive and fcrupulous care of two or three generations; and many alterations in the ftarry firmament, old ftars being nearly extinguifhed, and new emerging, would appear from a comparative ftate of the heavens

---

* Uranologion P. Petau.
† Banbridge, Ann. canicul.

heavens made for a feries of ages. And a Theban *Herfchel**
would have given us the hiftory of planets he then obferved,
which, after appearing for ages, are now vifible no more,
or have taken a different form.

The dial, or gold circle of Ofimandyas, fhews what an
immenfe progrefs they had made in aftronomy in fo little
time. This, too, is a proof of an early fall and revival of
the arts in Egypt, for the knowledge and ufe of Armillæ
had been loft with the deftruction of Thebes, and were not
again difcovered, that is, revived, till the reign of Ptolemy
Soter, 300 years before the Chriftian æra. I confider that
immenfe quantity of hieroglyphics, with which the walls
of the temples, and faces of the obelifks, are covered, as
containing fo many aftronomical obfervations.

I look upon thefe as the ephemerides of fome thoufand
years, and that fufficiently accounts for their number. Their
date and accuracy were indifputable; they were exhibited in
the moft public places, to be confulted as occafion required;
and, by the deepnefs of the engraving, and hardnefs of the
materials, and the thicknefs and folidity of the block itfelf
upon which they were carved, they bade defiance at once
to violence and time.

I know that moft of the learned writers are of fentiments
very different from mine in thefe refpects. They look for
myfteries

---

* An aftronomer greatly above my praife.

mysteries and hidden meanings, moral and philosophical treatises, as the subjects of these hieroglyphics. A sceptre, they say, is the hieroglyphic of a king. But where do we meet a sceptre upon an antique Egyptian monument? or who told us this was an emblem of royalty among the E- gyptians at the time of the first invention of this figurative writing? Again, the serpent with the tail in its mouth de- notes the eternity of God, that he is without beginning and without end. This is a Christian truth, and a Christian be- lief, but no where to be found in the polytheism of the in ventors of hieroglyphics. Was Cronos or Ouranus without beginning and without end? Was this the case with Osiris and Tot, whose fathers and mothers births and marriages are known? If this was a truth, independent of revelation, and imprinted from the beginning in the minds of men; if it was destined to be an eternal truth, which must have appeared by every man finding it in his own-breast, from the beginning, how unnecessary must the trouble have been to write a common known truth like this, at the expence of six weeks labour, upon a table of porphyry or granite.

It is not with philosophy as with astronomy; the older the observations, the more use they are of to posterity. A lecture of an Egyptian priest upon divinity, morality, or natural history, would not pay the trouble, at this day, of engraving it upon stone; and one of the reasons that I think no such subjects were ever treated in hieroglyphics is, that in all those I ever had an opportunity of seeing, and very few people have seen more, I have constantly found the same figures repeated, which obviously, and without dispute, allude to the history of the Nile, and its different periods of increase; the mode of measuring t, the Etesian winds; in short, such observations.

obfervations as we every day fee in an almanack, in which we cannot fuppofe, that forfaking the obvious import, where the good they did was evident, they fhould afcribe different meanings to the hieroglyphic, to which no key has been left, and therefore their future inutility muft have been forefeen.

I SHALL content myfelf in this wide field, to fix upon one famous hieroglyphical perfonage, which is *Tot*, the fecretary of Ofiris, whofe function I fhall endeavour to explain; if I fail, I am in good company; I give it only as my opinion, and fubmit it chearfully to the correction of others. The word *Tot* is Ethiopic, and there can be little doubt it means the dog-ftar. It was the name given to the firft month of the Egyptian year. The meaning of the name, in the language of the province of Siré, is an *idol*, compofed of different heterogeneous pieces; it is found having this fignification in many of their books. Thus a naked man is not a *Tot*, but the body of a naked man, with a dog's head, an afs's head, or a ferpent inftead of a head, is a *Tot*. According to the import of that word, it is, I fuppofe, an almanack, or fection of the phænomena in the heavens which are to happen in the limited time it is made to comprehend, when expofed for the information of the public; and the more extenfive its ufe is intended to be, the greater number of emblems, or figns of obfervation, it is charged with.

BESIDES many other emblems or figures, the common Tot, I think, has in his hand a crofs with a handle, as it is called *Crux Anfata*, which has occafioned great fpeculation among the decypherers. This crofs, fixed to a circle, is fuppofed to denote the *four elements*, and to be the fymbol of the influence

London Published December 1st 1789 by G. Robinson & Co

THE SOURCE OF THE NILE. 417

influence the fun has over them. Jamblichus* records, that this crofs, in the hand of Tot, is the name of the *divine Being* that travels through the world. Sozomen † thinks it means the *life* to come, the fame with the ineffable image of eternity, Others, ftrange difference! fay it is the *phallus*, or human genitals, while a later ‡ writer maintains it to be the mariner's compafs. My opinion, on the contrary is, that, as this figure was expofed to the public for the reafon I have mentioned, the Crux Anfata in his hand was nothing elfe but a monogram of his own name TO, and $\overset{o}{TT}$ fignifying TOT, or as we write Almanack upon a collection publifhed for the fame purpofe.

The changing of thefe emblems, and the multitude of them, produced the neceffity of contracting their fize, and this again a confequential alteration in the original forms; and a ftile, or fmall portable inftrument, became all that was neceffary for finifhing thefe fmall *Tots*, inftead of a large graver or carving tool, employed in making the large ones. But men, at laft, were fo much ufed to the alteration, as to know it better than under its primitive form, and the engraving became what we may call the firft elements, or root, in preference to the original.

The reader will fee, that, in my hiftory of the civil wars in Abyffinia, the king, forced by rebellion to retire to the province of Tigré, and being at Axum, found a ftone covered with hieroglyphics, which, by the many inquiries I made after

---

* Jamblich. de Myft. fect. 8. cap. 5.   † Sozomen, Eccles. Hift. lib. 7. cap. 15.
‡ Herw. theolog. Ethnica, p. 11.

after infcriptions, and fome converfations I had had with him, he guefled was of the kind which I wanted. Full of that princely goodnefs and condefcenfion that he ever honoured me with, throughout my whole ftay, he brought it with him when he returned from Tigré, and was reftored to his throne at Gondar.

It feems to me to be one of thofe private Tots, or portable almanacks, of the moft curious kind. The length of the whole ftone is fourteen inches, and fix inches broad, upon a bafe three inches high, projecting from the block itfelf, and covered with hieroglyphics. A naked figure of a man, near fix inches, ftands upon two crocodiles, their heads turned different ways. In each of his hands he holds two ferpents, and a fcorpion, all by the tail, and in the right hand hangs a noofe, in which is fufpended a ram or goat. On the left hand he holds a lion by the tail. The figure is in great relief; and the head of it with that kind of cap or ornament which is generally painted upon the head of the figure called Ifis, but this figure is that of a man. On each fide of the whole-length figure, and above it, upon the face of the ftone where it projects, are marked a number of hieroglyphics of all kinds. Over this is a very remarkable reprefentation; it is an old head, with very ftrong features, and a large bufhy beard, and upon it a high cap ribbed or ftriped. This I take to be the Cnuph, or Animus Mundi, though Apuleus, with very little probability, fays this was made in the likenefs of no creature whatever. The back of the ftone is divided into eight compartments*, from the top.

---

* I apprehend this is owing to the circumftances of the climate, in the four months, the time of the inundation, the heavens were fo covered as to afford no obfervations to be recorded.

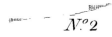

N.º 2

THE SOURCE OF THE NILE. 419

top to the bottom, and thefe are filled with hieroglyphics in the laft ftage, before they took the entire refemblance of letters. Many are perfectly formed; the Crux Anfata appears in one of the compartments, and Tot in another. Upon the edge, juft above where it is broken, is 1119, fo fair and perfect in form, that it might ferve as an example of caligraphy, even in the prefent times; 45 and 19, and fome other arithmetical figures, are found up and down among the hieroglyphics.

This I fuppofe was what formerly the Egyptians called a book, or almanack; a collection of thefe was probably hung up in fome confpicuous place, to inform the public of the ftate of the heavens, and feafons, and difeafes, to be expected in the courfe of them, as is the cafe in the Englifh almanacks at this day. Hermes is faid to have compofed 36,535 books, probably of this fort, or they might contain the correfpondent aftronomical obfervations made in a certain time at Meroë, Ophir, Axum, or Thebes, communicated to be hung up for the ufe of the neighbouring cities. Porphyry * gives a particular account of the Egyptian almanacks. "What is comprifed in the Egyptian almanacks, fays he, contains but a fmall part of the Hermaic inftitutions; all that relates to the rifing and fetting of the moon and planets, and of the ftars and their influence, and alfo fome advice upon difeafes."

It is very remarkable, that, befides my Tot here defcribed, there are five or fix, precifely the fame in all refpects, already

---

* Porpyhry Epift. ad Aneboncm.

ready in the British Museum; one of them, the largeſt of the whole, is made of fycamore, the others are of metal. There is another, I am told, in Lord Shelburn's collection; this I never had an opportunity of feeing; but a very principal attention feems to have been paid to make all of them light and portable, and it would feem that by theſe having been formed fo exactly fimilar, they were the Tots intended to be expoſed in different cities or places, and were neither more nor lefs than Egyptian almanacks.

Whether letters were known to Noah before the flood, is no where faid from any authority, and the inquiry into it is therefore ufelefs. It is difficult, in my opinion, to imagine, that any fociety, engaged in different occupations, could fubfift long without them. There feems to be lefs doubt, that they were invented, foon after the difperfion, long before Mofes, and in common ufe among the Gentiles of his time.

It feems alfo probable, that the firſt alphabet was Ethiopic, firſt founded on hieroglyphics, and afterwards modelled into more current, and lefs laborious figures; for the fake of applying them to the expedition of bufinefs. Mr Fourmont is fo much of this opinion, that he fays it is evident the three firſt letters of the Ethiopic alphabet are hieroglyphics yet, and that the Beta refembles the door of a houfe or temple. But, with great fubmiffion, the doors of houfes and temples, when firſt built, were fquare at the top, for arches were not known. The Beta was taken from the doors of the firſt Troglodytes in the mountains, which were rounded, and gave the hint for turning the arch, when architecture advanced nearer to perfection.

Others

OTHERS are for giving to letters a divine original: they say they were taught to Abraham by God himself; but this is no where vouched; though it cannot be denied, that it appears from scripture there were two sorts of characters known to Moses, when God spoke to him on Mount Sinai. The first two tables, we are told, were wrote by the finger of God, in what character is not said, but Moses received them to read to the people, so he surely understood them. But, when he had broken these two tables, and had another meeting with God on the mount on the subject of the law, God directs him specially not to write in the Egyptian character or hieroglyphics, but in the current hand used by the Ethiopian merchants, *like the letters* upon a signet; that is, he should not write in hieroglyphics by a *picture*, representing the *thing*, for that the law forbids; and the bad consequences of this were evident; but he should write the law in the current hand, by characters representing sounds, (though nothing else in heaven or on earth,) or by the letters that the Ishmaelites, Cushites, and India trading nations had long used in business for signing their invoices, engagements, &c. and this was the meaning of being *like the letters of a signet*.

HENCE, it is very clear, God did not invent letters, nor did Moses, who understood both characters before the promulgation of the law upon Mount Sinai, having learned them in Egypt, and during his long stay among the Cushites, and Shepherds in Arabia Petrea. Hence it should appear also, that the sacred character of the Egyptian was considered as profane, and forbid to the Hebrews, and that the common Ethiopic was the Hebrew sacred character, in which the copy of the law was first wrote. The text is very clear and explicit: " And the stones shall
" be

" be with the *names* of the children of Israel, twelve,
" according to their *names, like* the engravings of a *signet;* every
" one with his *name,* shall they be according to the twelve
" tribes*." Which is plainly, You shall not write in the way
used till this day, for it leads the people into idolatry; you
shall not type Judah by a *lion,* Zebulun by a *ship,* Issachar by
an *ass* couching between two burdens; but, instead of writing by pictures, you shall take the other known hand, the
merchants writing, which signifies *sounds,* not *things;* write
the names Judah, Zebulun, Issachar, in the letters, such as the
merchants use upon their signets. And, on Aaron's breastplate of pure gold, was to be written, in the same alphabet,
like the engravings of a signet, HOLINESS TO THE LORD †.

THESE signets, of the remotest antiquity in the East, are worn
still upon every man's hand to this day, having the name of
the person that wears them, or some sentence upon it always
religious. The Greeks, after the Egyptians, continued the
other method, and described figures upon their signet; the
use of both has been always common in Britain.

WE find afterwards, that, in place of stone or gold, for
greater convenience Moses wrote in a book, "And it came
" to pass, when Moses had made an end of writing the
" words of this law in a book, until they were finished;‡"—

ALTHOUGH, then, Moses certainly did not invent either,
or any character, it is probable that he made two, perhaps
more, alterations in the Ethiopic alphabet as it then stood,

with

---

* Exod. chap. xxviii. ver. 21. † Exod. chap. xxviii. ver. 36. ‡ Deut. chap. xxxi. ver. 24.

THE SOURCE OF THE NILE. 423

with a view to increase the difference still more between the writing then in use among the nations, and what he intended to be peculiar to the Jews. The first was altering the direction, and writing from right to left, whereas, the Ethiopian was, and is to this day, written from left to right, as was the hieroglyphical alphabet*. The second was taking away the points, which, from all times, must have existed and been, as it were, a part of the Ethiopic letters invented with them, and I do not see how it is possible it ever could have been read without them; so that, which way soever the dispute may turn concerning the antiquity of the application of the Masoretic points, the invention was no new one, but did exist as early as language was written. And I apprehend, that these alterations were very rapidly adopted after the writing of the law, and applied to the new character as it then stood; because, not long after, Moses was ordered to submit the law itself to the people, which would have been perfectly useless, had not reading and the character been familiar to them at that time.

It appears to me also, that the Ethiopic words were always separated, and could not run together, or be joined as the Hebrew, and that the running the words together into one must have been matter of choice in the Hebrew, to increase the difference in writing the two languages, as the contrary had been practised in the Ethiopian language. Though there is really little resemblance between the Ethiopic and the Hebrew letters, and not much more between
that

---

* Vide the hieroglyphics on the drawing of the stone.

that and the Samaritan, yet I have a very great fufpicion the languages were once much nearer a-kin than this difagreement of their alphabet promifes, and, for this reafon, that a very great number of words are found throughout the Old Teftament that have really no root, nor can be derived from any Hebrew origin, and yet all have, in the Ethiopic, a plain, clear, unequivocal origin, to and from which they can be traced without force or difficulty.

I shall now finifh what I have to fay upon this fubject, by obferving, that the Ethiopic alphabet confifts of twenty-fix letters, each of thefe, by a virgula, or point annexed, varying in found, fo as to become, in effect, forty-two diftinct letters. But I muft further add, that at firft they had but twenty-five of thefe original letters, the Latin P being wanting, fo that they were obliged to fubftitute another letter in the place of it. Paulus, for example, they called Taulus, Oulus, or Caulus. Petros they pronounced Ketros. At laft they fubftituted T, and added this to the end of their alphabet, giving it the force of P, though it was really a repetition of a character, rather than invention. Befides thefe there are twenty others of the nature of dipththongs, but I fhould fuppofe fome of thefe are not of the fame antiquity with the letters of the alphabet, but have been invented in later times by the fcribes for convenience.

The reader will underftand, that, fpeaking of the Ethiopic at prefent, I mean only the Geez language, the language of the Shepherds, and of the books. None of the other many languages fpoken in Abyffinia have characters for writing. But when the Amharic became fubftituted, in common ufe and converfation, to the Geez, after the reftoration

ration of the Royal family, from their long banifhment in Shoa, feven new characters were neceffarily added to anfwer the pronunciation of this new language, but no book was ever yet written in any other language except Geez. On the contrary, there is an old law in this country, handed down by tradition only, that whoever fhould attempt to tranflate the holy fcripture into Amharic, or any other language, his throat fhould be cut after the manner in which they kill fheep, his family fold to flavery, and his houfe razed to the ground; and, whether the fear of this law was true or feigned, it was a great obftacle to me in getting thofe tranflations of the Song of Solomon made which I intend for fpecimens of the different languages of thofe diftinct nations.

The Geez is exceedingly harfh and unharmonious. It is full of thefe two letters, D and T, on which an accent is put that nearly refembles ftammering. Confidering the fmall extent of fea that divides this country from Arabia, we are not to wonder that it has great affinity to the Arabic. It is not difficult to be acquired by thofe who underftand any other of the oriental languages; and, for a reafon I have given fome time ago, that the roots of many Hebrew words are only to be found here, I think it abfolutely neceffary to all thofe that would obtain a critical fkill in that language.

Wemmers, a Carmelite, has wrote a fmall Ethiopic dictionary in thin quarto, which, as far as it goes, has confiderable merit; and I am told there are others of the fame kind extant, written chiefly by Catholic priefts. But by far the moft copious, diftinct, and beft-digefted work, is that of Job Lu-dolf,

dolf, a German of great learning in the Eastern languages, and who has published a grammar and dictionary of the Geez in folio. This read with attention is more than sufficient to make any person of very moderate genius a great proficient in the Ethiopic language. He has likewise written a short essay towards a dictionary and grammar of the Amharic, which, considering the very small help he had, shews his surprising talents and capacity. Much, however, remains still to do; and it is indeed scarcely possible to bring this to any tolerable degree of forwardness for want of books, unless a man of genius, while in the country itself, were to give his time and application to it: It is not much more difficult than the former, and less connected with the Hebrew or Arabic, but has a more harmonious pronunciation.

CHAP.

CHAP. IV.

Some Account of the Trade Winds and Monsoons—Application of this to the Voyage to Ophir and Tarshish.

IT is a matter of real affliction, which shews the vanity of all human attainments, that the preceding pages have been employed in describing, and, as it were, drawing from oblivion, the history of those very nations that first conveyed to the world, not the elements of literature only, but all sorts of learning, arts, and sciences in their full detail and perfection. We see that these had taken deep root, and were not easily extirpated. The first great and fatal blow they received was from the destruction of Thebes, and its monarchy, by the first invasion of the Shepherds under Salatis, which shook them to the very foundation. The next was in the conquest of the Thebaid under Sabaco and his Shepherds. The third was when the empire of Lower Egypt (I do not think of the Thebaid) was transferred to Memphis, and that city taken, as writers say, by the Shepherds of Abaris only, or of the Delta, though it is scarcely probable, that, in so favourite a cause as the destruction of cities, the whole Shepherds did not lend their assistance.

These were the calamities, we may suppose, under which the arts in Egypt fell; for, as to the foreign conquests of Nebuchadnezzar and his Babylonians, they affected cities and the persons of individuals only. They were temporary, never intended to have lasting consequences; their beginning and end were prophesied at the same time. That of the Assyrians was a plundering expedition only, as we are told by scripture itself, intended to last but forty years *, half the life of man, given, for a particular purpose, for the indemnification of the king Nebuchadnezzar; for the hardships he sustained at the siege of Tyre, where the obstinacy of the inhabitants, in destroying their wealth, deprived the conqueror of his expected booty. The Babylonians were a people the most polished after the Egyptians. Egypt under them suffered by rapacity, but not by ignorance, as it did in all the conquests of the Shepherds.

After Thebes was destroyed by the first Shepherds, commerce, and it is probable the arts with it, fled for a time from Egypt, and centered in Edom, a city and territory, tho' we know little of its history, at that period the richest in the world. David, in the very neighbourhood of Tyre and Sidon, calls Edom the strong city; " Who will bring me into the " strong city? Who will lead me into Edom † ?" David, from an old quarrel, and probably from the recent instigations of the Tyrians his friends, invaded Edom ‡, destroyed the city, and dispersed the people. He was the great military power then upon the continent; Tyre and Edom were rivals; and his conquest of that last

great

---

* Ezek. chap. xxix. ver. 11. † Psalm. chap. lx. ver. 9. and Psal. cviii. ver. 10.
‡ 2 Sam. chap. viii. ver. 14. 1 Kings chap. x. ver. 15, 16.

THE SOURCE OF THE NILE.

great and trading ſtate, which he united to his empire, would yet have loſt him the trade he ſought to cultivate, by the very means he uſed to obtain it, had not Tyre been in a capacity to ſucceed to Edom, and to collect its mariners and artificers, ſcattered abroad by the conqueſt.

David took poſſeſſion of two ports, Eloth and Ezion-gaber *, from which he carried on the trade to Ophir and Tarſhiſh, to a very great extent, to the day of his death. We are ſtruck with aſtoniſhment when we reflect upon the ſum that Prince received in ſo ſhort a time from theſe mines of Ophir. For what is ſaid to be given by King David † and his Princes for the building of the Temple of Jeruſalem, exceeds in value eight hundred millions of our money, if the talent there ſpoken of is a Hebrew talent‡, and not a weight of the ſame denomination, the value of which was leſs, and peculiarly reſerved for and uſed in the traffic of theſe precious metals, gold and ſilver. It was, probably, an African or Indian weight, proper to the ſame mines, whence was gotten the gold appropriated to fine commodities only, as is the caſe with our ounce Troy different from the Averdupoiſe.

Solomon, who ſucceeded David in his kingdom, was his ſucceſſor likewiſe in the friendſhip of Hiram king of Tyre.

Solomon

---

* 1 Kings, chap. ix. ver. 26. 2 Chron. chap. viii. ver. 17. † 1 Chron. chap. xxii. ver. 14, 15, 16. Chap. xxix. ver. 3, 4, 5, 6, 7.—Three thouſand Hebrew talents of gold, reduced to our money, amount to twenty-one millions and ſix hundred thouſand pounds Sterling.

‡ The value of a Hebrew talent appears from Exodus, chap xxxviii. ver. 25, 26. For 603,550 perſons being taxed at half a ſhekel each, they muſt have paid in the whole 301,775 ; now that ſum is ſaid to amount to 100 talents, 1775 ſhekels only ; deduct the two latter ſums, and there will remain 300,000, which, divided by 108, will leave 3000 ſhekels for each of theſe talents.

Solomon vifited Eloth and Ezion-gaber* in perfon, and fortified them. He collected a number of pilots, fhipwrights, and mariners, difperfed by his father's conqueft of Edom, moft of whom had taken refuge in Tyre and Sidon, the commercial ftates in the Mediterranean. Hiram fupplied him with failors in abundance; but the failors fo furnifhed from Tyre were not capable of performing the fervice which Solomon required, without the direction of pilots and mariners ufed to the navigation of the Arabian Gulf and Indian Ocean. Such were thofe mariners who formerly lived in Edom, whom Solomon had now collected in Eloth and Ezion-gaber.

This laft-mentioned navigation was very different in all refpects from that of the Mediterranean, which, in refpect to the former, might be compared to a pond, every fide being confined with fhores little diftant the one from the other; even that fmall extent of fea was fo full of iflands, that there was much greater art required in the pilot to avoid land than to reach it. It was, befides, fubject to variable winds, being to the northward of 30° of latitude, the limits to which Providence hath confined thofe winds all over the globe; whereas the navigation of the Indian Ocean was governed by laws more convenient and regular, though altogether different from thofe that obtained in the Mediterranean. Before I proceed, it will be neceffary to explain this phænomenon.

It is known to all thofe who are ever fo little verfant in the hiftory of Egypt, that the wind from the north prevails in

---

* 2 Chron. chap. viii. ver 17.

THE SOURCE OF THE NILE. 431

in that valley all the fummer months, and is called the *Etefian winds;* it fweeps the valley from north to fouth, that being the direction of Egypt, and of the Nile, which runs through the midft of it. The two chains of mountains, which confine Egypt on the caft and on the weft, conftrain the wind to take this precife direction.

It is natural to fuppofe the fame would be the cafe in the Arabian Gulf, had that narrow fea been in a direction parallel to the land of Egypt, or due north and fouth. The Arabian Gulf, however, or what we call the Red Sea, lies from nearly north-weft to fouth-eaft, from Suez to Mocha. It then turns nearly eaft and weft till it joins the Indian Ocean at the Straits of Babelmandeb, as we have already faid, and may be further feen by confulting the map. Now, the Etefian winds, which are due north in Egypt, here take the direction of the Gulf, and blow in that direction fteadily all the feafon, while it continues north in the valley of Egypt; that is, from April to October the wind blows north-weft up the Arabian Gulf towards the Straits; and, from November till March, directly contrary, down the Arabian Gulf, from the Straits of Babelmandeb to Suez and the Ifthmus.

These winds are by fome corruptly called *the trade-winds;* but this name given to them is a very erroneous one, and apt to confound narratives, and make them unintelligible. A trade-wind is a wind which, all the year through, blows, and has ever blown, from the fame point of the horizon; fuch is the fouth-weft, fouth of the Line, in the Indian and Pacific Ocean. On the contrary, thefe winds, of which we have now fpoken, are called *monfoons;* each year they blow fix months from the northward, and the other fix months from the fouthward, in the Arabian Gulf: While in the Indian Ocean, without the Straits of Babelmandeb, they blow juft the contrary at the fame feafons; that is, in fummer from the fouthward, and in winter from the northward, fubject to a fmall inflexion to the eaft and to the weft.

THE reader will obferve, then, that, a veffel failing from Suez or the Elanitic Gulf, in any of the fummer months, will find a fteady wind at north-weft, which will carry it in the direction of the Gulf to Mocha. At Mocha, the coaft is eaft and weft to the Straits of Babelmandeb, fo that the veffel from Mocha will have variable winds for a fhort fpace, but moftly wefterly, and thefe will carry her on to the Straits. She is then done with the monfoon in the Gulf, which was from the north, and, being in the Indian Ocean, is taken up by the monfoon which blows in the fummer months there, and is directly contrary to what obtains in the Gulf. This is a fouth-wefter, which carries the veffel with a flowing fail to any part in India, without delay or impediment.

THE fame happens upon her return home. She fails in the winter months by the monfoon proper to that fea, that is, with a north-eaft, which carries her through the Straits of Babelmandeb. She finds, within the Gulf, a wind at fouth-caft, directly contrary to what was in the ocean; but then her courfe is contrary likewife, fo that a fouth-cafter, anfwering to the direction of the Gulf, carries her directly to Suez, or the Elanitic Gulf, to whichever way fhe propofes going. Hitherto all is plain, fimple, and eafy to be understood;

THE SOURCE OF THE NILE.

understood; and this was the reason why, in the earliest ages, the India trade was carried on without difficulty.

MANY doubts, however, have arisen about a port called *Ophir*, whence the immense quantities of gold and silver came, which were necessary at this time, when provision was making for building the Temple of Jerusalem. In what part of the world this Ophir was has not been yet agreed. Connected with this voyage, too, was one to Tarshish, which suffers the same difficulties; one and the same fleet performed them both in the same season.

IN order to come to a certainty where this Ophir was, it will be necessary to examine what scripture says of it, and to keep precisely to every thing like description which we can find there, without indulging our fancy farther. *First*, then, the trade to Ophir was carried on from the Elanitic Gulf through the Indian Ocean. *Secondly*, The returns were gold, silver, and ivory, but especially silver*. *Thirdly*, The time of the going and coming of the fleet was precisely three years †, at no period more nor less.

Now, if Solomon's fleet sailed from the Elanitic Gulf to the Indian Ocean, this voyage of necessity must have been made by monsoons, for no other winds reign in that ocean. And, what certainly shews this was the case, is the precise term of three years, in which the fleet went and came between Ophir and Ezion-gaber. For it is plain, so as to supersede the necessity of proof or argument, that, had this

---

* 1 Kings, chap. x. ver. 22.   † 1 Kings, chap. x. ver. 22. 2 Chron. chap. ix. ver. 21.

voyage been made with variable winds, no limited term of years ever could have been obferved in its going and returning. The fleet might have returned from Ophir in two years, in three, four, or five years; but, with variable winds, the return precifely in three years was not poffible, whatever part of the globe Ophir might be fituated in.

Neither Spain nor Peru could be Ophir; part of thefe voyages muft have been made by variable winds, and the return confequently uncertain. The ifland of Ceylon, in the Eaft Indies, could not be Ophir; the voyage thither is indeed made by monfoons, but we have fhewed that a year is all that can be fpent in a voyage to the Eaft Indies; befides, Ceylon has neither gold nor filver, though it has ivory. St. Domingo has neither gold, nor filver, nor ivory. When the Tyrians difcovered Spain, they found a profufion of filver in huge maffes, but this they brought to Tyre by the Mediterranean, and then fent it to the Red Sea over land to anfwer the returns from India. Tarfhifh, too, is not found to be a port in any of thefe voyages, fo that part of the defcription fails, nor were there ever elephants bred in Spain.

These mines of Ophir were probably what furnifhed the Eaft with gold in the earlieft times; great traces of excavation muft, therefore, have appeared; yet in none of the places juft mentioned are there great remains of any mines that have been wrought. The ancient traces of filver-mines in Spain are not to be found, and there never were any of gold. John Dos Santos*, a Dominican friar, fays, that on the

---

* Vid. Voyage of Dos Santos, publifhed by Le Grande.

THE SOURCE OF THE NILE.

the coaft of Africa, in the kingdom of Sofala, the mainland oppofite to Madagafcar, there are mines of gold and filver, than which none can be more abundant, efpecially in filver. They bear the traces of having been wrought from the earlieft ages. They were actually open and working when the Portuguefe conquered that part of the peninfula, and were probably given up fince the difcovery of the new world, rather from political than any other reafons.

JOHN DOS SANTOS fays, that he landed at Sofala in the year 1586; that he failed up the great river Cuama as far as Tetè, where, always defirous to be in the neighbourhood of gold, his Order had placed their convent. Thence he penetrated for above two hundred leagues into the country, and faw the gold mines then working, at a mountain called A-fura*. At a confiderable diftance from thefe are the filver mines of Chicoua; at both places there is great appearance of ancient excavations; and at both places the houfes of the kings are built with mud and ftraw, whilft there are large remains of maffy buildings of ftone and lime.

IT is a tradition which generally obtains in that country, that thefe works belonged to the Queen of Saba, and were built at the time, and for the purpofe of the trade on the Red Sea: this tradition is common to all the Cafrs in that country. Eupolemus, an ancient author quoted by Eufebius †, fpeaking of David, fays, that he built fhips at Eloth, a city in Arabia, and thence fent miners, or, as he calls

---

* See the map of this voyage.   † Apud Eufeb. Præp. Evang. lib. 9.

calls them, *metal-men*, to Orphi, or Ophir, an island in the Red Sea. Now, by the Red Sea, he understands the Indian Ocean*; and by Orphi, he probably meant the island of Madagascar; or Orphi (or Ophir) might have been the name of the Continent, instead of Sofala, that is, Sofala where the mines are might have been the main-land of Orphi.

The kings of the isles are often mentioned in this voyage; Socotra, Madagascar, the Commorras, and many other small islands thereabout, are probably those the scripture calls the *Isles*. All, then, at last reduces itself to the finding a place, either Sofala, or any other place adjoining to it, which avowedly can furnish gold, silver, and ivory in quantity, has large tokens of ancient excavations, and is at the same time under such restrictions from monsoons, that three years are absolutely necessary to perform the voyage, that it needs no more, and cannot be done in less, and this is Ophir.

Let us now try these mines of Dos Santos by the laws of the monsoons, which we have already laid down in describing the voyage to India. The fleet, or ship, for Sofala, parting in June from Ezion-gaber, would run down before the northern monsoon to Mocha. Here, not the monsoon, but the direction of the Gulf changes, and the violence of the south-westers, which then reign in the Indian Ocean, make themselves at times felt even in Mocha Roads. The vessel therefore comes to an anchor in the harbour of Mocha, and here she waits for moderate weather and a fair wind, which

---

* Dionysii Periegesis, ver. 38. and Comment. Eustathii in eundem. Strabo, lib. 16. p. 765. Agathemeri Geographia, lib. 2. cap. 11.

which carries her out of the Straits of Babelmandeb, through the few leagues where the wind is variable. If her courſe was now to the Eaſt Indies, that is eaſt-north-eaſt, or north-eaſt and by north, ſhe would find a ſtrong ſouth-weſt wind that would carry her to any part of India, as ſoon as ſhe cleared Cape Gardefan, to which ſhe was bound.

But matters are widely different if ſhe is bound for Sofala; her courſe is nearly ſouth-weſt, and ſhe meets at Cape Gardefan a ſtrong ſouth-weſter that blows directly in her teeth. Being obliged to return into the gulf, ſhe miſtakes this for a trade-wind, becauſe ſhe is not able to make her voyage to Mocha but by the ſummer monſoon, which carries her no farther than the Straits of Babelmandeb, and then leaves her in the face of a contrary wind, a ſtrong current to the northward, and violent ſwell.

The attempting this voyage with ſails, in theſe circumſtances, was abſolutely impoſſible, as their veſſels went only before the wind: if it was performed at all, it muſt have been by oars*, and great havock and loſs of men muſt have been the conſequence of the ſeveral trials. This is not conjecture only; the prophet Ezekiel deſcribes the very fact. Speaking of the Tyrian voyages probably of this very one he ſays, " Thy rowers have brought thee into great waters " (the ocean): the eaſt wind hath broken thee in the midſt of the feaſt†." In ſhort, the eaſt, that is the north-eaſt wind, was the very monſoon that was to carry them to Sofala, yet having no ſails, being upon a lee-ſhore, a very bold coaſt,

---

* Ezek. chap. xxvii. ver. 6.   † Ezek. chap. xxvii. ver. 26.

coaſt, and great ſwell, it was abſolutely impoſſible with oars to ſave themſelves from deſtruction.

At laſt philoſophy and obſervation, together with the unwearied perſeverance of man bent upon his own views and intereſt, removed theſe difficulties, and ſhewed the mariners of the Arabian Gulf, that theſe periodical winds, which, in the beginning, they looked upon as invincible barriers to the trading to Sofala, when once underſtood, were the very means of performing this voyage ſafely and expeditiouſly.

The veſſel trading to Sofala ſailed, as I have ſaid, from the bottom of the Arabian Gulf in ſummer, with the monſoon at north, which carried her to Mocha. There the monſoon failed her by the change of the direction of the Gulf. The ſouth-weſt winds, which blow without Cape Gardefan in the Indian Ocean, forced themſelves round the Cape ſo as to be felt in the road of Mocha, and make it uneaſy riding there. But theſe ſoon changed, the weather became moderate, and the veſſel, I ſuppoſe in the month of Auguſt, was ſafe at anchor under Cape Gardefan, where was the port which, many years afterwards, was called Promontorium Aromatum. Here the ſhip was obliged to ſtay all November, becauſe all theſe ſummer months the wind ſouth of the Cape was a ſtrong ſouth-weſter, as hath been before ſaid, directly in the teeth of the voyage to Sofala. But this time was not loſt; part of the goods bought to be ready for the return was ivory, frankincenſe, and myrrh; and the ſhip was then at the principal mart for theſe.

I suppose in November the veſſel ſailed with the wind at north-eaſt, with which ſhe would ſoon have made her voyage.

THE SOURCE OF THE NILE.

age: But off the coast of Melinda, in the beginning of December, she there met an anomalous monsoon at south-west, in our days first observed by Dr Halley, which cut off her voyage to Sofala, and obliged her to put in to the small harbour of *Mocha*, near Melinda, but nearer still to Tarshish, which we find here by accident, and which we think a strong corroboration that we are right as to the rest of the voyage. In the Annals of Abyssinia, we see that Amda Sion, making war upon that coast in the 14th century, in a list of the rebellious Moorish vassals, mentions the Chief of Tarshish as one of them, in the very situation where we have now placed him.

SOLOMON's vessel, then, was obliged to stay at Tarshish till the month of April of the second year. In May, the wind set in at north-east, and probably carried her that same month to Sofala. All the time she spent at Tarshish was not lost, for part of her cargo was to be brought from that place, and she probably bought, bespoke, or left it there. From May of the second year, to the end of that monsoon in October, the vessel could not stir; the wind was north-east. But this time, far from being lost, was necessary to the traders for getting in their cargo, which we shall suppose was ready for them.

THE ship sails, on her return, in the month of November of the second year, with the monsoon south-west, which in a very few weeks would have carried her into the Arabian Gulf. But off Mocha, near Melinda and Tarshish, she met the north-east monsoon, and was obliged to go into that port and stay there till the end of that monsoon; after which a south-wester came to her relief in May of the third year.

With

With the May monsoon she ran to Mocha within the Straits, and was there confined by the summer monsoon blowing up the Arabian Gulf from Suez, and meeting her. Here she lay till that monsoon, which in summer blows northerly from Suez, changed to a south-east one in October or November, and that very easily brought her up into the Elanitic Gulf, the middle or end of December of the third year. She had no need of more time to complete her voyage, and it was not possible she could do it in less. In short, she changed the monsoon six times, which is thirty-six months, or three years exactly; and there is not another combination of monsoons over the globe, as far as I know, capable to effect the same. The reader will please to consult the map, and keep it before him, which will remove any difficulties he may have. It is for his instruction this map has been made, not for that of the learned prelate * to whom it is inscribed, much more capable of giving additional lights, than in need of receiving any information I can give, even on this subject.

The celebrated Montesquieu conjectures, that Ophir was really on the coast of Africa; and the conjecture of that great man merits more attention than the assertions of ordinary people. He is too sagacious, and too enlightened, either to doubt of the reality of the voyage itself, or to seek for Ophir and Tarshish in China. Uninformed, however, of the particular direction of the monsoons upon the coast, first very slightly spoken of by Eudoxus, and lately observed and delienated

---

* Dr Douglas, Bishop of Carlisle.

THE SOURCE OF THE NILE.

lineated by Dr Halley, he was staggered upon considering that the whole distance, which employed a vessel in Solomon's time for three years, was a thousand leagues, scarcely more than the work of a month. He, therefore, supposes, that the reason of delay was owing to the imperfection of the vessels, and goes into very ingenious calculations, reasonings, and conclusions thereupon. He conjectures, therefore, that the ships employed by Solomon were what he calls *junks** of the Red Sea, made of papyrus, and covered with hides or leather.

PLINY † had said, that one of these junks of the Red Sea was twenty days on a voyage, which a Greek or Roman vessel would have performed in seven; and Strabo ‡ had said the same thing before him.

THIS relative slowness, or swiftness, will not solve the difficulty. For, if these junks ‖ were the vessels employed to Ophir, the long voyage, much more they would have been employed on the short one, to and from India; now they performed this within a year, which was all a Roman or Greek vessel could do, therefore this was not the cause. Those employed by Solomon were Tyrian and Idumean vessels, the best ships and sailers of their age. Whoever has seen the prodigious swell, the violent currents, and strong south-westers beyond the Straits of Babelmandeb, will not need any argument to persuade him, that no vessel made of papyrus, or leather, could live an hour upon that sea. The

---

* Vide L'Esprit des Loix, liv. xxi. cap. 6. p. 476. † Plin. lib. vi. cap. 22. ‡ Strabo, lib. xv.
‖ I know there are contrary opinions, and the junks might have been various. Vide Salm.

junks, indeed, were light and convenient boats, made to crofs the narrow gulf between the Sabeans and Homerites, or Cufhites, at Azab upon the Red Sea, and carry provifions from Arabia Felix to the more defert coaft of Azab. I have hinted, that the names of places fufficiently demonftrate the great lofs of men that happened to the traders to Sofala before the knowledge of the monfoons, and the introduction of the ufe of fails.

I SHALL now confider how far the thing is confirmed by the names of places in the language of the country, fuch as they have retained among them to the prefent day.

THERE are three Mochas mentioned in this voyage, fituated in countries very diffimilar to, and diftant from, each other. The firft is in Arabia Deferta, in lat. 30° nearly, not far from the bottom of the Gulf of Suez. The fecond is in lat. 13°, a fmall diftance from the Straits of Babelmandeb. The third Mocha is in lat. 3° fouth, near Tarfhifh, on the coaft of Melinda. Now, the meaning of Mocha, in the Ethiopic, is *prifon*; and is particularly given to thefe three places, becaufe, in any of them, a fhip is forced to ftay or be detained for months, till the changing of the monfoon fets her at liberty to purfue her voyage. At Mocha, near the bottom of the Gulf of Suez, a veffel, wanting to proceed fouthward to Babelmandeb, is kept here in prifon all winter, till the fummer monfoon fets her at liberty. At Mocha, in Arabia Felix, the fame happens to any veffel wanting to proceed to Suez in the fummer months; fhe may come up from the Straits of Babelmandeb to Mocha Road by the accidental direction of the head of the Gulf; but, in the month of May, the north-weft wind obliges her to put into Mocha, and

THE SOURCE OF THE NILE. 443

and there to stay till the south-easter relieves her in November. After you double Gardèfan, the summer monsoon, at north-east, is carrying your vessel full sail to Sofala, when the anomalous monsoon takes her off the coast of Melinda, and forces her into Tarshish, where she is imprisoned for six months in the Mocha there. So that this word is very emphatically applied to those places where ships are necessarily detained by the change of monsoons, and proves the truth of what I have said.

The last Cape on the Abyssinian shore, before you run into the Straits, is Cape Defan, called by the Portuguese, *Cape Dafui*. This has no meaning in any language; the Abyssinians, on whose side it is, call it *Cape Defan*, the Cape of Burial. It was probably there where the east wind drove ashore the bodies of such as had been shipwrecked in the voyage. The point of the same coast, which stretches out into the Gulf, before you arrive at Babelmandeb, was, by the Romans, called *Promontorium Aromatum*, and since, by the Portuguese, *Cape Gardefui*. But the name given it by the Abyssinians and sailors on the Gulf is, *Cape Gardefan*, the Straits of Burial.

Still nearer the Straits is a small port in the kingdom of Adel, called *Mete*, *i. e.* Death, or, he or they are dead. And more to the westward, in the same kingdom, is Mount Felix, corruptly so called by the Portuguese. The Latins call it Elephas Mons, the Mountain of the Elephant; and the natives, Jibbel Feel, which has the same signification. The Portuguese, who did not know that Jibbel Feel was Elephas Mons, being misled by the sound, have called it *Jibbel Felix*, the Happy Mountain, a name to which it has no sort of title.

The Straits by which we enter the Arabian Gulf are by the Portuguese called Babelmandeb, which is nonsense. The name by which it goes among the natives is Babelmandeb, the Gate or Port of Affliction. And near it Ptolemy * places a town he calls, in the Greek, Mandaeth, which appears to me to be only a corruption of Mandeb. The Promontory that makes the south side of the Straits, and the city thereupon, is *Diræ*, which means the Hades, or Hell, by Ptolemy † called Δηρη. This, too, is a translation of the ancient name, because Δηρη (or Diræ) has no signification in the Greek. A cluster of islands you meet in the canal, after passing Mocha, is called Jibbel Zekir, or, the Islands of Prayer for the remembrance of the dead. And still, in the same course up the Gulf, others are called Sebaat Gzier, Praise or Glory be to God, as we may suppose, for the return from this dangerous navigation.

All the coast to the eastward, to where Gardefan stretches out into the ocean, is the territory of Saba, which immemorially has been the mart of frankincense, myrrh, and balsam. Behind Saba, upon the Indian Ocean, is the *Regio Cinnamonifera,* where a considerable quantity of that wild cinnamon grows, which the Italian druggists call *canella*.

Inland near to Azab, as I have before observed, are large ruins, some of them of small stones and lime adhering strongly together. There is especially an aqueduct, which brought formerly a large quantity of water from a fountain in the mountains, which must have greatly contributed to the beauty,

---

* Pto'. Geog. lib. 4. cap 7.   † id. ibid.

beauty, health, and pleasure of Saba. This is built with large maffy blocks of marble, brought from the neighbouring mountains, placed upon one another without lime or cement, but joined with thick cramps, or bars of brafs. There are likewife a number of wells, not fix feet wide, compofed of pieces of marble hewn to parts of a circle, and joined with the fame bars of brafs alfo. This is exceedingly furprifing, for Agatharcides * tells us, that the Alileans and Caffandrins, in the fouthern parts of Arabia, (juft oppofite to Azab), had among them gold in fuch plenty, that they would give double the weight of gold for iron, triple its weight for brafs, and ten times its weight for filver; that, in digging the earth, they found pieces of gold as big as olivestones, but others much larger.

This feems to me extraordinary, if brafs was at fuch a price in Arabia, that it could be here employed in the meaneft and moft common ufes. However this be, the inhabitants of the Continent, and of the peninfula of Arabia oppofite to it, of all denominations agree, that this was the royal feat of the Queen of Saba, famous in ecclefiaftical hiftory for her journey to Jerufalem; that thefe works belonged to her, and were erected at the place of her refidence; that all the gold, filver, and perfumes came from her kingdom of Sofala, which was Ophir, and which reached from thence to Azab, upon the borders of the Red Sea, along the coaft of the Indian Ocean.

It will very poffibly be thought, that this is the place in which I fhould mention the journey that the Queen of Saba made into Paleftine; but as the dignity of the expedition itfelf,

---

* Agath. p. 60.

felf, and the place it holds in Jewiſh antiquities, merits that it ſhould be treated in a place by itſelf, ſo the connection that it is ſuppoſed to have with the foundation of the monarchy of Abyſſinia, the country whoſe hiſtory I am going to write, makes this particularly proper for the ſake of connection; and I ſhall, therefore, continue the hiſtory of the trade of the Arabian Gulf to a period in which I can reſume the narrative of this expedition without occaſioning any interruption to either.

CHAP.

CHAP. V.

Fluctuating State of the India Trade—Hurt by Military Expeditions of the Persians—Revives under the Ptolemies—Falls to Decay under the Romans.

THE prosperous days of the commerce with the Elanitic Gulf seemed to be at this time nearly past; yet, after the revolt of the ten tribes, Edom remaining to the house of David, they still carried on a sort of trade from the Elanitic Gulf, though attended with many difficulties. This continued till the reign of Jehosaphat*; but, on Jehoram's succeeding that prince, the Edomites † revolted and chose a king of their own, and were never after subject to the kings of Judah till the reign of Uzziah ‡, who conquered Eloth, fortified it, and having peopled it with a colony of his own, revived the old traffic. This subsisted till the reign of Ahaz, when Rezin king of Damascus took Eloth ‖, and expelled the Jews, planting in their stead a colony of Syrians.

---

* 1 Kings, chap. xxii. ver. 48.   2 Chron. chap. xx. ver. 36.   † 2 Kings, chap. viii. ver. 22.
2 Chron chap. xxi. ver. 10.   ‡ 2 Kings, chap. xiv. ver. 22.   2 Chron. chap. 26. ver. ii.
‖ 2 Kings, chap. xvi. ver. 6.

ans. But he did not long enjoy this good fortune, for the year after, Rezin * was conquered by Tilgath-pilefer; and one of the fruits of this victory was the taking of Eloth, which never after returned to the Jews, or was of any profit to Jerufalem.

The repeated wars and conqueft to which the cities on the Elanitic Gulf had been fubject, the extirpation of the Edomites, all the great events that immediately followed one another, of courfe difturbed the ufual channel of trade by the Red Sea, whofe ports were now confequently become unfafe by being in poffeffion of ftrangers, robbers, and foldiers; it changed, therefore, to a place nearer the center of police and good government, than fortified and frontier towns could be fuppofed to be. The Indian and African merchants, by convention, met in Affyria, as they had done in Semiramis's time; the one by the Perfian Gulf and Euphrates, the other through Arabia. Affyria, therefore, became the mart of the India trade in the Eaft

The conquefts of Nabopollafer, and his fon Nebuchadnezzar, had brought a prodigious quantity of bullion, both filver and gold, to Babylon his capital. For he had plundred Tyre †, and robbed Solomon's Temple ‡ of all the gold that had been brought from Ophir; and he had, befides, conquered Egypt and laid it wafte, and cut off the communication of trade in all thefe places, by almoft extirpating the
. people.

---

* 2 Kings, chap. xvi. ver. 6.
† Ezek. chap. xxvi. ver. 7. ‡ 2 Kings, chap. xxiv ver. 13. and 2 Chron. chap. xxxvi. ver. 7.

THE SOURCE OF THE NILE.

people. Immense riches flowed to him, therefore, on all sides, and it was a circumstance particularly favourable to merchants in that country, that it was governed by written laws that screened their properties from any remarkable violence or injustice.

I suppose the phrase in scripture, "The law of the Medes and Persians, which altereth not*," must mean only written laws, by which those countries were governed, without being left to the discretion of the judge, as all the East was, and as it actually now is.

In this situation the country was at the birth of Cyrus, who, having taken Babylon † and slain Belshazzer‡, became master of the whole trade and riches of the East. Whatever character writers give of this great Prince, his conduct, with regard to the commerce of the country, shews him to have been a weak one: For, not content with the prodigious prosperity to which his dominions had arrived, by the misfortune of other nations, and perhaps by the good faith kept by his subjects to merchants, enforced by those written laws, he undertook the most absurd and disastrous project of molesting the traders themselves, and invading India, that all at once he might render himself master of their riches. He executed this scheme just as absurdly as he formed it; for, knowing that large caravans of merchants came into Persia and Assyria from India, through the Ariana, (the desert coast that runs all along the Indian Ocean to

Vol. I.   3 L   the

---

* Dan. chap. vi. ver. 8. and Esther, chap. i. ver. 19.   † Ezra, chap. v. ver. 14. and chap. vi. ver. 5.   ‡ Dan. chap. v. ver. 30.

the Perfian Gulf, almoft entirely deftitute of water, and very nearly as much fo of provifions, both which caravans always carry with them), he attempted to enter India by the very fame road with a large army, the very fame way his predeceffor Semiramis had projected 1300 years before; and as her army had perifhed, fo did his to a man, without haing ever had it in his power to take one pepper-corn by force from any part of India.

The fame fortune attended his fon and fucceffor Cambyfes, who, obferving the quantity of gold brought from Ethiopia into Egypt, refolved to march to the fource, and at once make himfelf mafter of thofe treafures by rapine, which he thought came too flowly through the medium of commerce.

Cambyses's expedition into Africa is too well known for me to dwell upon it in this place. It hath obtained a celebrity by the abfurdity of the project, by the enormous cruelty and havock that attended the courfe of it, and by the great and very juft punifhment that clofed it in the end. It was one of thofe many monftrous extravagancies which made up the life of the greateft madman that ever difgraced the annals of antiquity. The bafeft mind is perhaps the moft capable of avarice; and when this paffion has taken poffeffion of the human heart, it is ftrong enough to excite us to undertakings as great as any of thofe dictated by the nobleft of our virtues.

Cambyses, amidft the commiffion of the moft horrid exceffes during the conqueft of Egypt, was informed that, from the fouth of that country, there was conftantly brought
a quantity

a quantity of pure gold, independent of what came from the top of the Arabic Gulf, which was now carried into Affyria, and circulated in the trade of his country. This fupply of gold belonged properly and exclufively to Egypt; and a very lucrative, though not very extenfive commerce, was, by its means, carried on with India. He found out that the people, poffeffing thefe treafures, were called *Macrobii*, which fignifies *long livers;* and that they poffeffed a country divided from him by lakes, mountains, and deferts. But what ftill affected him moft was, that in his way were a multitude of warlike Shepherds, with whom the reader is already fufficiently acquainted.

CAMBYSES, to flatter, and make peace with them, fell furioufly upon all the gods and temples in Egypt; he murdered the facred ox, the apis, deftroyed Memphis, and all the public buildings wherever he went. This was a gratification to the Shepherds, being equally enemies to thofe that worfhipped beafts, or lived in cities. After this introduction, he concluded peace with them in the moft folemn manner, each nation vowing eternal amity with the other. Notwithftanding which, no fooner was he arrived at Thebes (in Egypt) than he detached a large army to plunder the Temple of Jupiter Ammon, the greateft object of the worfhip of thefe *fhepherds;* which army utterly perifhed without a man remaining, covered, as I fuppofe, by the moving fands. He then began his march againft the *Macrobii*, keeping clofe to the Nile. The country there being too high to receive any benefit from the inundation of the river, produced no corn, fo that part of his army died for want of provifion.

ANOTHER detachment of his army proceeded to the country of the Shepherds, who, indeed, furnished him with food; but, exasperated at the sacrilege he had committed against their god, they conducted his troops through places where they could procure no water. After suffering all this loss, he was not yet arrived beyond 24°, the parallel of Syené. From hence he dispatched ambassadors, or spies, to discover the country before him, finding he could no longer rely upon the Shepherds. These found it full of black warlike people, of great size, and prodigious strength of body; active, and continually exercised in hunting the lion, the elephant, and other monstrous beasts which live in these forests.

THE inhabitants so abounded with gold, that the most common utensils and instruments were made of that metal; whilst, at the same time, they were utter strangers to bread of any kind whatever; and, not only so, but their country was, by its nature, incapable of producing any sort of grain from which bread could be made. They subsisted upon raw flesh alone, dried in the sun, especially that of the rhinoceros, the elephant, and giraffa, which they had slain in hunting. On such food they have ever since lived, and live to this day, and on such food I myself have lived with them; yet still it appears strange, that people confined to this diet, without variety or change, should have it for their characteristic that they were long livers.

THEY were not at all alarmed at the arrival of Cambyses's ambassadors. On the contrary, they treated them as an inferior species of men. Upon asking them about their diet,

and

THE SOURCE OF THE NILE. 453

and hearing it was upon bread, they called it *dung*, I suppose as having the appearance of that bread which I have seen the miserable Agows, their neighbours, make from seeds of bastard rye, which they collect in their fields under the burning rays of the sun. They laughed at Cambyses's requisition of submitting to him, and did not conceal their contempt of his idea of bringing an army thither.

They treated ironically his hopes of conquest, even supposing all difficulties of the desert overcome, and his army ready to enter their country, and counseled him to return while he was well, at least for a time, till he should produce a man of his army that could bend the bow that they then sent him; in which case, he might continue to advance, and have hope of conquest.—The reason of their reference to the bow will be seen afterwards. I mention these circumstances of the quantity of gold, the hunting of elephants, their living upon the raw flesh, and, above all, the circumstances of the bow, as things which I myself can testify to have met with among this very people. It is, indeed, highly satisfactory in travelling, to be able to explain truths which, from a want of knowledge of the country alone, have been treated as falsehoods, and placed to the discredit of historians.

The Persians were all famous archers. The mortification, therefore, they experienced, by receiving the bow they could not bend, was a very sensible one, though the narrative of the quantity of gold the messengers had seen made a much greater impression upon Cambyses. To procure
this

this treafure was, however, impracticable, as he had no provifion, nor was there any in the way of his march. His army, therefore, wafted daily by death and difperfion; and he had the mortification to be obliged to retreat into Egypt, after part of his troops had been reduced to the neceffity of eating each other *

DARIUS, king of Perfia, attempted to open this trade in a much more worthy and liberal manner, as he fent fhips down the river Indus into the ocean, whence they entered the Red Sea. It is probable, in this voyage, he acquired all the knowledge neceffary for eftablifhing this trade in Perfia; for he muft have paffed through the Perfian Gulf, and along the whole eaftern coaft of Arabia; he muft have feen the marts of perfumes and fpices that were at the mouth of the Red Sea, and the manner of bartering for gold and filver, as he was neceffarily in thofe trading places which were upon the very fame coaft from which the bullion was brought. I do not know, then, why M. de Montefquieu † has treated this expedition of Darius fo contemptuoufly, as it appears to have been executed without great trouble or expence, and terminated without lofs or hardfhip; the ftrongeft proof that it was at firft wifely planned. The prince himfelf was famous for his love of learning, which we find by his anxiety to be admitted among the Magi, and the fenfe he had of that honour, in caufing it to be engraved upon his tomb.

---

* Lucan lib. x. ver. 280.   † Vide Montefq. liv. 21. chap 8-

THE SOURCE OF THE NILE.

The expedition of Alexander into India was, of all events, that which moft threatened the deftruction of the commerce of the Continent, or the difperfing it into different channels throughout the Eaft: Firft, by the deftruction of Tyre, which muft have, for a time, annihilated the trade by the Arabian Gulf; then by his march through Egypt into the country of the Shepherds, and his intended further progrefs into Ethiopia to the head of the Nile. If we may judge of what we hear of him in that part of his expedition, we fhould be apt not to believe, as others are fond of doing, that he had fchemes of commerce mingled with thofe of conquefts. His anxiety about his own birth at the Temple of Jupiter Ammon, this firft queftion that he afked of the prieft, " Where the Nile had its fource," feemed to denote a mind bufied about other objects; for elfe he was then in the very place for information, being in the temple of that horned god*, the deity of the Shepherds, the African carriers of the Indian produce; a temple which, though in the midft of fand, and deftitute of gold or filver, poffeffed more and better information concerning the trade of India and Africa, than could be found in any other place on the Continent. Yet we do not hear of one queftion being made, or one arrangement taken, relative to opening the India trade with Thebes, or with Alexandria, which he built afterwards.

After having viewed the main ocean to the fouth, he ordered Nearchus with his fleet to coaft along the Perfian Gulf, accompanied by part of the army on land for their mutual affiftance, as there were a great many hardfhips which

---

* Lucan, lib. 9. ver. 515.

which followed the march of the army by land, and much difficulty and danger attended the fhipping as they were failing in unknown feas againft the monfoons. Nearchus himfelf informed the king at Babylon of his fuccefsful voyage, who gave him orders to continue it into the Red Sea, which he happily accomplifhed to the bottom of the Arabian Gulf.

WE are told it was his intention to carry on the India trade by the Gulf of Perfia, for which reafon he broke down all the cataracts and dams which the Perfians had built over the rivers communicating with the Euphrates. No ufe, however, feems to have been made of his knowledge of Arabia and Ethiopia, which makes me imagine this expedition of Alexander's fleet was not an idea of his own. It is, indeed, faid, that when Alexander came into India, the fouthern or Indian Ocean was perfectly unknown; but I am rather inclined to believe from this circumftance, that this voyage was made from fome memorials remaining concerning the voyage of Darius. The fact and circumftances of Darius's voyage are come down to us, and, by thefe very fame means, it muft be probable they reached Alexander, who I do not, believe ever intended to carry on the India trade at Babylon.

To render it impoffible, indeed, he could not have done three things more effectual than he did, when he deftroyed Tyre, and difperfed its inhabitants, perfecuted the Orites, or land-carriers, in the Ariana, and built Alexandria upon the Mediterranean; which laft ftep fixed the Indian trade in that city, and would have kept it there eternally, had the Cape of Good Hope never been difcovered.

THE

THE SOURCE OF THE NILE. 457

The Ptolemies, the wifeft princes that ever fat upon the throne of Egypt, applied with the utmoft care and attention to cultivate the trade of India, to keep up perfect and friendly underftanding with every country that fupplied any branch of it, and, inftead of difturbing it either in Afia, Arabia, or Ethiopia, as their predeceffors had done, they ufed their utmoft efforts to encourage it in all quarters.

Ptolemy I. was then reigning in Alexandria, the foundation of whofe greatnefs he not only laid, but lived to fee it arrive at the greateft perfection. It was his conftant faying, that the true glory of a king was not in being rich himfelf, but making his fubjects fo. He, therefore, opened his ports to all trading nations, encouraged ftrangers of every language, protected caravans, and a free navigation by fea, by which, in a few years, he made Alexandria the great ftore-houfe of merchandize, from India, Arabia, and Ethiopia. He did ftill further to infure the duration of his kingdom, at the fame time that he fhewed the utmoft difintereftednefs for the future happinefs of his people. He educated his fon, Ptolemy Philadelphus, with the utmoft care, and the happy genius of that prince had anfwered his father's utmoft expectations; and, when he arrived at the age of governing, the father, worn out by the fatigue of long wars, furrendered the kingdom to his fon.

Ptolemy had been a foldier from his infancy, and confequently kept up a proper military force, that made him every where refpected in thefe warlike and unfettled times. He had a fleet of two hundred fhips of war conftantly ready in the port of Alexandria, the only part for which he had apprehenfions. All behind him was wifely governed, whilft it enjoyed a moft flourifhing trade, to the profperity of which peace is neceffary. He died in peace and old age, after having merited the glorious name of *Soter*, or *Saviour of the kingdom*, which he himfelf had founded, the greateft part of which differed from him in language, colour, habit, and religion.

It is with aftonifhment we fee how thoroughly he had eftablifhed the trade of India, Ethiopia, and Arabia, and what progrefs he had already made towards uniting it with that of Europe, by a paffage in Athenæus*, who mentions a feftival and entertainment given by his fon, Ptolemy Philadelphus, to the people of Alexandria at his acceffion, while his father was alive, but had juft given up his crown.

There was in this proceffion a great number of Indian women, befides of other countries; and by Indians we may underftand, not only the Afiatic Indians, but the Abyffinians, and the inhabitants of the higher part of Africa, as all thefe countries were comprehended under the common appellation of *India*. Thefe were in the habit of flaves, and each led, or was followed by, a camel loaded with incenfe of Sheher, and cinnamon, befides other aromatics. After thefe came a number of Ethiopian blacks carrying the teeth of 600 elephants. Another troop had a prodigious quantity of ebony; and again others loaded with that fineft gold, which is not dug from the mine, but wafhed from the mountains by the tropical rains in fmall pieces, or pellets, which

---

* Athen. lib. 5.

THE SOURCE OF THE NILE. 459

which the natives and traders at this day call *Tibbar*. Next came a pack of 24,000 Indian dogs, all Afiatics, from the peninfula of India, followed by a prodigious number of foreign animals, both beafts and birds, paroquets, and other birds of Ethiopia, carried in cages; 130 Ethiopian sheep, 300 Arabian, and 20 from the Ifle Nubia*; 26 Indian buffaloes, white as fnow, and eight from Ethiopia; three brown bears, and a white one, which laft muft have been from the north of Europe; 14 leopards, 16 panthers, four lynxes, one giraffa, and a rhinoceros of Ethiopia.

When we reflect upon this prodigious mixture of animals, all fo eafily procured at one time, without preparation, we may imagine, that the quantity of merchandifes, for common demand, which accompanied them, muft have been in the proper proportion.

The current of trade ran towards Alexandria with the greateft impetuofity, all the articles of luxury of the Eaft were to be found there. Gold and filver, which were fent formerly to Tyre, came now down to the Ifthmus (for Tyre was no more) by a much fhorter carriage, thence to Memphis, whence it was fent down the Nile to Alexandria. The gold from the weft and fouth parts of the Continent reached the fame port with much lefs time and rifk, as there was now no Red Sea to pafs; and here was found the merchandife of Arabia and India in the greateft profufion.

3 M 2   To

---

* This is probably from Atbara, or the old name of the ifland of Meroe, which had received that laft name only as late as Cambyfes.

To facilitate the communication with Arabia, Ptolemy built a town on the coaft of the Red Sea, in the country of the Shepherds, and called it *Berenice**, after his mother. This was intended as a place of neceffary refrefhment for all the traders up and down the Gulf, whether of India or Ethiopia; hence the cargoes of merchants, who were afraid of lofing the monfoons, or had loft them, were carried by the inhabitants of the country, in three days, to the Nile, and there embarked for Alexandria. To make the communication between the Nile and the Red Sea ftill more commodious, this prince tried an attempt (which had twice before mifcarried with very great lofs) to bring a canal† from the Red Sea to the Nile, which he actually accomplifhed, joining it to the Pelufiac, or Eaftern branch of the Nile. Locks and fluices moreover are mentioned as having been employed even in thofe early days by Ptolemy, but very trifling ones could be needed, for the difference of level is there but very fmall.

This noble canal, one hundred yards broad, was not of that ufe to trade which was expected; merchants were weary of the length of time confumed in going to the very bottom of the Gulf, and afterwards with this inland navigation of the canal, and that of the Nile, to Alexandria. It was therefore much more expeditious to unload at Berenice, and, after three days journey, fend their merchandife directly down to Alexandria. Thus the canal was difufed, the goods paffed from Berenice to the Nile by land, and that road continues open for the fame purpofe to this day.

* Plin. lib. 6. cap. 23.   † Strabo, lib. 17. p. 932.

THE SOURCE OF THE NILE. 461

It should appear, that Ptolemy had employed the vessels of India and the Red Sea, to carry on his commerce with the peninsula, and that the manner of trading directly to India with his own ships, was either not known or forgotten. He therefore sent two ambassadors, or messengers, Megasthenes and Denis, to observe and report what was the state of India since the death of Alexander. These two performed their voyage safely and speedily. The account they gave of India, if it was strictly a true one, was, in all respects, perfectly calculated to animate people to the further prosecution of that trade. In the mean time, in order to procure more convenience for vessels trading on the Red Sea, he resolved to attempt the penetrating into that part of Ethiopia which lies on that sea, and, as historians imagine, with an intention to plunder the inhabitants of their riches.

It must not, however, be supposed, that Ptolemy was not enough acquainted with the productions of a country so near to Egypt, as to know this part of it had neither gold nor silver, whilst it was full of forests likewise; for it was that part of Ethiopia called Barbaria, at this day Barabra, inhabited by shepherds wandering with their cattle about the neighbouring mountains according as the rains fall. Another more probable conjecture was, that he wanted, by bringing about a change of manners in these people, to make them useful to him in a matter that was of the highest importance.

Ptolemy, like his father, had a very powerful fleet and army, he but was inferior to many of the princes, his rivals, in elephants, of which great use was then made in war. These Ethiopians were hunters, and killed them for their subsistence. Ptolemy, however, wished to have them taken alive,

alive, being numerous, and hoped both to furniſh himſelf, and diſpoſe of them as an article of trade, to his neighbours.

There is ſomething indeed ridiculous in the manner in which he executed this expedition. Aware of the difficulty of ſubſiſting in that country, he choſe only a hundred Greek horſemen, whom he covered with coats of monſtrous appearance and ſize, which left nothing viſible but the eyes of the rider. Their horſes too were diſguiſed by huge trappings, which took from them all proportion and ſhape. In this manner they entered this part of Ethiopia, ſpreading terror every where by their appearance, to which their ſtrength and courage bore a ſtrict proportion whenever they came to action. But neither force nor intreaty could gain any thing upon theſe Shepherds, or ever make them change or forſake the food they had been ſo long accuſtomed to; and all the fruit Ptolemy reaped from this expedition, was to build a city, by the ſea-ſide, in the ſouth-eaſt corner of this country, which he called Ptolemais Theron, or Ptolemais in the country of wild beaſts.

I have already obſerved, but ſhall again repeat it, that the reaſon why ſhips, in going up and down the Red Sea, kept always upon the Ethiopian ſhore, and why the greateſt number of cities were always built upon that ſide is, that water is much more abundant on the Ethiopian ſide than the Arabian, and it was therefore of the greateſt conſequence to trade to have that coaſt fully diſcovered and civilized. Indeed it is more than probable, that nothing further was intended by the expedition of the hundred Greeks, juſt now mentioned, than to gain ſufficient intelligence how this might be done moſt perfectly.

THE SOURCE OF THE NILE. 463

Ptolemy Evergetes, fon and fucceffor of Ptolemy Philadelphus, availed himfelf of this difcovery. Having provided himfelf amply with neceffaries for his army, and ordered a fleet to coaft along befide him, up the Red Sea, he penetrated quite through the country of the Shepherds into that of the Ethiopian Troglodytes, who are black and woolly-headed, and inhabit the low country quite to the mountains of Abyffinia. Nay [*], he even afcended thofe mountains, forced the inhabitants to fubmiffion, built a large temple at Axum, the capital of Sirè, and raifed a great many obelifks, feveral of which are ftanding to this day. Afterwards proceeding to the fouth-eaft, he defcended into the cinnamon and myrrh country, behind Cape Gardefan, (the Cape that terminates the Red Sea, and the Indian Ocean) from this, croffed over to Arabia, to the Homerites, being the fame people with the Abyffinians, only on the Arabian fhore. He then conquered feveral of the Arabian princes, who firft refifted him, and had it in his power to have put an end to the trade of India there, had he not been as great a politician as he was a warrior. He ufed his victory, therefore, in no other manner, than to exhort and oblige thefe princes to protect trade, encourage ftrangers, and, by every means, provide for the furety of neutral intercourfe, by making rigorous examples of robbers by fea and land.

The reigns of the latter Ptolemies were calculated to bring this commerce to a decline, had it not been for two great events, the fall of Carthage, deftroyed by Scipio, and that of Corinth, by the conful Mummius. The importance of thefe

---

[*] Mon. Aduli.

these events to Alexandria seems to have sustained the prosperity of Egypt, even against the ravages committed in the war between Ptolemy the VI. and VII. Alexandria was then besieged, and not only deprived of its riches, but reduced to the utmost want of necessaries, and the horrid behaviour of Ptolemy VII. (had it continued) would have soon rendered that city desolate. The consequence of such a conduct, however, made a strong impression on the prince himself, who, at once recalling his unjust edicts, by which he had banished all foreign merchants from Alexandria, became on a sudden wholly addicted to commerce, the encourager of arts and sciences, and the protector of strangers.

THE impolitic conduct in the beginning of his reign, however, had affected trade even in India. For the story preserved by Posidonius, and very improperly criticised by Strabo, seems to import little less. One day, the troops posted on the Arabian Gulf found a ship abandoned to the waves, on board of which was one Indian only, half dead with hunger and thirst, whom they brought to the king. This Indian declared he failed from his own country, and, having lost his course and spent all his provisions, he was carried to the place where he was found, without knowing where he was, and after having survived the rest of his companions; he concluded an imperfect narrative, by offering to be a guide to any person his majesty would send to India. His proposals were accordingly accepted, and Eudoxus was named by the king to accompany him. Strabo* indeed laughs at
this

---

* Strabo, lib. ii. p. 98.

THE SOURCE OF THE NILE. 465

this story. However, we must say, he has not seized the most ridiculous parts of it.

We are told that the king ordered the Indian to be taught Greek, and waited with patience till he had learned that language. Surely, before any person could thus instruct him, the master must have had some language in common with his scholar, or he had better have taught Eudoxus the Indian language, as it would have been as easy, and of much more use in the voyage he was to undertake. Besides, is it possible to believe, after the many years the Egyptians traded backwards and forwards to India, that there was not a man in Alexandria who could interpret for him to the king, when such a number of Egyptians went every year to India to trade, and stayed there for months each time? Could Ptolemy Philadelphus, at his father's festival, find 600 Indian female slaves, all at once, in Alexandria; and, after the trade had lasted so much longer, were the people from India decreased, or would their language be less understood? The king's wisdom, moreover, did not shew itself greatly, when he was going to trust a ship with his subjects to so skilful a pilot as this Indian, who, in the first voyage, had lost himself and all his companions.

India, however, and the Indian seas, were as well known in Egypt as they are now; and the magnificence and shew which attended Eudoxus's embassy seems to prove, that whatever truth there is in the Indian being found, Eudoxus' errand must have been to remove the bad effects that the king's extortions and robberies, committed upon all strangers in the beginning of his reign, had made upon the trading nations. Eudoxus returned, but after the death of Ptolemy, my. The neceffity, however, of this voyage appeared ftill great enough to make Cleopatra his widow project a fecond 'to the fame place, and greater preparations were made than for the former one.

But Eudoxus, trying experiments probably about the courfes of the trade-winds, loft his paffage, and was thrown upon the coaft of Ethiopia; where, having landed, and made himfelf agreeable to the natives, he brought home to Egypt a particular defcription of that country and its produce, which furnifhed all the difcovery neceffary to inftruct the Ptolemies in every thing that related to the ancient trade of Arabia. In the courfe of the voyage, Eudoxus difcovered the part of the prow of a veffel which had been broken off by a ftorm. The figure of a horfe made it an object of inquiry; and fome of the failors on board, who had been employed in European voyages, immediately knew this wreck to be part of one of thofe veffels ufed to trade on the weftern ocean. Eudoxus * inftantly perceived all the importance of the difcovery, which amounted to nothing lefs, than that there was a paffage round Africa from the Indian to the Atlantic Ocean. Full of this thought, he returned to Egypt, and, having fhewn the prow of his veffel to European fhipmafters, they all declared that this had been part of a veffel which had belonged to Cadiz, in Spain.

This difcovery, great as it was, was to none of more importance than to Eudoxus; for, fome time after, falling under the difpleafure of Ptolemy Lathyrus, VIIIth of that name,

---

* Plin. Nat. Hift. lib. 2. cap. 67.

THE SOURCE OF THE NILE. 467

name, and being in danger of his life, he fled and embarked on the Red Sea, failed round the peninfula of Africa, croffed the Atlantic Ocean, and came fafely to Cadiz.

The fpirit of inquiry, and defire of travelling, fpread itfelf inftantly through Egypt, upon this voyage of Eudoxus; and different travellers pufhed their difcoveries into the heart of the country, where fome of the nations are reported to have been fo ignorant as not to know the ufe of fire: ignorance almoft incredible, had we not an inftance of it in our own times. It was in the reign of Ptolemy IX. that Agatharcides * drew up his defcription of the Red Sea.

The reigns of the other Ptolemies ending in the XIIIth of that name, though full of great events, have nothing material to our prefent fubject. Their conftant expence and profufion muft have occafioned a great confumption of trading articles, and very little elfe was wanting; or, if there had, it muft have arrived at its height in the reign of the celebrated Cleopatra; whofe magnificence, beauty, and great talents, made her a wonder, greater than any in her capital. In her time, all nations flocked, as well for curiofity as trade, to Alexandria; Arabs, Ethiopians, Troglodytes, Jews, and Medes; and all were received and protected by this princefs, who fpoke to each of them in his own language†.

The difcovery of Spain, and the poffeffion of the mines of Attica from which they drew their filver, and the revolution

---

* Dodwell's Differtat. vol. 1. Scrip. Græc. Min. Id. Ox. 1698. 8vo.
† Plut. Vita. Ant. p. 913. tom. 1. part 2. Lubec. 1624. fol.

lution that happened in Egypt itself, seemed to have superseded the communication with the coast of Africa; for, in Strabo's time, few of the ports of the Indian Ocean, even those nearest the Red Sea, were known. I should, indeed, suppose, that the trade to India by Egypt decreased from the very time of the conquest by Cæsar. The mines the Romans had at the source of the river Betis*, in Spain, did not produce them above L. 15,000 a-year; this was not a sufficient capital for carrying on the trade to India, and therefore the immense riches of the Romans seem to have been derived from the greatness of the prices, not from the extent of the trade. In fact †, we are told that 100 *per cent.* was a profit in common trade upon the Indian commodities. Egypt now, and all its neighbourhood, began to wear a face of war, to which it had been a stranger for so many ages. The north of Africa was in constant troubles, after the first ruin of Carthage; so that we may imagine the trade to India began again, on that side, to be carried on pretty much in the same manner it had been before the days of Alexander. But it had enlarged itself very much on the Persian side, and found an easy, short inlet, into the north of Europe, which then furnished them a market and consumption of spices.

I MUST confess, notwithstanding, if it is true what Strabo says he heard himself in Egypt, that the Romans employed one hundred and twenty vessels in the Indian trade‡, it must at that time have lost very little of its vigour. We must, however, imagine, that great part of this was for the account,

---

* Strabo, lib. 3. † Plin. lib. vi. cap. 23. ‡ Strabo, lib. 2. p. 81.

THE SOURCE OF THE NILE. 469

account, and with the funds of foreign merchants. The Jews in Alexandria, until the reign of Ptolemy Phifcon, had carried on a very extenfive part of the India trade. All Syria was mercantile; and lead, iron, and copper, fupplied, in fome manner, the deficiency of gold and filver, which never again was in fuch abundance till after the difcovery of America.

But the ancient trade to India, by the Arabian Gulf and Africa, carried on by the medium of thefe two metals, remained at home undiminifhed with the Ethiopians, defended by large extenfive deferts, and happy with the enjoyment of riches and fecurity, till a frefh difcovery again introduced to them both partners and mafters in their trade.

One of the reafons that makes me imagine the Indian trade was not flourifhing, or in great efteem, immediately upon the Roman conqueft of Egypt, is, that Auguftus, very foon after, attempted to conquer Arabia. He fent Elius Gallus, with an army from Egypt into Arabia, who found there a number of effeminate, timid people, fcarcely to be driven to felf-defence by violence, and ignorant of every thing that related to war. Elius, however, found that they overmatched him in cunning, and the perfect knowledge of the country, which their conftant employment as carriers had taught them. His guides led him round from hardfhip to hardfhip, till his army almoft perifhed with hunger and thirft, without feeing any of thofe riches his mafter had fent him to take poffeffion of.

Thus was the Arabian expedition of Auguftus conceived with the fame views as thofe of Semiramis, Cyrus, and Cambyfes, defervedly as unhappy in its iffue as thefe firft had been.

That the African trade, moreover, was loft, appears from Strabo*, and his reafoning upon the voyage of Eudoxus, which he treats as a fable. But his reafoning proves juft the contrary, and this voyage was one foundation for opening this trade again, and making this coaft more perfectly known. This likewife appears clear from Ptolemy †, who, fpeaking of a promontory or cape oppofite to Madagafcar, on the coaft of Africa, fays it was inhabited by anthropophagi, or man-eaters, and that all beyond 8° fouth was unknown, and that this cape extended to and joined the continent of India ‡.

---

* Strabo, lib. ii. p. 98.   † Ptol. lib. iv. cap. 9. p. 115.   ‡ Ptol. lib. vii. cap. 3.

CHAP. VI.

Queen of Saba visits Jerusalem—Abyssinian Tradition concerning Her—Supposed Founder of that Monarchy—Abyssinia embraces the Jewish Religion—Jewish Hierarchy still retained by the Falasha—Some Conjectures concerning their Copy of the Old Testament.

IT is now that I am to fulfil my promise to the reader, of giving him some account of the visit made by the Queen of Sheba*, as we erroneously call her, and the consequences of that visit; the foundation of an Ethiopian monarchy, and the continuation of the sceptre in the tribe of Judah, down to this day. If I am obliged to go back in point of time, it is, that I may preserve both the account of the trade of the Arabian Gulf, and of this Jewish kingdom, distinct and unbroken.

We are not to wonder, if the prodigious hurry and flow of business, and the immensely valuable transactions they had with each other, had greatly familiarised the Tyrians

and

---

* It should properly be Saba, Azab, or Azaba, all signifying *South*.

and Jews, with their correspondents the Cushites and Shepherds on the coast of Africa. This had gone so far, as very naturally to have created a desire in the queen of Azab, the sovereign of that country, to go herself and see the application of such immense treasures that had been exported from her country for a series of years, and the prince who so magnificently employed them. There can be no doubt of this expedition, as Pagan, Arab, Moor, Abyssinian, and all the countries round, vouch it pretty much in the terms of scripture.

MANY* have thought this queen was an Arab. But Saba was a separate state, and the Sabeans a distinct people from the Ethiopians and the Arabs, and have continued so till very lately. We know, from history, that it was a custom among these Sabeans, to have women for their sovereigns in preference to men, a custom which still subsists among their descendents.

——————— *Medis levibusque Sabæis,*
Imperat hos sexus Reginarumque Jubarmis,
Barbariæ†, pars magna jacet. CLAUDIAN.

HER name, the Arabs say, was *Belkis;* the Abyssinians, *Maqueda*. Our Saviour calls her *Queen of the South*, without mentioning any other name, but gives his sanction to the truth of the voyage. " The Queen of the South (or Saba,
" or

---

* Such as Justin, Cyprian, Epiphanius, Cyril.
† By this is meant the country between the tropic and mountains of Abyssinia, the country of Shepherds, from *Berber*, Shepherd.

THE SOURCE OF THE NILE.

ª or Azab) shall rise up in the judgment with this genera-
" tion, and shall condemn it; for she came from the utter-
" most parts of the earth to hear the wisdom of Solomon;
" and, behold, a greater than Solomon is here *." No other
particulars, however, are mentioned about her in scripture;
and it is not probable our Saviour would say she came from
the uttermost parts of the earth, if she had been an Arab,
and had near 50° of the Continent behind her. The gold,
the myrrh, cassia, and frankincense, were all the produce
of her own country; and the many reasons Pineda † gives
to shew she was an Arab, more than convince me that she
was an Ethiopian or Cushite shepherd.

A strong objection to her being an Arab, is, that the
Sabean Arabs, or Homerites, the people that lived opposite
to Azab on the Arabian shore, had kings instead of queens,
which latter the Shepherds had, and still have. Moreover,
the kings of the Homerites were never seen abroad, and
were stoned to death if they appeared in public; subjects of
this stamp would not very readily suffer their queen to go
to Jerusalem, even supposing they had a queen, which they
had not.

Whether she was a Jewess or a Pagan is uncertain; Sabaism was the religion of all the East. It was the constant
attendant and stumbling-block of the Jews; but considering
the multitude of that people then trading from Jerusalem,
and the long time it continued, it is not improbable she was
a Jewess.

---

* Matth. chap. xii. ver. 42. Luke xi. 31.

† Pin. de reb. Solomon, lib. iv. cap. 14th.—Josephus thinks she was an Ethiopian, so do Origen, Augustin, and St Anselmo.

a Jewefs. "And when the queen of Sheba heard of the fame of Solomon concerning the name of the Lord, fhe came to prove him with hard queftions*." Our Saviour, moreover, fpeaks of her with praife, pointing her out as an example to the Jews †. And, in her thankfgiving before Solomon, fhe alludes to *God's blessing* on the *feed* of Ifrael for ever‡, which is by no means the language of a Pagan, but of a perfon fkilled in the ancient hiftory of the Jews.

SHE likewife appears to have been a perfon of learning; and that fort of learning which was then almoft peculiar to Paleftine, not to Ethiopia. For we fee that one of the reafons of her coming, was to examine whether Solomon was really the learned man he was faid to be. She came to try him in allegories, or parables, in which Nathan had inftructed Solomon.

THE learning of the Eaft, and of the neighbouring kings that correfponded with each other, efpecially in Paleftine and Syria, confifted chiefly in thefe: "And Joafh king of Ifrael fent to Amaziah king of Judah, faying, The thiftle that was in Lebanon fent to the Cedar that was in Lebanon, faying, Give thy daughter to my fon to wife: and there paffed by a wild beaft that was in Lebanon, and trode down the thiftle."—" Thou fayeft, Lo, thou haft
" fmitten

---

* 1 Kings, chap. x. ver 1. and 2 Chron. chap. ix. ver. 1.
† Matt. chap. xii. ver. 43. and Luke, chap xi. ver. 31.
‡ 1 Kings, chap. x. ver. 9. and 2 Chron. chap. ix. ver 8.

THE SOURCE OF THE NILE. 475

"smitten the Edomites, and thine heart lifteth thee up to boast: abide now at home, why shouldest thou meddle to thine hurt, that thou shouldest fall, even thou, and Judah with thee *?"

The annals of Abyssinia, being very full upon this point, have taken a middle opinion, and by no means an improbable one. They say she was a Pagan when she left Azab, but being full of admiration at the sight of Solomon's works, she was converted to Judaism in Jerusalem, and bore him a son, whom she called Menilek, and who was their first king. However strongly they assert this, and however dangerous it would be to doubt it in Abyssinia, I will not here aver it for truth, nor much less still will I positively contradict it, as scripture has said nothing about it. I suppose, whether true or not, in the circumstances she was, whilst Solomon also, so far from being very nice in his choice, was particularly addicted to Idumeans †, and other strange women, he could not more naturally engage himself in any amour than in one with the queen of Saba, with whom he had so long entertained the most lucrative connections, and most perfect friendship, and who, on her part, by so long a journey, had surely made sufficient advances.

The Abyssinians, both Jews and Christians, believe the xlvth psalm to be a prophecy of this queen's voyage to Jerusalem; that she was attended by a daughter of Hiram's from Tyre to Jerusalem, and that the last part contains a declaration

---

* 2 Chron. chap. xxv. ver. 18. 19.   † 1 Kings, chap. xi. ver. 1.

ration of her having a son by Solomon, who was to be king over a nation of Gentiles.

To Saba, or Azab, then, she returned with her son Menilek, whom, after keeping him some years, she sent back to his father to be instructed. Solomon did not neglect his charge, and he was anointed and crowned king of Ethiopia, in the temple of Jerusalem, and at his inauguration took the name of David. After this he returned to Azab, and brought with him a colony of Jews, among whom were many doctors of the law of Moses, particularly one of each tribe, to make judges in his kingdom, from whom the present Umbares (or Supreme Judges, three of whom always attend the king) are said and believed to be descended. With these came also Azarias, the son of Zadok the priest, and brought with him a Hebrew transcript of the law, which was delivered into his custody, as he bore the title of Nebrit, or High Priest; and this charge, though the book itself was burnt with the church of Axum in the Moorish war of Adel, is still continued, as it is said, in the lineage of Azarias, who are Nebrits, or keepers of the church of Axum, at this day. All Abyssinia was thereupon converted, and the government of the church and state modelled according to what was then in use at Jerusalem.

By the last act of the queen of Saba's reign, she settled the mode of succession in her country for the future. First, she enacted, that the crown should be hereditary in the family of Solomon for ever. Secondly, that, after her, no woman should be capable of wearing that crown or being queen, but that it should descend to the heir

THE SOURCE OF THE NILE.

heir male, however diftant, in exclufion of all heirs female whatever, however near; and that thefe two articles fhould be confidered as the fundamental laws of the kingdom, never to be altered or abolifhed. And, laftly, That the heirs male of the royal houfe, fhould always be fent prifoners to a high mountain, where they were to continue till their death, or till the fucceffion fhould open to them.

What was the reafon of this laft regulation is not known, it being peculiar to Abyffinia, but the cuftom of having women for fovereigns, which was a very old one, prevailed among the neighbouring fhepherds in the laft century, as we fhall fee in the courfe of this hiftory, and, for what we know, prevails to this day. It obtained in Nubia till Auguftus's time, when Petreius, his lieutenant in Egypt, fubdued her country, and took the queen Candace prifoner. It endured alfo after Tiberius, as we learn from St Philip's baptifing the eunuch* fervant of queen Candace, who muft have been fucceffor to the former; for fhe, when taken prifoner by Petreius, is reprefented as an infirm woman, having but one eye †. Candace indeed was the name of all the fovereigns, in the fame manner Cæfar was of the Roman emperors. As for the laft fevere part, the punifhment of the princes, it was probably intended to prevent fome diforders among the princes of her houfe, that fhe had obferved frequently to happen in the houfe of David ‡ at Jerufalem.

The

---

* Acts, chap. viii. ver. 27 and 38. † This fhews the falfehood of the remark Strabo makes, that it was a cuftom in Meroë, if their fovereign was any way mutilated, for the fubjects to imitate the imperfection. In this cafe, Candace's fubjects would have all loft an eye. Strabo, lib. 17. p. 777, 778.
‡ 2 Sam. chap. xvi. ver. 22. 1 Kings, chap. ii. ver. 13.

THE queen of Saba having made thefe laws irrevocable to all her pofterity, died, after a long reign of forty years, in 986 before Chrift, placing her fon Menilek upon the throne, whofe pofterity, the annals of Abyffinia would teach us to believe, have ever fince reigned. So far we muft indeed bear witnefs to them, that this is no new doctrine, but has been ftedfaftly and uniformly maintained from their earlieft account of time; firft, when Jews, then in later days after they had embraced chriftianity. We may further add, that the teftimony of all the neighbouring nations is with them upon this fubject, whether they be friends or enemies. They only differ in name of the queen, or in giving her two names.

THIS difference, at fuch a diftance of time, fhould not break feores, efpecially as we fhall fee that the queens in the prefent day have fometimes three or four names, and all the kings three, whence has arifen a very great confufion in their hiftory. And as for her being an Arab, the objection is ftill eafier got over. For all the inhabitants of Arabia Felix, efpecially thofe of the coaft oppofite to Saba, were reputed Abyffins, and their country part of Abyffinia, from the earlieft ages, to the Mahometan conqueft and after. They were her fubjects; firft, Sabean Pagans like herfelf, then converted (as the tradition fays) to Judaifm, during the time of the building of the temple, and continuing Jews from that time to the year 622 after Chrift, when they became Mahometans.

I SHALL therefore now give a lift of their kings of the race of Solomon, defcended from the queen of Saba, whofe device is a lion paffant, proper upon a field gules, and their motto,

motto, " *Mo Anbafa am Nizilet Solomon am Negadè Jude* ;" which fignifies, ' the lion of the race of Solomon and tribe of Judah hath overcome.' The Portuguefe miffionaries, in place of a lion paffant, which is really the king's bearing, have given him, in fome of their publications, a lion rampant, purpofely, as is fuppofed, to put a crofs into the paw of this Jewifh lion; but he is now returned to the lion paffant, that he was in the time of Solomon, without any fymbol either of religion or peace in his paws.

LIST OF THE KINGS OF ABYSSINIA,

FROM

MAQUEDA, QUEEN OF SABA, TO THE NATIVITY.

	Years.		Years.
Menilek, or David I. reigned	4	Katzina reigned,	9
Hendedya, or Zagdur,	1	Wazeha,	1
Awida,	11	Hazer,	2
Aufyi,	3	Kalas,	6
Sawé,	31	Solaya,	16
Gefaya,	15	Falaya,	26
Katar,	15	Aglebu,	3
Mouta,	20	Afifena,	1
Bahas,	9	Brus,	29
Kawida,	2	Mohefa,	1
Kanaza,	10	Bazen,	16

MENILEK fucceeded to the throne in the 986th year before Chrift; and this number of years muft be exhaufted in the reign of thefe twenty-two kings, when each reign, in that cafe, will amount to more than forty-four years, which is impoffible. The reign of the twenty-one kings of Ifrael, at a medium, is a little more than twenty-two years at an average, and that is thought abundantly high. And, even upon that footing of comparifon, there will be wanting a great deal more than half the number of years between Menilek and Bazen, fo that this account is apparently falfe. But I have another very material objection to it, as well as the preceding

THE SOURCE OF THE NILE. 481

preceding one, which is, that there is not one name in the whole lift that has an Ethiopic root or derivation.

The reader will give what credit he pleases to this very ancient lift. For my part, I content myself with disproving nothing but what is impossible, or contrary to the authority of scripture, or my own private knowledge. There are other lifts still, which I have seen, all of no better authority than this. I shall only observe, upon this last, that there is a king in it, about nine years before our Saviour's nativity, that did me the honour of using my name two thousand years before it came into Britain, spelled in the same manner that name anciently was, before folly, and the love of novelty, wantonly corrupted it.

The Greeks, to divert the king, had told him this circumstance, and he was exceedingly entertained at it. Sometimes, when he had seen either Michael, or Fasil *, or any of the great ones do me any favour, or speak handsomely of me, he would say gravely, that he was to summon the council to inquire into my pedigree, whether I was descended of the heirs-male of that Brus who was king nine years before the nativity; that I was likely to be a dangerous person, and it was time I should be sent to Wechné, unless I chose to lose my leg or arm, if I was found, by the judges, related to him by the heirs-male. To which I answered, that however he made a jest of this, one of my predecessors was certainly a king, though not of Abyssinia, not nine years before, but 1200 after our redemption; that the arms of my

Vol. I.   3 P   family

---

* What immediately follows will be hereafter explained in the Narrative.

family were a lion like his; but, however creditable his majesty's apprehensions as to Abyssinia might be to me, I could venture to assure him, the only connections I had the honour ever to have had *with him*, were by the *heirs-female*.

At other times, when I was exceedingly low-spirited, and despairing of ever again seeing Britain, he, who well knew the cause, used to say to the Serach Maffery, "Prepare "the Sendick and Nagareet; let the judges be called, and "the household troops appear under arms, for Brus is to be "buried: he is an Ozoro of the line of Solomon, and, for "any thing I know, may be heir to the crown. Bring like-"wife plenty of brandy, for they all get drunk at burials in "his country." These were days of sun-shine, when such jests passed; there were cloudy ones enough that followed, which much more than compensated the very transitory enjoyment of these.

Although the years laid down in the book of Axum do not precisely agree with our account, yet they are so near, that we cannot doubt that the revolt of the ten tribes, and destruction of Rehoboam's fleet which followed, occasioned the removal of Menilek's capital to Tigré*. But, whatever was the cause, Menilek did remove his court from Azab to a place near Axum, at this day called *Adega Daid*, the House of David; and, at no great distance, is another called *Azabo*, from his ancient metropolis, where there are old remains
of

---

* The temple which the Queen of Saba had seen built, and so richly ornamented, was plundered the 5th year of Rehoboam, by Sesac, which is 13 years before Menilek died. So this could not but have disgusted him with the trade of his ancient habitation at Saba.

of building of stone and lime, a certain proof that Axum was then fallen, else he would have naturally gone thither immediately upon forsaking his mother's capital of Azab.

That country, round by Cape Gardefan, and south towards Sofala, along the Indian Ocean, was long governed by an officer called *Baharnagash*, the meaning of which is, King of the Sea, or Sea Coast. Another officer of the same title was governor of Yemen, or Arabia Felix, which, from the earliest times, belonged to Abyssinia, down to the Mahometan conquest. The king himself was called *Nagash*, or Najashi, so were the governors of several provinces, especially Gojam; and great confusion has risen from the multitude of these kings. We find, for example, sometimes three upon the throne at one time, which is exceedingly improbable in any country. We are, therefore, to suppose, that one of these only is king, and two of them are the Najashi, or Nagash, we have just described; for, as the regulation of the queen of Saba banished the heirs-male to the mountain, we cannot conceive how three brothers could be upon the throne at the same time, as this law subsists to the present day. This, although it is one, is not the only reason of the confusion, as I shall mention another in the sequel.

As we are about to take our leave of the Jewish religion and government in the line of Solomon, it is here the proper place that I should add what we have to say of the Falasha, of whom we have already had occasion to speak, when we gave a specimen of their language, among those of the stranger nations, whom we imagine to have come originally from Palestine. I did not spare my utmost pains in inquiring into the history of this curious people, and lived in friendship with several esteemed the most knowing and learned among them, and I am persuaded, as far as they knew, they told me the truth.

THE account they give of themselves, which is supported only by tradition among them, is, that they came with Menilek from Jerusalem, so that they agree perfectly with the Abyssinians in the story of the queen of Saba, who, they say, was a Jewess, and her nation Jews before the time of Solomon; that she lived at Saba, or Azaba, the myrrh and frankincense country upon the Arabian Gulf. They say further, that she went to Jerusalem, under protection of Hiram king of Tyre, whose daughter is said in the xlvth Psalm to have attended her thither; that she went not in ships, nor through Arabia, for fear of the Ishmaelites, but from Azab round by Masuah and Suakem, and was escorted by the Shepherds, her own subjects, to Jerusalem, and back again, making use of her own country vehicle, the camel, and that her's was a white one, of prodigious size and exquisite beauty.

THEY agree also, in every particular, with the Abyssinians, about the remaining part of the story, the birth and inauguration of Menilek, who was their first king; also the coming of Azarias, and twelve elders from the twelve tribes, and other doctors of the law, whose posterity they deny to have ever apostatised to Christianity, as the Abyssinians pretend they did at the conversion. They say, that, when the trade of the Red Sea fell into the hands of strangers, and all communication was shut up between them and Jerusalem, the cities were abandoned, and the inhabitants relinquished the coast; that they were the inhabitants of these cities, by

trade

trade mostly brick and tile-makers, potters, thatchers of houses, and such like mechanics, employed in them; and finding the low country of Dembea afforded materials for exercising these trades, they carried the article of pottery in that province to a degree of perfection scarcely to be imagined.

BEING very industrious, these people multiplied exceedingly, and were very powerful at the time of the conversion to Christianity, or, as they term it, the Apostacy under Abreha and Atzbeha. At this time they declared a prince of the tribe of Judah, and of the race of Solomon and Menilek, to be their sovereign. The name of this prince was Phineas; who refused to abandon the religion of his forefathers, and from him their sovereigns are lineally descended; so they have still a prince of the house of Judah, although the Abyssinians, by way of reproach, have called this family Bet Israel, intimating that they were rebels, and revolted from the family of Solomon and tribe of Judah, and there is little doubt, but that some of the successors of Azarias adhered to their ancient faith also. Although there was no bloodshed upon difference of religion, yet, each having a distinct king with the same pretensions, many battles were fought from motives of ambition, and rivalship of sovereign power.

ABOUT the year 960, an attempt was made by this family to mount the throne of Abyssinia, as we shall see hereafter; when the princes of the house of Solomon were nearly extirpated upon the rock Damo. This, it is probable, produced more animosity and bloodshed. At last the power of the Falasha was so much weakened, that they were obliged to
leave

leave the flat country of Dembea, having no cavalry to maintain themselves there, and to take possession of the rugged, and almost inaccessible rocks, in that high ridge called the Mountains of Samen. One of these, which nature seems to have formed for a fortress, they chose for their metropolis, and it was ever after called the Jews Rock.

A GREAT overthrow, which they received in the year 1600, brought them to the very brink of ruin. In that battle Gideon and Judith, their king and queen, were slain. They have since adopted a more peaceable and dutiful behaviour, pay taxes, and are suffered to enjoy their own government. Their king and queen's name was again Gideon and Judith, when I was in Abyssinia, and these names seem to be preferred for those of the Royal family. At that time they were supposed to amount to 100,000 effective men. Something like this, the sober and most knowing Abyssinians are obliged to allow to be truth; but the circumstances of the conversion from Judaism are probably not all before us.

THE only copy of the Old Testament, which they have, is in Geez, the same made use of by the Abyssinian Christians, who are the only scribes, and sell these copies to the Jews; and, it is very singular that no controversy, or dispute about the text, has ever yet arisen between the professors of the two religions. They have no keriketib, or various readings; they never heard of talmud, targum, or cabala: Neither have they any *fringes** or *ribband* upon their *garments*, nor is there, as far as I could learn, one scribe among them.

I ASKED

---

* Numb. chap. xv. ver. 38, 39. Deut. chap. 22. ver. 12.

I ASKED them, being from Judea, whence they got that language which they spoke, whether it was one of the languages of the nations which they had learned on the coast of the Red Sea. They apprehended, but it was mere conjecture, that the language which they spoke was that of those nations they had found on the Red Sea, after their leaving Judea and settling there; and the reason they gave was certainly a pertinent one; that they came into Abyssinia, speaking Hebrew, with the advantage of having books in that language; but they had now forgot their Hebrew*, and it was therefore not probable they should retain any other language in which they had no books, and which they never had learned to express by letters.

I ASKED them, since they came from Jerusalem, how it happened they had not Hebrew, or Samaritan copies of the law, at least the Pentateuch or Octateuch. They said they were in possession of both when they came from Jerusalem; but their fleet being destroyed, in the reign of Rehoboam, and communication becoming very uncertain by the Syrian wars, they were, from necessity, obliged to have the scriptures translated, or make use of the copies in the hands of the Shepherds, who, according to them, before Solomon's time, were all Jews.

I ASKED them where the Shepherds got their copy, because, notwithstanding the invasion of Egypt by Nebuchadnezzar, who was the foreign obstacle the longest in their way,

---

* We see this happened to them in a much shorter time during the captivity, when they forgot their Hebrew, and spoke Chaldaee ever after.

way, the Ishmaelite Arabs had accefs through Arabia to Jerufalem and Syria, and carried on a great trade thither by land. They profeffed very candidly they could not give a fatisfactory anfwer to that, as the time was very diftant, and war had deftroyed all the memorials of thefe tranfactions. I afked if they really ever had any memorials of their own country, or hiftory of any other. They anfwered, with fome hefitation, they had no reafon to fay they ever had any; if they had, they were all deftroyed in the war with Gragné. This is all that I could ever learn from this people, and it required great patience and prudence in making the interrogations, and feparating truth from falfehood; for many of them, (as is invariably the cafe with barbarians) if they once divine the reafon of your inquiry, will fay whatever they think will pleafe you.

THEY deny the fceptre has ever departed from Judah, as they have a prince of that houfe reigning, and underftand the prophecy of the gathering of the Gentiles at the coming of Shiloh, is to be fulfilled on the appearance of the Meffiah, who is not yet come, when all the inhabitants of the world are to be Jews. But I muft confefs they did not give an explanation of this either clearly or readily, or feem to have ever confidered it before. They were not at all heated by the fubject, nor interefted, as far as I could difcern, in the difference between us, nor fond of talking upon their religion at all, though very ready at all quotations, when a perfon was prefent who fpoke Amharic, with the barbarous accent that they do; and this makes me conceive that their anceftors were not in Paleftine, or prefent in thofe difputes or tranfactions that attended the death of our Saviour, and have fubfifted ever after. They pretend that the book of Enoch

Enoch was the first book of scripture they ever received. They knew nothing of that of Seth, but place Job immediately after Enoch, so that they have no idea of the time in which Job lived, but said they believed it to be soon after the flood; and they look upon the book bearing his name to be the performance of that prophet.

MANY difficulties occur from this account of the Falasha; for, though they say they came from Jerusalem in the time of Solomon, and from different tribes, yet there is but one language amongst them all, and that is not Hebrew or Samaritan, neither of which they read or understand; nor is their answer to this objection satisfactory, for very obvious reasons.

LUDOLF, the most learned man that has writ upon the subject, says, that it is apparent the Ethiopic Old Testament, at least the Pentateuch, was copied from the Septuagint, because of the many Grecisms to be found in it; and the names of birds and precious stones, and some other passages that appear literally to be translated from the Greek. He imagines also, that the present Abyssinian version is the work of Frumentius their first bishop, when Abyssinia was converted to Christianity under Abreha and Atzbeha, about the year 333 after Christ, or a few years later.

ALTHOUGH I brought with me all the Abyssinian books of the Old Testament, (if it is a translation) I have not yet had time to make the comparison here alluded to, but have left them, for the curiosity of the public, deposited in the British Museum, hoping that some man of learning or curiosity would do this for me. In the mean time I must observe, that

that it is much more natural to suppose that the Greeks, comparing the copies together, expunged the words or passages they found differing from the Septuagint, and replaced them from thence, as this would not offend the Jews, who very well knew that those who translated the Septuagint version were all Jews themselves.

Now, as the Abyssinian copy of the Holy Scriptures, in Mr Ludolf's opinion, was translated by Frumentius above 330 after Christ, and the Septuagint version, in the days of Philadelphus, or Ptolemy II. above 160 years before Christ, it will follow, that, if the present Jews use the copy translated by Frumentius, and, if that was taken from the Septuagint, the Jews must have been above 400 years without any books whatsoever at the time of the conversion by Frumentius: So they must have had all the Jewish law, which is in perfect vigour and force among them, all their Levitical observances, their purifications, atonements, abstinences, and sacrifices, all depending upon their memory, without writing, at least for that long space of 400 years.

This, though not absolutely impossible, is surely very nearly so. We know, that, at Jerusalem itself, the seat of Jewish law and learning, idolatry happening to prevail, during the short reigns of only four kings, the law, in that interval, became so perfectly forgotten and unknown, that a copy of it being accidentally found and read by Josiah, that prince, upon his first learning its contents, was so astonished at the deviations from it, that he apprehended the immediate destruction of the whole city and people. To this I shall only add, that whoever considers the stiff-neckedness, stubbornness, and obstinacy, which were ever the characters

racters of this Jewish nation, they will not easily believe that they did ever *willingly* " receive the *Old* Testament from a " people who were the avowed champions of the *New*."

THEY have, indeed, no knowledge of the New Testament but from conversation; and do not curse it, but treat it as a folly where it supposes the Messiah come, who, they seem to think, is to be a temporal prince, prophet, priest, and conqueror.

STILL, it is not probable that a Jew would receive the law and the prophets from a Christian, without absolute necessity, though they might very well receive such a copy from a brother Jew, which all the Abyssinians were, when this translation was made. Nor would this, as I say, hinder them from following a copy really made by Jews from the text itself, such as the Septuagint actually was. But, I confess, great difficulties occur on every side, and I despair of having them solved, unless by an able, deliberate analysis of the specimen of the Falasha language which I have preserved, in which I earnestly request the concurrence of the learned. A book of the length of the Canticles contains words enough to judge upon the question, Whence the Falasha came, and what is the probable cause they had not a translation in their own tongue, since a version became necessary?

I HAVE less doubt that Frumentius translated the New Testament, as he must have had assistance from those of his own communion in Egypt; and this is a further reason why I believe that, at his coming, he found the Old Testament already translated into the Ethiopic language and character, because Bagla, or Geez, was an unknown letter, and the language unknown, not only to him, but likewife to every province in Abyssinia, except Tigré; fo that it would have coft him no more pains to teach the nation the Greek character and Greek language, than to have tranflated the New Teftament into Ethiopic, ufing the Geez character, which was equally unknown, unlefs in Tigré. The faving of time and labour would have been very material to him; he would have ufed the whole fcriptures, as received in his own church, and the Greek letter and language would have been juft as cafily attained in Amhara as the Geez; and thofe people, even of the province of Tigré, that had not yet learned to read, would have written the Greek character as eafily as their own. I do not know that fo early there was any Arabic tranflation of the Old Teftament; if there was, the fame reafons would have militated for his preferring this; and ftill he had but the New Teftament to undertake. But having found the books of the Old Teftament already tranflated into Geez, this altered the cafe; and he, very properly, continued the gofpel in that language and letter alfo, that it might be a teftimony for the Chriftians, and againft the Jews, as it was intended.

CHAP. VII.

Books in Use in Abyssinia—Enoch—Abyssinia not converted by the Apostles—Conversion from Judaism to Christianity by Frumentius.

THE Abyssinians have the whole scriptures entire as we have, and count the same number of books; but they divide them in another manner, at least in private hands, few of them, from extreme poverty, being able to purchase the whole, either of the historical or prophetical books of the Old Testament. The same may be said of the New, for copies containing the whole of it are very scarce. Indeed no where, unless in churches, do you see more than the Gospels, or the Acts of the Apostles, in one person's possession, and it must not be an ordinary man that possesses even these.

MANY books of the Old Testament are forgot, so that it is the same trouble to procure them, even in churches, for the purpose of copying, as to consult old records long covered with dust and rubbish. The Revelation of St John is a piece of favourite reading among them. Its title is, *the Vision of John Abou Kalamsis*, which seems to me to be a corruption of *Apocalypsis*.

lypsis. At the same time, we can hardly imagine that Frumentius, a Greek and a man of letters, should make so strange a mistake. There is no such thing as distinctions between canonical and apocryphal books. Bell and the Dragon, and the Acts of the Apostles, are read with equal devotion, and, for the most part, I am afraid, with equal edification; and it is in the spirit of truth, and not of ridicule, that I say St George and his Dragon, from idle legends only, are objects of veneration, nearly as great as any of the heroes in the Old Testament, or saints in the New. The Song of Solomon is a favourite piece of reading among the old priests, but forbidden to the young ones, to the deacons, laymen, and women. The Abyssinians believe, that this song was made by Solomon in praise of Pharaoh's daughter; and do not think, as some of our divines are disposed to do, that there is in it any mystery or allegory respecting Christ and the church. It may be asked, Why did I choose to have this book translated, seeing that it was to be attended with this particular difficulty? To this I answer, The choice was not mine, nor did I at once know all the difficulty. The first I pitched upon was the book of Ruth, as being the shortest; but the subject did not please the scribes and priests who were to copy for me, and I found it would not do. They then chose the Song of Solomon, and engaged to go through with it; and I recommended it to two or three young scribes, who completed the copy by themselves and their friends. I was obliged to procure licence for these scribes whom I employed in translating it into the different languages; but it was a permission of course, and met with no real, though some pretended difficulty.

A NEPHEW

A nephew of Abba Salama*, the Acab Saat, a young man of no common genius, afked leave from his uncle before he began the tranflation; to which Salama anfwered, alluding to an old law, That, if he attempted fuch a thing, he fhould be killed as they do fheep; but, if I would give *him* the money, he would permit it. I fhould not have taken any notice of this; but fome of the young men having told it to Ras Michael †, who perfectly gueffed the matter, he called upon the fcribe, and afked what his uncle had faid to him, who told him very plainly, that, if he began the tranflation, his throat fhould be cut like that of a fheep. One day Michael afked Abba Salama, whether that was true; he anfwered in the affirmative, and feemed difpofed to be talkative. " Then," faid the Ras to the young man, " your uncle de- " clares, if you write the book for Yagoube, he fhall cut " your throat like a fheep; and I fay to you, I fwear by St " Michael, I will put you to death like an afs if you don't " write it; confider with yourfelf which of the rifks you'll " run, and come to me in eight days, and make your choice." But, before the eighth day, he brought me the book, very well pleafed at having an excufe for receiving the price of the copy. Abba Salama complained of this at another time when I was prefent, and the name of *frank* was invidioufly mentioned; but he only got a ftern look and word from the Ras: " Hold your tongue, Sir, you don't know what you fay; you " don't know that you are a fool, Sir, but I do; if you talk " much you will publifh it to all the world."

AFTER

---

* I fhall have occafion to fpeak much of this prieft in the fequel. He was a moft inveterate and dangerous enemy to all Europeans, the piincipal ecclefiaftical officer in the king's houfe.

† Then Prime Minifter, concerning whom much is to be faid hereafter.

AFTER the New Teſtament they place the conſtitutions of the Apoſtles, which they call *Synnodos*, which, as far as the caſes or doctrines apply, we may ſay is the written law of the country. Theſe were tranſlated out of the Arabic. They have next a general liturgy, or book of common prayer, beſides ſeveral others peculiar to certain feſtivals, under whoſe names they go. The next is a very large voluminous book, called *Haimanout Abou*, chiefly a collection from the works of different Greek fathers, treating of, or explaining ſeveral hereſies, or diſputed points of faith, in the ancient Greek Church. Tranſlations of the works of St Athanaſius, St Bazil, St John Chryſoſtome, and St Cyril, are likewiſe current among them. The two laſt I never ſaw; and only fragments of St Athanaſius; but they are certainly extant.

THE next is the Synaxar, or the Flos Sanctorum, in which the miracles and lives, or lies of their ſaints, are at large recorded, in four monſtrous volumes in folio, ſtuffed full of fables of the moſt incredible kind. They have a ſaint that wreſtled with the devil in ſhape of a ſerpent nine miles long, threw him from a mountain, and killed him. Another ſaint who converted the devil, who turned monk, and lived in great holineſs for forty years after his converſion, doing penance for having tempted our Saviour upon the mountain: what became of him after they do not ſay. Again, another ſaint, that never ate nor drank from his mother's womb, went to Jeruſalem, and ſaid maſs every day at the holy ſepulchre, and came home at night in the ſhape of a ſtork. The laſt I ſhall mention was a ſaint, who, being very ſick, and his ſtomach in diſorder, took a longing for partridges; he called upon a brace of them to come to him,

3 and

THE SOURCE OF THE NILE.

and immediately two roasted partridges came *flying*, and rested upon his plate, to be devoured. These stories are circumstantially told and vouched by unexceptionable people, and were a grievous stumbling-block to the Jesuits, who could not pretend their own miracles were either better established, or more worthy of belief.

There are other books of less size and consequence, particularly the Organon Denghel, or the Virgin Mary's Musical Instrument, composed by Abba George about the year 1440, much valued for the purity of its language, though he himself was an Armenian. The last of this Ethiopic library is the book of Enoch*. Upon hearing this book first mentioned, many literati in Europe had a wonderful desire to see it, thinking that, no doubt, many secrets and unknown histories might be drawn from it. Upon this some impostor, getting an Ethiopic book into his hands, wrote for the title, *The Prophecies of Enoch*, upon the front page of it. M. Pierisc † no sooner heard of it than he purchased it of the impostor for a considerable sum of money: being placed afterwards in Cardinal Mazarine's library, where Mr Ludolf had access to it, he found it was a Gnostic book upon mysteries in heaven and earth, but which mentioned not a word of Enoch, or his prophecy, from beginning to end; and, from this disappointment, he takes upon him to deny the existence of any such book any where else. This, however, is a mistake; for, as a public return for the many obligations I had received from every rank of that most humane,

---

* Vid. Origen contra Celsum, lib. 5. Tertull. de Idolol. c. 4. Drus in suo Enoch. Bangius in Cœlo Orientis Exercit. 1. quæst. 5. and 6.

† Gassend in vita Pierisc, lib. 5.

humane, polite, and scientific nation, and more especially from the sovereign Louis XV. I gave to his cabinet a part of every thing curious I had collected abroad; which was received with that degree of confideration and attention that cannot fail to determine every traveller of a liberal mind to follow my example.

AMONGST the articles I configned to the library at Paris, was a very beautiful and magnificent copy of the prophecies of Enoch, in large quarto; another is amongst the books of scripture which I brought home, standing immediately before the book of Job, which is its proper place in the Abyssinian canon; and a third copy I have presented to the Bodleian library at Oxford, by the hands of Dr Douglas the Bishop of Carlisle. The more ancient history of that book is well known. The church at first looked upon it as apocryphal; and as it was quoted in the book of Jude, the same suspicion fell upon that book also. For this reason, the council of Nice threw the epistle of Jude out of the canon, but the council of Trent arguing better, replaced the apostle in the canon as before.

HERE we may obferve by the way, that Jude's appealing to the apocryphal books did by no means import, that either he believed or warranted the truth of them. But it was an argument, *a fortiori*, which our Saviour himself often makes use of, and amounts to no more than this, You, says he to the Jews, deny certain facts, which must be from prejudice, because you have them allowed in your own books, and believe them there. And a very strong and fair way of arguing it is, but this is by no means any allowance that they are true. In the same manner, You, says Jude, do not be-

lieve

lieve the coming of Chrift and a latter judgment; yet your ancient Enoch, whom you fuppofe was the feventh from A-dam, tells you this plainly, and in fo many words, long ago. And indeed the quotation is, word for word the fame, in the fecond chapter of the book.

ALL that is material to fay further concerning the book of Enoch is, that it is a Gnoftic book, containing the age of the Emims, Anakims, and Egregores, fuppofed defcendents of the fons of God, when they fell in love with the daughters of men, and had fons who were giants. Thefe giants do not feem to have been fo charitable to the fons and daughters of men, as their fathers had been. For, firft, they began to eat all the beafts of the earth, they then fell upon the birds and fifhes, and ate them alfo; their hunger being not yet fatisfied, they ate all the corn, all men's labour, all the trees and bufhes, and, not content yet, they fell to eating the men themfelves. The men (like our modern failors with the favages) were not afraid of dying, but very much fo of being eaten after death. At length they cry to God againft the wrongs the giants had done them, and God fends a flood which drowns both them and the giants.

SUCH is the reparation which this ingenious author has thought proper to attribute to Providence, in anfwer to the firft, and the beft-founded complaints that were made to him by man. I think this exhaufts about four or five of the firft chapters. It is not the fourth part of the book; but my curiofity led me no further. The cataftrophe of the giants, and the juftice of the cataftrophe, had fully fatisfied me.

I CANNOT but recollect, that when it was known in England that I had presented this book to the library of the King of France, without staying a few days, to give me time to reach London, when our learned countrymen might have had an opportunity of perusing at leisure another copy of this book, Doctor Woide set out for Paris, with letters from the Secretary of State to Lord Stormont, Ambassador at that court, desiring him to assist the doctor in procuring access to my present, by permission from his Most Christian Majesty. This he accordingly obtained, and a translation of the work was brought over; but, I know not why, it has no where appeared. I fancy Dr Woide was not much more pleased with the conduct of the giants than I was.

I SHALL conclude with one particular, which is a curious one: The Synaxar (what the Catholics call their Flos Sanctorum, or the lives and miracles of their saints), giving the history of the Abyssinian conversion to Christianity in the year 333, says, that when Frumentius and Œdesius were introduced to the king, who was a minor, they found him reading the Psalms of David.

THIS book, or that of Enoch, does by no means prove that they were at that time Jews. For these two were in as great authority among the Pagans, who professed Sabaism, the first religion of the East, and especially of the *Shepherds*, as among the Jews. These being continued also in the same letter and character among the Abyssinians from the beginning, convinces me that there has not been any other writing in this country, or the south of Arabia, since that which rose from the Hieroglyphics.

THE SOURCE OF THE NILE.

The Abyssinian history begins now to rid itself of part of that confusion which is almost a constant attendant upon the very few annals yet preserved of barbarous nations in very ancient times. It is certain, from their history, that Bazen was contemporary with Augustus, that he reigned sixteen years, and that the birth of our Saviour fell on the 8th year of that prince, so that the 8th year of Bazen was the first of Christ.

Amha Yasous, prince of Shoa, a province to which the small remains of the line of Solomon fled upon a catastrophe, I shall have occasion to mention, gave me the following list of the kings of Abyssinia since the time of which we are now speaking. From him I procured all the books of the Annals of Abyssinia, which have served me to compose this history, excepting two, one given me by the King, the other the Chronicle of Axum, by Ras Michael Governor of Tigré.

SHOA LIST OF PRINCES.

Bazen,	Araad,
Tzenaf Segued,	Saladoba,
Garima Asferi,	Alamida,
Saraada,	Tezhana,
Tzion,	Caleb, 522,
Sargai,	Guebra Mafcal,
Bagamai,	Conſtantine,
Jan Segued,	Bazzer,
Tzion Heges,	Azbeha,
Moal Genha,	Armaha,
Saif Araad,	Jan Asfeha,
Agedar,	Jan Segued,
Abreha and Atzbeha, 333,	Fere Sanai,
Asfeha,	Aderaaz,
Arphad and Amzi,	Aizor,

Del Naad, 960*.

THIS liſt is kept in the monaſtery of Debra Libanos in Shoa; the Abyſſinians receive it without any ſort of doubt, though to me it ſeems very exceptionable: If it were genuine, it would put this monarchy in a very reſpectable light in point of antiquity.

GREAT confuſion has ariſen in theſe old liſts, from their kings having always two, and ſometimes three names. The

---

* The length of theſe princes reigns are ſo great as to become incredible; but, as we have nothing further of their hiſtory but their names, we have no data upon which to reform them.

The first is their christened name, their second a nick, or byename, and the third they take upon their inauguration. There is, likewise, another cause of mistake, which is, when two names occur, one of a king, the other the quality of a king only, these are set down as two brothers. For example, Atzbeha is the *blessed*, or *the saint*; and I very much suspect, therefore, that Atzbeha and Abreha, said to be two brothers, only mean Abraham the *blessed*, or *the saint*; because, in that prince's time, the country was converted to Christianity; Caleb * and Elesbaas, were long thought to be contemporary princes, till it was found out, by inspecting the ancient authors of those times, that this was only the name or quality of *blessed*, or *saint*, given to Caleb, in consequence of his expedition into Arabia against Phineas, king of the Jews, and persecutor of the Christians.

There are four very interesting events, in the course of the reign of these princes. The first and greatest we have already mentioned, the birth of Christ in the 8th year of Bazen. The second is the conversion of Abyssinia to Christianity, in the reign of Abreha and Atzbeha, in the year of Christ 333, according to our account. The third the war with the Jews under Caleb. The fourth, the massacre of the princes on the mountain of Damo. The time and circumstances of all these are well known, and I shall relate them in their turn with the brevity becoming a historian.

Some ecclesiastical* writers, rather from attachment to particular systems, than from any conviction that the opinion they

---

* Caleb el Atsbeha, which has been made Elesbaas throwing away the t.
† Surius Tom. 5. d. 24. Oct. Card. Baronius. Tom. 7. Annal. A. C. 522. N. 23.

they espouse is truth, would persuade us, that the conversion of Abyssinia to Christianity happened at the beginning of this period, that is, soon after the reign of Bazen; others, that Saint Matthias, or Saint Bartholomew, or some others of the Apostles, after their mission to teach the nations, first preached here the faith of Christ, and converted this people to it. It is also said, that the eunuch baptized by Philip, upon his return to Candace, became the Apostle of that nation, which, from his preaching, believed in Christ and his gospel. All these might pass for dreams not worthy of examination, if they were not invented for particular purposes.

Till the death of Christ, who lived several years after Bazen, very few Jews had been converted even in Judea. We have no account in scripture that induces us to believe, that the Apostles went to any great distance from each other immediately after the crucifixion. Nay, we know positively, they did not, but lived in community together for a considerable time. Besides, it is not probable, if the Abyssinians were converted by any of the Apostles, that, for the space of 300 years, they should remain without bishops, and without church-government, in the neighbourhood of many states, where churches were already formed, without calling to their assistance some members of these churches, who might, at least, inform them of the purport of the councils held, and canons made by them, during that space of 300 years; for this was absolutely necessary to preserve orthodoxy, and the communion between this, and the churches of that time. And it should be observed, that if, in Philip's time, the Christian religion had not penetrated (as we see in effect it had not) into the court of Candace, so much nearer Egypt, it did not surely reach so early into the

more

THE SOURCE OF THE NILE.

more diftant mountainous country of Abyffinia; and if the Ethiopia, where Candace reigned, was the fame as Abyffinia, the ftory of the queen of Saba muft be given up as a falfehood; for, in that cafe, there would be a woman fitting upon the throne of that country 500 years after fhe was excluded by a folemn deliberate fundamental law of the land.

But it is known, from credible writers, engaged in no controverfy, that this Candace reigned upon the Nile in Atbara, much nearer Egypt. Her capital alfo was taken in the time of Auguftus, a few years before the Converfion, by Philip; and we fhall have occafion often to mention her fucceffors and her kingdom, as exifting in the reign of the Abyffinian kings, long after the Mahometan conqueft; they exifted when I paffed through Atbara, and do undoubtedly exift there to this day. What puts an end to all this argument is a matter of fact, which is, that the Abyffinians continued Jews and Pagans, and were found to be fo above 300 years after the time of the Apoftles. Inftead, therefore, of taking the firft of this lift (Bazen) for the prince under whom Abyffinia was converted from Judaifm, as authors have advanced, in conformity to the Abyffinian annals, we fhall fix upon the 13th (Abreha and Atzbeha, whom we believe to be but one prince) and, before we enter into the narrative of that remarkable event, we fhall obferve, that, from Bazen to Abreha, being 341 years inclufive, the eighth of Bazen being the firft of Chrift, by this account of the converfion, which happened under Abreha and Atzbeha, it muft have been about 333 years after Chrift, or 341 after Bazen.

But we certainly know, that the firft bifhop, ordained for the converfion of Abyffinia, was fent from Alexandria by

St Athanafius, who was himfelf ordained to that See about the year 326. Therefore, any account, prior to this ordination and converfion, muft be falfe, and this converfion and ordination muft have therefore happened about the year 330, or poffibly fome few years later; for Socrates* fays, that St Athanafius himfelf was then but newly elected to the See of Alexandria.

In order to clear our way of difficulties, before we begin the narrative of the converfion, we fhall obferve, in this place, the reafon I juft hinted at, why fome ecclefiaftical writers had attributed the converfion of Abyffinia to the Apoftles. There was found, or pretended to be found in Alexandria, a canon, of a council faid to be that of Nice, and this canon had never before been known, nor ever feen in any other place, or in any language, except the Arabic; and, from infpection, I may add, that it is fuch Arabic that fcarce will convey the meaning it was intended. Indeed, if it be conftrued according to the ftrict rule of grammar, it will not convey any fenfe at all. This canon regulated the precedency of the Abuna of Ethiopia in all after councils, and it places him immediately after the prelate of Seleucia. This moft honourable antiquity was looked upon and boafted of for their own purpofes by the Jefuits, as a difcovery of infinite value to the church of Ethiopia.

I shall only make one other obfervation to obviate a difficulty which will occur in reading what is to follow. The Abyffinian hiftory plainly and pofitively fays, that when
Frumentius

---

* Ludolf, vol. 2. lib. iii. cap. 2.

Frumentius (the apoſtle of the Abyſſinians) came firſt into that country, a queen reigned, which is an abſolute contradiction to what we have already ſtated, and would ſeem to favour the ſtory of queen Candace. To this I anſwer, That though it be true that all women are excluded from the Abyſſinian throne, yet it is as true that there is a law, or cuſtom, as ſtrictly obſerved as the other, that the queen upon whoſe head the king ſhall have put the crown in his life-time, it matters not whether it be her huſband or ſon, or any other relation, that woman is regent of the kingdom, and guardian of every minor king, as long as ſhe ſhall live. Suppoſing, therefore, a queen to be crowned by her huſband, which huſband ſhould die and leave a ſon, all the brothers and uncles of that ſon would be baniſhed, and confined priſoners to the mountain, and the queen would have the care of the kingdom, and of the king, during his minority. If her ſon, moreover, was to die, and a minor ſucceed who was a collateral, or no relation to her, brought, perhaps, from the mountain, ſhe would ſtill be regent; nor does her office ceaſe but by the king's coming of age, whoſe education, cloathing, and maintenance, ſhe, in the mean time, abſolutely directs, according to her own will; nor can there be another regent during her life-time. This regent, for life, is called *Iteghè;* and this was probably the ſituation of the kingdom at the time we mention, as hiſtory informs us the king was then a minor, and conſequently his education, as well as the government of his kingdom and houſehold, were, as they appear to have been, in the queen, or *Iteghè*'s hands; of this office I ſhall ſpeak more in its proper place.

MEROPIUS, a philosopher at Tyre, a Greek by nation, and by religion, had taken a paffage in a fhip on the Red Sea to India, and had with him two young men, Frumentius and Œdefius, whom he intended to bring up to trade, after having given them a very liberal education. It happened their veffel was caft away on a rock upon the coaft of Abyffinia. Meropius, defending himfelf, was flain by the natives, and the two boys carried to Axum, the capital of Abyffinia, where the Court then refided. Though young, they foon began to fhew the advantages attending a liberal education. They acquired the language very fpeedily; and, as that country is naturally inclined to admire ftrangers, thefe were foon looked upon as two prodigies. Œdefius, probably the dulleft of the two, was fet over the king's houfehold and wardrobe, a place that has been filled conftantly by a ftranger of that nation to this very day. Frumentius was judged worthy by the queen to have the care of the young prince's education, to which he dedicated himfelf entirely.

AFTER having inftructed his pupil in all forts of learning, he ftrongly impreffed him with a love and veneration for the Chriftian religion; after which he himfelf fet out for Alexandria, where, as has been already faid, he found St. Athanafius * newly elected to that See.

HE related to him briefly what had paffed in Ethiopia, and the great hopes of the converfion of that nation, if proper paftors were fent to inftruct them. Athanafius embraced that opportunity with all the earneftnefs that became his
ftation

---

* Vid. Baion, tom. 4. p. 331. et alibi paffim.

ſtation and profeſſion. He ordained Frumentius biſhop of that country, who inſtantly returned and found the young king his pupil in the ſame good diſpoſition as formerly; he embraced Chriſtianity; the greateſt part of Abyſſinia followed his example, and the church of Ethiopia continued with this biſhop in perfect unity and friendſhip till his death; and though great troubles aroſe from hereſies being propagated in the Eaſt, that church, and the fountain whence it derived its faith (Alexandria,) remained uncontaminated by any falſe doctrine.

But it was not long after this, that Arianiſm broke out under Conſtantius the Emperor, and was ſtrongly favoured by him. We have indeed a letter of St Athanaſius to that Emperor, who had applied to him to depoſe Frumentius from his See for refuſing to embrace that hereſy, or admit it into his dioceſe.

It ſhould ſeem, that this converſion of Abyſſinia was quietly conducted, and without blood; and this is the more remarkable, that it was the ſecond radical change of religion, effected in the ſame manner, and with the ſame facility and moderation. No fanatic preachers, no warm ſaints or madmen, ambitious to make or to be made martyrs, diſturbed either of theſe happy events, in this wiſe, though barbarous nation, ſo as to involve them in bloodſhed: no perſecution was the conſequence of this difference of tenets, and if wars did follow, it was from matters merely temporal.

2. CHAP.

CHAP. VIII.

War of the Elephant—First Appearance of the Small-Pox—Jews perse-cute the Christians in Arabia—Defeated by the Abyssinians—Mahomet pretends a divine Mission—Opinion concerning the Koran—Revolu-tion under Judith—Restoration of the Line of Solomon from Shoa.

IN the reigns of the princes Abreha and Atzbeha, the A-byssinian annals mention an expedition to have happen-ed into the farthest part of Arabia Felix, which the Arabian authors, and indeed Mahomet himself in the Koran calls by the name of the War of the Elephant, and the cause of it was this. There was a temple nearly in the middle of the peninsula of Arabia, that had been held in the greatest ve-neration for about 1400 years. The Arabs say, that Adam, when shut out of paradise, pitched his tent on this spot; while Eve, from some accident or other I am not acquaint-ed with, died and was buried on the shore of the Red Sea, at Jidda. Two days journey east from this place, her grave, of green sods about fifty yards in length, is shewn to this day. In this temple also was a black stone, upon which Jacob saw the vision mentioned in scripture, of the angels descending, and ascending into Heaven. It is likewise said, with more appearance of probability, that this temple was

built

THE SOURCE OF THE NILE. 511

built by Sefoſtris, in his voyage to Arabia Felix, and that he was worſhipped there under the name of Oſiris, as he then was in every part of Egypt.

The great veneration the neighbouring nations paid to this tower, and idol, ſuggeſted the very natural thought of making the temple the market for the trade from Africa and India; the liberty of which, we may ſuppoſe, had been in ſome meaſure reſtrained, by the ſettlements which foreign nations had made on both coaſts of the Red Sea. To remedy which, they choſe this town in the heart of the country, acceſſible on all ſides, and commanded on none, calling it Becca, which ſignifies the Houſe; though Mahomet, after breaking the idol and dedicating the temple to the true God, named it Mecca, under which name it has continued, the centre or great mart of the India trade to this day.

In order to divert this trade into a channel more convenient for his preſent dominions, Abreha built a very large church or temple, in the country of the Homerites, and nearer the Indian Ocean. To encourage alſo the reſort to this place, he extended to it all the privileges, protection, and emoluments, that belonged to the Pagan temple of Mecca

One particular tribe of Arabs, called Beni Koreiſh, had the care of the Caba, for ſo the round tower of Mecca was called. Theſe people were exceedingly alarmed at the proſpect of their temple being at once deſerted, both by its votaries and merchants, to prevent which, a party of them, in the night, entered Abrcha's temple, and having firſt burned,

burned what part of it could be confumed, they polluted the part that remained, by befmearing it over with human excrements.

This violent facrilege and affront was foon reported to Abreha, who, mounted upon a white elephant at the head of a confiderable army, refolved, in return, to deftroy the temple of Mecca. With this intent, he marched through that ftripe of low country along the fea, called Tehama, where he met with no oppofition, nor fuffered any diftrefs but from want of water; after which, at the head of his army, he fat down before Mecca, as he fuppofed.

Abou Thaleb (Mahomet's grandfather, as it is thought) was then keeper of the Caba, who had intereft with his countrymen the Beni Koreifh to prevail upon them to make no refiftance, nor fhew any figns of wifhing to make a defence. He had prefented himfelf early to Abreha upon his march. There was a temple of Ofiris at Taief, which, as a rival to that of Mecca, was looked upon by the Beni Koreifh with a jealous eye. Abreha was fo far mifled by the intelligence given him by Abou Thaleb, that he miftook the Temple of Taief for that of Mecca, and razed it to the foundation, after which he prepared to return home.

He was foon after informed of his miftake, and not repenting of what he had already done, refolved to deftroy Mecca alfo. Abou Thaleb, however, had never left his fide; by his great hofpitality, and the plenty he procured to the Emperor's army, he fo gained Abreha, that hearing, on inquiry, he was no mean man, but a prince of the tribe of Beni Koreifh, noble Arabs, he obliged him to fit in his prefence

fence, and kept him constantly with him as a companion. At last, not knowing how to reward him sufficiently, Abreha desired him to ask any thing in his power to grant, and he would satisfy him. Abou Thaleb, taking him at his word, wished to be provided with a man, that should bring back forty oxen, the soldiers had stolen from him.

ABREHA, who expected that the favour he was to ask, was to spare the Temple, which he had in that case resolved in his mind to do, could not conceal his astonishment at so silly a request, and he could not help testifying this to Abou Thaleb, in a manner that shewed it had lowered him in his esteem. Abou Thaleb, smiling, replied very calmly, If that before you is the Temple of God, as I believe it is, you shall never destroy it, if it is his will that it should stand: If it is not the Temple of God, or (which is the same thing) if he has ordained that you should destroy it, I shall not only assist you in demolishing it, but shall help you in carrying away the last stone of it upon my shoulders: But as for me, I am a shepherd, and the care of cattle is my profession; twenty of the oxen which are stolen are not my own, and I shall be put in prison for them to-morrow; for neither you nor I can believe that this is an affair God will interfere in; and therefore I apply to you for a soldier who will seek the thief, and bring back my oxen, that my liberty be not taken from me.

ABREHA had now refreshed his army, and, from regard to his guest, had not touched the Temple; when, says the Arabian author, there appeared, coming from the sea, a flock of birds called Ababil, having faces like lions, and each of them in his claws, holding a small stone like a pea, which he let fall upon Abreha's army, fo that they all were deftroyed. The author of the manufcript * from which I have taken this fable, and which is alfo related by feveral other hiftorians, and mentioned by Mahomet in the Koran, does not feem to fwallow the ftory implicitly. For he fays, that there is no bird that has a face like a lion, that Abou Thaleb was a Pagan, Mahomet being not then come, and that the Chriftians were worfhippers of the true God, the God of Mahomet; and, therefore, if any miracle was wrought here, it was a miracle of the devil, a victory in favour of Paganifm, and deftructive of the belief of the true God. In conclufion, he fays, that it was at this time that the fmall-pox and meafles firft broke out in Arabia, and almoft totally deftroyed the army of Abreha. But if the ftone, as big as a pea, thrown by the Ababil, had killed Abreha's army to the laft man, it does not appear how any of them could die afterwards, either by the fmall-pox or meafles

ALL that is material, however, to us, in this fact, is, that the time of the fiege of Mecca will be the æra of the firft appearance of that terrible difeafe, the fmall-pox, which we fhall fet down about the year 356; and it is highly probable, from other circumftances, that the Abyffinian army was the firft victim to it.

As for the church Abreha built near the Indian Ocean, it continued free from any further infult till the Mahometan conqueft of Arabia Felix, when it was finally deftroyed in the Khalifat † of Omar. This is the Abyffinian account, and this

---

* El Hameefy's Siege of Mecca.   † Fetaat el Yemen.

THE SOURCE OF THE NILE. 515

this the Arabian hiftory of the War of the Elephant, which I have ftated as found in the books of the moft credible writers of thofe times.

BUT it is my duty to put the reader upon his guard, againft adopting literally what is here fet down, without being fatisfied of the validity of the objection that may be made againft the narrative in general. Abreha reigned 27 years; he was converted to Chriftianity in 333, and died in 360; now, it is fcarcely poffible, in the fhort fpace of 27 years, that all Abyffinia and Arabia could be converted to Chriftianity. The converfion of the Abyffinians is reprefented to be a work of little time, but the Arab author, Hameefy, fays, that even Arabia Felix was full of churches when this expedition took place, which is very improbable. And, what adds ftill more to the improbability, is, that part of the ftory which ftates that Abreha converfed with Mahomet's father, or grandfather. For, fuppofing the expedition in 356, Mahomet's birth was in 558, fo there will remain 202 years, by much too long a period for two lives. I do believe we muft bring this expedition down much lower than the reign of Abreha and Atzbeha, the reafon of which we fhall fee afterwards.

As early as the commencement of the African trade with Paleftine, the Jewifh religion had fpread itfelf far into Arabia, but, after the deftruction of the temple by Titus, a great increafe both of number and wealth had made that people abfolute mafters in many parts of that peninfula. In the Neged, and as far up as Medina, petty princes, calling themfelves kings, were eftablifhed; who, being trained in the wars of Paleftine, became very formidable among the pacific

cific commercial nations of Arabia, deeply funk into Greek degeneracy.

PHINEAS, a prince of that nation from Medina, having beat St Aretas, the Governor of Najiran, began to perfecute the Chriftians by a new fpecies of cruelty, by ordering certain furnaces, or pits full of fire, to be prepared, into which he threw as many of the inhabitants of Najiran as refufed to renounce Chriftianity. Among thefe was Aretas, fo called by the Greeks, Aryat by the Arabs, and Hawaryat, which fignifies the *evangelical*, by the Abyffinians, together with ninety of his companions. Mahomet, in his Koran, mentions, this tyrant by the name of the Mafter of the *fiery pits*, without either condemning or praifing the execution; only faying, ' the fufferers fhall be witnefs againft him at the laft day '

JUSTIN, the Greek Emperor, was then employed in an unfuccefsful war with the Perfians, fo that he could not give any affiftance to the afflicted Chriftians in Arabia, but in the year 522 he fent an embaffy to Caleb, or Elefbaas, king of Abyffinia, intreating him to interfere in favour of the Chriftians of Najiran, as he too was of the Greek church. On the Emperor's firft requeft, Caleb fent orders to Abreha, Governor of Yemen, to march to the affiftance of Aretas, the fon of him who was burnt, and who was then collecting troops. Strengthened by this reinforcement, the young foldier did not think proper to delay the revenging his father's death, till the arrival of the Emperor; but having come up with Phineas, who was ferrying his troops over an arm of the fea, he entirely routed them, and obliged their prince, for fear of being taken, to fwim with his horfe to the neareft fhore. It was not long before the Emperor had croffed the Red Sea with his army; nor had Phineas loft any time in collecting his fcattered forces to oppofe him. A battle was the confequence, in which the fortune of Caleb again prevailed.

It would appear that the part of Arabia, near Najiran, which was the fcene of Caleb's victory, belonged to the Grecian Emperor Juftin, becaufe Aretas applied directly to him at Conftantinople for fuccour; and it was at Juftin's requeft only, that Caleb marched to the affiftance of Aretas, as a friend, but not as a fovereign; and as fuch alfo, Abreha, Governor of Yemen, marched to affift Aretas, with the A-byffinian troops, from the fouth of Arabia, againft the ftranger Jews, who were invaders from Paleftine, and who had no connection with the Abyffinian Jewifh Homerites, natives of the fouth coaft of Arabia, oppofite to Saba.

But neither of the Jewifh kingdoms were deftroyed by the victories of Caleb, or Abreha, nor the fubfequent conqueft of the Perfians. In the Neged, or north part of Arabia, they continued not only after the appearance of Mahomet, but till after the Hegira. For it was in the 8th year of that æra that Hybar, the Jew, was befieged in his own caftle in Neged, and flain by Ali, Mahomet's fon-in-law, from that time called Hydar Ali, or Ali the Lion.

Now the Arabian manufcripts fays pofitively that this Abreha, who affifted Aretas, was Governor of Arabia Felix, or Yemen; for, by this laft name, I fhall hereafter call the part of the peninfula of Arabia belonging to the Abyf-finians; fo that he might very well have been the prince who converfed with Mahomet's father, and loft his army

before

before Mecca, which will bring down the introduction of the fmall-pox to the year 522, juft 100 years before the Hegira, and both Arabian and Abyffinian accounts might be then true.

THE two officers who governed Yemen, and the oppofite coaft Azab, which, as we have above mentioned, belonged to Abyffinia, were ftiled *Najafhi*, as was the king alfo, and both of them were crowned with gold. I am, therefore, perfuaded, this is the reafon of the confufion of names we meet in Arabian manufcripts, that treat of the fovereigns of Yemen. This, moreover, is the foundation of the ftory found in Arabic manufcripts, that Jaffar, Mahomet's brother, fled to the Najafhi, who was governor of Yemen, and was kindly treated by him, and kept there till he joined his brother at the campaign of Hybarea. Soon after his great victory over the Beni Koreifh, at the laft battle of Beder Hunein, Mahomet is faid to have written to the fame Najafhi a letter of thanks, for his kind entertainment of his brother, inviting him (as a reward) to embrace his religion, which the Najafhi is fuppofed to have immediately complied with. Now, all this is in the Arabic books, and all this is true, as far as we can conjecture from the accounts of thofe times, very partially writ by a fet of warm-headed bigotted zealots; fuch as all Arabic authors (hiftorians of the time) undoubtedly are. The error only lies in the application of this ftory to the Najafhi, or king of Abyffinia, fituated far from the fcene of thefe actions, on high cold mountains, very unfavourable to thofe rites, which, in low flat and warm countries, have been temptations to flothful and inactive men to embrace the Mahometan religion.

A MOST

THE SOURCE OF THE NILE.

A most shameful prostitution of manners prevailed in the Greek church, as also innumerable heresies, which were first received as true tenets of their religion, but were soon after persecuted in a most uncharitable manner, as being erroneous. Their lies, their legends, their saints and miracles, and, above all, the abandoned behaviour of the priesthood, had brought their characters in Arabia almost as low as that of the detested Jew, and, had they been considered in their true light, they had been still lower.

The dictates of nature in the heart of the honest Pagan, constantly employed in long, lonely, and dangerous voyages, awakened him often to reflect who that Providence was that invisibly governed him, supplied his wants, and often mercifully saved him from the destruction into which his own ignorance or rashness were leading him. Poisoned by no system, perverted by no prejudice, he wished to know and adore his Benefactor, with purity and simplicity of heart, free from these fopperies and follies with which ignorant priests and monks had disguised his worship. Possessed of charity, steady in his duty to his parents, full of veneration for his superiors, attentive and merciful even to his beasts in a word, containing in his heart the principles of the first religion, which God had inculcated in the heart of Noah, the Arab was already prepared to embrace a much more perfect one than what Christianity, at that time, disfigured by folly and superstition, appeared to him to be.

Mahomet, of the tribe of Beni Koreish (at whose instigation is uncertain) took upon himself to be the apostle of a new religion, pretending to have, for his only object, the worship of the true God. Ostensibly full of the morality of the Arab, of patience and self-denial, superior even to what is made necessary to salvation by the gospel, his religion, at the bottom, was but a system of blasphemy and falsehood, corruption and injustice. Mahomet and his tribe were most profoundly ignorant. There was not among them but one man that could write, and it was not doubted he was to be Mahomet's secretary, but unfortunately Mahomet could not read his writing. The story of the angel who brought him leaves of the Koran is well known, and so is all the rest of the fable. The wiser part of his own relations, indeed, laughed at the impudence of his pretending to have a communication with angels. Having, however, gained, as his apostles, some of the best soldiers of the tribe of Beni Koreish, and persisting with great uniformity in all his measures, he established a new religion upon the ruins of idolatry and Sabaism, in the very temple of Mecca.

NOTHING severe was injoined by Mahomet, and the frequent prayers and washings with water which he directed, were gratifications to a sedentary people in a very hot country. The lightness of this yoke, therefore, recommended it rapidly to those who were disgusted with long fasting, penances, and pilgrimages. The poison of this false, yet not severe religion, spread itself from that fountain to all the trading nations: India, Ethiopia, Africa, all Asia, suddenly embraced it; and every caravan carried into the bosom of its country people not more attached to trade, than zealous to preach and propagate their new faith. The Temple of Mecca (the old rendezvous of the Indian trade) perhaps was never more frequented than it is at this day, and the motives of the journey are equally trade and religion, as they were formerly.

I SHALL

I shall here mention, that the Arabs begun very foon to ftudy letters, and came to be very partial to their own language; Mahomet himfelf fo much fo, that he held out his Koran, for its elegance alone, as a greater miracle than that of raifing the dead. This was not univerfally allowed at that time; as there were even then compofitions fuppofed to equal, if not to furpafs it. In my time, I have feen in Britain a fpirit of enthufiafm for this book in preference to all others, not inferior to that which poffeffed Mahomet's followers. Modern unbelievers (Sale and his difciples) have gone every length, but to fay directly that it was dictated by the Spirit of God. Excepting the command in Genefis chap. i. ver. 3. "And God faid, Let there be light; and there was light;" they defy us to fhew in fcripture a paffage equal in fublimity to many in the Koran. Following, without inquiring, what has been handed down from one to the other, they would cram us with abfurdities, which no man of fenfe can fwallow. They fay the Koran is compofed in a ftyle the moft pure, and chafte, and that the tribe of Beni Koreifh was the moft polite, learned, and noble of all the Arabs.

But to this I anfwer—The Beni Koreifh were from the earlieft days, according to their own * account, part cftablifhed at Mecca, and part as robbers on the fea-coaft, and they were all children of Ifhmael. Whence then came their learning, or their fuperior nobility? Was it found in the defert, in the temple, or did the robbers bring it from the fea? Soiouthy, one of thofe moft famous then for

---

* El Hameefy.

knowledge in the Arabic, has quoted from the Koran many hundred words, either Abyssinian, Indian, Persian, Ethiopic, Syrian, Hebrew, or Chaldaic, which he brings back to the root, and ascribes them to the nation they came from. Indeed it could not be otherwise; these caravans, continually crowding with their trade to Mecca, must have vitiated the original tongue by an introduction of new terms and new idioms, into a language labouring under a penury of vocabules. But shall any one for this persuade me, that a book is a model of pure, elegant, chaste English, in which there shall be a thousand words of Welsh, Irish, Gaelic, French, Spanish, Malabar Mexican, and Laponian? What would be thought of such a medley? or, at least, could it be recommended as a pattern for writing pure English?

WHAT I say of the Koran may be applied to the language of Arabia in general: when it is called a copious language, and professors wisely tell you, that there are six hundred words for a sword, two hundred for honey, and three hundred that signify a lion, still I must observe, that this is not a copious language, but a confusion of languages: these, instead of distinct names, are only different epithets. For example, a lion in English may be called a young lion, a white lion, a small lion, a big lion: I style him moreover the fierce, the cruel, the enemy to man, the beast of the desert, the king of beasts, the lover of blood. Thus it is in Arabic; and yet it is said that all these are words for a lion. Take another example in a sword; the cutter, the divider, the friend of man, the master of towns, the maker of widows, the sharp, the straight, the crooked; which may be said in English as well as in Arabic

THE

THE SOURCE OF THE NILE.

The Arabs were a people who lived in a country, for the moft part, defert; their dwellings were tents, and their principal occupation feeding and breeding cattle, and they married with their own family. The language therefore of fuch a people fhould be very poor; there is no variety of images in their whole country. They were always bad poets, as their works will teftify; and if, contrary to the general rule, the language of Arabia Deferta became a copious one, it muft have been by the mixture of fo many nations meeting and trading at Mecca. It muft, at the fame time, have been the moft corrupt, where there was the greateft concourfe of ftrangers, and this was certainly among the Beni Koreifh at the Caba. When, therefore, I hear people praifing the Koran for the purity of its ftyle, it puts me in mind of the old man in the comedy, whofe reafon for loving his nephew was, that he could read Greek; and being afked if he underftood the Greek fo read, he anfwered, Not a word of it, but the rumbling of the found pleafed him.

The war that had diftracted all Arabia, firft between the Greeks and Perfians, then between Mahomet and the Arabs, in fupport of his divine miffion, had very much hurt the trade carried on by univerfal confent at the Temple of Mecca. Caravans, when they dared venture out, were furprifed upon every road, by the partizans of one fide or the other. Both merchants and trade had taken their departure to the fouthward, and eftablifhed themfelves fouth of the Arabian Gulf, in places which (in ancient times) had been the markets for commerce, and the rendezvous of merchants. Azab, or Saba, was rebuilt; alfo Raheeta, Zeyla, Tajoura, Soomaal, in the Arabian Gulf, and a number of other towns on the Indian Ocean. The conqueft of the Abyffinian territories in

Arabia forced all thofe that yet remained to take refuge on the African fide, in the little diftricts which now grew into confideration. Adel, Mara, Hadea, Auffa, Wypo, Tarfhifh, and a number of other ftates, now affumed the name of kingdoms, and foon obtained power and wealth fuperior to many older ones.

The Governor of Yemen (or Najafhi) cŏnverted now to the faith of Mahomet, retired to the African fide of the Gulf. His government, long ago, having been fhaken to the very foundation by the Arabian war, was at laft totally deftroyed. But the Indian trade at Adel wore a face of profperity, that had the features of ancient times.

Without taking notice of every objection, and anfwering it, which has too polemical an appearance for a work of this kind, I hope I have removed the greateft part of the reader's difficulties, which have, for a long time, lain in the way, towards his underftanding this part of the hiftory. There is one, however, remains, which the Arabian hiftorians have mentioned, viz. that this Najafhi, who embraced the faith of Mahomet, was avowedly of the royal family of Abyffinia. To this I anfwer, he certainly was a perfon of that rank, and was undoubtedly a nobleman, as there is no nobility in that country but from relationfhip to the king, and no perfon can be related to the king by the male line. But the females, even the daughters of thofe princes who are banifhed to the mountain, marry whom they pleafe; and all the defcendents of that marriage become noble, becaufe they muft be allied to the king. So far then they may truly affert, that the Mahometan Governor of Yemen, and his pofterity, were this way related to the king of Abyffinia.

But

THE SOURCE OF THE NILE. 525

But the fuppofition that any heirs male of this family became muffulmen, is, beyond any fort of doubt, without foundation or probability.

Omar, after fubduing Egypt, deftroyed the valuable library at Alexandria, but his fucceffors thought very differently from him in the article of profane learning. Greek books of all kinds (efpecially thofe of Geometry, Aftronomy, and Medicine,) were fearched for every where and tranflated. Sciences flourifhed and were encouraged. Trade at the fame time kept pace, and increafed with knowledge. Geography and aftronomy were every where diligently ftudied and folidly applied to make the voyages of men from place to place fafe and expeditious. The Jews (conftant fervants of the Arabs) imbibed a confiderable fhare of their tafte for earning.

They had, at this time, increafed very much in number. By the violence of the Mahometan conquefts in Arabia and Egypt, where their fect did principally prevail, they became very powerful in Abyffinia. Arianifm, and all the various herefies that diftracted the Greek church, were received there in their turn from Egypt; the bonds of Chriftianity were diffolved, and people in general were much more willing to favour a new religion, than to agree with, or countenance any particular one of their own, if it differed from that which they adopted in the mereft trifle. This had deftroyed their metropolis in Egypt, juft now delivered up to the Saracens; and the difpofition of the Abyffinians feemed fo very much to refemble their brethren the Cophts, that a revolution in favour of Judaifm was thought full as feafible in the country, as it had been in Egypt in favour of the newly-preached, but unequivocal religion of Mahomet.

An independent sovereignty, in one family of Jews, had always been preserved on the mountain of Samen, and the royal residence was upon a high-pointed rock, called the Jews Rock: Several other inaccessible mountains served as natural fortresses for this people, now grown very considerable by frequent accessions of strength from Palestine and Arabia, whence the Jews had been expelled. Gideon and Judith were then king and queen of the Jews, and their daughter Judith (whom in Amhara they call *Esther*, and sometimes *Saat*, i. e. *fire**,) was a woman of great beauty, and talents for intrigue; had been married to the governor of a small district called Bugna, in the neighbourhood of Lasta, both which countries were likewise much infected with Judaism.

Judith had made so strong a party, that she resolved to attempt the subversion of the Christian religion, and, with it, the succession in the line of Solomon. The children of the royal family were at this time, in virtue of the old law, confined on the almost inaccessible mountain of Damo in Tigrè. The short reign, sudden and unexpected death of the late king Aizor, and the desolation and contagion which an epidemical disease had spread both in court and capital, the weak state of Del Naad who was to succeed Aizor and was an infant; all these circumstances together, impressed Judith with an idea that now was the time to place her family upon the throne, and establish her religion by the extirpation

---

* She is also called by Victor, *Tredda Gahez*.

THE SOURCE OF THE NILE.

extirpation of the race of Solomon. Accordingly she surprised the rock Damo, and flew the whole princes there, to the number, it is said, of about 400.

Some nobles of Amhara, upon the first news of the catastrophe at Damo, conveyed the infant king Del Naad, now the only remaining prince of his race, into the powerful and loyal province of Shoa, and by this means the royal family was preserved to be again restored. Judith took possession of the throne in defiance of the law of the queen of Saba, by this the first interruption of the succession in the line of Solomon, and, contrary to what might have been expected from the violent means she had used to acquire the crown, she not only enjoyed it herself during a long reign of 40 years, but transmitted it also to five of her posterity, all of them barbarous names, originating probably in Lasta: These are said to be,

> Totadem,
> Jan Shum,
> Garima Shum,
> Harbai,
> Marari.

Authors, as well Abyssinian as European, have differed widely about the duration of these reigns. All that the Abyssinians are agreed upon is, that this whole period was one scene of murder, violence, and oppression.

Judith and her descendents were succeeded by relations of their own, a noble family of Lasta. The history of this revolution, or cause of it, are lost and unknown in the country, and therefore vainly sought after elsewhere. What we know

know is, that with them the court returned to the Chriſtian religion, and that they were ſtill as different from their predeceſſors in manners as in religion. Though uſurpers, as were the others, their names are preſerved with every mark of reſpect and veneration. They are,

    Tecla Haimanout,
    Kedus Harbé,
    Itibarek,
    Lalibala,
    Imeranha Chriſtos,
    Naacueto Laab.

Not being kings of the line of Solomon, no part of their hiſtory is recorded in the annals, unleſs that of Lalibala, who lived in the end of the twelfth, or beginning of the thirteenth century, and was a ſaint. The whole period of the uſurpation, comprehending the long reign of Judith, will by this account be a little more than 300 years, in which time eleven princes are ſaid to have ſat upon the throne of Solomon, ſo that, ſuppoſing her death to have been in the year 1000, each of theſe princes, at an average, will have been a little more than twenty-four years, and this is too much. But all this period is involved in darkneſs. We might gueſs, but ſince we are not able to do more, it anſwers no good purpoſe to do ſo much. I have followed the hiſtories and traditions which are thought the moſt authentic in the country, the ſubject of which they treat, and where I found them; and though they may differ from other accounts given by European authors, this does not influence me, as I know that none of theſe authors could have any other authorities than thoſe I have ſeen, and the difference only muſt

must be the fruit of idle imagination, and ill-founded conjectures of their own.

• In the reign of Lalibala, near about the 1200, there was a great persecution in Egypt against the Christians, after the Saracen conquest, and especially against the masons, builders, and hewers of stone, who were looked upon by the Arabs as the greatest of abominations; this prince opened an asylum in his dominions to all fugitives of that kind, of whom he collected a prodigious number. Having before him as specimens the ancient works of the Troglodytes, he directed a number of churches to be hewn out of the solid rock in his native country of Lasta, where they remain untouched to this day, and where they will probably continue till the latest posterity. Large columns within are formed out of the solid rock, and every species of ornament preserved, that would have been executed in buildings of separate and detached stones, above ground.

This prince undertook to realize the favourite pretensions of the Abyssinians, to the power of turning the Nile out of its course, so that it should no longer be the cause of the fertility of Egypt, now in possession of the enemies of his religion. We may imagine, if it was in the power of man to accomplish this undertaking, it could have fallen into no better hands than those to whom Lalibala gave the execution of it; people driven from their native country by those Saracens who now were reaping the benefits of the river, in the places of those they had forced to seek habitations far from the benefit and pleasure afforded by its stream.

This prince did not adopt the wild idea of turning the course of the Nile out of its present channel; upon the possibility or impossibility of which, the argument (so warmly and so long agitated) always most improperly turns. His idea was to famish Egypt: and, as the fertility of that country depends not upon the ordinary stream, but the extraordinary increase of it by the tropical rains, he is said to have found, by an exact survey and calculation, that there ran on the summit, or highest part of the country, several rivers which could be intercepted by mines, and their stream directed into the low country southward, instead of joining the Nile, augmenting it and running northward. By this he found he should be able so to disappoint its increase, that it never would rise to a height proper to fit Egypt for cultivation. And thus far he was warranted in his ideas of succeeding (as I have been informed by the people of that country), that he did interfect and carry into the Indian Ocean, two very large rivers, which have ever since flowed that way, and he was carrying a level to the lake Zawaia, where many rivers empty themselves in the beginning of the rains, which would have effectually diverted the course of them all, and could not but in some degree diminish the current below.

Death, the ordinary enemy of all these stupendous Herculean undertakings, interposed too here, and put a stop to this enterprize of Lalibala. But Amha Yasous, prince of Shoa (in whose country part of these immense works were) a young man of great understanding, and with whom I lived several months in the most intimate friendship at Gondar, assured me that they were visible to this day; and that they were of a kind whose use could not be mistaken; that

he

THE SOURCE OF THE NILE. 531

he himfelf had often vifited them, and was convinced the undertaking was very poffible with fuch hands, and in the circumftances things then were. He told me likewife, that, in a written account which he had feen in Shoa, it was faid that this prince was not interrupted by death in his undertaking, but perfuaded by the monks, that if a greater quantity of water was let down into the dry kingdoms of Hadea, Mará, and Adel, increafing in population every day, and, even now, almoft equal in power to Abyffinia itfelf, thefe barren kingdoms would become the garden of the world; and fuch a number of Saracens, diflodged from Egypt by the firft appearance of the Nile's failing, would fly thither: that they would not only withdraw thofe countries from their obedience, but be ftrong enough to over-run the whole kingdom of Abyffinia. Upon this, as Amha Yafous informed me, Lalibala gave over his firft fcheme, which was the famifhing of Egypt; and that his next was employing the men in fubterraneous churches; a ufelefs expence, but more level to the underftanding of common men than the former.

Don Roderigo de Lima, ambaffador from the king of Portugal, in 1522 faw the remains of thefe vaft works, and travelled in them feveral days, as we learn from Alvarez the chaplain and hiftorian of that embaffy[*], which we fhall take notice of in its proper place.

Lalibala was diftinguifhed both as a poet and an orator. The old fable, of a fwarm of bees hanging to his lips

---

[*] See Alvarez, his relation of this Embaffy.

in the cradle, is revived and applied to him as foretelling the fweetnefs of his elocution.

To Lalibala fucceeded Imeranha Chriftos, remarkable for nothing but being fon of fuch a father as Lalibala, and father to fuch a fon as Naacueto Laab; both of them diftinguifhed for works very extraordinary, though very different in their kind. The firft, that is thofe of the father we have already hinted at, confifting in great mechanical undertakings. The other was an operation of the mind, of ftill more difficult nature, a victory over ambition, the voluntary abdication of a crown to which he fucceeded without imputation of any crime.

TECLA HAIMANOUT, a monk and native of Abyffinia, had been ordained Abuna, and had founded the famous monaftery of Debra Libanos in Shoa. He was a man at once celebrated for the fanctity of his life, the goodnefs of his underftanding, and love to his country; and, by an extraordinary influence, obtained over the reigning king Naacueto Laab, he perfuaded him, for confcience fake, to refign a crown, which (however it might be faid with truth, that he received it from his father) could never be purged from the ftain and crime of ufurpation.

IN all this time, the line of Solomon had been continued from Del Naad, who, we have feen, had efcaped from the maffacre of Damo, under Judith. Content with poffeffing the loyal province of Shoa, they continued their royal refidence there, without having made one attempt, as far as hiftory tells us, towards recovering their ancient kingdom.

RACE

RACE of SOLOMON banished, but reigning in SHOA.

>Del Naad,
>Mahaber Wedem,
>Igba Sion,
>Tzenaf Araad,
>Nagaſh Zaré,
>Asfeha,
>Jacob;
>Bahar Segued,
>Adamas Segued,
>Icon Amlac.

Naacueto Laab, of the houſe of Zaguè, was, it ſeems, a juſt and peaceable prince.

Under the mediation of Abuna Tecla Haimanout, a treaty was made between him and Icon Amlac confiſting of four articles, all very extraordinary in their kind.

The firſt was, that Naacueto Laab, prince of the houſe of Zaguè, ſhould forthwith reſign the kingdom of Abyſſinia to Icon Amlac, reigning prince of the line of Solomon then in Shoa

The ſecond, that a portion of lands in Laſta ſhould be given to Naacueto Laab and his heirs in abſolute property, irrevocably and irredeemably; that he ſhould preſerve, as marks of ſovereignty, two ſilver kettle-drums, or nagareets; that the points of the ſpears of his guard, the globes that ſurmounted his fendeck, (that is the pole upon which the colours,

colours are carried), fhould be filver, and that he fhould fit upon a gold ftool, or chair, in form of that ufed by the kings of Abyffinia; and that both he and his defcendents fhould be abfolutely free from all homage, fervices, taxes, or public burdens for ever, and ftiled Kings of Zaguè, or the Lafta king.

The third article was, That one third of the kingdom fhould be appropriated and ceded abfolutely to the Abuna himfelf, for the maintenance of his own ftate, and fupport of the clergy, convents, and churches in the kingdom; and this became afterwards an æra, or epoch, in Abyffinian hiftory, called the æra of partition.

The fourth, and laft article, provided, that no native Abyffinian could thereafter be chofen Abuna, and this even tho' he was ordained at, and fent from Cairo. In virtue of this treaty, concluded and folemnly fworn to, Icon Amlac took poffeffion of his throne, and the other contracting parties of the provifions refpectively allotted them.

The part of the treaty that fhould appear moft liable to be broken was that which erected a kingdom within a kingdom. However, it is one of the remarkable facts in the annals of this country, that the article between Icon Amlac and the houfe of Zaguè was obferved for near 500 years; for it was made before the year 1300, and never was broken, but by the treacherous murder of the Zaguean prince by Allo Fafil in the unfortunate war of Begemder, in the reign of Joas 1768, the year before I arrived in Abyffinia; neither has any Abuna native of Abyffinia ever been known fince that period. As for the exorbitant grant of one third

third of the kingdom to the Abuna, it has been in great meafure refumed, as we may naturally fuppofe, upon different pretences of mifbehaviour, true or alledged, by the king or his minifters, the firft great invafion of it being in the fubfequent reign of king Theodorus, who, far from lofing popularity by this infraction, has been ever reckoned a model for fovereigns.

END OF VOLUME FIRST.

Made in United States
Cleveland, OH
15 November 2024